Weimar Surfaces

Weimar and Now: German Cultural Criticism

Edward Dimendberg, Martin Jay, and Anton Kaes, General Editors

1. *Heritage of Our Times*, by Ernst Bloch
2. *The Nietzsche Legacy in Germany, 1890–1990*, by Steven E. Aschheim
3. *The Weimar Republic Sourcebook*, edited by Anton Kaes, Martin Jay, and Edward Dimendberg
4. *Batteries of Life: On the History of Things and Their Perception in Modernity*, by Christoph Asendorf
5. *Profane Illumination: Walter Benjamin and the Paris of Surrealist Revolution*, by Margaret Cohen
6. *Hollywood in Berlin: American Cinema and Weimar Germany*, by Thomas J. Saunders
7. *Walter Benjamin: An Aesthetic of Redemption*, by Richard Wolin
8. *The New Typography*, by Jan Tschichold, translated by Ruari McLean
9. *The Rule of Law under Siege: Selected Essays of Franz L. Neumann and Otto Kirchheimer*, edited by William E. Scheuerman
10. *The Dialectical Imagination: A History of the Frankfurt School and the Institute of Social Research, 1923–1950*, by Martin Jay
11. *Women in the Metropolis: Gender and Modernity in Weimar Culture*, edited by Katharina von Ankum
12. *Letters of Heinrich and Thomas Mann, 1900–1949*, edited by Hans Wysling, translated by Don Reneau
13. *Empire of Ecstasy: Nudity and Movement in German Body Culture, 1910–1935*, by Karl Toepfer
14. *In the Shadow of Catastrophe: German Intellectuals between Apocalypse and Enlightenment*, by Anson Rabinbach
15. *Walter Benjamin's Other History: Of Stones, Animals, Human Beings, and Angels*, by Beatrice Hanssen
16. *Exiled in Paradise: German Refugee Artists and Intellectuals in America from the 1930s to the Present*, by Anthony Heilbut
17. *Cool Conduct: The Culture of Distance in Weimar Germany*, by Helmut Lethen, translated by Don Reneau
18. *In a Cold Crater: Cultural and Intellectual Life in Berlin, 1945–1948*, by Wolfgang Schivelbusch, translated by Kelly Barry

19. *A Dubious Past: Ernst Jünger and the Politics of Literature after Nazism,* by Elliot Y. Neaman
20. *Beyond the Conceivable: Studies on Germany, Nazism, and the Holocaust,* by Dan Diner
21. *Prague Territories: National Conflict and Cultural Innovation in Franz Kafka's Fin de Siècle,* by Scott Spector
22. *Munich and Memory: Architecture, Monuments, and the Legacy of the Third Reich,* by Gavriel D. Rosenfeld
23. *The UFA Story: A History of Germany's Greatest Film Company, 1918–1945,* by Klaus Kreimeier, translated by Robert and Rita Kimber
24. *From Monuments to Traces: Artifacts of German Memory, 1870–1990,* by Rudy Koshar
25. *We Weren't Modern Enough: Women Artists and the Limits of German Modernism,* by Marsha Maskimmon
26. *Culture and Inflation in Weimar Germany,* by Bernd Widdig
27. *Weimar Surfaces: Urban Visual Culture in 1920s Germany,* by Janet Ward

Weimar Surfaces

Urban Visual Culture in 1920s Germany

JANET WARD

University of California Press
BERKELEY LOS ANGELES LONDON

University of California Press
Berkeley and Los Angeles, California

University of California Press, Ltd.
London, England

Library of Congress Cataloging-in-Publication Data

Ward, Janet, 1963–.
Weimar surfaces : urban visual culture in 1920s Germany / Janet Ward.
p. cm.—(Weimar and now ; 27)
Includes bibliographical references and index.
ISBN 0-520-22298-9 (cloth : alk. paper)—ISBN 0-520-22299-7
(pbk. : alk paper)
1. Arts, German. 2. Arts, Modern—20th century—Germany.
3. Modernism (Aesthetics)—Germany. 4. Popular culture—
Germany—Influence. 5. Germany—History—1918–1933.
I.Title. II. Series.

NX550.A1 W37 2001
306.4'7'094309042—DC21

00–055963

Manufactured in the United States of America

10 09 08 07 06 05 04 03 02 01
10 9 8 7 6 5 4 3 2 1

The paper used in this publication meets the minimum requirements of
ANSI / NISO Z39 0.48-1992(R 1997) (*Permanence of Paper*). ♾

For my parents,
Joan and Alfred Ward,
with love and gratitude

Contents

Illustrations

Acknowledgments

I am greatly indebted to the archivists and librarians of the various institutions where I gathered materials for this book during the summers of 1994, 1995, and 1996, at the Akademie der Künste (Sammlung Baukunst), Bundesarchiv-Filmarchiv, Bundesarchiv Koblenz, Deutsche Bücherei Leipzig, Geheimes Staatsarchiv Berlin, Hauptstaatsarchiv Stuttgart, Landesarchiv Berlin, Landesbildstelle Berlin, Deutsches Technikmuseum Berlin, Stadtarchiv München, Zentral- und Landesbibliothek Berlin, Staatsbibliothek 1 Berlin (Unter den Linden), Stiftung Deutsche Kinemathek, Stadtarchiv Stuttgart, and the Museum der Dinge. Special thanks are due to Janos Frecot (Berlinische Galerie); Michael Davidis (Deutsches Literaturarchiv); and Rainer Hering (Staatsarchiv Hamburg).

Various grants were received for the writing of this book, including a University of Colorado Twentieth-Century Humanities Grant; a National Endowment for the Humanities Summer Grant for Faculty; a German Academic Exchange Service Research Grant for Recent Ph.D.s and Ph.D. candidates; a National Endowment for the Humanities Summer Seminar for College Teachers; a University of Colorado Junior Faculty Development Award; and two Travel Grants from the University of Colorado's Graduate Committee on the Arts and Humanities.

This book owes its germination to a 1994 National Endowment for the Humanities seminar on Berlin and the Weimar Republic: my first thanks go to the seminar director, Anton Kaes, as well as to fellow participants for conversations that jump-started the issues pursued in this book. To my former dissertation advisor, Walter H. Sokel, I owe, as ever, a great deal for his constant mentorship on this new project. I am immensely grateful for invaluable feedback on the various chapters and their subject matter from the following friends and colleagues: Susan Buck-Morss, Marcus Bullock,

Kenneth Calhoon, Adrian Del Caro, Ian Foster, Gabrielle Gillner, Rolf Goebel, Werner Goehner, Erk Grimm, Sabine Hake, Andreas Huyssen, Clayton Koelb, Helmut Lethen, Susan Linville, Cecile Mazzucco-Than, Richard W. McCormick, Hans Morgenthaler, Klaus Phillips, Eric Rentschler, Christian Rogowski, Mary Roper, Elizabeth Sauer, and Anthony Vidler. This book also benefits from the helpful responses I received after presentations at such venues as the Conference on Literature and Film in Tallahassee, the German Studies Association, the International Society for the Study of European Ideas, the Modern Language Association, the Ninth Hollins College Colloquium on German Film, the Society for Cinema Studies, the Cornell German Cultural Studies Institute, and a Twentieth-Century Humanities lecture presented at the University of Colorado at Boulder. My students at CU-Boulder assisted with their enthusiastic comments on the primary source materials in my seminars on urban visual culture. The readers of this manuscript for the University of California Press also contributed significantly.

A pilot version of chapter four has appeared in *New German Critique* 76 (1999): 115–60. It is reprinted here by kind permission of the publishers.

The final word of thanks goes to my wonderful husband, David M. Wrobel, who gives me true partnership in life and humanism. I dedicate *Weimar Surfaces* to my parents, who were born in London while the Weimar Republic was still in full swing, and whose loving support of all my endeavors continues to inspire.

INTRODUCTION

Modern Surface and Postmodern Simulation

A Retrospective Retrieval

Denn was innen, das ist außen!
Johann Wolfgang von Goethe

AGENDAS OF SURFACE AND SIMULACRUM

It is in our time that the Enlightenment project has reached its ultimate implosion. In visual terms, the twentieth century of the western hemisphere will be remembered as the century in which content yielded to form, text to image, depth to façade, and *Sein* to *Schein.* For over a hundred years, mass cultural phenomena have been growing in importance, taking over from elite structures of cultural expression to become sites where real power resides, and dominating ever more surely our social imaginary. As reflections of the processes of capitalist industrialization in forms clad for popular consumption, these manifestations are literal and conceptual expressions of *surface:*[1] they promote external appearance to us in such arenas as architecture, advertising, film, and fashion. Located as we are at the outset of the new millennium, some may recognize with trepidation that mass culture is becoming so wedded to highly orchestrated and intrusive electronic formats that there seems to be less and less opportunity for any creative maieutics, or participatory "wiggle room." Modernity's surfaces, entirely site-and-street-specific yet mobile and mobilizing, have been replaced by the stasis of the fluid mobility granted to our perception by the technologies of television, the VCR, the World Wide Web, and virtual reality.[2]

Perhaps as a result of this underlying discomfort, we appear to have a case of what Fredric Jameson has called "inverted millenarianism":[3] rather than look forward at future developments, we choose, almost apotropaically, to look back at how mass culture emerged in the first place. In other words, postmodernity is living up to its name and engaging in a serious bout of nostalgia for modernity. Our culture of the copy without original, that is, of the "simulacrum" or the "hyperreal"—as the most extreme prophet of postmodern neocapitalism, Jean Baudrillard, has adapted Plato's term—induces us, quite naturally, to feel a nostalgia for the real.[4] We turn, then, from our technologized surface culture to look not for metaphysical origins but for a time when surface played a different, more dynamic, meaningful role in mass cultural formation.

We do not, indeed, have to look far. Germany of the 1920s offers us a stunning moment in modernity when surface values first ascended to become determinants of taste, activity, and occupation—a scene of functioning that shows us there was in fact a time when the new was not yet old, modernity was still modern, and spectacle was still spectacular. Certain arenas of Weimar urban spectacle revalorized surface as the dominant "social space" of the era, to use Henri Lefebvre's phrase.[5] It would not be an exaggeration to claim for the culture (or cult) of surface in 1920s Germany the status of the visual embodiment of the modern per se. In order to recapture this spirit of the Weimar modern—both as *material condition* (modernity) and as *aesthetic output* (modernism)—it is first necessary to traverse back through the current condition of the "overexposure and transparence of the world," to cite Baudrillard,[6] toward a time when exposure and transparency first offered themselves as emancipatory advances.

Rather than dismiss modernist practice for being—despite its avant-gardistic focus on surface as the predominant generator of cultural activity—perpetually in depth-seeking error and in search of transformative social hope that postmodernism has long since cynically eclipsed in some undefinably superior way, I find enormous value in examining the tangible perceptual ways in which the modern era is still part of our own. I propose, then, that we reenact the surface terrain of Weimar Germany as one of the most dazzling examples of the modern period and reassess it according to its own merits. While nonetheless admitting that the gate to the immediate contemporariness of modernity is forever closed to us, located as we are within a later historical era,[7] I believe there are more ways to understand the modern era than exclusively through the postmodern lens of recording modernity's representational and conceptual shortcomings; similarly, postmodernist thought cannot, in all intellectual honesty, continue to use modernity to define itself along authoritative lines. A postmodernism that purifies itself from the modernist pursuit of pure form is only engaging in a new kind of epistemological error. Instead, it is the interconnectedness between the visual codes of these historical and political alternative cultures that draws us like moths to the Weimar flame.

Most crucially, what attracts the contemporary mind to these years is the basic sense of (self-)recognition: for so much of today's electronically simulational environment was literally *in vitro* during the high points of Western modernity's "culture of momentum."[8] A close attention to Weimar is of particular value as an ongoing "bridging" scenario between modernism and postmodernism: Weimar can be seen as the singular era of transition from the modern to the postmodern. In key ways, Weimar design initiated our current state of saturation regarding the visual codes of consumerism. Our contemporary relation to the visual culture of the German 1920s is therefore much closer than we might think, even as we exaggerate and intensify its political and aesthetic trajectories. Hence what is needed is not a reclamation of modernity as any contemporary alternative to postmodernity; the more interesting endeavor lies in a reengagement with those modern elements that still underpin postmodern expression.

The spectacularization of consumerist display contained the germination of surface culture's emergence as a powerful conceptual and exterior entity, which Guy Debord dates as occurring in the mid-1920s.[9] Debord's study *The Society of the Spectacle* (1967) was written within the Marxist artistic movement of the Situationist International in France (1957–1972); in it, he offers a devastating critique of the (American, "diffused"—as opposed to Soviet, "concentrated") spectacle as the *con* of consumerism and the dominant *Weltanschauung* of modernity and postmodernity alike. Even though Debord's student-protest-era reaction against consumptionism has retrospectively been dubbed "paranoid," or as "Adorno gone mad," or at best a "lone voice of virtue and ethics in a corrupt world,"[10] he remains a clear inspiration for current (and especially for Baudrillard's) theories about how postmodern society actually functions. And, despite Michel Foucault's attempt to guide us away from Debord ("Our society is not one of spectacle but of surveillance"),[11] the latter's theory illuminates how the spectacle, as the twentieth-century's visual codification of consumption, is a true descendant of modernity's homogenizing Benthamite panopticon.[12]

Debord recognizes how today's panoramically soaked "spectacle is *capital* accumulated to the point where it becomes image," a condition that was made acute by the fact that "commodities are now *all* that there is to see; the world we see is the world of the commodity."[13] His most pathbreaking insight, and one that Baudrillard subsequently builds upon, is that commodity aesthetics is no longer a cover for any deeper meaning, but has become the only option for capitalistic representation, that is, both signifier and signified unite/collapse in an entirely totalizing sense:

> [The spectacle] is not something *added* to the real world—not a decorative element, so to speak. On the contrary, it is the very heart of society's real unreality. . . . It is the omnipresent celebration of a choice *already made* in the sphere of production, and the consummate result of that choice. In form as in content the spectacle serves as total justification for the conditions and aims of the existing system.[14]

Writing on the eve of electronic interfaces with modern surfaces, Debord presents an all-out condemnation of how our spectacular society represents to itself, in the guise of the parade of the "autonomous image," only nonmemory, antihistory, death, deceit, control, and the "autonomous movement of non-life":[15]

> Understood on its own terms, the spectacle proclaims the predominance of appearances and asserts that all human life, which is to say all social life, is mere appearance. But any critique capable of apprehending the spectacle's essential character must expose it as a visible negation of life—and as a negation of life that has *invented a visual form for itself.*[16]

For Debord, then, the spectacle, as a spirally negative source of self-reflexivity, is the very furthest from the visual pleasure of consumer freedom that it appears to be.

Baudrillard, removing the tragic tone from Debord's analysis even as he remains entirely indebted to the latter's thesis, finds that electronic technology has enacted ineradicable perceptual shifts on the spectacle. There is now no more "surface" in the modern sense; there is no more distinction between depth/shadow on the one hand and that which is situated above or outside, because there is no more "original." Surface culture has become so endemic and our contact with the phenomenal world so permanently mediated that all we have left is an environment of simulation in which even warfare appears more real as a signifier than as an actual event, thanks to (say) the media coverage of the Gulf War of 1991.[17] This state of displacement from the experiential real to the mediated hyperreal is so acute that the Three Mile Island nuclear accident happened, Baudrillard suggests, as much as a contagious reflection of the film *The China Syndrome* as of anything else, since "it is simulation that is effective, never the real."[18] This is the point that Jameson also makes in his assessment of the late capitalist era that has been witness to an "emergence of a new kind of flatness or depthlessness, a new kind of superficiality in the most literal sense"—a paradigm that no longer even cares to ask dialectical questions about "essence and appearance."[19]

Baudrillard's rather deterministic vision of the shift from modernity to postmodernity gains self-supporting strength from his emphasis on that epochal break at which, along the post-WWII continuum of exponential growth in communications technologies, the spectacle becomes what Baudrillard refers to as the hyperreal without a site-specific referent. Baudrillard points, with thinly disguised relish, to the pornographic ecstasy of our latter condition:

> [Modern] consumer society lived . . . under the sign of alienation, as a society of the spectacle. But just so: as long as there is alienation, there is spectacle, action, scene. It is not obscenity—the spectacle is never obscene. Obscenity begins precisely when there is no more spectacle, no more scene, when all becomes transparence and immediate visibility, when everything is exposed to the harsh and inexorable light of information and communication.[20]

There is now only surface as postmodern *simulation,* rather than modern *stimulation:* an invasion of electronic imagery into all things, a "forced extroversion of all interiority"[21] that is our postmodern condition—in short, a *perversion of surface culture.* We have killed off our amazement at spectacle *in situ* in much the same way as we previously killed off God (according to Friedrich Nietzsche, in an excess of rationalism): we have developed technologies that turn the display button to an eternal "on," and in the Global Village there is no difference left between public and private, outer and inner space. There is nothing more to show—no more desire for spectacle in the modernist sense of the word—because we are always constantly displaying all. What we have instead "is the obscenity of the visible, of the all-too-visible, of the more-visible-than-the-visible," as Baudrillard effusively claims.[22]

How, then, can we best explain the gap between these bleak contemporary fin-de-millennium configurations of surface and the early twentieth-century celebratory "primal scene" of the same? In defining the modern, Ernst Bloch's "synchronicity of the non-synchronous" or "contemporaneity of the non-contemporaneous" (*Gleichzeitigkeit des Ungleichzeitigen*) is often applied, a phrase whose spatio-temporal sense of crisis initially appears at odds with any timely celebration of the new.[23] But, as social historians of Weimar Germany like Detlev Peukert and Peter Fritzsche have noted, it is precisely out of post-WWI Germany's highly *un*even landscape of modernization that such creative intensity of cultural change (and belief in cultural changeability) also emerged.[24] In defining the postmodern, we find instead an ostensible emphasis on celebration, but not coupled with any motivating Blochian sense of contradictory urgency: this causeless playfulness tires quickly. The "key words" of modernity have been updated to appear like mere pastiches of the old (that is, modern): industrialized capitalism has become postindustrial late capitalism; surface, simulation; visible electricity, invisible electronics; film, channel-surfing (or surfing the Web); real place, virtual reality; political engagement, deconstructionist play (or now, its latest form, socially conscious cultural studies). In a state of exhaustion, the modernist new has passed over into what counts as the traditions of postmodernism: Jameson states that the writings of Marcel Proust and the designs of Frank Lloyd Wright, once revolutionary, are now canonical.[25] Media theorist Norbert Bolz tries to put a positive spin on this shift:

> Modernity was an organized distrust of the senses. Today we are told by depthless surfaces to trust our senses again. The modernist insight went into depth, was revelatory, and tore off the veil from appearances—today we search for the meaning of surface on the surface. That is why we are changing our style of perception: instead of reaching into the depths, we are surfing on the crests of the waves.[26]

Bolz appears to replicate Marshall McLuhan's vision for the role of electronic media in the postmodern age. Nonetheless our era has produced, for the most part, not McLuhan's sought-after postvisual, electronically alert and interactive "extended" human being, but rather a visually overdependent, stimuli-deadened, debt-laden mass consumer.[27]

There is more going on here than just an epistemic dualism of modernist past and postmodernist present: material, technological and perceptual differences notwithstanding, we find ourselves today in a state of exchange referred to by the sociologist Mike Featherstone as the "*trans*-modern."[28] The creative complexities of the Weimar modern provide us, of course, with an important case-in-point.[29] Of this "both/and" aspect Susan Buck-Morss has stated:

> Modernism and postmodernism are not chronological eras, but political positions in the century-long struggle between art and technology. If modernism expresses utopian longing by anticipating the reconciliation of social function and aesthetic form, postmodernism acknowledges their nonidentity and keeps fantasy alive. Each position thus represents a partial truth; each will recur "anew," so long as the contradictions of commodity society are not overcome.[30]

Because the contradictions of our involvement with consumerism continue to deepen along sociopolitical lines, the postmodern voice should not automatically claim that modernity has by now been emptied out. Perhaps we would do better to hope, along with the (unfashionably modernist) voice of Jürgen Habermas, that on some levels at least "the project of modernity has not yet been fulfilled" (significantly, for Habermas, in the direction of an era beyond that of postmodernity).[31]

Adopting the notion of the "trans-modern," the following chapters redress the balance so that the many voices of aesthetic and intellectual modernism, as well as the myriad material facets of everyday life in modernity, are not drowned out by a postmodern revisionism that seeks (even if inadvertently) to reduce all of the modern in a supererogatory gesture to something that on some fundamental level "led to" the Holocaust, Stalinism, and Hiroshima. Jacques Derrida perhaps overeagerly assumes an end to modernity's "domination" agenda with the advent of postmodernity;[32] such claims aside, the entire project of modernity is not going to be leveled off as a false construction to which postmodernity usefully provides a clever deconstruction. Miriam Hansen warns against enacting such reductionism, lest the postmodern critic slide into the same conceptual "totalitarianism" that (s)he is trying to replace:

> The critical fixation on hegemonic modernism to some extent undercuts the effort to open up the discussion of modernism from the traditional preoccupation with artistic and intellectual movements and to understand the latter as inseparable from the political, economic, and social processes of modernity and modernization, including the development of mass and media culture. In other words, the attack on hegemonic modernism tends to occlude the material conditions of everyday modernity which distinguish living in the twentieth century from living in the nineteenth, at least for large populations in western Europe and the United States.[33]

This is why Hansen calls for inquiry that seeks to "reconstruct the liberatory appeal of the 'modern' for a mass public—a public that was itself both product and casualty of the modernization process."[34] This book is a response to such a call.

Linked to Hansen's antitotalitarian call for fresh approaches to the study of modernity is my focus on visuality. Evidently, the study of Weimar German mass cultural phenomena runs in its emotional core somewhat against the grain of the anti-graven-image (*Bilderverbot*) inheritance of Frankfurt School theory. We would do well to remind ourselves that the postwar influence of the Frankfurt School has had, since Nazism, an understandably problematic effect on the study of visual culture per se. This often unacknowledged nervousness before "graven images" must not lead primary sources of visuality to be regarded peremptorily as symptoms of capitalist social disease in need of ideologically informed dialectical redemption. Nor has this rejection of images been limited to the German intellectual sphere: in *Downcast Eyes: The Denigration of Vision in Twentieth-Century French Thought* (1993), Martin Jay has delineated French linguistic resistance to ocular metaphoricity in general, a trend that occurred in precise conjunction with ocularity's cultural ascendance.[35]

My study, then, is couched within what W. J. T. Mitchell has termed the "pictorial turn,"[36] and provides the reader with an unabashed entrée to Weimar Germany's visual plethora of historiographical-cum-aesthetic symbols of everyday life, to be studied in their own right. I seek to retrieve the consumerist spectacle of Weimar German visual modernity on primarily *asymptomatic* terms—not always as a proto-Nazi illness or just plain old capitalist "false consciousness," the manifestations of which are thus eternally in error, but instead as a cultural blueprint of visual life that shows us where our images today have come from. This approach also highlights where our images have journeyed—into postmodernism's subsequent transformation of modern street-based surface into electronically based simulation. Modernity's obsession with and representations of surface may yet surprise us, if found to contain a greater degree of conceptual clarity (and even playful joy) than is presently the case in postmodern versions of the same. Despite this book's return to modernity through the use of New Historicist tactics applied to visual history, it does not engage in a mere duplication of non-self-reflexive positivism: rather, Weimar visuality is resurrected here more as a "communal creation" of then and now, of constantly interacting aesthetic, social, political, filmic, architectural, and economic discourses.[37] My scholarly intention here is a balance of historiography that Jean Starobinski defined, and Martin Jay more recently advocates, as one that touches both a panoramic perspective (*le regard surplombant*) as well as a more intimate, ground-level, close-up gaze.[38] This hermeneutically double approach of applying philosophical and social theory to open up contextual source texts can be understood as a combination of theoretical with archival study.

WEIMAR SURFACES NOW

In what can be for our eyes a refreshing respite from today's infinitely variable, unstable, and hence often confusingly schizophrenic hybridity of products and clientele, the style and visual effects of Weimar Germany operated as a significantly streamlined phenomenon. The sites of surface in the German 1920s were aestheticizations of *function.* They were the latest in artistic design and yet served the everyday public, and were very much part of the industrial economy of the era, having been built up along the model of the new industrial technologies' production lines. Taylorism and Fordism's demiurgic principles of infinite expansion and efficiency—techniques that determined the predominant system of labor, products, and capital for most of the twentieth century[39]—were adhered to in Weimar Germany with a unique fanaticism born of a collective need to repair wounded nationhood in the wake of the humiliations of the Treaty of Versailles and the ensuing loss of colonial and military strength. Fordist-Taylorist focus on the machine climaxed particularly in the context of the relative wealth of the Weimar Republic's economic "stabilization" or "boom" years, after the inflation crisis of November 1923 and before the Wall Street crash of October 25, 1929. As David Harvey comments, conceptions and practices of space and time change according to a knife-edged capitalist dialectic, such that "capitalism perpetually strives . . . to create a social and physical landscape in its own image and requisite to its own needs at a particular point in time, only just as certainly to undermine, disrupt and even destroy that landscape at a later point in time."[40] In this way, the cult of surface was hewn out of Weimar Germany for a period during the mid-1920s, so as to reflect modernity's idealized self-image back to itself.[41]

Consequently, it is not at all coincidental that in the relative boom phase of 1924–1929, Weimar society enjoyed a concomitant upswing in architectural output that entirely matched the economic philosophy of this period. Known as functionalism or *Neue Sachlichkeit* (New Sobriety or New Objectivity)[42] and operative not just in architecture but also in all areas of design, art, and photography, the new constructivist-realist focus replaced expressionism's rough, religious warmth with smooth, logical coolness. New Objectivity's "nonstyle," or rejection of decorative style, constitutes this century's most concentrated systematization of surface, and has become one of European modernism's best-known visual codes. Its discursive figures include such terms as "façade culture," "glamour," "asphalt," and "surface" (*Fassadenkultur, Glanz, Asphalt, Oberfläche*), which appeared repeatedly in the media and literature of the era to describe the modern urban, commercial experience. Moreover, the intensity of people's conception of the city was amplified by the fact that, due to the Wilhelmine era's intense industrialization, Weimar Berlin was the world's third largest city (after New York and London), its population rising to 4.24 million.

Thus entering the "roaring twenties" with bravado, Berlin acquired the position of industrial and cultural leadership over the rest of interwar Europe.[43] The capital was host to 2.5 million workers, or ten percent of all those working in Weimar Germany.[44] By 1929, more than one in four of the total population of 64.4 million Germans lived in cities of more than one hundred thousand.[45]

Evidence of Weimar Germany's New Objectivist "surface" style was inscribed most strongly in the following ways: the transformation induced by modern architecture and the latter's relation to parallel metamorphoses in fashion; the interrelation of outdoor electric advertising with the city street; the evolution of the Weimar film industry, with its movie palaces and film set designs as the respective extrinsic and intrinsic "surfaces" of German silent cinema; and the display of actual commodities in shrinelike store display windows. These, then, are the various *topoi,* the literal surface areas, that form the subjects of the four ensuing chapters in this book—namely, the radical social and aesthetic changes invoked by modern architecture in Weimar Germany, and its relation to the fashion of the New Woman (chapter one); the new architectural spatiality and human sensory perception inspired by electric advertising (chapter two); Weimar cinema as architectural event, both in film production and film reception (chapter three); and the function of the display window as a nexus of Weimar consumerism (chapter four).

Thus each chapter that follows is indicative of how in the middle years of the Weimar Republic there emerged a marked celebration of surface culture in everyday urban life. In these chapters' Geertzian "thick descriptions"[46] of surface, where the topographies of high and low culture become almost seamlessly enmeshed, the joint aim is a cross-sectional hermeneutics of Weimar society—a spatial freeze-frame of surface phenomena as they developed during the New Objectivity years of 1924 to 1929. In an intersecting series of collations of surface phenomena produced during the stabilization years, I present here a synchronically based iconology of the German mid-1920s, in order to relocate and re-present that short, even fragile, period of "stable" creative output during which Weimar visual culture was at its most stunning and most sustained.[47]

Only in Weimar Germany did modernity's cult of surface extend uniformly into *all* visual fields and come to dominate cultural and business production so simultaneously and so distinctively. How and when, then, was Weimar urban spectacle expressed? A useful preliminary exercise in this regard is to chronicle a selection of events that are characteristic of the speed of German interwar modernization, in order to gain a sense of the actual "trope" of mid-Weimar surface culture. The Weimar surface era first developed, however, through the U.S.-assisted economic recovery after the inflation of 1923—the year that Henry Ford's autobiography was translated into German and became, as Jost Hermand and Frank Trommler term it, the "bible of the Weimar stabilization epoch."[48] In 1924, the Rentenmark was able to stabilize postinflation currency, the *Bubikopf* (page boy) hairstyle for women was introduced to Germany from France, and the first part of the Berlin railway was electrified. One year later, the effect of the Dawes Plan took hold and a steep escalation of visually oriented modernization events began: the year witnessed, for example, the opening of the Osram electric company's "House of Light" (*Osram-Lichthaus*) in Berlin, for research into electricity; the prominent installation of the very first "traffic tower" (*Verkehrsturm*), the predecessor of the traffic light, at Berlin's Potsdamer Platz, Europe's busiest intersection; the first escalator in Germany at the Tietz department store on the nearby Leipziger Straße; the advertising journal *Seidels Reklame* marking its first quarter-century of promoting the German advertising industry; the Ford Motor Company's first opening of a German subsidiary; the American dancer Josephine Baker's arrival in Berlin; the opening of Weimar Berlin's premiere movie theater, the Ufa-Palast-am-Zoo; Eugen Schüfftan perfecting his trick effect of mirrors for use in filmic architecture (the "Schüfftan-technique"); the display window competition "Then and Now" (*Einst und Jetzt*) in Berlin; the popularization of the Charleston dance; the founding of the first German national window dressers' guild (Bund der Schaufensterdekorateure Deutschlands); and dozens of exhibitions in Berlin, of, for example, automobiles, shoes, clothing, furniture, radio, hotels, film and photography, and "hygiene."

This incredible pace of production and display was maintained during 1926, the year of several key beginnings, such as those of the Berlin exhibition area with its new radio tower; the movie theaters Gloria-Palast and Capitol opposite the Kaiser Wilhelm Memorial Church (Kaiser-Wilhelm-Gedächtniskirche), marking the completion of the cinema area in central Berlin; Parufamet, the German-American film treaty in which the United States bailed out Ufa, the Universal Film-Aktiengesellschaft; and, most radically, Walter Gropius's ultrafunctionalist Bauhaus building in Dessau (fig. 1). In 1927, the Weissenhof Housing Project (*Weissenhofsiedlung*), organized by the German Werkbund, opened in Stuttgart. 1928 was famous for such technological events as the "Berlin in Light" (*Berlin im Licht*) week, followed by electric display weeks in other German cities; the Mercedes Benz eight-cylinder automobile, which was billed as the "biggest

Figure 1. Bauhaus building, Dessau, designed by Walter Gropius (1926).

event of the year"; and the Zeppelin airship that flew across Berlin and then on to the U.S.—events the like of which were responsible for the trade journal *AEG-Mitteilungen* doubling the length of its issues during that year. By 1929 (the ten-year anniversary of the signing of the Weimar Republic's constitution, and the last expansionist year before the onset of economic depression after the Great Crash), the Berlin railway had been fully electrified; the rebuilding of Berlin's Alexanderplatz was finally completed; the Karstadt department store opened in Berlin-Neukölln; Ufa built its first sound studios at Neubabelsberg; and Germany's largest movie palace, the Ufa-Palast in Hamburg (with 2,667 seats), was opened.

The heterogeneous events of the above chronicle of Weimar surface culture during the New Objectivity years all reflect the rise of a pervasive urban spirit. *Tempo,* or being constantly "on the go," was not just the name of these surface times—although in 1929 it literally became a German brand name (for pocket paper tissues, appropriately enough).[49] The pattern emerging from these "exterior" events entirely matched an "interior" rise of antimimesis in aesthetic modernism, which signified an abrupt end to the dominance of realism in art and writing during the nineteenth century. For the art historian Clement Greenberg, archchronicler of modern art's shift toward the abstract, it was the new focus on visuality as pure, "flat" form that was taking industrial society's obsession with surface one vital step further toward aesthetic iconoclasm. This was the case with cubism's self-predication on the eye as the sole verifying agent that could see mechanically in the manner of aerial photography (just developed in World War I)—a mode of vision by which, stated Greenberg, the "world was stripped of its surface, of its skin, and the skin was spread flat on the flatness of the picture plane."[50] Because, however, modernist thought was both obsessed with and repelled by visuality's rapid expansion into the social imaginary, modernism was also host to an uncomfortable rivalry between visuality and textuality, resulting in a schizoid (antimimetic) condition of representation. As Jay points out in *Downcast Eyes,* modernism brought with it not just a scopic fascination but also its opposite, namely "visual spleen as well as visual euphoria."[51]

This tension within aesthetic modernism helps form an interesting feedback loop for Weimar modernity's surface images, mirroring and influencing the desires of the urban masses on the street. In the German 1920s, the lines between the world of business and the world of the avant-garde become at times more than blurred: to adopt Jay's terms for visuality's role in modernism, it is increasingly impossible to differentiate between a purportedly avant-gardistic "ocularphobia" at work in high culture and a surface-oriented "ocularcentrism" operating in popular culture. Instead, we find in the Weimar years continual crossovers in art and architecture between artist and society—the Bauhaus sought to realize its mission in applied arts for the masses, such as deornamentalized typography, kitchen units and other mass-produced furniture, chinaware, and utensils, while architects like Erich Mendelsohn or Hans Poelzig built some of their most radical designs for the display needs of consumerism and the film industry. Similarly, applied arts like advertising were entirely adept at using those same formal shock techniques of visual crisis that were also the trademark of modernist writing, art and film. Modernist representations, then, as both afterimages and prophecies of industrialization, dared to draw new polysemous distinctions, the bold preconditions for the postmodernist epigenesis to come.

TACTILITY IN THE CITY

Modern urban surface culture was experienced as an outdoor "reading" of the city's commercial life force, namely the street. These streets of surface in which zones of business, dwelling, advertising, and entertainment all simultaneously coexisted and intermingled were naturally located in the city center. City centers like New York, London, Rome, and Paris vied with each other for "world-city" status. Berlin, likewise, was an active competitor: "Everyone once in Berlin" was the bid of a tourism slogan about the German capital, and a tourist poster circa 1929 declared that "Germany Wants To See You." But the world financial markets of the postwar years have since brought about a tectonic shift of urban identities away from their heterogeneous sites of modernity, and toward what social theorist Saskia Sassen has determined to be a far more streamlined postmodern condition of globalization. In *The Global City* (1991) and *Cities in a World Economy* (1994),[52] Sassen shows us how modernity's streets of *flânerie*—which were located in the metropolis, itself in turn the main showplace of the nation-state—have since given way to an erosion of national borders and new transnational market spaces, at least in certain selected cities like New York, London and Tokyo, whose financial markets guide the world economy and out of which worldwide corporations are headquartered. The global city, according to Sassen, is still governed by the rules of agglomeration and centralization, but it has more in common with its interrelated sister global cities than it does with its own host nation. Sassen therefore takes issue with the doomsayers of the urban in postmodern times, pointing out that globalization has not, after all, resulted in total decentralization of power out of the city. From the *Weltstadt* of modernity, we have thus reached the global city of postmodernity.[53]

Despite Sassen's compelling depiction of the global city's role within the new world economy, we need to account for the modern street experience's demise in the contemporary metropolis. Here we can refer to French theorist Paul Virilio, who, in "The Overexposed City" (1984), investigates how we have lost the immediacy of street apperception that was so vital to the culture of 1920s Berlin or New York. "Does the greater metropolis still have a façade?" he asks, in the sense of a socio-spatial façade providing a break, boundary, or "urban wall" between the intramural metropolitan area and that which is outside the city.[54] The answer, in Virilio's dystopic vision, is no. Suburbia has denuded the city's street-fronts of their modern discursivity. Worse yet: electronic transparency is replacing the traditional opacity of buildings' surfaces to the extent that we are "no longer ever in front of the city but always inside it": there is only the "interfaçade of monitors and control screens."[55] In the computer age, continues Virilio, there is a loss of urban tactility, and the "architectonic element begins to drift": "urban space" has lost its "geographical reality."[56] Here, Virilio is transferring to the spatial logic of the city Baudrillard's thesis of the postmodern "ecstasy of communication," where a "nonreflecting surface, an immanent surface where operations unfold" has replaced the Platonic "mirror and scene."[57] As Baudrillard also states of the new virtual urban condition: "To grasp . . . [the] secret [of America], you should not then begin with the city and move inwards toward a screen; you should begin with the screen and move outwards towards the city."[58] But unlike Baudrillard's ambiguous poetics, Virilio's vision of the contemporary-futuristic metropolis, where the new production mode of "interface man/machine replaces the façades of buildings and the surfaces of ground on which they stand," is wholly negative.[59] This electronic-human syncretism has supplanted the physicality of humans interacting with the city street and the ensuing act of "tact and contact": instead we have the "elimination of attention, of human confrontation, of the direct face-à-face, of the urban vis-à-vis."[60] When Virilio looks back at the urban landscape of modernity he sees it sadly as a "'Monument Valley' from a pseudolithic era, . . . a ghostly landscape, the fossil of past societies for which technology was still closely associated with the visible transformations of substance."[61]

Virilio's epitaph for the tangibility of the modern city is extreme in its pessimism and is unresponsive to Sassen's recognition that urbanism is doggedly persisting into the era of the postmodern world economy, albeit under a new understanding of what centralization actually entails. The site-specificity of the modern street is now the globalized centrality of transnational capital. In this context, we can refer back to Weimar Germany both as the apex of the urban modern and as the germination of the urban postmodern. Weimar spectacle no longer encouraged the directionless dandyism of the Parisian nineteenth-century arcades, nor was it (yet) today's virtual (i.e., immobile) nonexperience of the TV-supplied living room; rather, it demanded one's physical presence on the city street. "Berlin by night" was both actual and fabulated; that is, it was both real on the Friedrichstraße and "reel" in the genre of the "street film" (*Straßenfilm*) with its film-set urbanity. The *flânerie* that took place during the 1920s in such "world cities" as Berlin and Manhattan was rationalized, applied window shopping—a systematic feminization of the masses, as Andreas Huyssen has defined urban modernity,[62] that bespoke the Fordist dictates of mass production and consumption, but was still host to a definite sense of *place* for the visual effects, a location for the action, a path for the participant (the mass character of the *flâneuse*). Weimar visual display was created as a spatial experience whose location was still phenomenological and still on the (newly asphalt-covered) street.

Postindustrial cities today, in contrast, certainly make use of, but no longer in fact *require*, a series of commercial streets to be the site of spectacle. They differ conceptually very much from the vision of the city called for by functionalist architect Le Corbusier, who wanted the street to be a "traffic machine," a new factory "organ," but *not* yet eclipsed as a display carrier by vehicular traffic's demands.[63] The electronically commanded surfaces of the renovated Times Square may shine brighter and better than ever before, but even this exterior glory is being undermined from within by Walt Disney and virtual reality arcades setting up shop under its very nose. Window shopping does not, for the most part, take place on the street anymore, but in the electronic home or, at best, in atrium-filled malls: even the recreation of Berlin's Potsdamer Platz into a millennium-site of urban entertainment amply indicates this shift toward IMAX-enhanced interior space. Walter Benjamin's claim that "streets are the dwelling of the collective" is no longer true.[64] As Anton Kaes has stated, film director Godfrey Reggio's postmodern commentary on technology run amok, *Koyaanisqatsi* (*Life Out of Balance,* 1983), has overtaken Walther Ruttmann's modern film-poem of machinic celebration, *Berlin, Symphony of a City* (*Berlin, Sinfonie der Großstadt,* 1927).[65] Such, then, is our loss of tactile urban living for which Virilio is so nostalgic. The majority of Americans no longer actually *walk* in the city. The city comes to us via the media wherever we live, so there is no more need to experience urban surface culture firsthand. "Real" modern manufacturing industry has sold out to "unreal" service industry, outsourcing, and a sheer excess of retailing. Our age is all but devoid of what Michel de Certeau calls "pedestrian street acts,"[66] and the still extant *flânerie* of old, rich industrial cities has become all but impossible to duplicate.

We may well ask: is there any such thing, then, as postmodern *flânerie?* Yes, but only in those few urban spaces whose infrastructure was established during industrial modernity (especially Manhattan, Boston, and San Francisco, or European city centers like Amsterdam, London, Paris—or even parts of reconstructed Berlin, and this despite its fractured inner city where the Wall once was).[67] Or again yes, but only when the *flânerie* concerned is not based on actually walking in the city itself. Think of Stairmasters and other recreation-center regimentations of postmodern America's required level of "strolling"—fitness in as condensed a temporal and spatial span as possible. The only places currently being designed to be *walked* (in the United States, but increasingly so in Europe as well) are suburban shopping malls, and even they are increasingly fashioned like Disneyland/Disneyworld/EuroDisney as the replacement village greens of today.[68] Indeed, the simulational theme park of postmodernity has replaced the spectacular world trade fair of modernity. Outside of Disney in the postmodern urban dystopia, strolling in the city is all too often associated with the loitering of street persons: as Anne Friedberg states, the *flâneuse* has become a bag lady; and in "imagineered" shopping malls, where limited walking does take place but only in a safe interior, such ugly sights are banned.[69] We can stroll in Disneyland, but when we do so we are moving within a "*simulation of the third order,*" as Baudrillard states: it "exists in order to hide that it is the 'real' country"; its function is to make us think it is imaginary, disguising that "the real is no longer real, and thus . . . saving the reality principle."[70] Umberto Eco agrees, finding the step from Disney's "total fake" to the "totally real" of hyperreality to be an instant one.[71] Las Vegas's Strip now promotes itself as a pedestrian zone, but one that is an electronic film set intended to seduce the walker-gambler into the casinos waiting behind the constantly performing film-façades that reach out to the sidewalk.[72] For Friedberg, the only thing that actually moves with us in the postmodern city is our "spatially and temporally fluid visuality": if we engage in *flânerie,* we are not so much street-smart as virtually guided.[73]

The Weimar German urban street experience, on the other hand, even when driven rather than walked, was still set up for a spectatorship commanded by the peripatetic eye. While Weimar Berlin was one of the first (and last) metropolises to successfully combine mass transit (of train, tram, and bus), pedestrianism, and the new car culture, Los Angeles was the first city whose infrastructure fully superseded foot travel. Already boasting more cars in the 1920s than any other city in the world, L.A. signaled, in 1929, the end of the city-walking era with the opening of Bullocks Wilshire department store: its main entrance was in fact at the back of the building, to suit customers emerging from their cars in the massive parking lot; this back entrance was decorated with a ceiling fresco fittingly entitled "Spirit of Transportation."[74] The rise of the suburban automobile culture that decentered L.A. before any other city did not go unnoticed in the early 1930s by Nazi Germany's castoffs—the left-wing, Jewish, or otherwise banned antifascist exiles, who soon began to sense that in joining the diaspora to L.A. they had left behind what was, by comparison, the intellectual "depth" of Weimar Berlin and traded it for, as Bertolt Brecht felt, the false spatiality of the city of the angels.[75]

In short, in ways far beyond the surface culture of 1920s Berlin, Los Angeles of the subsequent two decades preempted the postmodern emptying-out of the metropolis—even as it seemed initially to fulfill the heavenly garden-city promise as dreamed of by expressionist antiurban utopianists like Bruno Taut.[76] As urban critic Mike Davis explains in his *City of Quartz* (1990), boosterist Los Angeles engaged in a dialectical coalescence of façade "sunshine" and film-set "noir": devoid as it was (and is) of any "*civitas* of public places," L.A. became the "ultimate city of capital, lustrous and superficial, negating every classical value of European urbanity."[77] Erich Maria Remarque, in exile from his native Berlin, complained of his adoptive city's surface paradise that "real and false were fused here so perfectly that they became a new substance."[78] It was due to the ubiquitous L.A. mode of movie-set-inspired "façade landscapes"[79] that Theodor W. Adorno and Max Horkheimer felt justified in subsuming their attack on the Culture Industry within their wholesale rejection of the Enlightenment for having produced masses so ready for synchronization (*Gleichschaltung*) that they would consume or vote Nazi in the same blind breath—a process of massification that facilitated the reduction of the Jews by the Nazis to nonhumans fit only for extermination. The new "hygienic" bungalows on the edges of L.A. make Adorno and Horkheimer nervous in the uncanny resemblance of these "living cells" to the throwaway, transitory architecture ("unsolid structures") of modernity's exhibition era; both building-types appear to have been made only to "toss them away after short usage like cans of food."[80] The latter-day "panopticon shopping malls" at which L.A. excels these days are, states Davis, even more unsettling, born as they are of a desire not just to "kill the street" but to "kill the crowd":[81] thus the very harbinger of the urban modern, the (now multiracial) masses, are being eradicated at the same time that the street is being stripped of its walkable traces.

EXHIBITING SUPERFICIES

And yet postmodern urbanity is not completely without steps toward reinstating *flânerie*, even in the suburban, electronic age. There are indications that the modern street experience can be revived, if only on the level of postmodern public monuments, which self-consciously lend themselves to the cause. A site of urban spectacle can be created that self-consciously plays with the architectonics of surface and material superficiality: indeed, a longstanding landmark of this is Renzo Piano and Richard Rogers's Pompidou Center (a.k.a. Beaubourg, 1972–1977) in Paris, an exhibition structure that is painted as bright as a playhouse and shows its interior plumbing on the outside, much to the delight of tourists who come for the tactile experience of enjoying its insane surfaces, riding its transparently encased escalators along the exterior wall, and neglecting the exhibits within.[82] Another will occur if the artist Christo succeeds in gaining municipal permission to create his temporary Central Park Project: a series of yellow, cloth-draped gateways positioned along the paths of Central Park, designed for people to walk under and view from both near and afar, underneath and aerially, as interconnecting curves. Frank Gehry's new Guggenheim Museum in Bilbao, Spain, which opened in October 1997, places the postmodern attempt at spectacle (a titanium-covered, silvery play of complex spherical structures, arising as if in whimsical, organic motion out of the ground) in ironically suggestive, dialogic counterpoint to the straightforward city streets around it.[83] The most immediate effect of such postmodern re-creations of the walkable city is indeed recreational: for a surface spectacle that encourages, even demands, a participatory pedestrian experience is first and foremost a sign of urban self-confidence, and play.

In this way, Christo and Jeanne-Claude's *Wrapped Reichstag* (*Verhüllter Reichstag*) of 1995 (fig. 2), twenty-four years in the making, constituted an acknowledgment of postmodern nostalgia for the advantages of the modern city experience, in that it obstinately sought, for two weeks, to recreate the ludic power of modern urban display and individual *flânerie*.[84] As anyone knows who was there that summer, the only way to experience this event was to go right up to the building and touch it, and then revisit it under a different sky so as to catch the alternating effects of the 330,000 square feet of aluminum-coated fabric covering the façades and the roof of the building—and of course to enjoy the ongoing street-festival atmosphere that its presence produced for the two million people who came to spectate and celebrate. "I have made a building out of a building," said Christo at the time of construction: "For that I needed material, the structure of a material."[85] Its massive vertical folds sought to create a temporal pause in which surface could rebecome, in an quasi-retro way, the site of new spectacle: a veiling (*Verhüllung*, the Christos insisted, and not the more commercially inclined term for wrapping, *Verpackung*)[86] that aimed for revelation (*Enthüllung*) via the play of material surfaces. It was a playful version of Heideggerian *alētheia*, whereby Christo's *technē* inspires a moment of truth that lies, conversely, in the "concealedness" of folding the veil rather than in any unfolding or "unconcealedness."[87]

Figure 2. *Wrapped Reichstag* by Christo and Jeanne-Claude, Berlin, 1995.

Christo's literal surface-art also had a special meaning for Germany. By draping itself over the German *Volk* inscription and transforming the architectonic "horizon of expectations" of the building into something quite new, the fabric cover of 1995 temporarily detoxified, or dislodged, the overweighty monumentalism that the 101-year-old Reichstag had always signified for Germans, and opened up the conceptual surface area of the building to new possibilities beyond that of its burning in the Nazi spring of 1933 and its Cold War role as a bulwark of the West against the Berlin Wall only a few yards away.[88] Christo's wrapping, then, can be seen as an optimistic gesture that anticipated the Reichstag's 1999 grand reopening with its Norman Foster glass dome. One German newspaper article insisted on finding a protofascist sense of foreboding in the wrapping of the Reichstag, linking it to a photograph of the monumental sculpture *Kameradschaft* (Comradeship) by the Nazi sculptor Josef Thorak in its wrapped condition before the opening of the German pavilion at the Paris Exhibition of 1937.[89] Nonetheless, a more accurate hermeneutical gauge would be to state that the rarity of Christo's *Wrapped Reichstag* is constituted precisely in the way its monumentality was turned on its head into a masterful *Verfremdungseffekt,* thanks to being remade out of surface, and hence could be experienced guilt-free.[90] As Huyssen states, Christo's Reichstag is a "monumentality that can do without permanence and without destruction, that is fundamentally informed by the modernist spirit of a fleeting and transitory epiphany, but that is no less memorable or monumental for that."[91]

The brevity of the Wrapped Reichstag reminds us that surface architecture is a self-conscious expression of the transitoriness of the modern metropolitan experience. Nineteenth-century European exhibition architecture began this mode, with an unashamed emphasis on surface appearance such as the world had never seen before. This utopian construction style, from the Crystal Palace of London's Great Exhibition of 1851 onwards, emerged in order to best display and fetishize, as in a museum, the industrial nations' latest technological achievements and colonially gathered goods, promising even greater things to what soon rose to millions of world fair visitors (14,837 in 1851; 32 million at the Paris Exposition of 1889; 27.5 million at Chicago's Columbian Exposition in 1893; 50.8 million in Paris again in 1900).[92] In 1896 the social theorist Georg Simmel suggested that such architectonics of temporary excess was not only permissible but even desired, in that the "exhibition with its emphasis on amusement attempts a new synthesis between the principles of external stimulus and the practical functions of objects, and thereby takes this aesthetic superadditum to its highest level."[93] Simmel was thus the first to promote a clear "exhibition style" in such architecture: a liberated, experimental style that is unabashedly oriented toward surface and transience rather than toward depth and permanence.[94]

World fairs thus offered the viewer-participant an aesthetic of display on the grandest possible scale, and spectators were to be induced by the extravagance of exhibition architecture into thinking more highly of the commodities on display, which became in turn indivisible from their settings.[95] As Buck-Morss emphasizes, here the spirit of advertising was born: "At the fairs the crowds were conditioned to the principle of advertisements: 'Look, don't touch,' and were taught to derive pleasure from the spectacle alone."[96] Likewise, Eco stresses the "semantic apparatus" of exhibitions: "In an exposition, architecture and design explode their dual communicative nature, sacrificing denotation to very widespread connotation. . . . [I]n an exposition we show not the objects but the exposition itself."[97] All of this had of course a pragmatic reason for existing, as the Weimar cultural critic Siegfried Kracauer noted: the Parisian frenzy for "joy and glamour" (*Freude und Glanz*) was occasioned and stimulated by its serial hosting of world trade exhibitions in the latter part of the nineteenth century; these in turn stimulated the world economy.[98] Benjamin, in "Paris—Capital of the Nineteenth Century," declares: "Exhibitions are the places of pilgrimage for the fetish Commodity. . . . World trade exhibitions glorify the exchange value of commodities. They create a space in which their use value diminishes. They open up a phantasmagoria into which people enter in order to let themselves be distracted."[99] Benjamin finds industrial exhibitions to be a globalizing "synthesis of the arts," a *Gesamtkunstwerk* of nineteenth-century aims.[100] He invokes Faust for the modern age in the guise of the bourgeoisie who call out to the exhibition's wondrous show of order, property and production: "Oh tarry yet, thou art so fair."[101]

The most decadent, overblown example of the exhibition age's excesses in ephemeral surface occurred in the World's Columbian Exposition in Chicago, which produced a White City style of neoclassical, white-clad buildings south of the city. It was a surface event, in that it was literally built that way—as fakery. The overly ornate structures looked like marble to last the ages, but they were for the most part not real buildings at all but mere façades composed of "staff" (plaster and fibrous binding over wood and steel), which burned down weeks after the fair closed (the only remaining structure is now the Museum of Science and Industry). This act of consumptive squander notwithstanding, Chicago's self-image and boosterism were certainly aided by the event: in their famous *Plan of Chicago* of 1909, Daniel H. Burnham and Edward H. Bennett referred with pride to the grand "transitory city" of the World's Fair as a galvanizing motor in city planners' dreams for designing the new, materially purified Chicago.[102] Fittingly, it was this exhibition that first introduced picture postcards (as miniature mirror-surfaces of itself) to the world.

For modernist tastes, however, such as Lewis Mumford's, the Chicago fair was a corrupt veneer, a false "municipal cosmetic" whose "monumental façades" concealed rather than revealed or improved housing conditions for the masses.[103] Likewise, after having heaped praise on the glass architecture and the Eiffel Tower born of the French exhibitions, architectural critic Sigfried Giedion dismissed the Columbian Exposition's plaster architecture as the beginning of the end for the exhibition age.[104] This point of view is echoed by Stuart and Elizabeth Ewen, who, in their analysis of modern consumerism, satirize Chicago's 1893 Venetian mock-up for being a "city that was primarily surface, true to the priorities of the age," namely modernity's "logic of consumption."[105] But herein, precisely, lies the importance of the Chicago fair: the American modern ethic of instant mass production and swift consumption that was so characteristic of the exhibition was played out here as an architectural narrative. Even though the Columbian Exposition's surface architecture was impossibly ornate—a nostalgic shell with which to line the future-oriented technological items on display within—its strength lay in its performance ethos of great spectacle and proliferation of goods, which encouraged an unapologetic eye for the façade, both architectural and commercial. Indeed, we can only imagine that for visitors at this fair, where almost all the states of the U.S. were represented, the playground of surface architecture facilitated a sense of America as a unified entity, wherein social disjunctions could be temporarily set aside.[106] The Chicago fair's emphasis on colonial prowess notwithstanding,[107] the rapturous play-experience effected by Christo's Reichstag does not, in this sense, seem so very far removed.

Yet we should not go so far as to think that because the world exhibition age is dead, we have no more equivalent displays of grand self-consumption on the scale of an entire metropolis. Indeed, more contemporary versions of the White City would include Olympic cities, which are created and unmade in the space of months—a recent example being the rapid makeover of temporary, media-clad architecture at Georgia Tech shortly before the 1996 Olympics in Atlanta.[108] Then there is Las Vegas, whose "decorated shed" architectural style Robert Venturi suggested in 1972 we learn from: a freely applied sign-city of urban commercial sprawl, rich in symbolic iconography.[109] But the new Las Vegas of the millennium, America's fastest growing city, has become the ultimate exhibition-city for the postmodern age. Las Vegas today, as Ada Louise Huxtable comments, is "the real, real fake at the highest," where it "has finally all come together: the lunar theatrical landscape of the Strip and the casino hotels, the amusement park and the shopping mall, all themed and prefabricated and available as a packaged vacation for all."[110] A dozen or so of the world's largest hotels are here, including the largest of all, the MGM Grand, with its 5,005 rooms. Each superhotel is a theme park in itself (the Venetian, the Paris, Treasure Island, Excalibur, New York–New York, or Luxor);[111] each is a "mini-city," a "synthetic play world" in itself.[112] In Las Vegas, we may *think* we are experiencing the urban, but it is always and only the urban-as-simulacrum; and unlike Christo's events, its deracinated surfaces nonetheless seek the conviction of permanence. If it gives to visitors a sense of American identity, it is a Culture Industry character far in excess of the media-oriented commercialism of either Christo's art or the Chicago Columbian Exposition. The whole city has been effectively rewrapped to become the top tourist destination in the country, the most unabashed example of surface-play, of architecture as "gaming" (the postmodern word for gambling).

PHILOSOPHIES OF COUNTERFEIT

In an important sense, Las Vegas's latest metamorphosis is to be expected. If we are honest readers of ourselves and of our relation to the world—so the prime philosopher of cultural modernity, Nietzsche, tells us—we should admit that on some basic level we all enjoy surface; for human nature has always wanted a play-state of surface values. Nietzsche's insight into truth covering up for lies reminds us that we naturally desire to glide over the surface of things and envision forms rather than content. His posthumously published essay "On Truth and Lies in an Extra-Moral Sense" (1904) explains how established language covers up its own metaphoricity, claiming it as metaphysical truth;[113] and this mere linguistic sleight of hand, perceives Nietzsche, is what disguises human awareness of illusion and dream-image, like the aesthetic Apollonian shield covering over Dionysian abysmal insight. Indeed for Nietzsche, in his transformatory role as architect of surface values and grand proto-postmodern debunker of the Platonic order of representation, there is greater truth in recognizing the meaninglessness of the origin and the ensuing importance of the tangible, superficial-yet-impenetrable world, than in searching for immaterial origins and metaphysical depth.[114] In his notes of 1880, he undermines the Kantian premise of the "thing-in-itself" by suggesting: "If we try to look at the mirror-in-itself, we discover nothing but things. If we want to grasp things, then we end up arriving at nothing but the mirror again."[115] All we have is our ability to "scan" relations; we cannot reproduce the world mimetically.[116] Underlying the philosopher's pursuit of truth, asserts Nietzsche, there is an instinct even more basic to all life and pleasure: namely the Will to Power, which asserts itself through what may also be termed a Will to Surface. At the heart of all things, Nietzsche finds affective forces eternally and agonistically inclined toward supremacy and play, toward destructiveness and creation, toward illusionary nonknowledge and forgetting. Those who know what true "depth" is, he suggests in *The Gay Science* (1882), prefer to exist on the surface, "like flying fish, playing on the peaks of the waves": they possess a certain "skin-coveredness" (*Hautlichkeit*).[117]

Such a focus on *Hautlichkeit* is also a trademark of the urban culture of the Weimar Republic's stabilization years. For the purposes of this study, we can infer that Nietzsche's high praise, in his 1887 preface to *The Gay*

Science, for the ancient Greeks' surface culture is indeed transferable onto Weimar Berliners: "Oh, those Greeks! They knew how to live. What is required for that is to stop courageously at the surface, the fold, the skin, to adore appearance, to believe in forms, tones, words, in the whole Olympus of appearance. Those Greeks were superficial—*out of profundity.*"[118] But something has ineluctably changed since the Greeks, and even since the Weimar Berliners: the twentieth century's creation of mass culture, particularly the cult of consumerism in an urban environment, has overtaken Nietzsche's perception, and has made our all-too-human predilection for display into an absolutely unavoidable optical value system. The way power is nowadays unremittingly located within the realm of commodity display would not have pleased Nietzsche, if his criticism of the Wagner cult is anything to go by. This composer, argues Nietzsche in *The Case of Wagner* (1888), instigated the "rise of the actor" into music, a new decadent age in which the "whole no longer exists: it is put together, planned, artificial, an artefact."[119] With respect to modern mass consumerism, the "art of appearance," Nietzsche offers in *Human, All Too Human* (1878) an aristocratic-Luddite critique of mass taste and of the mechanization of production: "All that impresses the eye and is inexpensive will now gain the upper hand."[120]

The unintended great irony of Nietzsche is that he is both a herald of the surface-era of modernity in the realms of philosophy and morality (and of its subsequent technocultures in the postmodern age)[121] and a Zarathustran naysayer of the leveling (for him socialistic, democratic), mass consumer manifestations of precisely this transvaluation of values. Indeed, he abhors modern urban society for being so surface-oriented, for the way it "outwardly demands mannerliness and the newest fashions, and inwardly insists on rushed understanding and exploitation of the ephemeral, even the momentary—and nothing besides!"[122] The transitoriness of modernity can of course be approached with less conservative resistance than Nietzsche. But for Nietzsche's aristocratic radicalism, modernity in the material sense of the word signifies the age of the democratized Last Man, the era of the merely journalistic: "the three M's—of the moment, opinions, and fashion" (*des Moments, der Meinungen und der Moden*).[123]

Nietzsche's fin-de-siècle vision of the downside to surface culture came entirely too late to alter the path of urbanization and its effect on the psyche.[124] Other voices acknowledged the ineluctability of this process. In a Baudelairean vein, Simmel recognized the importance not of dismissing but of delineating the tiniest or most superficial instances of modernity's new "concrete" culture in all its material but short-lived manifestations and permutations.[125] In his 1903 essay "The Metropolis and Mental Life" ("Die Großstadt und das Geistesleben"), Simmel posits that an "atrophy" of what is surely Nietzsche's highest tenet, namely "individual culture," is the unavoidable consequence of modern massification.[126] Urban surface culture encourages social independence but not private creativity. The new metropolitan dweller, states Simmel, cultivates a "blasé attitude" of rational superficiality and indifference in order to survive the onslaught of perceptual and psychological stimuli brought on by "each crossing of the street, . . . [by] the tempo and multiplicity of economic, occupational, and social life."[127] The emergence of surface-attitudes among city-dwellers is thus a Darwinian strategy for adapting to life in the industrial age; as far as the actual consequences of the shocks of urbanization for those who fail to successfully adapt, Simmel prefers to sit on the intellectual fence.

Simmel's vision of modernity and its effects upon the individual is decidedly based on the money economy. In his essay on the 1896 Berlin trade exhibition, for example, Simmel notes the ambiguous parallel between the exhibited objects of world trade fairs and the metropolitan individual: in the environment of competitive display, there exists a risk-benefit situation of (self-)depreciation versus (self-)accentuation. The very multiplicity involved in the "stimulus of appearance" offers the metropolitan type, like the value of the items on display, both the very real danger of "levelling and uniformity" (as Nietzsche recognized) as well as the tempting high of further self-aggrandizement.[128] Simmel, sharing Karl Marx's insights if not his transformatory zeal, perceives that the capitalist circulation of money "with all its colorlessness and indifference" is the unstoppable wheel or *perpetuum mobile*[129] of the economy, forever turning these transformations of the collective urban psyche and all ensuing visual expressions of surface culture; for money alone "hollows out the core of things, their individuality, their specific value, and their incomparability."[130] Most significantly, Simmel bases his analysis of the money economy not on Marxist production value but on exchange (i.e., exhibited, sign) value, and the effect that exchange value as driving force has on people.[131] Marx's insight into the modern human condition as one of alienation before the magical autonomy of commodities is thus transformed by Simmel into an oscillating ride with both reifying *and* liberating experiences—at least for those who are permitted to participate.[132] This view of continuous circulation is reiterated as an ideal articulation in urban planning during the Weimar years: improving the flow of money becomes synonymous with improving the flow of traffic. In plans of 1930 for the Hindenburg Platz intersection at the Stuttgart railway station (fig. 3), or in

Figure 3. Hindenburg Platz, Stuttgart (1930).

Hans Scharoun's unrealized design of 1925 for the Berlin exhibition area (fig. 4), the streamlining of building façades and street directionality alike is seen, in true Simmelesque fashion, as a facilitator of traffic flow and as a marker of street-smart efficiency for the urban denizen.

A second respondent to Nietzsche's concerns about modernity is Benjamin, whose unfinished magnum opus, *The Arcades Project* (*Das Passagen-Werk*, 1927–1940), likewise enters into the consequences and effects of surface exteriority in modern urban culture from the perspective of an unabashed metropolitan participant who was raised in turn-of-the-century Berlin, attended Simmel's lectures, and lived through the German 1920s. *The Arcades Project* effectively gives us the prehistory of Weimar modernity with a vast collection of archival notes on the rise of the fetishistic nature of commodities (and hence the origins of surface culture) in Second Empire Paris. From his enforced exile in Paris from Nazi Germany during the 1930s, Benjamin writes about this city as the implicit forerunner of the Weimar metropolis, while at the same time sketching a de facto epitaph of the latter, for the experimental atmosphere of Weimar urban surface culture had by then been thoroughly condemned by the

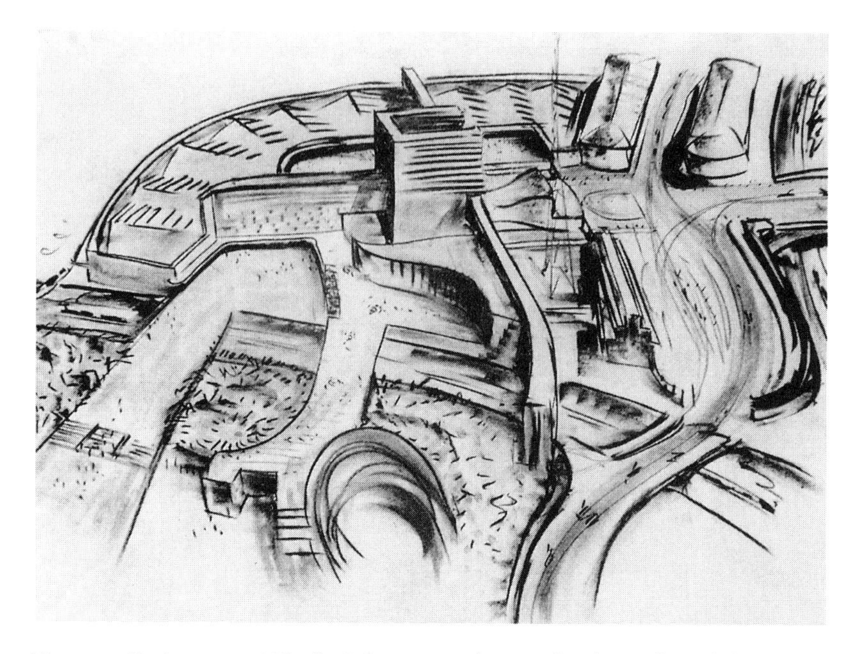

Figure 4. Design entry ("Spider") by Hans Scharoun for the Berlin exhibition area competition, 1925.

Nazis as one of morally, racially, and politically bankrupt "asphalt literature" (*Asphaltliteratur*). By calling forth the materiality of this system of commodified display in the act of writing, Benjamin finds he can create an historical picture of "dialectics at a standstill," in which "that which has been comes together like lightning into a constellation with the now."[133]

By far the most important dialectical pictures in Benjamin's key work on the consumerist mentality of industrial modernity are the Parisian *galeries* or *passages*,[134] the panoramas of shopping desire that appeared after 1800 in response to the growth of the textile industry and immediately predated the era of grand department stores. Drawing heavily from Giedion's *Building in France: Building in Iron, Building in Concrete* (*Bauen in Frankreich: Bauen in Eisen, Bauen in Eisenbeton*, 1928)—whose smooth-surfaced typography was the work of Bauhaus photographer László Moholy-Nagy—Benjamin states that "construction plays the role of the *subconscious*"[135] and is not merely a consequence of the *ratio;* in this way, Benjamin views the Parisian arcade-constructions as allegorical "dreams around the scaffolding of these body processes." He is alert to the light-giving function of the arcades' glass-covered roofs, and their role as the true predecessors of the contemporary Weimar urban pedestrian experience in that they were "both house and street" for the *flâneur*—who, as the perambulating spectator of urban life, became therein both within and without, private and public, seller and commodity, in the manner of the prostitute.[136] For as long as the *flâneur* could stroll in the arcades, the "traffic" of commodification was disrupted and disruptable.[137] The Parisian arcades are metropolitan modernity's first site of "dream houses of the collective"; they preempt the late nineteenth century's rise of the department store in that they are "houses or walkways that have no outside [*keine Außenseite*]—like the dream."[138]

Through the wandering vision of the *flâneur* or the camera-eye, Benjamin's Paris most clearly resembles a *Gesamtkunstwerk*—not a Wagnerian one, but a deconstructed "total artwork" that highlights, rather than veils over, its origins of production and processes of technique. Benjamin muses that the Parisian city map could be rendered into a "passionate film" that could portray, in half an hour, the transformation through the centuries of this labyrinthine network or "concentration" of streets, arcades, *métro*, and boulevards.[139] Note that the Benjaminian city enters the realm of the "total work of art" by the back door, and creates a different kind of vision of the same: the ultimate Parisian monument, the Eiffel Tower, is defined by Benjamin as adhering to the "yardstick of the 'smallest,'" that is, to the *genus loci* of the arcades' own construction motif of iron-and-glass montage.[140] Both Eiffel Tower and arcades accentuate the modern city as "trace" (*Spur*).[141] That is to say, Benjamin knows how a modern city's surface traces are montage-Babels and can organically deflate any monumentalism being imposed upon them. The Eiffel Tower is the epitome of this double discourse: built as a display item for the Paris Exhibition of 1889, its twelve thousand metal components are held together by the "principle of montage." Benjamin thus approves of this implicit presence of the labyrinth within the monument.

The collective yet cacophonic vision that *The Arcades Project* reconstructs, with its surrealism-inspired tableaux of infinite reflections and distortions, is Benjamin's acknowledgment that what modernity really signifies is at odds with Max Weber's dictate regarding industrialization. Weber assessed modernity thus:

> The increasing intellectualization and rationalization does *not* . . . signify an increasing general knowledge of the conditions of life under which one exists. Rather it means for us something different: knowledge thereof or belief therein: that one, if one only *wanted to, could* find the answer at any time, that there are therefore basically no secret incalculable forces that play a role here, that on the contrary one can in

> principle *control* all things through *calculation.* But this means: the disenchantment of the world.[142]

The tale of modernity's reenchantment charted by Benjamin's montage-epic asserts the other, less often shown side of the Weberian coin, which normally reflects the stamp of modernity's "disenchantment of the world" (*Entzauberung der Welt*) as the high price to pay for the rationalization of all spheres. Hence the collective unconscious of the modern industrial age was to be found in the apparently functionalist realm of glass transparency that consistently exteriorized the interior. As Buck-Morss states: "On an unconscious 'dream' level, the new urban-industrial world had become fully reenchanted. In the modern city, as in the ur-forests of another era, the 'threatening and alluring face' of myth was alive and everywhere."[143]

This new mythic dream-state of surface culture, particularly in Benjamin's own Weimar era, constituted at first impression an antimyth, for it was obsessed with reproducing an anti-auratic, antiornamental, efficient functionality in the name of capitalist profit margins. Nonetheless, Benjamin finds its displacement effect entirely mythologizing; for, rather than serve the masses on the path toward critical self-understanding of their roles in the capitalist production-and-display process, all the surface dream does is support them (and now us) narcotically in a delusionary condition of isolating conformity and unfulfillable desire. Against this Benjamin posits a neo-Enlightenment reading of his *Arcades Project*, which was to have provided a stimulus to social change and greater autonomy for the reader-consumer.[144] While this dream was being continued in modernized, "objectified" format in the Weimar era, it is by extension still being dreamed today, albeit in the electronic media's far more intrusive acts of simulation. This, indeed, is why we should care about the Benjaminian desire for epiphany, for a wake-up call from our continued virtual slumbering.

Yet if Benjamin is open to the active participation of the consumer, his openness remains contingent on various transformations required for the new dream-world of commodity fetishism. What Benjamin is seeking and what he demonstrates in his own texts is not a retrogressive ornamental style, but instead a surface-orientation that is less rigid and will permit a (Nietzschean, or proto-postmodern) play between the traces of surfaces. In *One-Way Street* (1926)—his first exploration of material, local, street culture—he suggests an almost Gnostic vision of the modern world's fallen state of disintegration, noting how the best hermeneuts, namely children, are (like dada-artists) fascinated by "detritus" (*Abfall*) of all kinds, by "any site where things are being visibly worked on," where there is building, gardening, housework, et cetera going on: their imaginary games with discarded materials permit them to redeem a new microcosmic "world of things" (*Dingwelt*) within the larger world.[145] If, then, we could create with commodities (the ultimate surface-items for grown-ups) in the same way that children create a "new, intuitive relationship" within the materials and debris they play with, then we would be responding to modernity as Benjamin would have us do.[146]

Michel de Certeau echoes Benjamin's sentiment when he writes: "The child still scrawls and daubs on his schoolbooks; even if he is punished for this crime, he has made a space for himself and signs his existence as an author on it."[147] This sort of creative, subversive act from within is, moreover, not so dissimilar from the resistance of the colonized vis-à-vis the colonizer described by Edward Said.[148] But despite this visionary claim, even Benjamin senses that for Weimar Germans, particularly after the inflation crisis of 1923, any sense of *Geist* has been eradicated from the "brazen solidity" (*schamlose Massivität*) in the display of luxury goods—the strength of which is so complete that "all the mind's shafts break harmlessly on their surface."[149] His underlying unease with his contemporary consumer culture (and, moreover, with the ensuing Nazi adaptation of the same) is perhaps most apparent in his preference, as an exiled writer during the 1930s, for ensconcing himself primarily not in the present crisis of fascist Europe but in a genealogical re-creation of the (by then already buried) social imaginary of nineteenth-century Paris.

Benjamin's prophecy, his belief in the power of texts to create a new collective subjectivity among readers, one that might awaken them from their repressed state of alienation hidden within the dream factory of urban surface culture, is shared (albeit in a less visionary, less revolutionary way) by Siegfried Kracauer, fellow Weimar discussant and former student of Simmel. Kracauer's attention to German modernity's cult of surface is particularly conscientious and astute, due in no small part to the fact that his first profession (until 1919) was as an architect.[150] Although Kracauer left behind his rather uninspiring experience with late Wilhelmine architecture—to become, during the Weimar years, a novelist, journalist, literary and film critic, newspaper editor, and social theorist, often all at once—the "primacy of the optical that architecture requires," as Adorno relates, "remained with him in sublimated form."[151] Even more than Benjamin, Kracauer finds greater social reality in deciphering the "hieroglyphics of any spatial picture" in his vicinity than in more distant metaphysical constructs.[152] Unlike Benjamin, however, he finds in surface culture not so much a new dream-world emerging out of Weberian rationality, but an intensification and multiplication of rationalized work-scenes operating even within that dream.

Kracauer's critiques of social phenomena, particularly those of the Weimar metropolis, remain indebted to Simmel as a master theorist of surface. Through analyzing the material world around him with its "distorted conceptual petrifications," Kracauer hopes, in a Simmelesque gesture, to ascend above a recognition of the alienated modern condition to an "aware[ness] of the many-sidedness of things" and an ability to interpret "relations between phenomena."[153] But this surface-dance does not quell a desire to penetrate to what lies beneath the upper (*Ober-*) part of surface (*Fläche*). In his 1920–1921 essay on Simmel, for example, Kracauer praises an archaeological-cum-Maeterlinckian approach of defamiliarization that "advances from the surface of things to their spiritual/intellectual substrata" in order to demonstrate that "this surface is symbolic in character": "All dullness and shabbiness disappear from the world's external surface, as if it had suddenly become as transparent as glass, enabling one to look in and through it into otherwise hidden layers of being which it reveals and simultaneously covers up."[154] Note that Kracauer retains here, in the cause of sociopolitical awareness-raising or exiting from the dream of commodity fetishism, a firmly Platonic belief in the conceptual depth that still remains beneath the fog of material *Oberfläche.*

The opening statement of Kracauer's landmark essay on Weimar mass culture, "The Mass Ornament" ("Das Ornament der Masse," 1927), resonates as the author's plaidoyer for a social history version of a critical hermeneutics of psychological "deep surface."[155] Kracauer declares that what appear to be superficial phenomena in his and indeed any historical era function in fact as nonsupervenient manifestations of the collective unconscious:

> The position that an epoch occupies in the historical process can be determined more strikingly from an analysis of its inconspicuous surface-level expressions [*Oberflächenäußerungen*] than from that epoch's judgments about itself. Since these judgments are expressions of the tendencies of a particular era, they do not offer conclusive testimony about its overall constitution. The surface-level expressions, however, by virtue of their unconscious nature, provide unmediated access to the fundamental substance of the state of things. Conversely, knowledge of this state of things depends on the interpretation of these surface-level expressions. The fundamental substance of an epoch and its unheeded impulses illuminate each other reciprocally.[156]

Thus the task of the anthropologist of material culture is to explain these structures of surface signification. Kracauer reminds us transversely of Claude Lévi-Strauss's geological metaphor of cultural analysis as an enterprise of digging up the surface to reveal both synchronic and diachronic patterns.[157] Michel Foucault updates this proposition in *The Archaeology of Knowledge* (1969): archaeological (genealogical) exploration seeks not origins but an analysis of the "already-said," of the "discursive formation, and the general archive system to which it belongs."[158] Foucault's essay "The Discourse of Language" extends this plaidoyer for surface: referring to his method of "exteriority" or "materiality" in reading historical discourse, he insists that "we should look for its external conditions of existence, for that which gives rise to the chance series of these events and fixes its limits."[159]

During his 1921–1933 tenure at the *Frankfurter Zeitung* (for which he wrote nearly two thousand articles),[160] Kracauer repeatedly selected topics that allowed him to excavate the discursive potential provided by the material, exterior phenomena of Weimar culture. As the 1920s progressed, however, and increasingly after his absorption of Marxist theory in 1925, Kracauer displays a more resigned acceptance of the opacity of surface.[161] Writing in 1930, for example, about the demise of Berlin's nineteenth-century arcades, he asks somewhat helplessly: "What good is an arcade in a society that itself is only an arcade?"[162] While the method of inquiry exactly matches the object of inquiry in the Kracauerian universe of Weimar Berlin, the author himself is far from an easygoing observer of what he sees and measures. His comments for the *Frankfurter Zeitung* on the newly redesigned Alexanderplatz in 1932, for example, indicate that he respects this wholly rationalized, lake-sized area as a "model of organization," as indeed a pinnacle of Weimar functionalism—but his tone teeters on abjection when he considers what lies beneath the literal surface of this sublime immensity: namely, the "hygienic brightness" (*hygienischen Glanz*) of the Alexanderplatz's three metro stations, whose inhuman "fanaticism for order" is far from user-friendly and stands in stark contrast to the lives of the working people who must use it.[163] Or again, in an article on Christmas decorations for children in a Berlin department store in 1930, he voices concern that the miniature fantasy worlds presented there are too perfect an illusion, too Taylorized and well organized to be true fantasies, with guards ensuring the children walk through the displays toward the exit at an appropriate pace ("Keep moving! No standing still!")—a sure reminder for the children that "no place in paradise is assured them."[164]

Kracauer thus presents contemporary readers with an intriguing conundrum, because he uses the surface-worship so symptomatic of the Weimar Republic as an inspirational focus and stylistic methodology for his own cultural critique, but only in order to get beneath and beyond it to the needs of surface culture's audience, the masses. His writings on film and mass urban culture of the Weimar 1920s betray a certain contradictoriness: as journalistic yet simultaneously intellectual articles, they are surface-texts intended to be read not by the masses but by what remains of the *Bildungsbürgertum*, the German educated elite; they are essays ostensibly in league with, yet at times transparently condescending toward, the mass Other (particularly when that Other is gendered female).[165] But we also see here his socialist concern for these deluded, disadvantaged masses—a caring that generates both his occasional impatience at their gullibility before the Weimar system of image-production and his constant faith (before, that is, the years of Nazism) that they will nevertheless meet him halfway.

As both Benjamin and Kracauer intimate, the 1920s witnessed a massification of the work of art into entertainment forms that mirrored the Taylorized working reality of the Weimar masses and matched the psychological need of the modern metropolitan type for distractions on an equivalent scale. The average working week fell from just over fifty hours in 1925 to just over forty-one hours in 1932.[166] The weekend was created as a leisure-time institution for the newly urbanized working and middle classes; the movie houses lured people from their homes of an evening. Benjamin's exoteric image is of the Berlin Lunapark's bumper cars (*Wackeltöpfe*) throwing off-duty factory workers around, not only as a "taste of the drill" of mechanized employment but also as the "art of being off center" (*die Kunst des Exzentriks*) that *un*employment (like the experience of war, or economic crisis) may induce.[167] Kracauer also refers to the Lunapark as a place where "pleasure is organized. . . . here the production line rules."[168]

Kracauer's most famous illustration for this understanding of Blochian *Gleichzeitigkeit* of entertainment and work is contained in the fragmented, mechanized body parts of the (originally English) Tiller Girls dance troupe (fig. 5). Their revues constitute for Kracauer a typical pluralized surface phenomenon of Fordist functioning, what he terms the "mass ornament" par excellence of the commodified substrata of Weimar society. The Tiller Girls are the entertainment end of a culture that, the spiritualistic Alfred Döblin rather gloomily concurs in 1924, is driven by a "naturalistic," "technical," and necessarily urban impulse; in this engineering age no "deepening, [no] spiritualization of the impulse" can occur.[169] The Girls'

Figure 5. The Tiller Girls (1929).

synchronized, collective body (referred to at the time as "one entity with twenty-four legs") could endlessly form, unform, and reform itself in myriad shapes for the enjoyment, both erotic and militaristic, of the (male) spectators.[170] For Joseph Roth, however, in his 1925 review of the revue phenomenon, the dancers' sexuality was not remotely sexual because it functioned only "in the service of hygiene," efficiency, and production: these were the bourgeois virgin "girls" who would later in life give birth to future soldiers.[171] Kracauer extends this de-eroticized sexual-soldier notion to find in the Tiller Girls revue a machinically abstract aesthetics that unwittingly reflects the rationalized "linear system" of capitalism: "The girl-units drill in order to produce an immense number of parallel lines, the goal being to train the broadest mass of people in order to create a pattern of undreamed-of dimensions. The end result is the ornament, whose closure is brought about by emptying out all the substantial constructs of their contents."[172] Likewise, in the later essay "Girls and Crisis"

("Girls und Krise"), Kracauer finds in the dance of a similar troupe, the Alfred Jackson Girls, the "machinic activity" of a factory shift; but, writing now in 1931, he notes that their mythologized mission of Americanism, namely to represent the "*functioning* of a blooming economy" back to itself, has become, after the Great Crash of 1929, only an "emptied-out montage," a shadow of its former self.[173]

Kracauer's judgment of the mass ornament is laced with, on the one hand, his optical delight in the Girls, who, like all the surface phenomena of New Objectivity, so efficiently reflect the masses back to themselves, and who display a new grace of movement and supraconsciousness of the kind only dreamed about by Heinrich von Kleist in his essay "On the Marionette Theater" ("Über das Marionettentheater," 1810); and, on the other, a disgust for the same masses' proclivity toward remythologizing these ornaments into depthlike meanings which can, by dint of their own structure, have no meaning. Kracauer's position vis-à-vis the mass ornament is thus an ambivalent one. First, one could say that he is, as a low-flying observer of all the localities of urban mass culture, glad that the massification-cum-modernization of life has brought about a socialization of art; whatever the masses produce and are entertained by, it is certainly a healthy step beyond the history of ideas or elitist art practices, which are, he opines, left far behind in terms of social power and relation to the real.[174] He finds it more praiseworthy than blameworthy that Berlin audiences preferred the "surface glamour [*Oberflächenglanz*] of the stars, films, revues, and spectacular shows" to high art, for only here, "in pure externality" (*im reinen Außen*), could the masses encounter their own true image.[175] However, since whatever engages Western mass culture is congenitally linked to profit and to the capitalist system of values, this certainly damages the mass ornament's claims to be a total "end in itself," if all it does is mirror capitalism's own *Selbstzweck* of infinite production, expansion, and reproduction.[176] If an irrationality is born out of the incessant, capitalistic *ratio*—for the latter is *not* synonymous with reason—then the "ornament's conformity to reason is . . . an illusion."[177]

Not surprisingly, then, Kracauer's Weimar-era writings resonate with fears for the loss of *Mündigkeit* in the age of the mass ornament, a mummifying of intellectual spirit before the still-new visually oriented cultural power, but he continues to hope that it can be worked through. He gives somewhat naive credence to the "cult of distraction" only as "improvisation, as a reflection of the uncontrolled anarchy of our world."[178] But neither can one deny—and Kracauer certainly does not wish to deny—an obsessive exhilaration in the mass ornament as the single most impressive factor of the masses: this is their focus on display, on showing and reshowing their liberation within the state of fragmented exteriority. The display-focus of Weimar urban culture is the latter's dazzling mirror held up to modernity and attracts us today as kinaesthetic descendants of this period. Only when petrification steps in and the Wagnerian, self-mythologizing "total artwork of effects" (*Gesamtkunstwerk der Effekte*) is attempted does the mass ornament fail its own people, and a system of entrapment arises out of the visual pleasure.[179]

Kracauer's most negative sentiment concerning Weimar surface emerges in his strong criticisms of any passive or blind acceptance of façade culture. It is indicative of his concern that behind the consumerist motto of (self-) aggrandizement the social condition of most people, particularly the uprooted millions who migrated from the countryside to the cities during the Wilhelmine and Weimar years, in fact worsened. According to Kracauer in his study *The White-Collar Workers* (*Die Angestellten*, 1929), a keyword of surface culture, namely "glamour" (*Glanz*), proves itself to be a mere "pseudoglamour [*Similiglanz*] of counterfeit social heights."[180] This delusionary attraction to the "shelter" provided by *Glanz* was particularly endemic to German white-collar workers, whom Kracauer decries as being "intellectually homeless,"[181] yet whose numbers exploded to three-and-a-half million in the Weimar years, multiplying by a factor of five while blue-collar workers' numbers only doubled.[182] Elsewhere, Kracauer ironically refers to hotels and stores with display windows as "shelters for the homeless"[183]—an epithet repeated in his account of the glittering boulevards of Paris during the Second Empire as another such shelter for the "homeless" (this time upper-class dandies).[184] Kracauer takes pains to point out how the value-system of the new middle classes dooms them to false consciousness because of their hypnotic self-identification with the upper classes as the latter are represented in advertising and film. In this context, it is less surprising that the orphanlike white-collar workers would subsequently—in the wake of the Great Depression and in the ruins of their faith in all that Weimar surface glamour could bring them—constitute the largest constituency of National Socialist vote.

RESISTANCES TO WEIMAR SURFACE

What emerges here is a tension in Weimar modernity—between the apparent ludic pleasure and liberation inherent in surface culture, and a new form of punishment or internalized (self-)reification if one buys into surface culture too completely. The obvious ideational fascination with surface culture evidenced in the writings of Simmel, Benjamin, and Kracauer is for all these authors' ambiguity and discomfort, wholly positive in contrast to the crisis-ridden plebiscites drawn up by more negative Weimar observers. Warnings against the dangers of surface culture arose alongside the hype: at the height of the mass ornamentation of Weimar society, when architectural, literary, and artistic modernism attempted gestures parallel to Fordist functionality by wiping the representational slate clean and promoting only efficient functionality in all spheres, doubts were raised about the implacability of these transformations. Stefan Zweig, for example, was a vocal defender of the by-now seriously endangered German "inwardness" (*Innerlichkeit*); in his 1925 essay "The Monotonization of the World" ("Die Monotonisierung der Welt"), Zweig bitterly predicts that mechanized standardization on all cultural levels, owing to the "conquest of Europe by America," will flatten out German individuality onto a single, monotonous plane of surface: "Everything is becoming more uniform in its outward manifestations, everything leveled into a uniform cultural schema. . . . [M]onotony necessarily penetrates beneath the surface. Faces become increasingly similar through the influence of the same passions, bodies more similar to each other through the practice of the same sports, minds more similar for sharing the same interests."[185] Massification through the flatland of surface values becomes the ultimate nightmare for the educated German Nietzscheanist.

The need for resistance is seen in Franz Kafka's stories as a necessary, if unattainable, exit to the law that is nightmarish modernity. Kafka's narrative environments have been read as both timeless—as stories happening within a nameless, placeless psyche—and, more recently, as clear historical contextualizations. The latter occur in his stories, notes, letters, and novels both on the level of favorable, mirrorlike responses to the aesthetic and architectural avant-garde's critique of ornament in the declining years of the Habsburg fin de siècle,[186] and also as scathing commentaries on the systematization of surface in industrial modernity. His tales preempt the path of "Weimarization" in that they occur with agonized protagonists nonetheless fixed in a recognizable modernity that is hopelessly bureaucratized and absorbed in an ongoing reification of the self.[187] Turning the Kafkan vision outwards, the French observer Léon Daudet damned slavish embrace of bureaucracy, technology, and commerce in the German 1920s as merely the "latest form of fatalism. . . . The rushing, almost automatic development has turned the German people into a big barracks full of brand manufacturers." Instead of knowledge and *Geist,* all that is left of German culture is an "enormous information office."[188]

A related but reactively anti-American sense of urgency pervades the writing of the extreme right-wing Weimar author Gertrud Bäumer, for whom in 1926 the Weimar era has a "public that loves the crisis-ridden as a kind of stimulation for the soul."[189] Following Oswald Spengler's account in *The Decline of the West* (*Der Untergang des Abendlandes,* 1918–1922) of the fall of Western culture and the rise of the technical-capitalistic age, and also Thomas Mann's distinction in *Observations of a Non-Political Man* (*Betrachtungen eines Unpolitischen,* 1918) between alien *Zivilisation* and German *Kultur,* Bäumer sees a direct correlation between the demise of European spirituality and the rise of American imported surface-values as the "threat to the soul by the outer style of life . . . the flattening-out and the objectification of human relations . . . the alienation [*Veräußerlichung*] of life."[190] Another conservative nationalist, Friedrich Schönemann, was more direct: he couched his complaint about the egregious effects of the propagandistic "mass influence" of Americanization on Germany on the claim that it was a disguised continuation of America's anti-German propaganda campaign during the Great War.[191]

Antipathies to Weimar surface culture arose on both ends of the political spectrum: on the *völkisch* right, surface was retaliated against wherever it was deemed to threaten or destabilize the status quo of autonomous nationhood, social elitism, and high culture; on the left, it was blamed where it contributed to rather than broke through the false consciousness promoted by capitalism. The Marxist critic Georg Lukács, writing in 1922, depicts social alienation as a literal surface related to the bourgeoisie's spiritual entrapment, or reification (*Verdinglichung*), by the phantasmagorical hold of commodity fetishism. Commodities facilitate a superstructural world of false consciousness that can yet be broken through to reach the "concrete" relations of the base beneath and thus cause change in social practices. Lukács is confident that surface culture is a crust that is "cracking . . . because of the inner emptiness."[192] Yet even Lukács does not deny that his era is witness to a "quantitative increase of the forms of reification, their empty extension to cover over the whole surface of manifest phenomena."[193] Ever in search of hermeneutical meaning in art as in class struggle, he attacks the ensuing absorption of realist mimesis into the spectacle of empty surface-worship in impressionism and naturalism.[194] Nonetheless, Lukács asserts that by rendering conscious that which has been made immanent or unconscious, this layer of reification can yet be undone for workers: the structure of commodity fetishism "can be overcome only by *constant and constantly renewed efforts to disrupt the reified structure of existence by concretely relating to the concretely manifested contradictions of the total development.*"[195] Lukács' words echo those of Kracauer when the latter promotes the insight that the apparent order of Weimar social space would soon "burst apart" to show up the "*disorder*" underneath—as indeed it eventually would in 1933, but not in the political direction Kracauer and Lukács had hoped for.[196]

The issue of whether the cult of surface in German modernity results in an emancipatory dream-world or a collective denial of free will (for those who ingest it unthinkingly, or who are trampled on as they resist others who profit from it) engendered some particularly critical literary visions of the latter scenario, such as in Ernst Toller's late expressionist drama *Hurrah, We're Alive!* (*Hoppla, wir leben!*), which was staged by Erwin Piscator in 1927. In Toller's parabolic rise of the Weimar Republic out of the ashes of the failed civil revolution, the façade of the Grand Hotel setting is opened up to reveal governmental and capitalistic corruption within, and is on stage literally exchanged for the façade of a lunatic asylum, because "today there [is] no border between madhouse and world."[197] The drama depicts Toller's socialistically inspired desire to actively resurrect a holistic form of humanity out of modernity's fragmented state of exteriority; but the overwhelming pessimism of such works cathectically reenacts a melancholic reflection of this reified human condition, as if in a broken mirror. Similarly, in Erich Kästner's darkly satirical novel of late Weimar's bankrupt values, *Fabian* (1931), the eponymous protagonist has a ghoulish dream in which people literally fall into a mirror-machine of modernity, and thence through the mirror (of surface culture) become their own reflected selves, trapped like insects in amber beneath the glass layer.[198]

In the end, it was not the critics of the self-celebratory stance of the Weimar surface era that defeated it, but rather the aftereffects of the 1929 "Black Friday" stock market crash. By 1933, the last year of the Weimar Republic, the surface dream was over: Berlin, reeling in economic crisis, showed every sign of desperation and degeneration in its frantic price wars in store windows over items that no one could afford to buy.[199] The average wage (for those who still had one) sank to pre-1924 levels.[200] Everywhere in Berlin buildings were for rent, and new construction practically ceased.[201] For the keen observer Kracauer, writing in 1931, the widespread poverty was clearly visible under the surface, despite occasional luxury cars and prevailing "glamour attitudes" (*Glanzperspektiven*) of denial: he sees that the "signals [of need] are pointing up rather like masts of sunken ships over the mirror-smooth surface" of a Weimar era in its final phase.[202] Novels such as Kästner's *Fabian* and Christa Anita Brück's *A Girl Manager* (*Ein Mädchen mit Prokura*, 1932), a novel of the banking crisis, reflect the dire state of economic, spiritual, and moral exhaustion of a German democracy that no longer believed in itself or in modernity's project. New Objectivity, which had begun as an earnest term for faith in progress and Fordism, declined as a satirical one when surface values failed to deliver. The once-successful merger of New Objectivity's aesthetics and consumerist pragmatism became lost in the midst of failed businesses and the unemployment of more than five million. But the intoxicating tempo of modernity continued, straight into the fatal elections that elevated the *new* façade, Hitler, to power.

Nonetheless, the enunciation of a new mass cultural superstratum that began in the 1920s is still in force. In our condition as postmodern epigones we are still inevitably responding to the heritage of Weimar urban culture. To retrospectively study the German modern is the furthest from engaging in *memento mori*. Unlike our state of excess spectacle (Debord's view), or the totalizing invasion of the hyperreal into our field of vision (Baudrillard's), Weimar surface was, or at least appeared to be in its autocentric concatenations, a sign of life. Rather than dismiss the vitality of 1920s visual culture as a Debordian "negation of life,"[203] as carrying the seeds of future postmodern destruction within itself, we can instead promote this era as an opportunity for heuristic anamnesis. Weimar still surfaces; its exegesis is still very much "now."

SURFACE, ACADEMY, AND WORLD

As a final note to this introductory chapter, I would like to comment on the ironic predicament that I, as author of a book on surface culture, face, and indeed that all intellectuals face (since the very act of intellection suggests abstraction and profundity), in an era when cultural power arises out of simulational entertainment rather than philosophical depth. In *The Illusions of Postmodernism* (1996), Terry Eagleton mocks Baudrillardian discourse and those who emulate it for selling out to consumerism even as they dare to step out of the ivory tower of *Geist:* "The epistemology of the disco or shopping mall," he states laconically, "is hardly the epistemology of the jury, chapel or voting booth." Eagleton finds that the "terrors and allures of the signifier" are but a "glamorous substitute for baulked political energies, an ersatz iconoclasm in a politically quiescent society."[204] In a related vein, the late Bill Readings, in *The University in Ruins* (1996), finds that the university's traditional educational mission has been commodified to the point of paradigmatic collapse, a situation compounded by the apparently radical epistemology of race-class-gender studies by postmodern intellectuals engaged in cultural studies, whose work amounts in fact to nothing more than a servile reproduction of consumerist dictates: "Rather than posing a threat, the analyses provided by cultural studies risk providing new marketing opportunities for the system."[205]

Eagleton and Readings thus express their distrust of postmodernists' tendency to gloss over the inability of the contemporary intellectual to actively contribute to and change society; the problem is not so much the loss of the now-defunct system of self-formation (*Bildung*) at the university level, but postmodernist academicians who claim they are enacting change when all they are doing is mimetically reproducing that which Pierre Bourdieu defines as their own rubric of existence, namely "cultural capital"—the "aesthetic disposition" that presupposes a "sort of withdrawal from economic necessity."[206] But even Bourdieu is still too idealistic in his conception of cultural capital: while the weightings of the latter may vary across national and ethnic borders, it has become wholly part of the age of total commodification. Rather than enjoy a distance to the economy, today's intellectuals are cultural capitalists: this is how intellectual-aesthetic expression is actually valorized. Eagleton and Readings feel they cannot just sit by as they watch the academic discourse of cultural studies effectively share corporate values, especially when it claims to subvert the status quo from within.

Weimar Surfaces does not claim such pseudorevolutionary status for itself, but neither does it reject a certain degree of preconditioning by the current commodification of intellectual life. Bourdieu's epithet for the production of knowledge is fitting in that modern visuality in Weimar Germany was cultural capital in the earlier etiological sense of reflecting the commodification of mass culture back to itself (as well as actively constituting it); so there is little reason for aspiring toward any different appellation for the object of the present study. This may in fact be the best way to write historiographies of visual culture; as W. J. T. Mitchell recently pointed out, it "may be time to rein in our notions of the political stakes in a critique of visual culture and to scale down the rhetoric of the 'power of images'"; for Mitchell, the more interesting question remains the desire, rather than the power, operative in visuality—creating thereby a "model of the subaltern" that can be "invited to speak."[207]

To the degree that modern visual culture needs to be uncovered from its subsumption within postmodernity's totalizing mechanism, which tends to claim modernity's innovations as its own, Mitchell's suggestion is a helpful one. In what follows, I attempt a reactivation of ocular cultural memory: I strive to rescue and engage dialogically the traces of modern surface out of their immanent eclipse within the postmodern. Weimar Berlin simply understood what we have since ceased to appreciate due to our overexposure, namely the dynamic side to façadism: "spectacle, action, scene."[208] The need for retrospective retrieval is something Benjamin knew all too well:

> The true picture of the past flits by. The past can be seized only as an image which flashes up at the instant when it can be recognized and is never seen again. . . . For every image of the past that is not recognized by the present as one of its own concerns threatens to disappear irretrievably. . . . History is the subject of a structure whose site is not homogeneous, empty time, but time filled by the presence of the now [*Jetztzeit*].[209]

As we enter the twenty-first century, our awareness grows of twentieth-century modernity's surface culture as a former *Jetztzeit,* as an image that flashes up just when it is about to fade from urban memory. This recognition grows as a comparative dose for what is glaringly absent from the postmodern "suburbiascape." We who have come after modernity may no longer feel required to share any Marxist-modern *Angst* before consumer culture's inherent negativity and fetishistic disguises (the vast majority of our students certainly do not). However, whether we are Marxist, centrist, or otherwise, we would do well to remember, at least, that this capitalist "false consciousness" is precisely what postmodern culture is essentially predicated upon. Let's not pretend the absence of the historical and literal processes located surreptitiously behind the theoretical-cum-virtual façade!

1 Functionalist Façades
The Reformation of Weimar Architecture

Reine Konstruktion ist das Kennzeichen
der neuen Formenwelt.

Hannes Meyer

THE BUILDING'S NEW FACE

"No more façade," announced the architectural critic Adolf Behne in 1925.[1] Weimar Germans evidently agreed, albeit with a sense of the absurdity that this proclamation entailed: in 1929, for example, a cartoon in the *Berliner Illustrirte Zeitung* parodied the current spate of façade-renewal on buildings in the German metropolis with before-and-after mug shots of a man in front of a building (fig. 6). The overblown Wilhelmine ornamentation on the building's façade, and in the man's own outer appearance, is shown liberated, streamlined, rejuvenated, technologized—a makeover that projects efficiency and dynamism: in short, both man and building have undergone a process of "New Objectification." The cartoon's comparison clearly satirizes the typical "architectonic 'facial operation'"[2] that many urban German buildings underwent during the 1920s, from old, impotent inefficiency to new, potent austerity (as in fig. 7)—but the foregrounding of a human male is suggestive of the polysemous levels of signification included in the transformative motion of architectural cleansing.

Another depiction of such change can be found in a 1929 issue of the *Berliner Zeitung*, where an upbeat article, dedicated to how Berlin is "changing its face overnight" through these "rejuvenated façades," describes both the general upheaval and excitement in the neighborhood caused by the temporary veiling of a building with scaffolding. Inhabitants feared break-ins by *Fassadenkletterer* (burglars accessing apartments via the scaffolding); local businesses whose storefronts were under wraps

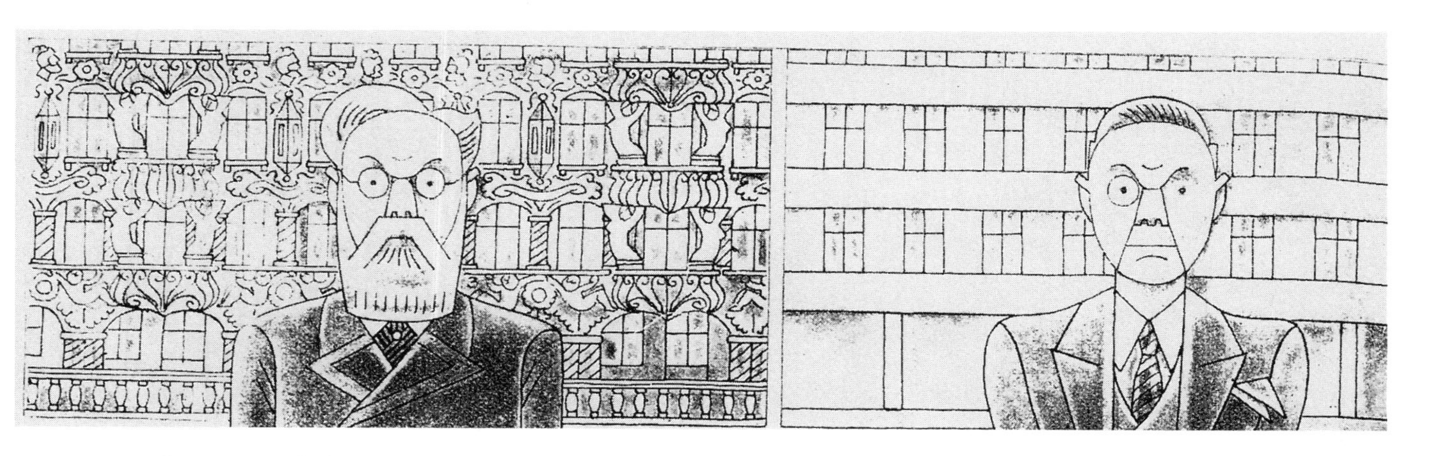

Figure 6. "Modernization: The house-owner Gieselmann before and after the renovation of his façade" (*Modernisierung: Der Hausbesitzer Gieselmann vor und nach der Erneuerung seiner Fassade*), by H. Abeking (1929).

Figure 7. Before-and-after sketch of the corner of Uhlandstraße and Kurfürstendamm, Berlin (1929).

reduced prices ever further in order to attract customers; the builders knocked off all the old decorations (balustrades, garlands, cherubs etc.) and, behind a curtain, began the process of adding the building's "new garment," this time made of smooth mortar mixed on the street below; and finally, after about a month, the locals gathered to wonder at the newly revealed façade. As one observer noted, 1920s fashions of architecture and fashion were of a pair: "Look there, the house has had a page boy haircut!" (*Kiek mal, das Haus hat sich einen Bubikopf schneiden lassen!*)[3]

A third illustration of such humor is in the satirical journal *Der Querschnitt* of the same year, which stressed the extremism of the functionality-fad in an article whose own form reads as telegrammatically as the electric advertising texts on the Weimar city street:

> For we live in an age of objectivity. A chair is for sitting—stop—a bed for sleeping—stop—a book for reading—stop—and a façade for renting out spaces for electric ads. That both saves space and uses space. And whoever knows the street scene of Berlin by night thanks his creator for the scratched-off doll-like façades [*abgekratzten Puppen*]. These flat surfaces don't spare and cover anything up anymore, they are . . . a truth-bound affirmation of a soberly thinking and calculating people, without any pale ideals.[4]

From such tongue-in-cheek comments, we can infer that the debate over façade-renewal was more than might appear to just meet the eye: it affected and reflected city-dwellers' individual and collective identity as much as it did urban design.

The façade-renewal of modernity was first and foremost a purification of the surface, a purification that then consciously exposed precisely this surface.[5] It emerged as a cleansing motion from the late nineteenth century's phase of extravagant decoration, the swan song of which was the 1900 Paris Universal Exhibition, with its incredibly complex, Orientalesque exhibition halls obstinately looking back at the past rather than into the new century.[6] Modern architecture was, in contrast, intended as the promotion of a structure's (bare, hence authentic) face without need for any (extra, hence inauthentic) mask. The general call of Weimar architectural modernity was for the building thus changed (as well as its inhabitants, their attitudes, their habits, and the clothes they wore) to present only essence, no more and no less: namely, "smooth forms, pure lines, and the origin of function [*Ursprünglichkeit des Zwecks*]."[7] The Weimar spirit of building against the grain of the decorative monumentalism from the Wilhelmine decades pervaded all display-areas of life, including the text: Behne and Martin Wagner, Berlin's city planner, as editors of the volume *The New Berlin* (*Das neue Berlin,* 1929), proudly announced the format of their publication as one of consciously ornament-free display: "We do not want to give this journal any façade, and we do not want to stylize its front."[8] The difference between the old Wilhelmine and the new Weimar style was seen as the fruits of technological progress—an increased demand for architectural-cum-societal honesty, for "*much greater* clarity and lucidity."[9]

The architectural cleansing taking place, an integral part of "life in the big city" of Weimar Germany, was a "multiple weaving of surfaces" guided by a mindset that was far from utopian.[10] It was recognized, for example, that "the Modernist gospel of bold, bare surfaces" had definitely capitalist uses in focusing the public's attention when on the street. Hence the most incisive effect of all the architectural reenvisioning came with its commercially oriented contributions—such as in a 1929 design by Johann Emil Schaudt for a new Tietz department store in Berlin-Schöneberg, with a horizontally streamlined façade; or in the curved façade designed by Hans and Wassily Luckhardt and Alfons Anker for an office block on the Potsdamer Straße.[11] Or again, the advantages of artificial light, especially, dictated that the "shop-sign" façades of movie palaces should be nonornamental and unfenestrated; this was seen to be an economy born of the requirement of "plain surfaces irradiated by light."[12]

In short: the modern architectural cult of surface was blatantly mined by Germans for the purposes of their capital city's aggrandizement. Façade renewal lent a confidently visible, tangible tone to the "*world-city spirit*" sought for Berlin, staging itself as metropolis of the world.[13] A symptomatically popular publication of this ilk was *The Rise of Berlin as a World-City* (*Berlins Aufstieg zur Weltstadt,* 1929), which, while acknowledging that the spate of façade removals over the last several years had been less than perfect in all instances, nonetheless valorized it positively:

> Houses of the [18]90s, lathered in the worst ornamental entrails, with façades of clueless apportionment, were suddenly rejuvenated, in that their first floor or even several of the lower storeys were seized and conjured into one of the modern store surprises. This often led to strange contradictions between individual parts of the thus-changed house. The upper and lower parts would not go together any more. The rapidity of conversion in the structural praxis became apparent, sometimes to a comical degree. But the result was nonetheless positive, since impossible buildings that had looked at the new age like pathetic ghosts of a died-out fashion now received at least in their essentials a new sense of life.[14]

In texts such as the above, the connection between the modernizing transformation of the buildings' façades and the new city- (or even empire-) building on behalf of a renewed Germany is made transparent. At stake here is Weimar Germany's particular application of modern architecture's emphasis on building a rejuvenated collective spirit to match the rapid tempo of the mechanized era. For that end, the loss of a city's recent architectural memory seemed to many Germans to be more than worthwhile: the eradication of the Wilhelmine building style signified a convenient eradication of the empire's defeat in World War I.

The fact that the urge to renew façades extended beyond individual buildings to the reformation of the metropolis as a synecdochal emblem of the collective is attested by Wagner's unrealized project of 1929 for Berlin's Potsdamer/Leipziger Platz, to cure the congestion of traffic and Wilhelmine buildings alike with a drastic stripping-away of all unnecessary items, all in the name of speedier circulation (fig. 8). Indeed, in Weimar Germany, architecture-as-surface never stood alone from national identity, despite its "international" tag; during the stabilization years in particular it was regarded as contributing positively to a sense of national pride—so much so that the German pavilion for the 1929 world trade exhibition in Barcelona was designed by the functionalist architect Ludwig Mies van der Rohe. One also thinks here of Hans Poelzig's still-standing semicircular Broadcasting House (Haus des Rundfunks, 1930—now part of Sender Freies Berlin), with its sliced-off front of reflective brown tiles and windows, directly facing the then-newly-completed exhibition area (*Messegelände*)—an imposing double-act of shiny new façades for showing off Berlin to the visiting world.[15]

Weimar German exhibition mania—an economic and symbolic desire to tell the international community about Germany's newly modernized

Figure 8. Project for the Potsdamer/Leipziger Platz, designed by Martin Wagner (1929).

surfaces in all spheres—was never a neutral, unpolitical event. 1923 saw the founding of the Berlin trade fair association (Gemeinnützige Berliner Messe- und Ausstellungsgesellschaft GmbH), which was consolidated in 1925 into the Ausstellungs-, Messe- und Fremdenverkehrs-Amt der Stadt Berlin (Amefra) to encourage a plethora of exhibitions year-round in the capital.[16] In 1927, two years after Germany had been excluded from the Paris world trade fair, a national exhibition organization was formed (Deutsche Ausstellungs- und Messe-Amt) as a conscious "self-help movement," aiming to "*reestablish international relations torn apart by the war*" and hence revamp Germany's tarnished reputation.[17] Sharing this nationalistic-capitalistic dream were, as members of the organization's board, a significant proportion of the German-Jewish business elite.[18]

In a 1928 lecture to the national exhibition organization, Ernst Jäckh defined national "exhibition politics" (*Ausstellungspolitik*) as an "instrument, as a function of politics, but also in the other inverted sense: as the politics of exhibiting, its instrumentation and organization," and as a "unity of economics, politics, and culture."[19] This assertion of the syndicated triadic status of exhibitions was more than mere verbiage, for Germany's national organization launched an immediate overkill of its mission, arranging a total of 249 trade fairs and exhibitions in its first year alone.[20] In his call for new German *Ausstellungspolitik,* Jäckh wanted "greater recognition for the organic totality of culture, economics, and politics."[21] Otto Neurath agreed that the mission of exhibitions should be raised to that of *Sozialpädagogik.*[22] In 1928, Mies van der Rohe ascribed a more metaphysical significance to German *Ausstellungen:* only if the "central problem" of today, namely the "intensification of life," is addressed by these exhibitions will they succeed in fulfilling their role as transformative indicators of the modern world.[23] Thus, just as the display window reflected the modern city back to itself—a gesture reiterated by the glass skyscraper designs of Mies—so too was the same function fulfilled by trade exhibitions, but on a far larger scale.

Indeed, these various schillerizations of the Weimar metropolis, from refaçading individual buildings to reshaping the city by means of world trade fairs, are not so far removed from postmodern architect Rem Koolhaas's rereading of the revolution constituted by "Manhattanism" in the first part of the twentieth century. Koolhaas's "retroactive manifesto" for the city draws attention to the ways in which a congested proliferation of monumental fantasies gave rise to modern New York,[24] issuing forth a deflection and deflation of any original strict utopianism; so too, in the high point of Germany's New Objectivity, we can nonetheless find a pragmatic ousting of both expressionist architectural idealism and overly stringent urban replanning, in favor of a more down-to-earth, hands-on approach to metropolitan life whereby celebratory commercialism takes over as the dominant metaphor.[25]

In this chapter, we will analyze the visual articulations and social-cum-aesthetic consequences of modern architecture's surface-voiding technique, especially in its Weimar German apogee. Modern architecture's reenvisioning of the façade constituted a unique historical moment, when the relation between built space and the functioning of society was as closely matched as it has ever been (before or since). This focus on surface was akin to a face-lift, on which the new decorations of the modern era (such as fashion, advertising text, neon lighting, cinematic performance, and glass display of commodities) would not be just afterthoughts but would be quintessentially at home as key elements in the art of construction itself. The following discussion serves as an exegetical rediscovery of the very new sense of spatiality invoked by modern architecture, and of the utterly credible sense of freedom inspired by European modernity's stringent clearing of the façade. At the same time, we can perceive in the "New Objectively" cleansed German male in figure 6 an evocation of a far more ambiguous sentiment concerning this modern condition(ing)—a condition expressed by Karl Jaspers in *The Spiritual Situation of Our Times* (*Die geistige Situation der Zeit,* 1932) as a mechanical stripping-down from humankind of all its former beliefs, leaving only the modern New Objective hero's "activity without glamour." "The individual," cautions Jaspers, "is sublated into function."[26]

DECORATION DO'S AND DON'TS

Design in German modernity constituted a radical opposite of the *horror vacui* that had traditionally hidden behind architecture's need to decorate (cover up) the exterior and interior surfaces of buildings. This is particularly important for us today, because when we as millennium-critics elegiacally re-view the modern from the postmodern perspective, we must first absorb or confront architect Robert Venturi's ludic acuity in his replacement of Mies van der Rohe's "less is more" dictum with his own "less is a bore."[27] Venturi's joke, however, like postmodernism in architecture generally, is not so much targeted at the architectural revolution inspired by the modernist conceptual realm of the 1920s as against its decidedly nonludic, exaggerated aftermath carried out in the 1950s and 1960s. After the Museum of Modern Art's 1932 exhibition introduced modern architecture to the U.S.,[28] the result was ultimately a self-implosion in the post-WWII years—an event literally and symbolically illustrated in 1972, as Charles Jencks has said, by the destruction by dynamite of the Pruitt-Igoe housing development in St. Louis.[29] Architectural modernism has therefore been given a bad name, but only if we neglect its original prewar context and drive.

In our postwar/postmodern times, we have witnessed a renewed architectural awareness concerning the surfaces of buildings, but one that, in contrast to that of the Weimar era, renews the façade not by a surgical operation but by overfill and opacity for the purposes of aesthetic, nostalgic play. Façades of the past are now toyed with, resulting in architectural theme parks, as emblematically realized in Las Vegas, Christo's Reichstag, or Charles Moore's busily eclectic Piazza d'Italia in New Orleans (1975–1978).[30] Such is our situational palimpsest today, and it must lead us first to the problematic of the "decorated shed." This definition of unabashed ornament by Venturi has come to stand for what postmodern architectural theorists understand by their own architecture, specifically in its apparent advance over modernism's indebtedness to symbolic form—the latter being dubbed, again by Venturi, as the modernist "building-becoming-sculpture," or "duck" (which, he admonishes, produces only "dead ducks" when it is emulated in postmodern times).[31] As we learn from Venturi in *Learning from Las Vegas*, postmodernism's decorated shed (Venturi's own self-proclaimed style) offers, in contrast, a broader realm of construction to which the symbol of ornament can be self-reflexively applied.

Does this judgment passed on architectural modernism by postmodernists mean, therefore, that the Weimar façade (a term derived from the Italian *facciata* [front of a building], and, like "surface," related to *faccia* [face], with the Latin roots *facia* and *facies*) must be mocked for having, simply, the wrong expression? Are the rejuvenated "faces" of Weimar modern architecture, according to Venturi's logic, inevitably misplaced in their self-paring processes, right down to the building's form?[32] A recent response to Venturi is given by Karsten Harries in his study *The Ethical Function of Architecture*.[33] Harries draws our attention to the fact that postmodernists who favor ornament as playful pastiche and "guerrilla warfare" bear more similarity than they would prefer to the late nineteenth century's own overly decorative addiction to borrowed ornamentation and stuccoed façades. Ornament (whether nostalgic Wilhelmine or hybrid postmodern) can thus be understood as an aesthetic flight from the functioning of the technologized world in its absolute sense. While nonetheless acknowledging the failure of functionalism and the Bauhaus to deliver on their promises for healing the rift between art and technology, or beauty and reason,[34] Harries does offer us the useful reminder that the modern movement in architecture, in its reformist agenda of creating surfaces that more authentically matched the respective functions that buildings actually enact in their social contexts, was aimed toward something that will necessarily rearise from time to time. This something is the "modernist hope" that architecture can, and ultimately should, fulfill an ethical, transformative role even while still engaging in playfulness—that it can provide something more than an aesthetics of disguise and avoidance, a cover-up over the void, or a dysfunctional hiding of the form hidden below the carefully distracting surface.[35]

Harries's proposal for designers today is to move away from what amounts to the simplistically dichotomous syndrome of decorated box versus duck, and become oriented instead toward an archaeologically informed "arche-tecture" more in tune with one's time, community, and surroundings.[36] For Harries, ornament and ornament-bearer (building) should not compete but have an organic relationship well suited one to the other.[37] As Harries has suggested, there is a middle path for the role of surfacing in architecture: perhaps the best way for ornament to live on is to first "die as ornament" and then be reborn in order to "serve the ornament-bearer, as a bracelet should serve the arm it circles."[38] Here Harries follows Hans-Georg Gadamer, who, in *Truth and Method,* finds that ornament is not additive but, instead, ontologically necessary, so long as it is the genuine fit for the wearer: "The concept of decoration must be freed from this antithetical relationship to the concept of art of experience and be grounded in the ontological structure of representation. . . . Ornament is not primarily something by itself that is then applied to something else but belongs to the self-presentation of its wearer. Ornament is part of the presentation. But presentation is an ontological event; it is representation."[39] While postmodern architecture still has to come to grips with this, Weimar modernism successfully performed this deaestheticization.

Hence it is precisely this organic compatibility of surface and structure that the Weimar modern achieved, albeit briefly. The brief coincidence of avant-gardistic vision and popular culture during the heyday of New Objectivity from 1924 to 1929 brought forth an oxymoronic condition of ornament-free ornamentation that was not escapist decoration over the void (nor yet its eventual, post-WWII exclusion of the all-too-human needs of dwelling), but wholly functional and authentic within the society whence it came. "Modern ornament is lack of ornament," proclaimed Viennese-trained designer Frederick Kiesler in 1930, who knew exactly what was to be avoided.[40] With the uncluttered surface of modern architecture, the structural "truth" about buildings could be revealed. By destylizing and revealing the bare surface for what it is, the underlying *form*—whether architectural or human—was highlighted and put under a new scrutiny.

In Weimar terms, the resurfacing of architecture was always couched in terms of its applications—hence the attainment of a form that was authentic to the function of the construction under consideration became recognized as the main goal. For Kiesler, "the new beauty must be based on EFFICIENCY and not on decorative cosmetics."[41] Likewise, in a poem celebrating the opening of his Schocken department store in Nuremberg on October 11, 1926, architect Erich Mendelsohn defended the industrial rhythm of modernity and the (his) new architecture that this "efficiency, clarity, simplicity" of form produced.[42] Or again, *Die Form* (design journal of the Werkbund, the German Arts and Crafts movement) contained an announcement in its opening pages of 1922 by its editor, Walter Riezler, of a new valuation of form as an architectonic, aesthetic, and social category: "For us, 'form' does not refer to that which is external in art, against which the 'essence,' 'being,' or 'soul' could be contrasted as the actual important item. . . . 'Form' is not a cover, but equally the kernel, not the opposite of essence, but itself the essence of inner life. Yes, it is life itself. . . . We know of no life that does not rush toward form."[43] Riezler's enthusiastic words betray the dizzy sense of an anti-auratic, reiterative "condition of exteriority" as the driving force in artistic and architectural design, a "shifting" of "architecture's meaning to the outside," that is, from the private interior to "public, cultural space."[44]

In this way, surface rose in stature toward a new visibility, linked in no small measure to the geometric shapes of modern abstract art's new spatial perspective and its interest in foregrounding texture. A professional manifesto of modern art's gradual accession (through expressionism, cubism, and constructivism) to the nonornamental, wholly structural goal of modern architecture was given by the ultrafunctionalist architect Ludwig Hilberseimer in his self-consciously Nietzschean-sounding essay "The Will to Architecture" ("Der Wille zur Architektur," 1923)—namely, a manifesto of "grasping actual things," "finding an adequate form for them," and, through a new "creative rationalism," even "giving order to the world and to human relations."[45] In accordance with Hilberseimer's tenets, Sigfried Giedion, one of the best psychoanalysts of architectural modernity, suggests in his *Space, Time and Architecture* (1941) that the early twentieth century marked the moment when the truth of construction rose for the first time to the surface of architectural form as the new unconscious of the modern age:

> Surface, which was formerly held to possess no intrinsic capacity for expression, and so at best could only find decorative utilization, has now become the basis of composition. . . . With the cubist's conquest of space, and the abandonment of one predetermined angle of vision which went hand in hand with it, surface acquired a significance it had never known before. Our powers of perception became widened and sharpened in consequence. The human eye awoke to the spectacle of form, line, and color—that is, the whole grammar of composition. . . . [46]

Thus, in the work of Picasso, Léger, Mondrian, Lissitzky, and Braque, as well as in the artists of dadaism and Soviet constructivism, we find the first articulations of urban modernity's new space-time configurations: these artists boldly display both the interior and the exterior of an object simultaneously, often in a fragmented and abstract way.[47] While the modern architectural style evidently could not duplicate all the perspectival distortions of cubism, it could and did reflect a nascent sense for the beauty of functional construction itself, as portrayed by clear contours and sheer surface-display.

BRAVE NEW WORLD

How, then, did the architectural shift toward the display of bare surface come about? What was the significance of the new building materials (iron and glass, steel and reinforced concrete) and the concomitant new construction techniques for these new acts of surfacing? And what role did surface have in the functionalist architectural revolution in Weimar Germany—prior, that is, to its disastrous subsequent "deformations,"[48] as Jürgen Habermas not inaccurately complains, in the post-WWII International Style?

In the 1920s building designs of such architects as German modernists Walter Gropius, Mies van der Rohe, and Mendelsohn, or De Stijl architect J. J. P. Oud, and especially in such cities as Berlin, Amsterdam, and Prague, a new ornament-free surface rose in stature and visibility. Walter Curt Behrendt, in *The Victory of the New Building Style* (*Der Sieg des neuen Baustils,* 1927), defined the "lack of all ornament" as "externally the most noticeable, striking trademark of modern architecture"; in a 1928 essay on "The Aesthetics of Architecture," Bruno Taut spoke of his "love for clean smoothness"; and Swiss-born Le Corbusier, in a 1929 article for *Die Form,* called for the liberation of the façade from its former heaviness as a starting point for the new architecture.[49] The De Stijl group in Holland coined the phrase "Functional Horizontalism," made possible by cantilevered floors and an elastic "Tensionism": "Instead of ornament, plain walls; instead of art, architecture" as the "urge of the age."[50]

"Objectivity" was not, as such, "new" to the mid-1920s; for *Sachlichkeit* was a term first used in 1902 by the architect Hermann Muthesius to praise the style of modern bridges, steamships, et cetera: "Here we notice a rigorous, one might say scientific objectivity [*wissenschaftliche Sachlichkeit*], an abstention from all superficial forms of decoration [*Enthaltung von allen äußern Schmuckformen*], a design following strictly the purpose that the work should serve."[51] This new attention to contour likewise permitted Frank Lloyd Wright in his turn-of-the-century houses—following through the trajectory of form following function begun by Louis Sullivan—to create plane surfaces, arranged in a rectilinear juxtaposition, as if cut out of a machine.[52] Indeed, Wright was the among the first to strip the wall down to a mere surface state, to open up interior space, and to demolish the former barriers of inside and outside, and he exercised considerable influence on the subsequent Weimar generation of architects.

The fresh focus on the façade by proponents of the New Building (*Neues Bauen*) movement of the 1920s, as they combined glass with iron, steel, and reinforced concrete, removed all extraneous elements from the face of the building, thereby undermining the former solidity of the outer wall as a barrier between the interior of a building and its exterior, bringing attention instead to precisely the point at which both met: the surface, the wall, the façade. These new spatial techniques of openness, moreover, once applied to the industrial or public building, could now influence and invade those of the private dwelling, which itself in turn turned outwards.[53] The outer walls, for example, of the single-storey house that Mies van der Rohe built in 1931 to display the "Dwelling of our Time" for the Building Exhibition in Berlin were entirely of glass: hence there were no windows per se. Indeed, it was this construction of Mies's that prodded a perspicacious Kracauer to declare: "If anywhere, Wilhelminism is defeated here."[54]

The Viennese fin-de-siècle architect Otto Wagner is often regarded as the father of rejuvenated surface. He is known as the originator of the maxim "Light, hygiene, plain surfaces, genuineness of material."[55] Here he was reacting to the late nineteenth century's swan-song of ornament as a nonrepresentational artistic expression (*Kunstwollen*) in its own right, as elaborated by fellow Viennese Alois Riegl in his art histories, *Problems of Style* (*Stilfragen*, 1883) and the unfinished *Historical Grammar of the Plastic Arts* (*Historische Grammatik der bildenden Künste*, 1897–1899).[56] This renewal of ornament is most apparent in the façade details on Wagner's Postal Savings Building (1904–1906), the outer walls of which, marble slabs attached by oversized transversal bolts made of aluminum, ostentatiously display themselves as a plane surface and announce a new era for decoration.[57] While still stylized, Wagner's surfaces offer a radically simplified, machine-oriented departure from the Klimt-based ornamentation predominant in the Secessionist *Gesamtkunstwerk*, and paved the way for Karl Kraus's subsequent critique of the same.

The foray that Wagner began into the deconstruction of architectural surface for urban modernity was taken a radical step further by his pupil, Adolf Loos. Loos understood the primacy of surface as the external covering of the building, for "cladding" (*Bekleidung*), he states, is in fact the origin of all architecture, in that animal skins were worn to provide the body with protection against the elements and were subsequently hung up as a shelter.[58] Thus, functional garmenting serves authentic architecture, while excess ornament—as eroticized, "extra," feminine—detracts from the same. Loos's minimalist "law of cladding" is demonstrated not only by his radical emptying of interior surfaces to the point that they resemble the equally streamlined exterior, as in his Moller House (1928) in Vienna, but also in the parallel use of interior and exterior space in his project of the same year for a house for Josephine Baker in Paris.[59] The latter structure is striking not only for the dominant use of zebralike stripes on the façade, suggestive of the dancer's much-hyped animalism, but for the indoor swimming pool lit by a skylight and voyeuristically surrounded, like a stage or film set, by transparent windows that descended into the pool, permitting spectators to observe Baker's famous nude body on public display in the water, in a play of reflective surfaces and light-effects.[60]

Despite the obvious eroticism of the Baker house design, it is for his moralizing attack on the exaggerated use of ornament (specifically in art nouveau) that Loos became most (in)famous. In his stance against the Wiener Werkstätte and Henry van de Velde for importing the English style of ornamentation prized by William Morris and the Arts and Crafts movement, Loos aimed to defalsify the (for him) degenerate fin-de-siècle addiction to infinitely decorating objects and surfaces—an implicit extension of society's obscene fetishization of commodities.[61] The Loosian call for the removal of ornament from the exterior of a building was a major contributor to the early twentieth century's demystification of the exterior's formerly stable role as guardian of any possible secrets held by the interior.[62] In an 1898 essay, "Ladies Fashion" ("Damenmode"), Loos states quite mercilessly: "The lower the culture, the more apparent the ornament. Ornament is something that must be overcome."[63] As Beatriz Colomina points out, Loos's attack on ornament is homophobic: real men don't decorate.[64] And again, in his most controversial essay, "Ornament and Crime" ("Ornament und Verbrechen," 1908)—indebted to Louis Sullivan's rechannelling of architectural energy into a more efficient form[65]—Loos promotes society's advance beyond the passing fads of decoration. When he presented this lecture in Prague in 1911, Loos even influenced Kafka's decision to drop all cloying literary ornament from his own writing style.[66] On a par with Nietzsche's attack on Wagnerian composite decadence in music and art,[67] Loos's essay denigrates ornament to the rank of the overblown Viennese *Sachertorte* or the dirty, sexually explicit tattooing on the bodies of primitives: "*The evolution of culture is synonymous with the removal of ornament from objects of daily use.* . . . The lack of ornament is a sign of intellectual power."[68] By way of contrast, it is the plumber, along with the latest in technological plumbing achievements, that constitutes for Loos the sober emblem of Germanic civilization and cleanliness across the globe[69]—an evolving process of abstraction matching that of the modern art world.

The evangelism inherent in the Loosian revolution for desensualizing architecture's social presence is matched by the tone of the Communist architect Hannes Meyer (head of the Bauhaus after Gropius, from 1928 to 1930), who, in "The New World" manifesto of 1926, proudly heralds the internationalizing "will for renovation breaking out everywhere." This prose poem is dedicated to the technological age for its procommunal world-regulation and its mass functionalization of art and design in a machinic nonstyle that can be shared by all: "Hangars and dynamo halls are the cathedrals raised to the spirit of our age. . . . Freed of the ballast of classical airs, artistic conceptual confusion, or the need for a decorative wrapping, the witnesses of a new epoch rise in their [the elders'] place; trade fair, grain silo, music hall, airport, office chair, standard ware. All of these things are products of the formula, function times economy. They are not artworks; art is composition, while purpose is function."[70] Meyer's *Weltanschauung* on architecture's new leavening renovation of the surfaces of all products, services, and surrounding constructions is ecstatic, yet unbending; small wonder, then, that during his brief tenure the Bauhaus went through serious unrest, not just externally from the Nazi threat but internally from members who disagreed with Meyer's intense anti-aestheticism. His new world seems scarily reifying in its lack of room for the outmoded sentiments (i.e., ornaments) that weigh buildings down. Similarly, emotionalism is identified as the "temperamental" problem of Wilhelmine overdecoration. As *Das Kunstblatt* editor Paul Westheim complained in 1926, "Façades and the façade attitude are in any case our woe, and not only in architecture."[71]

We find the same unyieldingly puritanical drive in the development of Le Corbusier—whose early interfaces with German modern architecture are clear from the fact that he had studied with Peter Behrens, and from his translation of Loos's "sensational" "Ornament and Crime" essay in the 1920 issue of *L'Esprit nouveau*.[72] Surface is defined by Le Corbusier in *Towards a New Architecture* (*Vers une architecture*, 1923) as the "envelope of the mass," as an entity that can "diminish or enlarge the sensation the latter gives us"; mass and surface together are generated by the plan.[73] The cancerous "iconology" of decoration and custom must be eradicated in favor of the home as a factory-produced "machine for living in."[74] Of all his contemporaries, Le Corbusier issues the most austere call for purism (containing, some would say, sinister undercurrents, given the architect's subsequent dallying with designs for totalitarian regimes).[75] Le Corbusier's architectural "truth" ("Decoration is dead and the spirit of architecture is asserting itself")[76] remains at its best when inserted into the realm of modern commerce and design, rather than seeking to control urbanism through razing existing city plans, as he wished to do for Paris and New York.

New Objective artworks that best express Le Corbusier's commandments for the nascent era of cleansed architectural surface include Oskar Schlemmer's 1932 *Bauhaus Stairway*, with its denizens' bodies and cladding in literal step with the functionality of the school's ascent of glass, cement, and steel (fig. 9). Another related image is George Grosz's 1921 sketch *The New Man* (*Der neue Mensch*; fig. 10), which, in ways similar to Grosz's equally functionalist *Boxer* (1920/1921) or *Diabolo Player* (1921), depicts the geometrically configured man for modernity, who, as the epitome of Ulrich in Musil's novel *The Man Without Qualities*, strides in his room between various psychotechnical instruments of measurement and performance, all suggesting to the viewer the broad range of ultramodern professions that he practices: an engineer's design for a piston, an architect's T-square, a boxer's punching bag. Such is the New Man, the embodiment of Weimar surface; for Kracauer he is the detective-type, the representative of the *ratio*, and the neutral fact-finder of New Objectivity. Kracauer summarizes the New Man thus: "Cleanly shaved face, whose cool features, apart from being characterized by intellect, renounce any individual meaning; a 'conditioned sportsman's body, controlled movements' . . . ; moreover, inconspicuous behavior and clothing according to fashion and situations: such is the typical appearance of the detective."[77] This new constructor-figure should emulate (say) the well-ordered engineering style of ocean liners and so lose any fear of the "geometrical constituents of surfaces," for, states Le Corbusier, "contour and profile are the touchstone of the architect": his task is to "vitalize the surfaces which clothe [the] . . . masses, but in such a way that these surfaces do not become parasitical, eating up the mass and absorbing it to their own advantage."[78] Not just the outside but the inside of the building must project this state of revitalization (including furniture, as with built-in closets);[79] even the roof of a house, now that it is flat, presents a usable surface. Indeed, a major tenet of Le Corbusier is the "free façade":[80] no longer the bearers of weight, the reinforced, "ferro"-concrete walls were openly exposed, adhering to the lines of the steel skeletal structure behind them.[81]

Le Corbusier was among the dominant functionalist architects to join organizer Mies van der Rohe for the German Werkbund's 1927 exhibition in Stuttgart, "The Dwelling" ("Die Wohnung").[82] The sixty houses of the exhibition became known as the Weissenhof Housing Project (*Weissenhof Siedlung*), and as the epitome of architecture as monochrome surface—even if only one-third were actually white. Not surprisingly given its Stuttgart locale, there was an immediate outcry over Weissenhof's flat roofs and cubelike surfaces, as well as over the metal, minimalist furniture

Figure 9. *Bauhaus Stairway,* by Oskar Schlemmer (1932).

within its plain walls (designed by Marcel Breuer, for example). The Stuttgart building inspectors immediately found fault with almost every aspect of the Weissenhof houses: fire prevention, ceiling height, position and separation of the rooms, design of sanitary installations, etc. Such conservative reactions found validation when the exorbitant cost was discovered for what were ostensibly models for future mass housing. The total planned budget came to 1,492,000 RM, but the actual costs were much higher, and the city of Stuttgart had to pay for the many repairs.[83]

Controversy over the new surfaces of the Weissenhof project caused reactions like the statement by Paul Bonatz in 1926 about the colony's alienating resemblance to a "suburb of Jerusalem."[84] This helped ferment conditions ripe enough for a proto-Nazi postcard to appear, in which the houses received a caricatural makeover into an "Arab Village Housing Project" (*Siedlung Araberdorf*). But Kracauer, at least, was full of praise when he reviewed the houses for the *Frankfurter Zeitung,* finding a stringent

Figure 10. *Der neue Mensch,* by George Grosz (1921).

beauty in the sublation (*Auflösung*) of the house that was particularly visible in Mies van der Rohe's apartment block. Kracauer's words concerning the houses' skeletal purity serve as a direct reminder of Grosz's clean, lean configuration of the mechanically adept New Man: "Hygiene; no fuss. A skeleton, thin and agile like a person in sportshirt and pants."[85]

GLASS CULTURE

The discourse of purity within the rejuvenation brought forth by architectural resurfacing in the 1920s was intimately linked to the role of glass in architecture. As the prime facilitator of the new streamlining of design, as the man-made version of pure crystal, and as the medium *par excellence* of clean, clear surface, glass undeniably brought about the most dazzling transformation to date of architectural apperception. Modernity's combined desire for hygienic openness, social utopianism, and spaces to show off the unadulterated spectacle of commodity fetishism found its answer in the architecture of transparency. For the presence of glass, as Anthony Vidler has observed, enables even the most monumental of structures to appear "reticent," "invisible"—and, at any rate, lighter than the laws of gravity. In the decades of West German public and governmental architecture, glass has long been associated with postwar sensibilities of democratic openness.[86] And, after its initial postmodern trashing under the "sign of opacity," transparency in architecture is nowadays making a strong comeback—as I. M. Pei's *grand projet* pyramid of glass in the Louvre's courtyard, the glass-walled staircase for his ongoing extension to Berlin's Deutsches Historisches Museum, or Rem Koolhaas's design for the new Dutch embassy in the German capital all demonstrate.[87]

Before the 1920s functionalist approach to sheer surfaces could gain a foothold, the initial revolution occurred in the late nineteenth century's introduction of glass-and-iron techniques,[88] which single-handedly gave rise to what Susan Buck-Morss has termed a "landscape of techno-aesthetics, a dazzling, crowd-pleasing dreamworld that provided total environments to envelop the crowd."[89] In this way, bold transformations became possible in building, a direction initiated by Joseph Paxton's iconic Crystal Palace built for the first international exhibition in Hyde Park, London (1851)—a construction so tall that it encompassed mature trees growing in the park, but accomplished (incredibly) at a time when the largest pane of glass was only four feet long.[90] Habermas draws our attention to the way in which the "interior of the centerless repetitive London Crystal Palace must have had the effect of transcendence of all known dimensions of designed space."[91] And yet this new architectonic sublime of glass was just the beginning, for just four years later the Palais de l'Industrie for the international exhibition in Paris doubled the vaulting of the Crystal Palace from twenty-two to forty-eight meters across.[92] In subsequent French exhibitions, the major exhibition glass house was the Galerie des Machines, culminating in the 1889 Paris exhibition's glass construction with a span of 115 meters; and a showpiece for Paris's 1900 fair was the glass-and-iron domed Grand Palais, designed by Charles Girault. For Giedion, the fundamental innovation witnessed in such a fantastic rate of agglomeration in massive glass-house design lies in the "union and interpenetration" between interior and exterior space, from which grew a "completely new limitlessness and movement" that best reflected the audacity of the machines exhibited within.[93] Public spaces—especially in train stations, shopping arcades, winter gardens, and department stores[94]—could now be housed inside these gigantic glass-iron showcases, while the potential for opening up interior, private space was created as never before.

Expressionist Paul Scheerbart is generally regarded as the seminal creative force for the preeminence of glass in modern architectural thought.[95] In Scheerbart's science fiction novel of 1913, *Lesabéndio* (the subject of a lost Benjamin essay, "The True Politician" ["Der wahre Politiker"]),[96] a glass monument to light is depicted as the ultimate achievement of the planet Pallas: the mammoth "light-tower" (*Lichtturm*) is built of a special steel that permits it to reach up into the stars as it shines forth into the night.[97] In his 1914 treatise, Scheerbart links modernity's exhibition-spirit to glass architecture, suggesting a "permanent" exhibition of and for architectural experiments in this transparent medium, such as a room with a glass floor lit from below.[98] An archproponent of the use of electric power for flood-lights, Scheerbart foresees that "all towers must become light-towers in the reign of glass architecture."[99]

Bruno Taut's *Alpine Architecture,* a cosmic picture-book of 1919, is a direct promulgation of his friend Scheerbart's elysium for building with glass, this time in a Zarathustran mountain realm that seeks to revitalize the metropolis by escaping it.[100] First known as the *Fassadenkünstler,* or "façade artist," for his commissions in colorful renovations of building fronts, Taut gave himself the code name of "Glass" for his leading role in the expressionist group of architects behind the Crystal Chain Letters (*Die gläserne Kette,* 1919–1920), a publication of visionary art and design for a post-WWI age. Nostalgic for an earlier time in which ornamentation on buildings was an authentic cultural expression, akin to a sacred "incantation,"[101] Taut clearly fetishized the very glass structure that had just been purifyingly exposed by advances in building technologies. In Taut's alpine vision, the glass skyscraper is a centripetal force, a "city crown" (*Stadtkrone*), and is injected with a transfigurative power to raise mankind above the squalor of the city and the defeated agony of the First World War, up toward a new harmony of glass-crystal in the alpine land of ice-crystal. Taut's vision was even envisaged as fanciful facelift for the Potsdamer Platz, with a glass fountain lit up red by night.[102] Taut's unrealized film project, *The Galoshes of Fortune* (*Die Galoschen des Glücks,* 1920), tells of a futuristic realm of glass rooms, a city of flames, and a radiant cathedral: such visionary architecture bestows bliss on its human subjects worn down from warfare and paltry tenement-existences.[103] For this overidealized ontology, the principle of glass is not simply a new industrial building material but has been returned to its psychophysical, sacral function of Gothic times.[104]

The Taut-Scheerbartian expressionist avatar of glass architecture managed to elude, if not the tendency toward ethereal overvaluation, then at least that which Benjamin critiques as the negative "poverty" of overtly nonauratic experience that remains (if not remedied by other means) modernity's distinct downside. Taut encapsulated a more fertile vision of glass culture with his 1914 colored glass dome for the Mittag department store in Magdeburg, or again with his design for the Werkbund Exhibition in Cologne the same year: a fourteen-sided prism topped by a dome, called the Glass House.[105] Its ascending blue, green, and gold glass panels reflected the sky brilliantly—even if on cloudy days it looked yellowish and earned the nickname "Asparagus Head" (*Spargelkopf*). The Glass House provoked both a metaphysical and a self-reflexive attitude toward its material: by night, for example, a thousand watts of electricity lit it up from within, and inside the dome, the kaleidoscopic patterns of the myriad glass panels were reflected in the surface of a cascade of running water; yet there was also a parodic element, in that Scheerbart wrote fourteen tongue-in-cheek couplets for the Glass House, of which six were actually inscribed around the façade, such as "If you have no glass abode you will find that life's a load."[106] These self-mocking couplets on the power of glass form a gleeful counterpart to Meyer's or Le Corbusier's pedagogies, as well as an apposite pre-site of Weimar exhibitionism, electric advertising, and cinematic distraction.

The fantastical and exhibitionist architecture of Scheerbart and Taut soon gave way, however, to the functionalist application of building with glass that took its cue from modern factory design. An inspiration for architectural functionalism was Peter Behrens's neoclassical temple to industrialism, the Turbine Factory (1908–1909) for the General Electric Company AEG (Allgemeine Elektricitäts-Gesellschaft), with its steel supports, cement, and multistorey glass windows.[107] Taut himself moved with the times during the New Objectivity years, and designed wholly functionalist architecture for low-cost housing projects in Berlin, wishing to replace the Wilhelmine concept of façade (termed by Taut the "sheep's clothing" for the "wolf" of the "intrigue"-ridden interior) with a new tectonic honesty of surface.[108] The *Deutsche Bauzeitung,* Germany's foremost architectural journal, wrote eudaemonistically in 1929 of the "cultural mission of glass."[109] Most significantly, the Weimar-Dessau-Berlin Bauhaus promoted an "unconditional use of pure materials,"[110] honestly juxtaposing glass, iron, steel, and reinforced concrete. For Gropius, the first Bauhaus leader, glass facilitated the way in which design now arose out of the "*essence* of the building, out of the function that it is to fulfill."[111]

Gropius and Adolf Meyer's glass wall design for the Fagus shoe factory in Alfeld (1911–1914) is considered the first attempt at the pure glass façade, or curtain wall construction. Despite its history of rust problems that broke the glass panes, the Fagus works was the first building to have pendant-effect corners of translucent glass and even featured interior glass walls.[112] And, in Gropius' subsequent correlative model (*Fabrik*) for the 1914 Werkbund exhibition, the façade was extended further to include a radically obtruding spiral corner staircase whose outer walls were entirely of rounded glass, allowing one to see the revolutions of the screwlike stairwell within.[113] As Giedion states of Gropius's later Dessau workshop building with its famous three-storey curtain wall of glass (1925–1926) and accompanying dematerialization of the glass corners, here the "interior and the exterior of a building . . . are presented simultaneously."[114] Art and technology had never come closer than in this first moment of the façade's total transparency.

It was at this point, according to Henri Lefebvre's analysis of Weimar functionalist architecture, that the "*façade*—as face directed towards the observer and as privileged side or aspect of a work of art or a monument—*disappeared.*"[115] That is to say, with the transparency provided by glass, Loos's call for the outer surface of a building to be demoted was fully realized: the façade lost thereby its signification as marker of social status, as loud division between inside and outside. Gropius asserts that joy, not despair, is to be the result of this nudity at the core of *Neues Bauen:*

> The New Architecture throws open its walls like curtains to admit a plenitude of fresh air, daylight and sunshine. Instead of anchoring buildings ponderously into the ground with massive foundations, it poises them lightly, yet firmly, upon the face of the earth; and bodies itself forth, not in stylistic imitation or ornamental frippery, but in those simple and sharply modelled designs in which every part merges naturally into the comprehensive volume of the whole.[116]

In Gropius's praise of glass's "gaiety" and "sparkling insubstantiality," we find the Nietzschean crossing of the abysmal void that the empty façade reveals.[117] As Mark C. Taylor observes of this purifying disfiguration of building constituted by the Dessau Bauhaus, "the void is more a sign of presence and plenitude than of absence and emptiness. In this gay wisdom, the unbearable lightness of building creates a liberating sense of levity."[118]

Despite its sheer, glassy lack of extrusion, a characteristic of the new façade was its skill at invoking a sense of machinelike motion.[119] Mendelsohn heralded how a "new rhythm is grabbing the world, a new movement."[120] This was especially prevalent in the tendency to use glass in the act of rounding the building's corners—such as the BEWAG (Berliner

Kraft- und Licht-Aktiengesellschaft) electric company's Shell House, built by Emil Fahrenkamp from 1930 to 1931 and one of Berlin's first skeletal steel structures. Recently renovated, the BEWAG building radically invigorates the entire notion of the newly smoothed-out façade by having its rows of windows snake along the building in zigzag fashion. Indeed, the logical consequence of the curved, transparent corner was the totally circular construction, as in the Luckhardt Brothers' unbuilt design for Haus Berlin (1931), a glass and metal circular skyscraper for the Potsdamer Platz.

An early, highly influential example of this kinaesthetic cornering-effect is Mendelsohn's façade-renewal of 1921–1923 for the Rudolf Mosse company's *Berliner Tageblatt* publishing house, on Jerusalemerstraße in the newspaper area of Berlin (fig. 11).[121] Mendelsohn wrote of his redesign for the previously Wilhelmine-style Mosse House that it was not an "uninvolved observer" of the street life around it; through his renovation, it had become instead an "element of motion."[122] Here Mendelsohn does not so much dissent from his functionalist colleagues as accentuate their static geometric designs into a bolder, more visually stimulating relief. Indeed, Behne finds the "element of movement" to be a characteristic not just of the Bauhaus style but of Italian futurism and Soviet constructivism alike.[123] But it was Mendelsohn who set the tone for corners of curved glass that veritably leapt out at passersby. Conscious emulations of Mendelsohn's corners include not only such Ku-Damm landmarks as Otto Firle's late Weimar renovation for the Grünfeld department store, but also postmodern glass structures such as Jean Nouvel's Galeries Lafayette department store on the Friedrichstraße. Nouvel's 1996 building, while a totalizing statement of glass cornering and an early strong participant in the ongoing post-Wall commercial renaissance of Berlin-Mitte, has attained more notoriety than fame due to the continual falling of shards from the glass panels only three years after its opening.

The height of Weimar glass culture's aspirations is expressed most forcefully in the famous early Weimar skyscraper designs of Mies van der Rohe, namely Mies' unrealized 1921 Glass Skyscraper model and his equally radical project for the triangular site of the 1921–1922 Berlin Friedrichstraße competition (fig. 12). Unlike, say, Hans and Wassily Luckhardt's entry for the same competition, which offered the compromise of a glass and iron cafe-house standing in front of a nonglass skyscraper, the windowless sheerness of Mies' skyscraper is free of all such use-oriented constraints. Hilberseimer christened it a "skin of mirrored glass."[124] Its nickname, the "Honeycomb," is suggestive of its collage technique of twenty storeys holding multiple, cellular cubicles of glass between the

Figure 11. Mosse House, Berlin, designed by Erich Mendelsohn (1926).

inner steel structure of the three towers. The most startling feature of the design (a surprise even to Mies himself)[125] was that the outer façade of undulating convex and concave glass surfaces would not so much reveal the metal skeleton within as reflect and refract, in the multitudinous fashion of a distorted mirror, not only light and shade but the surrounding buildings and the skyscraper itself (as in Le Corbusier's *City of Tomorrow* of 1929).[126]

Mies' skyscraper project could in this way literally highlight its own surface qua surface, in the spiritually empty, self-referential manner of the Kracauerian mass ornament;[127] it is hence in full architectural kinship with Simmel's blasé metropolitan type, precursor of the New Man. As a building project of modernity, Mies' glass tower is desirous not only of accurately reflecting the true urban condition to itself, but also of further ennobling the subject's apperception. This basic trait in the Weimar discourse of the modern skyscraper returns us infallibly to its Tautian expressionist roots, no matter how functionalist the program. As Manfredo Tafuri has noted in *The Sphere and the Labyrinth,* the "skyscraper—put forward as a

Figure 12. Project for a Glass Skyscraper, by Ludwig Mies van der Rohe (1921).

providential 'exception' through which the language of matter expresses itself—intervenes to 'save,' not to change, the existing community" and "proclaims the socialist victory over space."[128]

THE PAINS OF TABULA RASA

A caveat against the necessity and clean-slate dictates of the new architecture came midway through its heyday in the mid-1920s. Functionalist design innovation had proven Loos's earlier tenets more than right, to the point of prompting even Loos to a qualification against purist overkill of his own antiornamentalism. After all, in the words of Theodor W. Adorno, the surface decorations that Loos sought to eradicate were themselves often no more than "vestiges of outmoded means of production," and even functionalism must have a strong aesthetic: its "pure forms of purpose are nourished by ideas—like formal transparency and graspability—which are in fact derived from artistic experience."[129] As if prescient of Adorno's subsequent criticism of functionalism, the later Loos (perhaps honestly facing up to his own sustained use of elegantly minimalist decoration in his own designs for furniture and interiors) suggested that "lack of ornament is not without charms; rather, it is effective as a new charm, it invigorates"[130]—suggesting thereby an imaginative-rational parity.

This sort of concern led the architect Hermann Muthesius, in his "emperor's new clothes" essay, the posthumously published "Art and Fashion Trends" ("Kunst und Modeströmungen," 1927),[131] to offer his contemporaries a last word of advice: even the antifashion and nonornament of the New Objective parallelepiped are nonetheless part of fashion and ornament, and are hence just as transitory. "The essence of the cubistic way of building has nothing to do with realities," states Muthesius, so it ought not to be defended as an ergonomic necessity by its proponents. Rather, it is for all its purism an architectural style, as attractive and prone to fashion as any other (and here Muthesius lets the cat out of the functionalist bag): it betrays a certain "romanticism of construction" (*Konstruktionsromantik*)—and is hence as exaggerated a stance as *Jugendstil* ever was. And, as another Weimar observer put it in 1932, the walls of New Objectivity are "decorated with decoration-free surfaces" (*ornamentiert mit ornamentlosen Flächen*)—hence the nonstyle is, obstinately, still a style.[132]

A practical observer of this problematic was Ernst Pollak, a Berlin publisher and author of a 1928 publication on the modern refitting of German stores. Pollak neatly relativizes any inherent tendency toward rational absolutism in the new relation between function and design:

> Each piece of work which is simply or primarily true to itself and its function [*um seiner selbst und seines Zweckes willen*] is now categorized under the rather confusing term of "New Objectivity."
>
> We must be quite clear that there is no absolute, unsullied objectivity, other than as an abstract theory. Because of our present awareness there is only an improved type of objectivity which is nothing more than a rejection of outmoded hackneyed phrases and worn-out valuations [*ein Abstoßen überlebter Floskeln, abgenutzter Gefühlswerte*], which, for the modern man, include representation. In the euphoria of his newly found freedom he believes that he has given priority to pure objectivity.[133]

Here Pollak sounds rather like Nietzsche with his definition of truth in language as a pack of metaphorical lies: New Objectivity, while valuable in its refreshing outreach toward the machinic spirit of the age, is in point of fact no closer to architecture's misplaced mimetic goal than were the styles that New Objectivity had to reject.

Muthesius's and Pollak's gentle yet lucid reminders of the unavoidable façade housed within the new façade found more negative echoes. For ex-architect Kracauer, the Weimar nonstyle was ultimately a hypocritical construct: "The characteristic of New Objectivity is precisely that it is a façade that hides nothing, that it does not wrest itself from depth but simulates it."[134] And in the radical façade renewal of urban buildings, Kracauer espies a more serious ailment, namely the loss of a city's personal history. The street has become thereby a "street without memory": "From many houses they have torn down the ornament that used to form a kind of bridge to yesteryear. Now the robbed façades stand there without a footing in time and are the impression of an ahistorical transformation taking place behind them."[135] Kracauer is not imagining this, for surface culture at its most radical came with Hilberseimer's suggestion to tear down and replace "old" structures every twenty-five years or so.[136] And Mies van der Rohe's plans for the Alexanderplatz involved, essentially, a ruthless voiding of the terrain that would hold back the congested old city behind the walls of its surrounding skyscrapers. What had begun with a renewal of the surface thus became a renewal of the entire structure or area, now that designs of previous eras had lost their value in New Objective eyes, and were to be, as Martin Wagner concurred, regularly re-formed in their "flight lines" according to the "motion lines" of traffic and consumer needs.[137] As a result of this emptying-out of metropolitan memory, Kracauer writes of a nightmarish "fear" that assaults him as he walks in the streets of Berlin-West, a panic caused by screams he hears. But this screaming does not, he suggests, originate with humans; rather, it is the "streets themselves" who are "screaming out their emptiness."[138] This dehumanized tectonics, then, appears as the negative apotheosis of modernity's insistent, architectural urge to renew and recreate surface.

Kracauer's concern about the void enunciated by glass culture is also made clear in his comments on the Weissenhof Housing Project, where there was a special room designed by Mies van der Rohe and Lilly Reich that had walls of sheer glass—a "glass box" (*Glaskasten*) that entranced and yet perplexed Kracauer thus:

> Every fixture and every movement in . . . [neighboring rooms] conjures up shadow-plays on the wall—immaterial silhouettes that hover through the air and become mixed with the mirror-images from the glass room itself. The raising of this impalpable glassy ghost, which transforms itself like a kaleidoscope or light reflex, signifies that the new dwelling is not the last solution. . . . No matter how kitschy the struck-down ornaments were, that which remains does not replace

> what was intended with them. . . . [I]t would be good if the sorrow at the renunciation that . . . [the new houses] must endure could be better articulated than is the case here—that farcical sorrow that clings to the images that have been banished into the glass surface. For the house-skeletons are not an end in themselves; rather they are the necessary bridge to an abundance that will not require any more points of departure and today can only be witnessed negatively in sorrow. They will flesh out only when the human being climbs out of the glass.[139]

With this rumination, Kracauer longs for the day when the designs of the new glass culture are fully functional in society and the glass environment is sufficiently natural for its denizens; until that point is reached, however, he predicts that the interim phase will be one of light-plays of "this impalpable glassy ghost" (*dieses ungreifbaren gläsernen Spuks*), and moreover of nostalgia for the lost ornament, as well as mourning over the ensuing emptiness that these surfaces produce.

Far more vituperative than Kracauer's, Ernst Bloch's critique espies in the 1920s cult of functionality an empty "railway stationness" (*Bahnhofhaftigkeit*) that induces only a creative paralysis for architecture and a hypertropic worship by white-collar workers.[140] Bloch is highly critical of the "technoid" inspiration lurking behind the rationalization of the façade: "[New] Objectivity has its ornament in not having any. It has not been pure functional form for a long time; rather it is covered with technoid decorations. Its machinic model has long since become an end in itself, serving as ersatz ornament and to no other end than that of strengthening the façade."[141] Façade renewal has for Bloch degenerated into an unthinking machine-mimesis in matters of architectural style; he hates the "hollow space" (*Hohlraum*) that New Objectivity has promoted.[142] Also in tune with Bloch is Adorno's retrospective essay on the 1920s, wherein the author critiques the era's "clear-as-glass order," a mode of excess revealingly linked (more for our understanding of Adorno than to surface culture) to the "hopelessly commercialized sex drive of the Kurfürstendamm."[143]

Nonetheless, in modernity's new architectural age, any resistance to the new purifying externalization may appear doomed, or at best shortsightedly bourgeois. Behne, in a 1919 essay, "Glass Architecture," cannot disguise his glee at the antibourgeois connotation of glass: "The European is right when he fears that glass architecture might become uncomfortable. Certainly, it will be so. And that is not its least advantage. For first the European must be wrenched out of his coziness [*Gemütlichkeit*]. Not without good reason the adjective "gemütlich" intensified becomes "saugemütlich" [swinishly comfortable]. Away with comfort! Only where comfort ends, does humanity begin."[144] Behne's schadenfreude amounts, in fact, to the frankly merciless tabula rasa spirit of modern urban planning, as witnessed even more hauntingly in the project for a "skyscraper city" (*Hochhausstadt,* 1924) by Hilberseimer—a vision that presents itself as the extreme consequence of modernity's deornamentation in design, a dystopian utopia lost in an abstract zone of euphorically geometric yet spiritually voided streets.[145]

In 1931, the ever-polyvocal Benjamin indicated his reservations concerning the effects of glass culture, in a prose-poem description of the "destructive character," a descendant of Simmel's metropolitan type. Benjamin paints here a transparent portrait of those proponents of the façade renewals, both material and spiritual, that were going on during the years of New Objectivity in all cultural spheres. But his words also transport the contemporary reader to an Ayn Randian architectural realm,[146] one where an infinite series of Miesian Seagram buildings is unleashed on what was once the private domain:

> The destructive character knows only one watchword: make room; only one activity: clearing away. . . .
>
> The destructive character is young and cheerful. For destroying rejuvenates in clearing away the traces of our own age. . . .
>
> The destructive character is always blithely at work. . . .
>
> No vision inspires the destructive character. He has few needs, and the least of them is to know what will replace what has been destroyed. First of all, for a moment at least, empty space, the place where the thing stood or the victim lived. . . .
>
> The destructive character is the enemy of the *etui*-man. The *etui*-man looks for comfort, and the case is its quintessence. The inside of the case is the velvet-lined track [*Spur*] that he has imprinted on the world. The destructive character obliterates even the traces of destruction.[147]

Benjamin's implicit self-inscription here as *etui*-collector of the traces of interiors and of interiority[148] is confronted with and negated by this new destructive spirit inherent to the era of trace-free bare surface: "That is what the new architects have achieved with their glass and their steel: they created spaces in which it is not easy to leave behind a trace."[149] Presentist glass surfaces, operating as if in an excess of Nietzsche's "critical history" mode,[150] can bear no memory or trace of private, individual *Geist* inscribed upon them. Citing Scheerbart's ecstatic predictions of the imminent rise of "glass-culture" ("The new glass-milieu will completely transform mankind"),[151] Benjamin offers here a more complex version of the same. Even as he looks forward to a Scheerbartian transformation of visual culture, Benjamin repeats his nostalgia for traces of interiority in the essay "Experience and Poverty" ("Erfahrung und Armut," 1933): "Not for nothing is glass such a hard and smooth material to which nothing can attach itself. It is also cold and sober. Things of glass have no 'aura.' Glass is basically the enemy of the secret. It is also the enemy of ownership."[152] Indeed, the Hausmannian "destructive character" as critiqued by Benjamin—the logocentric "glass man," which was literally constructed as a star exhibit for the German Hygiene exhibition of 1934[153]—is clearly personified by Le Corbusier, when the latter as avid (or some would say, concerning his plans for Paris and New York City, rabid) urban planner speaks dismissively of the "detritus of dead epochs" and his desire to "clear . . . away from our cities the dead bones that putrefy in them."[154] A more giving approach to one's environment, in contrast, is given by Mendelsohn, whose advice to architects includes the commandment not to forget that "individual creativity" can only be understood "within the totality of temporal appearances" and the "relativity of its facts."[155]

SURFACE ART AT HOME

Weimar functionalism's impact on surfaces extended, however, beyond the possibilities and practices of building with glass, toward the actual housing needs of German 1920s society. Major new spatial arrangements were conceived of by functionalist architects in their designs for mass-produced apartment blocks, intended to rehouse Germany's urban working classes out of the crowded conditions of tenement buildings (*Mietskasernen*) from the Wilhelmine era. Such buildings were the daily living reality for most Weimar Berliners (the working classes, which included the new white-collar workers, the *Angestellten*).[156] Alfred Döblin knew that these tenements did not partake of Weimar surface culture—they were for their inhabitants literally, and solely, "empty façade after empty façade."[157] To the credit of functionalist architects, efforts were made to improve the lot of the majority amongst the general revolutionary current of modern architecture.

The need was acute. The "new building" movement in the domain of mass housing, led by Germany's chief urban planners, among them Martin Wagner (Berlin) and Ernst May (Frankfurt a.M.), contributed significantly to rebuilding the broken nation after World War I. Taut estimated the republic needed three million apartments, to be built over a ten-year period (a vision that diminished after the worldwide economic crisis of 1929).[158] The nation's psychosocial need also remained an intensely pragmatic one—on average, a rental building in mid-Weimar Berlin housed almost seven times as many people as did an equivalent building in London.[159] The aim was, according to Taut, to move beyond the fake-castle illusionism and baroque Biedermeierism of the nineteenth century and have the new rationalized building reflect its actual function as, simply, "a true house for living" (*ein wahres Wohnhaus*), thereby saving on space and expenditure.[160] Moreover, these building projects were successful: indeed, in Berlin alone more than fourteen thousand units were built between 1924 and 1933, mostly by the housing agency Gemeinnützige Heimstätten-Aktiengesellschaft (GEHAG).[161]

One key rearrangement of surface in the new mass housing projects that were built on the outskirts of German cities (not just Berlin but also Magdeburg, Dessau, Frankfurt a.M., and Hannover, as well as Vienna) during the 1920s occurred literally and sociopolitically with the introduction of the flat roof. Conservative resistance against the flat roof for the private dwelling was so great, however, that twenty-seven of the most prominent functionalist architects of the day (among them Behrens, Gropius, Hugo Häring, Hilberseimer, the Luckhardt Brothers, May, Mendelsohn, Mies, Poelzig, Taut, his brother Max Taut, and Wagner) felt it necessary to form a group known as "The Ring" in order to publish statements in defense of its use and in defense of the new architecture. Writing in 1927 about this "pulse of the new era," May, as head architect for Frankfurt a.M.'s mass housing projects, presented his side of the *Flachdach oder Steildach* debate: the flat roof, he asserts, gives its overworked inhabitants a private open space for relaxation; it produces a new "unity" in the aspect of the city; and when properly built (i.e., when not leaking!), it provides a new "irreproachable roof-skin" (*einwandfreie Dachhaut*).[162]

As for Taut, the fact that flat roofs could be successfully blended with a wooded setting was ample proof of the aesthetic pleasure of this new act of horizontal surfacing. The respectfully symbiotic use of preexisting, hundred-year-old fir trees formed, in fact, one of the distinguishing features of a massive (albeit not working class) GEHAG housing project ("Onkel Toms Hütte," named after a popular restaurant in the area) that Taut headed in Berlin's upscale Zehlendorf, built from 1926 to 1932 for fifteen thousand inhabitants.[163] Here Taut is downplaying his own role in what became known as the "Zehlendorf roof war," one result of which was the smaller housing project right next door to Taut's: the decidedly bourgeois houses of Am Fischtal led by Heinrich Tessenow, solely intended to demonstrate the viability of traditional tiled roofs in steeply sloping "saddle" style. It opened in 1928 as a "Building and Living" exhibition.[164] Perhaps the most famous of such experiments with serial housing for the working poor was Wagner and Taut's GEHAG Horseshoe Project (Hufeisensiedlung) in Berlin-Britz, a thousand-unit strong series of colorfully painted apartments around a central horseshoe arc, built from 1925–1931 (fig. 13)—a success from the Tautian "garden city" point of view, if not in creating actual low rents. As Taut complained in his *Building* study of 1927, no amount of rationalization in costs (through both the removal of nonfunctional aspects and the use of industrially made building parts) was sufficient to overcome Weimar banks' unwillingness to reduce their lending rates.[165]

The surface-renewal of living spaces for the masses was not confined to the outsides of buildings. Taut and his fellow functionalists had a heartfelt need to go beyond the building's new "good face" and achieve "real architecture" by means of the extension of "cleanliness and clarity" politics far into the interior.[166] The Weimar Republic's strong movement of *Sozialpolitik* under the banner of public hygiene was thus theoretically in favor of such ideas. Hilberseimer stressed the need to create a Taylorized "typology" not only in planning the metropolis (as delineated in his radical book *City Architecture* [*Groszstadtarchitektur*], 1927), but also in renewing surfaces for the "spatial unities" *inside* the new apartments, so that the various living functions of sleeping, cooking, eating, washing, et cetera, could be separated room by room. Such hygienically intended division of indoor living space could be achieved on a small (hence cheap) ground plan, wrote Hilberseimer, so long as closets and cupboards were already built-in, and nondecorative furniture replaced the cluttered "junk shop" appearances of old.[167] Giedion lent his praise to this trend with his comments for a photobook of 1929 entitled *Liberated Dwelling* (*Befreites Wohnen*).[168] Such streamlining of all living areas was matched by the prefabrication of materials: in short, a cellular minimalization. One practically had to be a Groszian ascetically reformed *neuer Mensch* to live there.

In the wave of rationalization of the domestic living space, women became the objects, or carriers, of a new-found pragmatism in the home, insofar as women were, despite their WWI-induced entry into the workforce, still the primary organizers of and consumers for the household. The carrot that Taut used in his popular text *The New Apartment—Woman as Creator* (*Die neue Wohnung—Die Frau als Schöpferin*, 1924), which sold twenty-six thousand copies in four years, was that women's work in the home would be significantly reduced, so long as they followed his radical tenets of interior design.[169] Here Taut offers a more realizable, down-to-

Figure 13. Horseshoe Housing Project (Hufeisensiedlung), Berlin-Britz, designed by Bruno Taut and Martin Wagner (1925–1931).

earth version of Scheerbart's domestic "box" of the future:[170] "The practical and the aesthetic are a unity," proclaims Taut, "therefore the ideal apartment is entirely beautiful. A contour of the human being, one's protection, one's container of first and last thoughts, words and deeds, one's 'nest.'"[171] In both Hilberseimer's and Taut's visions of interior design, we perceive the influence of the Japanese mode of voided rooms (and the resultant spatial liberation of the interior). Japanese tenets were used by Taut as a major guide to his renovation plans for the mass dwelling and women's work therein,[172] much as the silhouette of the (male) Japanese kimono became in the early 1920s an originating leitmotif for Paris's concomitant revolution of women's fashion into the "flapper" style, with its straightening-out of the ideal torso and deemphasizing of the waist and bust.

Taut's spirit hovers over Erna Meyer's even more best-selling compendium for housewives, *The New Household* (*Der neue Haushalt*, 1926), which went through more than thirty printings during the Weimar years. In Meyer's text, the conjunction between the contours of the New Objective home and the shape of the New Woman's lifestyle has become complete. She offers her readers a total systematization of the home, addressing budgeting, cooking, cleaning, furnishing, and child-raising all in one.

Marriage was no longer a "haven" but a machinic organism to be kept functioning at optimal horsepower by means of the wholly rationalized home.[173] This active state of efficiency was heralded by Meyer in Zarathustran/ecstatic terms as a spiritual "freedom to" rather than a servile "freedom from"[174]—even if the New Woman's every movement is now measured and assessed. The creature that Meyer writes into existence is a new "professional" working woman, who yet remains the "creative mistress" of housework,[175] aligning her new hygienic efficiency with the (as yet rather costly) electrification of the home.[176] Meyer looks forward with positive "*longing*" to the time when all households will have such appliances as electrically heated boilers, refrigerators, and washing machines (in the 1920s, most German women could afford, at most, an electric iron).[177] Meyer's text is symptomatic of the process by which, as historian Atina Grossmann points out, Weimar women underwent a rather naive internalization of progressive factory-Fordism in their domestic lives, yearning for gadgets they could not, for the most part, afford: "The new woman consumer was created ideologically before she was materially possible."[178]

Beyond this creation of the New Woman as consumer for the new home, women were also partial initiators of the same drive. Even single working women were recognized as worthy of having apartment blocks built specifically for them.[179] It is undeniable that women occupied only a marginal presence in the actual design of modern architecture—the Bauhaus school excluded women from its architecture program,[180] and in 1920 Gropius even tried to reduce the number of women students; women who did enroll were pushed into weaving, for example, which soon became known as the "women's class."[181] Nonetheless, Weimar women *were* involved in organizing exhibitions on the latest in interior design, albeit for areas considered their natural domain: the designer Lilly Reich, for example, was responsible for the domestic appliances display at the Stuttgart Weissenhof exhibition of 1927, and at the German Building Exhibition in 1931, she designed a show of materials used in modern interior design, accentuating the contrasting surfaces of these various materials in relation to one another (wood, marble, etc.). At the same exhibition, Elisabeth Lüders designed the home appliances section, Lillian Gilberth the "American" kitchen, and the layout of Peter Behrens's exhibition building (*Ring der Frauen*) was arranged by his partner, Else Oppler-Legband, as a designated area for one hundred women's associations to organize lectures and musical performances by women during the exhibition. The curvature of the building was evidently intended to be feminine in the sense of the "prettiest 'Objectivity'";[182] and, indeed, it received the most media attention of any construction at the fair.[183] The interior walls served to guide the observer in making the correct purchases for interior decoration, in that they were decorated with nothing except display windows of silk, rayon, jewelry, and so forth.

Similarly, the famous "Frankfurt kitchen," the cheap new kitchen for the masses, consisting of six square meters and mass-produced cupboards, was designed in 1925 by Viennese architect Grete Schütte-Lihotzky, for Frankfurt a.M.'s housing projects. The Bauhaus, during its Dessau design phase, likewise focused on the rationalized working kitchen. Not surprisingly, the new kitchen forms the center of Meyer's book—in particular the *Reformküche* by the BEWAG company, with its cupboard-sections that could be assembled in multiple combinations. The functional kitchen was to be a work of art of totally preplanned positionality for the woman as user; but even Meyer herself admitted that this immaculate, modern kitchen was for most women still an expensive, imaginary tune (*Zukunftsmusik*).[184] Moreover, the apparently rational separation of cooking space and its appliances into a "working kitchen" only ended up removing the mother from the sphere of activities of her children; families also began eating in this cramped space (which replaced the larger, mixed-use "live-in kitchen" [*Wohnküche*]).[185]

Meyer is far from acknowledging such inconsistencies of surface-renewal for the Weimar home. Furnishings in the New Woman's home followed the same law introduced by Meyer's plan for electric housewifery: all surfaces should be bright and sheer, not dark and cluttered. Following Taut's woman-directed guidelines in *The New Apartment* and the functional furniture designs of the Bauhaus—what Helmut Lethen refers to as the anti-atavistic "cold interior" of the 1920s[186]—Meyer calls for her readers to muster their courage and get rid of (or store) all fussy, hard-to-clean Wilhelmine-era porcelain and glass ornaments, and to organize instead an emptied-out series of rooms. Living spaces should contain as few kitschy "sentimental pictures" (*Herzensbilder*) as possible to maintain the new aesthetic of "suitableness" (*Zweckmäßigkeit*).[187] The point of all this transformation, for Meyer, goes beyond any merely visual aesthetic to the practical-cum-emancipatory consideration of saving the ex-oppressed housewife "two-thirds of cleaning work"—which in turn would grant her a "secure footing in the shining-forth of her spiritual strength into her home environment."[188] That this increased productivity of kitchen, laundry, and cleaning activities would not, in fact, liberate women, but instead increase the time pressures put on them to achieve more with their "saved" time, was something not yet foreseen. There was, indeed, a certain degree of contradiction between architectural functionalism and the practical functioning of the home, as one Weimar housewife, Ilse Reicke, remarked: in the ultimate modernist home, one's labors would only be increased with cleaning all the glass windows and interior doors. Reicke also notes how structures were being erected by the late 1920s in climates unsuited to the equation of "form = function"—flat roofs, for example, were hardly appropriate to Scandinavian climates where it might snow for months on end.[189]

The New Objective rule of re-surfacing the home within and without coincided with the modern era's obsession with hygiene. The cleansing spirit of social hygiene is reflected in one of Le Corbusier's early, and most severe, trademarks of his philosophy of surface: his "Law of Ripolin" insists on painting inner and outer walls white, not as a cover but as a membrane.[190] Henry Ford, whose translated autobiography and defense of capitalism was an immediate bestseller when published in Germany in 1923 (*Mein Leben und Werk*), likewise applied the Law of Ripolin to further his bottom line, and to banish thereby any potential moral evils and work-related inefficiencies: he painted the interior of his factories white and turned every angle into a surveyable, clean surface.[191] In point of fact, however, Weimar modern architecture, unlike that of Le Corbusier, did not ignore the relation of form to color: colors were consistently applied to the rejuvenated façades and new buildings of the era, especially in Taut's housing projects; and Paul Klee and Wassily Kandinsky painted the walls and ceilings of the house they shared as "Bauhaus masters" in Dessau in the very brightest and warmest of colors.[192] In the bright, ostensibly cheerful colors used to offset the lack of exterior and interior ornament, we see an inherited kinship with German expressionist art, and back again to impressionism and fauvism.

On the domestic level, hygiene was effectively constituted, as one ad claimed in the *Berliner Zeitung* in 1929, by the "victory of the vacuum cleaner principle across the globe."[193] One brand of vacuum cleaner was even called the insect-catching "Vampire."[194] Taut's *New Apartment* is (dare one say) littered with an obsessive call to create efficient surfaces that do not harbor dust.[195] For Meyer, the work of the electric vacuum cleaner (expensive, but available on credit) is cut even more when the only furnishings present are "a few smooth objects and light materials."[196] Meyer continues her logical, hygienically inclined horror of unnecessary extra surface, or "decoration" (*Schmuck*), and the grime it collects, with an attack on patterned wallpaper, borders, upholstery, and heavy curtains, all of which would disturb the modern, light, dust-free, and eminently washable apartment with its minimalist, mass-produced furniture and bare, blank walls.[197] Even the archanalyst of Weimar surface culture, Kracauer, refers to the vacuum-cleaner principle in his description of mass urban entertainment literally sweeping up the blues of the working world, removing the "dust of the everyday."[198]

Domestic hygiene explicitly expanded into social planning with the Dresden Hygiene exhibition of 1930, which was hailed as a trade fair specifically for the female gender: "Everything today that has to do with hygiene originates somehow with woman."[199] There were displays on make-up, reproduction, diet, body culture, fashion, dwelling, work, family, and even on eugenics and hereditary ailments, at which women spectators were protofascistically encouraged to "keep their blood clean and thus provide the basis for healthy offspring."[200] Despite the immediate application of the Law of Ripolin by the Nazis in their hygiene policies of extermination against Jews, Gypsies, and the mentally and physically retarded, we would be in error to assume any total discreditation of social hygiene as a trend in postwar years. For the hygiene fashion during the German 1920s was not an isolated phenomenon: in post-Vichy France, for example, Weimar tenets rearose in a general surface cult of machinic cleanliness. Both were, in fact, scenarios of mass regeneration (literal and cultural acts of cleansing, under American tutelage) in the face of recent national defeat.[201] France of the 1950s needed to present a clean image of itself much as Weimar Germany had wanted to secure an international status for itself by rationalization processes.[202] And in both sociohistorical instances, hygiene was inscribed most effectively over the body of woman.

FASHIONING THE FEMALE BODY

Inferred in both Taut's and Meyer's texts is the assumption that the physiological surfaces of the major occupant of the new home, namely the New Woman (*Neue Frau*), would fully complement the psychogeographically revamped exterior and interior surfaces of her living space. Indeed, this functionalist-cum-feminine ideal that was in tandem with the goals of *Neues Bauen* was repeated consistently across the spectrum of the Weimar popular media. Georg Simmel defined fashion in 1911 as one of the ways in which humans follow a tendency toward Aristotelian mimesis and communal similarity, and yet simultaneously work against this tendency using its opposite, namely the will toward individuality and change.[203] What Simmel could not predict, however, was the massification of the fashion industry, which exploded class differentiations still so visible on the human

Figure 14. "The spirit of the new fashion corresponds to the spirit of the new architecture." Cover for the *Lette-Haus* fashion magazine (1929).

body until World War I, and simultaneously liberated the female form from its socially immobile prewar condition.

The fashion of the 1920s, especially its stylizations of the New Woman, was wholly part of the aspirations of Weimar German modernization in general, wherein form and function could be matched in a such a way to bring beauty (nature, sex appeal) and industry (efficiency, commercial profits) together.[204] As the cover page for a Weimar journal of 1929 proclaimed, the "spirit of the new fashion" for women went hand in hand with the "spirit of the new architecture" (fig. 14). Here, a figure of the New Woman rises gigantically above the twin towers proposed by the Luckhardt Brothers and Alfons Anker for the Alexanderplatz competition: the lines of her body adhere to the contours of the high-rise office buildings in the picture, and the lines decorating her outfit correspond at right angles to

Figure 15. Front cover for *Die Reklame* (1929).

the stark horizontal lines crossing the buildings' façades.[205] Similarly, the New Woman was employed in advertisements as an imaginary consumer of automobiles, because the sexually charged, angular linearity and energy of one entirely matched that of the other. A cover page of 1929 for *Die Reklame,* an advertising trade magazine, configured a female mannequin's head rising before a row of skyscrapers that literally support the title of the magazine (fig. 15). Advertising, architecture, and the new female identity are merged here into the unified functionalism of sheer surface.

Of course, being stripped of ornament was not the same as being ornament-free: just as the cleansed façades of Weimar buildings were immediately redecorated with advertising and other signs of commercial modernity, so too was the visage of the New Woman the first bearer of (now respectable) make-up—as witnessed by one newspaper's April Fool's joke, a machine for applying make-up (fig. 16).[206] Ads urged women to attract men by using hair-removal cream on their bodies, and to avoid urban living's stress and aging by using skin-elasticizing lotion on their

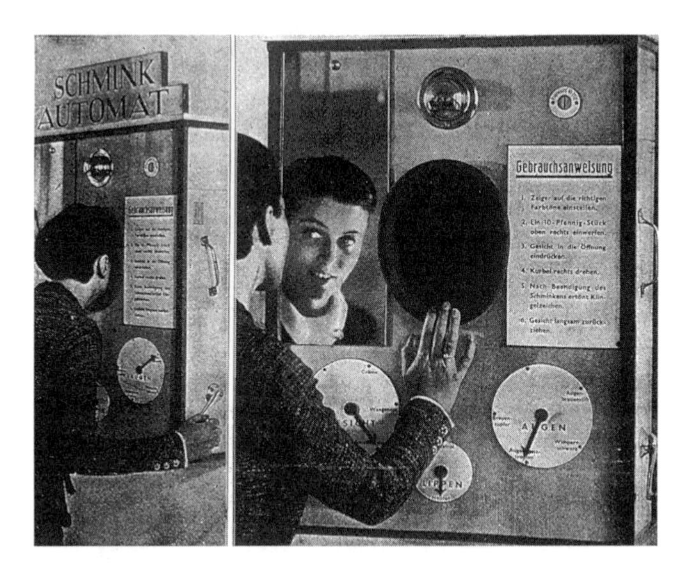

Figure 16. "The make-up machine" (*Der Schmink-Automat,* 1931).

faces (fig. 17).[207] Mark Wigley's assertion in *White Walls, Designer Dresses* that "modern architecture ends up being stitched ever more tightly to the realm of dress" can thus be extended to the reshaping of the female body itself.[208]

The New Woman, a full participant in Weimar surface culture, was an essentially tripartite conglomeration.[209] First, she was an unabashed import, drawing on both the radical innovations of the Parisian fashion houses and the American culture industry's creation of the 1920s flapper; her mediated and idealized presence in women's popular magazines (*Illustrierte*) such as *Neue Frauenkleidung und Frauenkultur* and *Die Dame*[210] influenced and gave rise to reality in a highly Baudrillardian manner. Second, she constituted a Fordist by-product of Weberian efficiency principles,[211] the aim of which was to benefit businesses' profit margins by putting women to work (albeit in positions permanently subservient to men, as popular pulp novels by Rudolf Braune and Christa Anita Brück depict).[212] Third, the New Woman was a stunning surface projection, as depicted on screen by the Hollywood/Babelsberg star-system of female icons, of an apparently emancipated sexuality (think of Colleen Moore, Louise Brooks, Betty Amann, Asta Nielsen, or Marlene Dietrich).

Nonetheless, it would be mistaken to dismiss the Weimar New Woman's various artifices of identity as merely a borrowed import or a passive, imaginary product. For she nonetheless "existed" and had a mas-

Figure 17. "The woman of today!" Advertisement for Creme Mouson (1929).

sive impact within the social imaginary, on both women and men. Robert Musil was aware of how, through the New Woman, women could stop being man's ideal and instead conceive of their own desired imago (*Wunschbild*).[213] Occasionally, as in the highly incisive story of Doris, the working-class heroine of the novel *The Artificial Silk Girl* (*Das kunstseidene Mädchen*, 1932) by Irmgard Keun, it is precisely in the increasingly obvious gap between the individual's sorry lot and her dream of reaching the stellar, auratic level of a *Glanz*—a New Woman as depicted in the movies and magazines, hence an active part in Weimar surface culture—that most of the learning curve for the protagonist (and hence also the *readership* of Weimar women) actually occurs.[214] Doris basically prostitutes herself with boyfriends in order to get a decent wardrobe, which enables her to give the world the impression of being a New Woman. Keun's protagonist provides us with a double metaphor of both self-subsumption within and resistance to modern surface culture—for though Doris never becomes the *Glanz* she thinks she deserves to be, by the end of her tale she demonstrates a learned independence of authentic action and thought that more assuredly grants her the status of New Woman after all.

The predicament of Doris as the "artificial silk girl" all at sea amid Weimar surface culture points up how, despite her theft of a fur coat, Doris's outfit, like her luck, generally remains on the level of artificial silk (i.e., rayon, the 1920s' most dynamic fashion material), never attaining the socioeconomic status of real silk.[215] Here one should bear in mind that a huge 25 percent of the average Weimar German income was spent on clothing:[216] the astronomical cost of modernity's first era of fashion for the masses can thus be assessed in relation to today's worldwide *prêt-a-porter* market. Nonetheless, the use of rayon democratized female dress like no other before it. Cities like Leipzig (in 1926) and Hamburg (1927) began a series of trade shows exhibiting the new material, so as to acquaint German retailers with its possibilities for the public, and there was even a national committee that organized rayon exhibitions. One commentator in 1932 bemoaned the way in which the "goddess of rayon" had brought down the common denominator of consumption, making even Berlin-West's elegant Tauentzienstraße into a deaestheticized market.[217] In magazines, artificial silk was hyped as a surefire way to succeed on a date, and artificial silk stockings could now be worn by women of all classes—all the better to highlight the newly revealed and hence fetishized body part, the back of the knee.[218]

Rather than negate the plight of Doris or the artificiality of the New Woman as the dreams of little Kracauerian shopgirls,[219] we can find according to Pierre Bourdieu's theory of social habitus a path wherein the image of the New Woman is one that was altered and transformed by women according to their own ongoing lifestyle identifications and tastes.[220] The role of women in the Weimar culture industry of surface, specifically the necessary, indivisible relation between woman's body and her clothing—where, in the words of Simone de Beauvoir in *The Second Sex,* the latter puts the former "on display" and makes her into a permanent source of commodified spectacle[221]—need not all be reduced to a reactive positionality for the wearer. We should not regard her, then, as merely a "media myth or a demographer's paranoid fantasy," but rather, with Grossmann, as a "social reality" of rationalization: the interesting question is to consider the "perception of change and rupture" that she so forcefully represented.[222] When it comes to images of women for feminist liberation, the New Woman surely remains one of the strongest images to date.

One key consequence of the architecturalization of the body of the New Woman according to the surfaces of New Objectivity was that her image became not that of a mature woman but of a practically prepubescent girl, who more closely resembled the athletic, slim-hipped, broad-shouldered Greek male youth of Western art than any previous female body ideal. The Girl's most obvious characteristic was hence her masculinity. There was a competition in 1928 for the "Most Beautiful Female Portrait," organized by the Elida shampoo, face cream, and soap firm, with 365 artists submitting entries for the ten-thousand-Rentenmark prize. The more daring depictions of the aggressive *garçonne* were not favored by the conservative jury; nonetheless, the winning entry, *Girl Standing* (*Stehendes Mädchen*) by Willy Jaeckel, shows off the short-skirted sporty vitality of the New Woman as a normal girl-next-door, standing head on, legs astride, in a confident but unassuming, erect but curvingly inclined, stance.[223]

Part of the New Woman's architecturalization as Girl—tying in completely with contemporary demands placed on the female body image in millennial U.S. culture—was the emphasis on motion. The hip-tied dress may have been unformed, but it was also uniformed; the newly gained mobility was gained only along the lines of rationalized, regimented expectations of fitness.[224] The calisthenic requirements imposed on women by the *Neue Sachlichkeit* of dress were severe ones: "Woman has become strong and self-assured through this work [of body culture], woman has become a complete human being; for her freedom today in all spheres stands in close relation to her physical liberation."[225] As Fritz Giese pronounced of the New Woman in his *Girlkultur* (1925): "[She] . . . must be a girl-type, youthful and lithe, unconnected to things that have to do outwardly with motherhood."[226] For Kiese it is clear that this recontouring shift amounts to a both a sweetening kitschification and an incipient eugenicization of the female form; he hopes that in the epidemic rush to emulate the Tiller Girl type there is already the "beginning of the end of their fashion."[227] The surface-ethos of the Girl is "doomed to imitation and flattening-out";[228] Giese would clearly prefer that something deeper, and originally "German," emerge instead. Giese's critique of the New Woman's precarious androgyny alerts us to the fact that for all the apparent emancipation of the female form from its various artificial surfaces of the nineteenth century to its natural physical surfaces of the 1920s—that is, out of the corset, via the uncorsetted "reform garment" (*Reformkleid*) movement of the fin-de-siècle,[229] to what Peter Wollen refers to as the unrestricted "modernist body"[230] wearer of the short, unwaisted tunic—Weimar society was not truly ready to accept the new sociosexual mobility now permitted women by their defeminized fashions. And yet it is on the body of the New Woman that Weimar surface culture was most vividly inscribed in all its force—despite the fact that the figure of modernity was predominantly male, and despite the traditional view of woman as a figure of *Unsachlichkeit*.[231]

Hence the ultrarational modernization of the 1920s was, despite its masculine credo, far from being at odds with the feminine per se, as might initially be presumed. Instead, a rare confluence of the two occurred, by which the transformation of the New Woman reflected and accentuated—and yet did not merely serve—the New Man's own makeover into the clean-cut façadism of New Objectivity. A leading fashion magazine announced in 1926, for example, that there was practically no difference any more between the American-style male and female bathing costumes.[232] The masculine streamlining of women's fashion was perceived to have a clear effect on sexual relations, as Döblin complained about the quasi-machinic "indifference" that had set in under the guise of "objective love."[233] With the onset in the mid-1920s of the New Woman's most extreme form, the wholly masculinized *Garçonne* in pantsuit and monocle, cartoons appeared in the press worrying about the "spirit of fashion" crossing over the female gender into the domain of the male, and vice versa.[234] Articles were written mocking women's new cropped *Bubikopf* haircuts as "circumcision" for women, or forecasting the day when men's hair would be braided and waistlength.[235] Lesbianism, like the rise in public visibility of male homosexuality in Weimar metropolitan life, was termed by Emil Lucka as a "parallel eroticism," the becoming-similar of both sexes, hence very much a part of the new "antipolar" tendencies of fashion.[236] For Lucka, the *Bubikopf*, sported by the likes of Coco Chanel and Isadora Duncan as of 1920 and by the masses a few years later, was, like smoking or wearing trousers, likewise part of this new antipolarity, a "necessary symptom of a leveling feeling of the sexes with respect to each other."[237]

What becomes clear from this blurring of sexual differences is that Weimar modernity signified the merging of the traditional design dichotomy regarding gender (namely, lack of ornament, male; ornament, female). New Objective design thus moved Nietzsche's own revalorization of feminine decadence and masquerade out of the late nineteenth century's decorative realm of metaphoricity[238] and into the twentieth century's deaestheticized world of functionality. As Patrice Petro has indicated, magazines like *Die Dame* quasi-innocently projected the inverse of Joan Rivière's 1929 thesis on sociosexual role-play of "womanliness as a masquerade"[239]—namely a bold and "self-consciously *masculine* masquerade" of female identity, and hence also a destabilization of male power by the coopting of its visual artifices.[240]

Conservative circles reacted strongly against the New Woman's unfeminine efficiency in favor of the traditional body type and function of the *Vollweib* or "full woman", à la Leni Riefenstahl as she depicted herself in her 1932 film *The Blue Light*. In Ernst Jünger's archconservative opinion, the rationalized female form lost its fertility and original sexual power: "How is it that these tremendous female bodies, in shape, suntanned and delineated with every cosmetic means, are as tasteless for one's appetite as Californian apples?"[241] Nor were the critics of the New Woman's assembly-line image entirely without justification, especially when one considers the bleakness inherent in such phrases as: "The clothing of the modern woman, like the revolutionary reshaping of her hairstyle, is in its deepest origin nothing other than the drive toward 'rationalization,' the functional, and the objective."[242] A fat woman's body did not go well with the Taylorized *Bubikopf* and obligatory short, sleek dresses or even pants. Amidst this enforced idealization of thinness, with diet pills and vitamins, it is no coincidence that anorexia and bulimia began in earnest in the 1920s. The Weimar New Woman's affinity with surface culture was also read as one of cynicism and self-regard—perhaps best personified by the character of Cornelia Battenberg and her theory of the "consumerist character of love" in Erich Kästner's satirical novel *Fabian: The Story of a Moralist* (*Fabian. Die Geschichte eines Moralisten,* 1931).[243] This geosexual displacement away from natural female roots was launched by the (future Nazi) feminist lecturer Gertrud Bäumer: in *Woman in the Crisis of Culture* (*Die Frau in der Krisis der Kultur,* 1926), Bäumer declares that the soul of woman in Weimar times "lies like earth underneath the asphalt."[244] Perturbed by how modernity has atomized, rationalized, and alienated woman from her mythical sources, Bäumer condemns, *inter alia,* the ostensibly liberated sexuality of the New Woman (i.e., loving as freely as a man, without ties to motherhood).[245]

Ironically, Bäumer and Kracauer would have agreed on the nefarious effect on white-collar workers of the cult of surface appearances in modern commodified society. Kracauer comments scathingly on the feminization of all salesmen in *Die Angestellten:* one's looks (*Äußere*) are now what count most for one's advancement, and a "pleasant appearance" (*angenehmes Aussehen*) is required for sales assistants.[246] Thus the fear of looking old (i.e., older than thirty), once the domain of women who did not marry out of the workforce, now applies to their male working colleagues as well. Youth becomes the "fetish of the illustrated magazines and their public," and aging is both devalued and repressed.[247] With regard to the slavish conformity of office and shop workers to the body ideal of surface culture, and employers who effectively promote it through the "selective breeding" of whom they hire and fire, Kracauer's sarcasm knows no bounds: "A moral-pink skin tint—this conceptual combination renders the everyday transparent in one fell swoop, filled as it is with display-window decorations, white-collar workers, and illustrated magazines. Its morality is to be tinted pink, its pink morally primed. That is how it is desired by those on whom the selection is incumbent. They would like life to be covered with a coat of varnish that would veil over its far from rosy reality."[248] Following Kracauer's study, Alice Rühle-Gerstel argues that being an employee encourages women to emphasize their "outward appearance," thereby erotically expressing their hopes of career advancement.[249] Accordingly, such office work, Rühle-Gerstel continues, is for women but a pseudo-job, an "artificial silk profession, artificial silk like the stockings and blouses of the little shop girls, artificial silk like their temperament and their world of ideas"—such is the result of putting female proletarians into a male, bourgeois work environment: "Iridescent figures [*schillernde Gestalten*], often with iridescent charms, but just as often of iridescent doubtfulness, but at any rate full of iridescent conviction of their social and spiritual existence."[250]

The end of New Woman had already occurred by Hitler's accession to power in January 1933, when the journalist Gabriele Tergit wrote that the era of the New Woman—of "becoming somebody" in the practical world of careers—was now an event of yesterday.[251] After the heyday of New Objectivity came a new retro-urge for women in society—the "new affection" (*neue Herzlichkeit*).[252] As Lucka noticed in 1929, the year of the stock market crash, the New Woman's fashion was becoming the fashion of yesterday, with women's hair beginning to lengthen again, and indeed the entire surface of clothing asserting a new (yet familiar) difference from the severe sheath-effect of the New Objectivity years: "The new attire is no longer a thin skin over the skin of the body, it is gaining a new life, bows and frills are appearing, the firmly delineated forms are being given up; something light and airy, perhaps something bell-like is again draping over the female body."[253] In the same year, author Marieluise Fleisser welcomed the "new line" for women, who were permitted to have curves once more: "Fashion is becoming feminine again."[254] The New Woman was effectively killed off by the demise of faith in Weimar architectural modernism; a pragmatic product, not an idealistic or ideological movement, she went under when the economy and politics demanded her demise.[255]

Weimar fashion, then, and its wearer, the New Woman, were anthropomorphizations of the German modern movement's radical stripping away of the surfaces that had defined nineteenth-century architecture. Neither the cladding of the body nor that of the building was a mere rubber-stamping of the sempiternal, technologically informed "rational" over the temporary, fashion- and ornament-bound "irrational." For all its apparent bareness of sobriety, we should understand that modern surface culture was itself a transitory cover(-up) or superficies that functioned as no more and no less than a passing statement of fashion, of modernity's essential being and faith in itself. After all, Charles Baudelaire, for whom *la modernité* and *la mode* were synonymous terms, liked to celebrate his own role as the "painter of the passing moment."[256] Baudelaire dedicated his poetic art to charting the beauty of "the ephemeral, the fugitive, the contingent," as he so famously defined modernity in 1863.[257] His suggestion to the modern artist is to pay specific attention to such literal surface fabrications as satin, cosmetics, and the latest contemporary style in ladies' fashion, because their barometer nature would guide the artist—and hence also the Weimar architect—best.

A concluding consideration can be gleaned from social theorist Gilles Lipovetsky's timely provocation in *The Empire of Fashion* (1987): "What is at stake is not at all a vision of modernity that would affirm the progress of rational universality through the dialectical play of individual tendencies, but the autonomy of a society structured by fashion, where rationality functions by way of evanescence and superficiality, where objectivity is instituted as a spectacle, where the dominion of technology is reconciled with play and the realm of politics is reconciled with seduction."[258] Lipovetsky's faith in the role of modern fashion (like that of advertising) is drawn from its ability to foster a public space of creativity, even for women: "Fashion does not bring about the definitive alienation of the masses; it is an ambiguous but effective vector of human autonomy, even though it functions via the heteronomy of mass culture."[259] The insight to be gained from Lipovetsky, then, is that (despite Loos's polarizations) we are not dealing in the modern era with a conundrum of sensible, ornament-free rationality versus trivial, decorative fashion (whether in clothing or in architecture); rather, we need to reencounter the process of modernization in the West as one in which rationality and fashion have coincided interstitially in a condition of symbiotically fertile rapprochement. Nowhere more than in New Objective Germany was there such a prime site for these cross-processes of modernity.

2 Electric Stimulations

The Shock of the New Objectivity in Weimar Advertising

Alles Göttliche auf Erden ist ein Lichtgedanke nur.
Friedrich von Schiller

ADVERTISING AS POWER

The advertising realm of the Weimar Republic offers us today a remarkable visual record of the reenchantment of modernity via apparently rational means. It is a particularly apposite example of the relentless functioning of surface culture that was so characteristic of German modernity in its commercial, urban setting. This chapter focuses on the shocks targeted at the psyche of the modern city-dweller by the new stimulants employed in Weimar advertising, and on the strategies involved in the displacement of the spectator's literal and psychological perception—a necessary process for any effective advertisement.

Weimar modernity's term for advertising, *Reklame,* was adopted from the French verb *reclamer* (with the Latin origin meaning "to call out"), suggesting a more expansive commercial situation than the German version, *Werbewesen* or *Werbung* (for all its parallel connotations to sexual courting).[1] As Walter Benjamin states, the rise of the French word was concomitant with the "enthronement of the commodity" in the Parisian arcades during the second half of the nineteenth century.[2] Advertising, which began as just one discourse among many (like the church, or the state), developed at the beginning of this century into a key denominator of modern industrial life.[3] Moreover, during the Weimar years, advertising was discovered as a science worthy of investigation: in a highly Teutonic version of American Fordism that reflected Germany's post–Treaty of Versailles need for acceptable international status, a new industry grew up around the opportunities that advertising offered. Weimar Germany's import of *Amerikanismus* resulted in tendencies of rationalization and New Objectivity in everything from art to kitchen design. It was reabsorbed by German business as a *Heimat* ("homeland") type of product, as an economic and psychological boost to the darkness of the ignominious defeat of World War I. While the National Socialist party of the 1920s insisted on seeing in the new urban consumerist culture elements of the Jewish threat, advertising nonetheless remained a highly efficient national self-promotion, or warfare by other means. The battle of materials, the *Materialschlacht,* did not end in 1918; rather, the technological war on the senses was just beginning.

The turn of the century witnessed the gradual implosion of advertising into art, and art into advertising. Decisive in the development of advertising aesthetics and in bringing art and industry closer together was the Werkbund, founded in Munich in 1907 by Friedrich Naumann, with such luminaries on board as Henry van de Velde, Fritz Schumacher, and Hermann Muthesius.[4] Peter Behrens continued this direction when he spearheaded a series of minimalist advertising designs that complemented his electrical goods for the German nation's first electric company, AEG, founded in 1883 by Emil Rathenau; these ads by the future father to the Bauhaus created one of the first corporate identities, provided further witness to the industrial application of art and architecture, and were part of a general shift in power and action away from the *Bildungsbürgertum* and toward the tastes of the urban masses. Weimar advertising also inherited a significant psychological identity from the Great War, which introduced the tactics of visual propaganda graphics, accentuated the agonies and ecstasies of expressionist art, and inspired the dada movement's aesthetics of shock. The *Gesamtkunstwerk* could never quite recover its aura "whole" again; from this point on, advertising was always in its midst.[5]

The primary location for the phantasmagorical investiture provoked by 1920s advertising was in the public sphere of the metropolis, specifically *on the street.* Given the way the masses moved about the modern city, outdoor electric advertisements were referred to (in the U.S.) as stationary "spectaculars," about which the market could freely "circulate."[6] As the locus of the modern masses, the street was the most effective place by far for advertising: in Weimar Germany, street media included display windows (*Schaufenster*), free-standing display boxes (*Schaukasten*), and posters on electrically lit advertising columns (*Litfaßsäulen*) and their cousins, clock-towers (*Normaluhren*) lit from within (figs. 18 and 19).[7] There were even walking advertisements—men employed to wear placards

Figure 18. Advertising column (*Litfaßsäule*, 1931).

or even human-sized promotional packages of the actual product, like the giant blackface puppets for the Bullrich Salt company shown parading between the trams in Walther Ruttmann's 1927 documentary *Berlin, Symphony of a City.* Add to this the new cinematic affines, namely slides projected at the movie theaters between film screenings, and the nascent genre of advertising films, and it is easy to see how the face of modern advertising was being changed forever, with such visually and mechanically oriented media clearly outshining the more traditional written formats for ads and announcements in newspapers, illustrated magazines, and flyers.

Advertising is, primarily, a discourse of visually harnessed, or applied, power. Bruno Taut, the expressionist architect who went through a per-

Figure 19. Electric clock tower (*Normaluhr*) advertising Sarotti chocolates (1925).

sonal makeover into a New Objectivity architect of mass housing projects in Berlin during the later Weimar years, wrote a newspaper article in 1922 urging the active participation of the public in shaping the future of urban advertising: ever one to grab the moment, Taut uses an electrical metaphor to say that if you do not plug yourself into advertising as the new "current of life," then you will effectively switch yourself off from the creative possibilities of modernity.[8] He stresses the essential discourse of advertising as that of the visually applied strength of the human will-to-power: it is a colorful "noise not for the ears," he says, "but for the eyes."

The dramatic scientization of advertising in Weimar Germany reflects a strong awareness of this power to entertain and to distract. Even though the advertising industry in Germany did not regain its pre-WWI levels until after 1923[9]—the number of advertisements in newspapers and magazines was literally halved by the war, the fledgling republic's ensuing civil unrest, and the inflation crisis[10]—it nonetheless expanded enormously during the mid-Weimar years. Indeed, one of the duties of the Weimar

Ministry of Culture (*Reichskunstwart*), founded in January 1920 after a parliamentary decree in October 1919, was to establish in the immediate post-WWI years a systematic, national approach to the use of advertising, initially in the postal and rail services.[11] If the Great War could not be won by military maneuver, then it could perhaps—at least after the introduction of the Rentenmark and until the economic depression caused by the stock market crash of October 1929—be won again by German advertising strength.

As if in response to such a call, advertising was made a university subject (*Werbewissenschaft*) in 1925,[12] and the stabilization years witnessed a veritable plethora of self-promotional advertising trade journals, such as *Die Auslage, Seidels Reklame, Reklamekunst, Die Reklame,* and *Zeitschrift für Waren- und Kaufhäuser.* By 1929 there were fifteen professional advertising and marketing associations in Germany (e.g., Deutscher Werbeklub, Deutscher Reklame-Verband, and the Reklameschutzverband).[13] In this era of incipient market segmentation,[14] the aesthetic style of efficient, antiornamental, promachinic *Neue Sachlichkeit* made perfect sense: "The position of our fatherland demands a rebuilding with all means," ran the opening line of a 1924 trade journal article by a Hamburg architect: whoever understands the "influence abroad of German spiritual life," especially architecture, will also understand "what duty outdoor advertising has to perform in Germany."[15] The exponential growth of advertising culminated in a gesture of self-referentiality when Berlin hosted the 1929 Reklameschau, an international trade fair dedicated to exhibiting advertising as a product in and of itself—the poster for the event shows the printing of its own poster (fig. 20). The exhibition even built its own model "advertising city" (*Reklamestadt*). It was announced at this event that Germany was spending nine hundred million RM on advertising per year (more per capita than the U.S.); one in thirty German workers was engaged full-time in the field.[16]

Industrially applied psychology was first imported from the United States to Germany by Harvard professor Hugo Münsterberg, who, with his book *Psychology and Economic Life* (*Psychologie und Wirtschaftsleben*) of 1912, was the first to psychologize the advertising act for Germans.[17] Interwar Germany was almost exaggeratedly swift to adopt the new field: by 1922, 170 German firms had separate divisions using "*Psychotechnik*"; and to get a job in a major department store or factory, one had to first pass a series of exams measuring aptitude and reaction time.[18] "Psychotechnicians," the first business consultants of the twentieth century, found lucrative employment consulting for German firms intent on

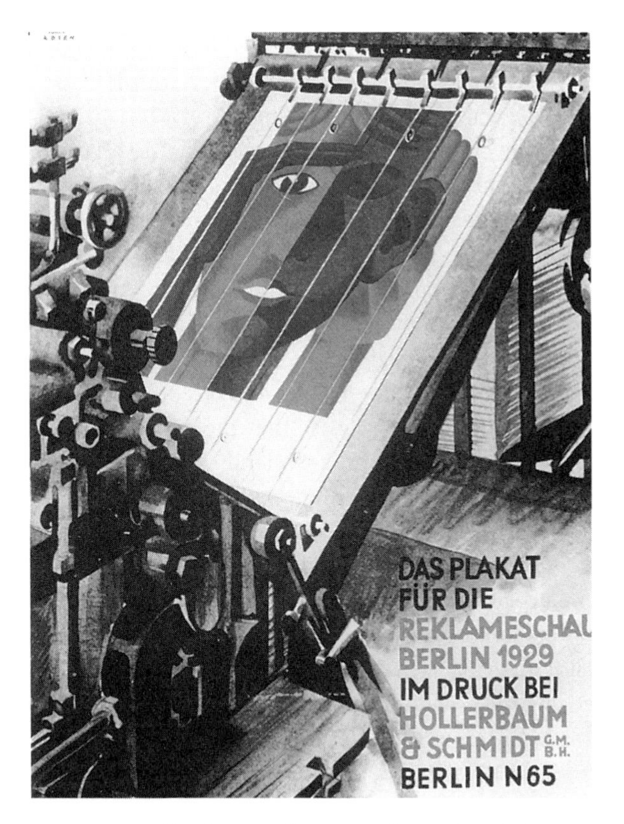

Figure 20. Official poster for the Berlin trade exhibition on advertising (*Reklameschau*, 1929).

modernizing their procedures. By 1932, even after the economic crisis of 1929 had forced the demise of many commercial psychotechnics agencies, the subject was being taught at thirty-three German universities and institutes.[19]

Clearly, the Weimar advertising cult was wholly in step with the machinic regimentation of the modern age. According to Kracauer in his commentaries on Weimar culture, the urban masses went in search of distraction that would match the stimulation of their mechanized, bureaucratized work patterns: however, before they even reached their entertainment destinations in the movie palaces or the Lunapark, they were successfully distracted by the advertising shapes dominating the city center, "electric advertising . . . , whose colored signs, words and lines control the heights."[20] In Kracauer's fascination with the role of advertising in people's lives, we espy also his view of its darker relation to the process of modernization—its function as an invasive, producer-manipulated entity that bullied the unconscious masses into the faithful shapes capitalism required of them, even in their leisure time.[21]

At the same time, modern advertising was the first textual presence on the street to give expression to the very power of mass culture—to create what we understand today as the masses' (our) relatively active ability to coauthor an individual lifestyle.[22] For Alfred Döblin, advertising constituted no less than the "people's poetry," the most authentic living language of the modern city, spoken *by* (as opposed to *at*) the "little man."[23] Many of the famous montage passages from his 1929 novel *Berlin Alexanderplatz* are authentic re-creations—a new form-oriented mimesis, in fact—of the multileveled advertising discourse that the author so admires: in one memorable section, Döblin's camera-eye and -ear of a narrator walks and glides across the "Alex," catching snippets of advertising slogans that could be read from the buildings or on the trams.[24] From the text it is impossible to tell precisely who among the crowd is reading these sound bites: it is as if the Alexanderplatz itself is talking with its denizens. Döblin's pieces about Berlin's commercial streets constitute a unique prose form that Weimar advertising first made possible: they are the novelist's combined version of the absurdist dada-photomontages by Raoul Haussmann and Hanna Höch and the more socially satirical photomontages by John Heartfield for the *Arbeiter Illustrierte Zeitung* (*AIZ*), incorporating the technology worship present in New Objective photo collections of urban living, such as Albert Renger-Patzsch's *The World is Beautiful* (*Die Welt ist schön*).[25]

While the veritable power of successful advertisements resides precisely in the role of coauthorship between public and mediated product, this is not the impression one receives from the ways in which the German advertising industry understood its role in the 1920s. The era's intense involvement with psychotechnical reasoning was responsible for Weimar advertising's intoxicated preoccupation not so much with human participatory acts as with the sheer strength of advertising's *functioning* in and of itself. A 1929 advertising study, *Allgemeine Werbelehre* by Rudolf Seyffert, offers a definition of advertising that is rather telling in this regard: its purpose, he says, is to provide a totally seamless combination of a will imposed from without and individual decision-making from within—a "*form of influence, which through the systematic application of methods, aims to bring about a voluntary reception, implementation, and continued fertilization of the goal that it offers.*"[26] Seyffert does at least problematize the issue of influence somewhat, when he detects advertising's tendency toward "exaggeration," and expresses some concern about the industry's latent potential to lie, or transfer its skills in mass manipulation toward religious or political applications.[27]

What we find in 1920s trade literature is a total faith in the industrial aesthetic of advertising, aimed at climaxing in the moment of consumption. Not for nothing did the German trade journal *Reklamekunst* (The Art of Advertising) change its name in 1927 to *Die Propaganda.* Exhaustive psychotechnical studies were carried out, echoing American guides such as Daniel Starch's *Principles of Advertising* (1923),[28] to pinpoint which pages and page sections of the newspaper best capture the reader's gaze, which sections of the store window caught the attention of an average passer-by, and even how long someone would normally stare at display windows (sixteen seconds, on average, a long pause indeed by our postmodern channel-surfing standards). Initial forays were performed into what nowadays count as market analysis and marketing strategy.[29]

An unquestioning faith regarding the efficacy of psychotechnics in the visual field of advertising is demonstrated by Karl Marbe in a 1927 study. Marbe favors the shock-techniques of electric advertising that induce "intensive perceptions of the senses, contrasting strongly with the environment," precisely for their "attention-principle" (*Aufmerksamkeitsprinzip*) that can summon the individual out of his or her blind, automatic reverie: "The advertising medium should be raised out . . . of the arena of the unconscious and into that of bright consciousness, into the so-called visual point [*Blickpunkt*] of attention."[30] Assuming the voyeuristic principle, he adds that street advertising has to stay in one's consciousness longer than the image of an attractive (female) passer-by. Kurt Friedlaender, in a 1922 study,[31] concentrates on the psychology of advertising attraction, interest, attention, and association, treating the human range of reactions as something entirely quantifiable and predictable so long as the correct stimuli are given.

Another psychotechnician, C. H. von Hartungen, gave a diagrammatic list in 1926 of the various ethically positive attitudes ("psychic receptors") that advertising was meant to induce: for example, patriotism, social responsibility, parental care, pity, thrift, self-survival, intellectual curiosity, aesthetic sensibility, humor, and creativity,[32] all induced by advertising's ability to create "sensory enjoyment" (*Sensationslust*), temporarily and hence repeatedly.[33] The entire spectrum of emotive human responses was considered to be a measurable, controllable entity. Likewise, Mia Klein in her 1929 book on department stores offers related definitions of *Propaganda, Werbung,* and *Reklame,* since all three terms aim for the same thing: the realization of a particular goal (*Zweck*) aimed at the masses.[34] She speaks of a "readiness of will" to be created by advertising in five stages: arousal of attention; effect on memory; creation of pleasurable feeling (*Lustgefühl*); arousal of value-motive; and overcoming of psychological hesitation.[35] In her account, department stores led advertising "campaigns" with military precision throughout the calendar year.[36]

Klein's unproblematized use of warfare terminology in the processes of Weimar advertising is repeated in the "advertising campaign" (*Werbefeldzug*) displayed as a model exhibit by the Mosse publishing house at the 1929 Reklameschau.[37] The purpose of the three-dimensional display was to show off the company's system for getting a product off the ground and into the hands of the consumer. The model incorporated a thirty-foot-long layout that topographically explained its warlike "campaign" with toy soldiers (a.k.a. advertising textwriters, graphic artists, psychotechnicians, and salesmen), as in battle plans from yesteryear. In constant lengthwise motion across the table, brightly colored cords traveled across the various sections of "Market Analysis," "Layout," et cetera, indicating the speed with which a new product could move from concept to profit, as well as the "lively, unstoppable forward movement that in the life of the present reveals itself most clearly in advertising." Indeed, the entire Reklameschau was described by a media commentator as a military "campaign" led by the generals of the advertising world.[38]

The military analogy leads one to want to draw conclusions about why, even though Münsterberg maintained that psychotechnics served only the national economic interest and was politically neutral at its core, so many of the very same psychotechnicians of Weimar commerce went on, in a seemingly effortless case of "synchronization," (*Gleichschaltung*) to become the (anti-Freudian, anti-Jewish) psychotechnicians of the Nazi regime.[39] As was the case with the Weimar era's discovery of (and plaidoyer for) technological "hygiene" in the home, it was all too easy for Nazism to adopt the psychotechnically dominated tendencies of the Weimar advertising industry for its own noncommercial aims of mass cultural rebirth.[40] As early as 1922, Kracauer offered a word of caution about the myriad "partial-selves" (*Teil-Iche*) that urban modernity was spewing forth. The uniform nonindividuality of these masses was forged by collective activity, such as that idealized by psychotechnical logic for the workplace, or for the ways people responded to advertising: only as a group could people become a "pure *tool of the idea.*"[41] Yet psychotechnics did not "lead" to Nazi propaganda, nor is advertising, simply in its application of psychological persuasion, inherently protofascistic. It should not be forgotten, for example, that at the same time as the rise of Nazism in Weimar Germany, Freud's American nephew, Edward Bernays (known nowadays to M.B.A. students as the father of marketing strategy), was busy promoting the very same skill-sets and values of *Psychotechnik* in his New York and Vienna advertising offices.[42]

ELECTRIC MODERNITY

We can thus chart a *mise-en-scène* of how advertising metastasized from its late nineteenth-century beginnings into a twentieth-century mechanism that radically reshaped the experience of idle *flânerie* into distraction with an applied purpose. What most transformed the power of outdoor advertising as a mass of visual signifiers was the use of electricity. At the turn of the century, America led the way with the recognition that "electrical advertising is a *picture medium.* Moreover, it is a *color* medium of motion, of action, *of life, of light,* of compulsory attraction."[43] Germany was quick to emulate and develop such techniques. One succinct way of depicting the changes that electric advertising brought was the so-called "Manoli" effect: in 1898, the electric ad for the Manoli tobacco firm—a revolving wheel of light high up on the rooftops of Berlin—promptly became a Wilhelmine synonym for "insanity" and the epitome of modernity's maddening changes in human apperception.[44] Even before World War I, it had become possible to have alternating electric advertisements rotating temporally in the same ad spot by using different "fields." After this came the shift to actual electric pictures, and finally electric movement itself: a 1912 Berlin ad for Kupferberg champagne showed not just the liquid "flowing" into the glass, but also the bubbles rising within it. The First World War brought a total ban on electric advertising, more for economic reasons than anything else—a blackout that lasted until the early 1920s.[45]

Not until the postinflation stabilization did Germany first make significant use of electric advertising, in a concerted effort to play catch-up in the race for industrial and economic prestige. Literal consequences of the Rentenmark's effect on Weimar urban life were the newly asphalted surfaces for city streets (for motor traffic, not for horse-drawn carriages), new urban planning for the installation of gas and electricity, and the concomitantly increased street lighting: "The streets became clean again. Holes grew over. New asphalt glistened. . . . Gaslights and electric lights increased in the nighttime streets, as if light had been sown."[46] From 1924 to 1928, enjoying the sinking costs of electricity use in Europe, and no longer lagging behind the U.S., Germany used twice as much electric advertising as in prewar years.[47] The point was more than aesthetic—it was to make people shop in the evening, for, as a commentator opined in 1929: "This is the time when retail shops have their greatest turnover and the desire to purchase is highest."[48]

While Paris had indeed been the City of Light in the nineteenth century, Berlin rose quickly to become the early twentieth century's "paradise of electricity."[49] In bids for world-city status, one defined a metropolis by its amount of artificial light; it was sincerely believed in 1920s Germany that the sparkle or *Glanz* of other world-cities was due more to their electricity than to anything else.[50] The architect Hermann Muthesius, coiner of the term *Sachlichkeit* for modern architecture, called in 1925 for an ordered, artistically tasteful "good form" for electric advertising to match Germany's already accepted status in display window designs.[51] Hence the German arena mandated on several levels that its electric applications should in significant ways outperform the more haphazard creations of (say) London or New York.[52] Weimar advances in the field were understood to be operating not randomly but under a unified approach,[53] "the light-economic idea" (*der lichtwirtschaftliche Gedanke*).[54] Before the stock market crash of 1929 forced the Weimar electric apex to decline, Germany's capital city had three thousand electric advertisements on display, at an estimated cost of nine million Reichsmarks and using up to 109.5 million kilowatt-hours per year.[55]

Here, economic and national pragmatism matched visionary qualities: it was, after all, the expressionist visionary Paul Scheerbart who, in his futuristic treatise *Glass Architecture* (*Glasarchitektur,* 1914), had predicted an "architecture of illumination," the effects of which would be so "indescribable" and immense that astronomers would be forced to build their telescopes far away from cities in order to see the stars through the competition of Earth's new "sea of colored lights."[56] Babelesque dream-towers are clearly present here, as in an unrealized design of 1926 for a fiery "House of Electricity," an entry in the architectural competition for Berlin's exhibition area.[57] Scheerbart's vision was no doubt based on the electricity spectacles already provided by the world's fairs. Edison's incandescent lighting was first displayed at the 1881 Paris exhibition; eight years later, an electric beacon was installed at the top of the Eiffel Tower. The 1891 International Electrotechnical Exhibition in Frankfurt a.M. showed off Wilhelmine Germany to the industrialized world and made Frankfurt, albeit temporarily, into a fairy-tale "city of lights."[58] The prize exhibit of the Chicago Exposition of 1893 was the Electricity building containing Edison's Kinetoscope, and the 1900 Paris exhibition, despite its overly decorative architectural style, clearly spoke Edison's new language of electricity for the new age: it had a Palace of Electricity with a façade of thousands of colored light bulbs shimmering before a cascading water fountain—a fantasy palace suggestive of a premodernist realization of Scheerbart's visionary architecture.[59] By the turn of the century, exhibitionist fancy had become translated into theme park reality: New York's masses could enjoy a nightly visual feast of 1,300,000 light bulbs on the towers decorating Coney Island's Luna Park.

The groundwork for the massive impact of electricity on commercial and private life during the Weimar Republic was laid during the Wilhelmine years. Between 1885 and 1900 the capital of the electric company AEG rose from five to 60 million RM, confirming its status as a world player among the industrial monopolies.[60] By the 1920s, AEG's impact in Berlin was shared by the city electric company, BEWAG (Berliner Kraft- und Licht-Aktiengesellschaft); and the Osram electric bulb company posited itself as Weimar Germany's version of Edison, taking the weight of the nation's economic renaissance after the Great War on its ubiquitous shoulders—in the realms of industry, offices, consumerist display, and street lighting, as its advertisements suggested (fig. 21). In 1925, Osram developed a way of shaping the bulb into letters or other symbols, which significantly expanded the application of neon advertising.[61]

Neon light originated with Geissler's tubes (cathode rays) and had first been used for Queen Victoria's Diamond Jubilee in 1897. The first large neon display in Germany was in Leipzig in 1922.[62] Neon permanently enhanced electric advertising: since it was not blinding, it facilitated the creation of real forms and dynamic lines in electric lighting that matched modern architecture's "purified" façades, as well as improving the effect of *Normaluhren*.[63] The new "tonal values and different light qualities" of neon light "have awakened in us a physiologically based refinement in sensitivity to light and color," remarked Giedion as he studied the spatio-temporal links between modern art and architecture.[64] Colors other than the primary ones of red, green, and blue were developed for neon during the mid-1920s; but, due to the timing of technological advances in this medium, it was in fact the Nazi years that expanded the use of color in neon street advertising, before the blackout caused by World War II.[65]

From our present postmodern position, amidst home-immanent means of advertising like TV and the Web, we must bear in mind the contextual significance of the neon revolution—as fundamental a shift for modernity, according to German cultural historian Wolfgang Schivelbusch, as the concurrent revolution in German typography from *Fraktur* to modern

Figure 21. Advertisement for Osram Nitra electric light bulbs (late 1920s).

script.[66] Moreover, with art's incorporation of the commercially applied electric medium, as Mark C. Taylor theorizes, the tectonics of artistic production irrevocably shifted toward the postmodern: "The medium of the work of art changes from paint to neon. Things become 'unbearably light.'"[67]

As both the public and private realms of the western world became electrified, metaphors to describe the effects were rewritten along with the changes in medium. According to Benjamin, Paris's "fairy-grotto" effect during the years of gas lighting was lost when the Louvre began electric lighting in 1857.[68] Another stage occurred after the turn of the century, when the image of electricity as female, magical, Medusan Other[69] began to give way to a more internalized approach to rationally appropriating the function of electric power for the modern (male) individual. The 1917 poem "Light-Vision," by future Bauhaus photographer László Moholy-Nagy, begins with a demand, "Recognize the light-structure of your life," and ends with the satisfied proclamation: "Light, total light, creates the

Figure 22. "The city in advertising's sea of lights" (*Die Großstadt im Lichtmeer der Reklame,* 1926).

whole person."[70] Similarly, it is the strange combination of New Objectivity and Expressionism in Lang's film *Metropolis* of 1927 that permits dual depictions of machinic power, namely both the male (rationalized) workers and the female (sexualized) robot.[71]

The prominent analogy to war used in Weimar advertising discourse can be better explained with reference to Germany's experience in the Great War than with any cause-and-effect tale pointing ineffectually toward Nazism. Germany's internalized acceptance of seeing the world and oneself electrically was a rapid transformation enforced by the experience of World War I, as a result of which the lights of the city immediately became equated with the *Materialschlacht.* A 1926 illustration for *Seidels Reklame* suggests such a residual transference of the scene of air battles to the lit-up metropolis (fig. 22). The words of expressionist Ludwig Meidner at the outbreak of war in 1914 already paint the urban setting as one of electric warfare: "Light seems to flow. It fragments things. We clearly feel shreds and beams and parcels of light. . . . In between high rows of houses we are blinded by a tumult of light and dark. Light surfaces lie right across the walls. Right in the middle of a sea of heads, a light explosive goes off. . . . Light mobilizes all things in space."[72] Meidner's metaphor exemplifies how, as Martin Jay reminds us in *Downcast Eyes*, the greatest "crisis of visual primacy" of the modern age came with the Great War.[73] The spatio-temporal decentering it wrought upon mankind was on a par with Copernicus's discovery—in the words of Gertrude Stein in 1938, this war was a "composition that had neither a beginning nor an end, a composition of which one corner was as important as another corner, in fact the composition of cubism."[74] A disruption in the surface plane of one's expected horizon can cause a literal flight response: in the case of early cinema, the Lumière brothers' film *Arrival of a Train at a Station* caused the audience to run when it was first shown on December 28, 1895, because the train was perpendicular to the screen.[75] The Cubist sense of infinite surveillability was in itself discomforting enough for anyone's prewar visual horizon, but the ground-level experience of WWI technology was far worse: it brought a disorientation and objectification of the human greater than the technologies of peacetime (like film or train), and paralleled in practice the transcendental loss already drawn up by Nietzsche.[76]

By the mid-1920s, when the experiential focus of electric light had become more settled as a transformer of the urban context, its presence was a fixture of more coolly ironic, New Objectively functional representations. In "City," a 1931 poem by George A. Goldschlag, electricity is but one of a staccato factual list of features epitomizing the fierce tempo of the modern metropolis: "Bands of light shoot across ravines of houses. / Steep façades stand to attention."[77] New Objective ways of understanding electricity's presence were used with great success in advertising itself. As a tourism poster of 1925 announced, Berlin wanted to "see you" on its streets, like the ones shown spinning around the Kaiser Wilhelm Memorial Church—so that the city could behold itself in its proconsumer scenes of electric spectacle. Paris's attempted transformation out of its nineteenth-century image was marked by the Eiffel Tower's electric advertisement for Citroen—a vertically descending column with the company name alternating with a pattern of light—the largest in the world during the 1920s, and likened in its effect to the monumental way in which Niagara Falls was enhanced electrically by night.[78]

An archproponent of the New Objective call for consummation with the electric city was the Werkbund architectural critic Walter Riezler, who in 1928 proposed a posthumanist metaphysics of artificial, man-made electric light. In an essay suggesting that the prime beneficiary of the Weimar light culture was not so much buildings but the street itself and its traffic, Riezler implies that humankind must fit within the auspices of the new electric urban universe: "Light, as a living, moving force, has become in effect the reality of the city by night. . . . A veritable frenzy of light will brighten the metropolis of the future, one that no imagined dazzle from old fairy tales can come close to."[79] This "frenzy of light" is recognized equally, but more ironically, by Kracauer, who in a brief essay, "Seen from the Window" ("Aus dem Fenster gesehen," 1931), understands Berlin-by-night, centered on the electrically lit-up tower (*Funkturm*, designed by Heinrich Sträumer) at the Berlin exhibition area, to be the epitome of Weimar-as-surface, a single "field of lights." Kracauer's text is also highly suggestive of an Osram poster of the same tower (fig. 23): "Out of the middle of the tumult that has no depth rises a beaming tree: the broadcasting tower, emitting a cone of light all around. The revolving light scans the night, ever turning, and when the storm howls it flies over the high waters, whose waves wash the acres of railway."[80] Indeed, it was the very ubiquitousness of the new street-electricity that prompted Ernst Bloch to mock the "beautifully made distraction" of neon light for only "increasing the darkness."[81]

Germany's ultimate interwar self-salvaging attempt through electric aggrandizement occurred with the "Berlin in Light" (*Berlin im Licht*) week of October 13–16, 1928, when for four nights a full illumination of the city's monuments and commercial buildings was staged by the city's major retail association (Verein der Kaufleute und Industriellen). "Light is life," proclaimed the Osram electric company's adornment of the Siegessäule (Großer Stern), which was clad with a sixty-six-foot-high surface of electric light, admired by a journalist as a "tower of pure fire" (fig. 24).[82] Trees on Unter den Linden were decorated with thousands of light bulbs, and there was even a Bauhaus light-sculpture in front of the Brandenburg Gate.[83] In response to this electric celebration, there were parades and open-air concerts, while retail stores of all kinds treated the event like Christmas, with a citywide competition for the best window display and storewide sales (*weisse Wochen*), all of which functioned as huge light-events in and of themselves—one almost dangerously so, when an electric fault caused a fire in a display window being decorated for the competition at the Tietz department store at Dönhoffplatz.[84] The Luft Hansa company operated flight tours above the shining city, and thousands of Berliners packed the streets for the four evenings of the light festival, which was mostly funded by private sources. Poems were written to both praise and bury the Berlin in Light week's ethos;[85] a hit song, "Berlin in Light," was composed and written by Kurt Weill;[86] and journalists wrote essays link-

Figure 23. The Berlin exhibition area lit by the Osram electric company (1929).

ing the electricity of the street to the latest electric applications for women's work in the home.[87]

In Nietzschean terms, the celebration of the Berlin in Light week constituted an Apollonian glaze over the blind spots caused by Dionysian night—that is to say, it provided Berliners with a comforting, controlled, indeed celebratory repetition of the shock of modernity on the psyche. For Nietzsche, conceptual truth lay more in the darkness of the Will than in the daylight of rationalism: his poetic-satirical, aphoristic advice "to a Light-Lover" is: "If you don't want your eyes and mind to fade, / Pursue the sun while walking in the shade."[88] Cartoons appearing in Berlin newspapers reflected a sense of Nietzsche's little joke, depicting the murkier sides of Berlin's nightlife as temporarily impaired by the totalizing electrification of the city, which left no room for criminal, poor, unseemly, or otherwise marginal activities.[89] But the official stance was to favor the temporary gloss afforded by the Light Week. New modernist buildings like the AEG's "Haus der Technik,"

Figure 24. The Osram company's electric adornment for the Siegessäule during the Berlin in Light week in October 1928.

shining bright blue on the Friedrichstraße, or the white-lit BEWAG building on the Schiffbauerdamm were featured as examples of the latest in *Lichtarchitektur.* Artificial light graced the museums and churches for the first time, lending a Parisian glamour to Berlin,[90] and definitively bringing the advertising lights of the Kurfürstendamm to the Schinkel buildings of old. The Light Week provided yet more proof that the *Glanz* of the city was lent it not by its palaces and ministries but by its commercial areas instead.

The incredible agenda for the Berlin in Light week was, moreover, a consciously staged part of finalizing the German metropolis's position on the world map. "For four days all of Berlin, this rushing, blossoming world-city, will show to its inhabitants and guests a performance that, in glamour and color, splendor and beauty, cannot be matched in the centers of the

Figure 25. Postcard of the "Edison-Spike" for the Amsterdam light week (1929).

world."[91] A newspaper cartoon featured "Heaven's Guardians" remarking from their position up in the stars that Berlin's lights were outdoing not only other world-cities but also Heaven's own light-sources;[92] indeed, the thirteen thousand light bulbs decorating the Leipziger Straße temporarily lent the epithet "Milky Way" to the street. The event also spawned a mimetic string of electric weeks organized by other German cities, such as the Frankfurter Lichtfest (December 1927), or the 1931 Hamburg im Licht week, for which even the housefronts of the traditional Binnenalster were lit up. It facilitated the entrée of electric advertising into Cologne's hitherto off-limits area surrounding the cathedral,[93] and it even spread abroad to Amsterdam's "Edison Light Week" in 1929 (fig. 25).

THE ARCHITECTURE OF LIGHT

In this way, then, the great era of electric advertising helped make the major urban centers of the 1920s—New York's Times Square and Broadway ("the Great White Way"), London's Piccadilly Circus and Leicester Square, Berlin's Potsdamer Platz and Friedrichstraße—into something far more than the sum of their buildings. Manhattan in particular inspired Weimar producers of architecture: Mendelsohn, for example, in his transatlantic photobook homage, *America* (1926), waxes in an ecstatic commentary on the "light circus" of the New York metropolis with its "texts of flames," its "rocket fires of moving electric advertisements diving up and down, disappearing and exploding over the thousands of cars and the merry rush of people."[94] In Germany more than anywhere else, however, the perceptual interference that electric advertising caused in the city street was fundamental to the *Schauspiel* of spatial disruptions caused concurrently by modern architecture. As a result of such architectural innovations, by the mid-1920s Berlin was no longer borrowing from Manhattan or London for advertising ideas. In Weimar Germany, for the first time, buildings were conceived of (or their former façades were removed and redesigned) in relation not just to their material monumentality by day but to their illusionary monumentality by night. The new smooth surfaces and horizontal streamlining of urban buildings' façades set the stage for the use of exterior advertising text, not as something fanciful but something organized and efficient (*sachlich*).

Modern architecture thus felt no discrepancy between design and outdoor advertising, for it was all one; the latter was "no longer tolerated against one's will," it was "planned and even required."[95] The façade, especially the new clean space between storeys, was now but a bare visage on which electric ads could be put. Expressionist architect Hans Scharoun's entry (bearing the rather telling motto "Inside and Outside") for the Berlin Friedrichstraße skyscraper competition of 1921–1922 was one of the first buildings to take into account *at the design stage* the presence of advertising on its outside walls. Scharoun's unrealized skyscraper design featured large advertising text between practically all the storeys, and there were to be prominent show windows at street level. Passers-by would find their gaze arrested further by the dynamic heterogeneity of Scharoun's building, with an enormous glass prism for the main entrance.[96] In 1922, Bruno Taut predated and predicted the façade-shift of the New Objectivity years in his claim that it was better to change the house's façade to match the advertisement than to have an advertisement that does not suit the house, in order that both might speak the same language of advertising.[97] Architecture by the Luckhardt Brothers, such as their office-building façade on Berlin's Tauentzienstraße, was particularly effective in this regard; similarly, their 1928 design for the Berlin House on the Potsdamer Platz was conceived of with a huge "Chlorodont" text ad halfway up the building.[98] Mendelsohn had likewise intended the façade of his Columbus House on the Potsdamer Platz, in which the architect had his own office (before it was occupied by the Gestapo a year after construction ended in 1932), as rows of spaces for advertising letters to be inserted between the windows of the seven upper storeys.[99]

In this way, more and more architects were designing electrically powered advertising structures that were, so to speak, always already plugged in.[100] Architect Hugo Häring noted that the "nighttime picture" of a building, and its concomitant advertising needs for the façade, were overtaking the "daytime picture"[101]—so much so that the prime function of a new "monumental building" on the Ku-damm, advertised in a 1929 issue of the *Berliner Tageblatt,* was precisely to be *Lichtreklame* (light-advertisement) and nothing else (fig. 26).[102] The design-stage inclusion of electric display also affected far smaller, free-standing structures on the Weimar city street: a public telephone was made into a *Telefonsäule,* or a bus stop into a *Haltesäule*—advertising columns lit up by night by their sponsoring companies. Other buildings particularly suited to exterior walls of neon (*Lichtbauten*) were the new gas stations, as well as exhibition pavilions, such as at the various trade fairs during the 1920s, or the Berlin tourist office pavilion on Unter den Linden.

This "architecture of light" developed as the architecture of pure façade in both the literal and metaphorical sense, for here structure was built with the single intent of advertising. *Lichtarchitektur* was defined in the *Reichsfilmblatt* in 1929 as a diurnal form of advertising construction in which "light is used as a building element, in the form of shining surfaces and shapes composed of the latter."[103] Light-architecture corresponded to the same buildings in daytime like a photographic negative to a positive,[104] and *Lichtarchitekten* were considered to be the latest subgenre or specialization of the profession. The architectural mission strove as a result toward a bold new synthesis of light and form, as the Weimar lighting expert and self-proclaimed innovator of light-architecture, Joachim Teichmüller, theorized in 1927:

> It is the task of the architect to employ, in full awareness of the power of light (and shadow) to form space, the means offered him by modern artificial light. . . . [T]he light engineer . . . learns that we do not only illuminate in order to see—that is what the art of lighting does—but in order to create [gestalten]—that is what the architecture of light does.
>
> In other words: by lighting and illuminating we also give form, thus blending the creation of form and the giving of light into a unity.[105]

Figure 26. Advertisement for a "Monumental Building, the focal point of traffic" (1929).

Exterior space and surface could now be accentuated and extended by night in ways unconnected with their daytime aspects. Where necessary, electric advertising was used to transform the shape of an otherwise unwieldy, old-fashioned building into something wholly modern by night. And in the same way, indoor architecture and light fixtures were becoming, thanks to new methods of indirect lighting (such as in pillars and ceilings lit from within), fully integrated one with another for the first time.[106]

Weimar German innovations with representations of artificial light pursued that which postmodern media theorist Norbert Bolz has recognized (following Marshall McLuhan) as the harnessing of electricity to achieve a new purity of transmittance, for the "message of electric light is the pure information of its beam."[107] In the city of the present and of the future, as Riezler asserts in his 1928 essay "Light and Architecture," the determinant of buildings is and will be their ability to integrate, reflect, and promote the purest surface of all, namely electric light: "The surfaces [of buildings] must be bright and smooth (so that shadows from a ledge do not interfere with the light) and large (so that light can assert itself in peace amidst all the agitation of its surroundings). For even here it is not the construction, but light that matters most. . . . [The building] functions not as a building, i.e., as a spatial-physical creation, but only as a phenomenon of immaterial surfaces, whose substance nobody thinks of."[108] Riezler is convinced that producing buildings in such a light-oriented manner will lead to a formidable "empire" of "indestructibility" and "unbroken developability." In this context, it was not at all a coincidence that Lang staged the monumental scene of the space rocket leaving the hangar in his 1929 film *Woman in the Moon* (*Die Frau im Mond*) as a nighttime scene of light-architecture on a massive scale.

Here it is crucial to realize that the demands of Fordist consumerism added a new twist to these revelatory renovations: the old Wilhelmine decorations that were so religiously removed from buildings' façades in the radical architectural face-lifts of the functionalist 1920s *Neues Bauen* were, ironically, reapplied and redecorated (but in a New Objective way) in the service of technologically amplified "light advertising" (*Lichtreklame*). The use of billboards, but more crucially electric text and imagery on the exterior of buildings, received an official confirmation in 1928 from the state art advisor (*Reichskunstwart*), Erwin Redslob, who called it the "great ornamental motif of our time"—not as something stuck onto buildings as an afterthought, but as a wholly architectural-industrial factor, a recognized part of the whole.[109] "The house, *the light-swallower* that sucks in the sunlight into its interior, *becomes a light-dispenser,*" continued Redslob,[110] a beacon beaming out light into the world—and a natural conduit for advertising's needs. Such was also the defining characteristic of the Berlin Reklameschau's symbolic design, "The Skyscraper of Light," drawn as an emblem of the exhibition.[111]

The new clean façades of Weimar city buildings had to be "fit for electric advertising" (*lichtreklamefähig*), since the old Wilhelmine ones were so inappropriate.[112] Having received such a makeover, the individual structure could enter into a new relationship with the night, as Berlin commentator Max Osborn enthused: "Architecture used to go to sleep as soon as it got dark. It disappeared and did not communicate. Only the display window shone out. The building itself did not exist any more, its contours faded away with the black sky. Today architecture awakens in the evening to a new, fantastical existence."[113] Perhaps the most significant aspect of the "fantastical existence" induced by the new light-architecture was that a *plurality* of buildings, once separate and disjointed even if next to each other, could now be unified via light: a whole new discursivity of

Figure 27. Design entry for Alexanderplatz competition, presumed to be by Johann Emil Schaudt (1929).

the street as a spatial entity framed by façade-lines of light now emerged. *Lichtarchitektur* was considered to be a power of glass and electricity that could unify a cityscape by night into an "organically membered communal entity," its "taut rhythm" bringing "order and character" to the otherwise opaque street.[114] An unrealized design for the Alexanderplatz competition of 1929, attributed to Johann Emil Schaudt,[115] suggests one such wholly interlinked application of electricity and buildings: the lit-up façades and lines of electric advertising text are intended to unify the contextual space of the Alexanderplatz in an amazing, massive configuration (fig. 27).

Thus it was that advertising became, as Riezler noted, "indivisible from the façade," indeed "part of architecture" itself: only the stagelike façade as a "boundary wall of the street itself" (*Begrenzungswand der Straße selbst*) counted anymore.[116] The need to include electric advertising at the initial stages of design, not just for buildings but for entire streets and public squares, was officially sanctioned by Ernst May, head architect for the city of Frankfurt a.M.; but he also cautioned that advertising should at all times fit itself into, and not thoughtlessly confront, the general urban picture.[117] Nonetheless, advertising was definitely no longer just a "palimpsest"[118] on the building structure of old. Indeed, the direction that the 1920s began to take toward the sublation of the architectural referent into that which Schivelbusch refers to as the "neon electropolis," or Tom Wolfe as "electrographic architecture,"[119] finds its postmodern expression not only in today's Las Vegas but also in the new towers of Potsdamer Platz in the Berlin-by-night of the millennium. Along the same lines, Jean Nouvel recently suggested the use of "lightscript-façades" (*Leuchtschriftfassaden*) as an act of "bordering, lining" the Friedrichstraße to celebrate its regained status, providing thereby a "new core for public animation day and night" to replace the "lobotomy and mummification of space" that was the Wall.[120]

SHOCK TREATMENTS

Weimar Berlin's aggressive street advertising constituted the first significant assault on the original "harmony" and "unity" of urban architecture,[121] distracting the passer-by into lingering, looking, and longing. "Every living organism reacts to stimulation," and particularly to that caused by light, stated von Hartungen in his 1921 study on advertising.[122] Benjamin went so far as to praise the action of Berlin's electric advertising signs as superior to the vast emptiness of the rooftops in Moscow: the Soviet capital could not apply the "big eye-catching motto" of firm names to advertise goods.[123] The words of an impressed visitor to the German capital in 1928 reiterate this sense of Berlin's visual supremacy: "Chains and streams of light accompany and swarm all around . . . [the visitor], light-architecture rises up, chinks of light appear from the fronts of palaces, then disappear and reappear, glittering towers grow tall, collapse, grow tall again. Fiery wheels swirl, words appear letter by letter and are obliterated as if on Belshazzar's Wall. . . . "[124] Indeed, the way in which electric ads revealed their wares in a "rhythmically dissected" fashion reminded Fritz Giese, in his 1925 analysis of American "girl-culture" in Germany (which in turn influenced Kracauer's own reading), of the metronomically controlled tempo of modern urban work and the Tiller Girls' dance revues.[125]

Furthermore, it was clear that the techniques of electric advertising had to keep pace with the public's perception skills, now accustomed to filmic motion. In 1926, advertising analyst Fritz Pauli demonstrated how kinetic ads adhered to the rhythm, or "resonance of lights and syllables," of the eye reading the message displayed for (say) Bergmann cigarettes—urban modernity's version of the electronic bullet-points appearing sequentially on a PowerPoint screen.[126] Accordingly, kinetic-electric advertisements

Figure 28. "Persil stays Persil" moving electric advertisement, Berlin.

(*Tricklichtreklame* or *Wanderschrift-Lichtreklame*) were considered the most sophisticated: like the segments of a cartoon film, a series of pictures or words was released to the viewer at such a pace as to convey chronological-linear movement of the elements depicted.[127] In 1929, the "Persil stays Persil" advertisement in Berlin was a high point in this protean development (fig. 28): four thousand bulbs alternated in position and color to show the "performance" of a dirty shirt being cleaned into a white one, with water pouring from a yellow tap into a red pot, and Persil powder falling from a green packet.[128] Similarly, the famous "Protos Corner" (housing the Grünfeld department store) became an advertising landmark, with a total of seven different flashing text messages promoting the use of electric Protos appliances in the home (fig. 29).

Figure 29. The Protos Corner on the Ku-Damm, Berlin (1927).

Weimar commercial architecture bears particular witness to the influence of Erich Mendelsohn. Despite all the architect's pronouncements favoring the severe rationalization of construction principles, his designs stand out because of their essentially nonrational, animalistic energy—a stimulation effect that consistently mirrors the tempo of the street, and that aestheticizes the machinic rhythm of the modern age. Accordingly, the Weimar architectural critic Adolf Behne portrays Mendelsohn's style as anthropomorphically "dramatic," with roots "wholly within Expressionism": "The entrance 'sucks in', the walls 'lead', the steps 'sway', etc."[129] With designs like the corner building for the textiles store Rudolf Petersdorff in Breslau in 1927, Mendelsohn introduced a series of buildings that were both neo-expressionistic and New Objective: the railwaylike horizontal lines of his striated façades fully bespoke the dynamic directionality of the street below.[130] The Petersdorff store concentrated its effect on the narrow cylindrical corner projection that rose up six storeys, each divided and accentuated by illuminated windows and solid ledges: it looked as if at any moment the building would move, like its contemporary the *Bremen* ocean liner, out of its immobility toward the passer-by below (fig. 30).

Two unmistakable principles emerge in what became known during the Weimar years as Mendelsohnian dynamism in architecture: namely, curvature and horizontalism.[131] These dual aspects were always situated against or within a radically deornamentalized façade and interior, the very bareness of which contributed to a further accentuation of their shock-effects. An architectonic harmony could, according to Mendelsohn, be created in the contrapuntal unification of the horizontal and the vertical planes (as, for example, in Bach's fugue theme),[132] as well as in the thematic bridging of curved with straight lines, suggestive of a machine in motion. These special effects were accentuated even further in his buildings' nighttime phases as sheer *Lichtarchitektur.* While medieval man had, according to Mendelsohn, a sacred, static, "vertical" relation to God and the heavens, the modern architectural inventor could pilot the skies aerodynamically in a "horizontal" (air)plane.[133] Thus Mendelsohn, the arch-architect of urban commercial modernity, became a master of the domains that Michel Foucault states are not normally within the purview of the architectural profession—namely "territory, communication, and speed."[134]

Paul Virilio, theorist of urban and technological (post)modernity, relates, however, a cautionary tale with respect to Mendelsohn's dynamic style, recognizing therein a direct "*neotechnological*" inheritance from World War I—an architectural rendering of the euphoric forces of futurist-Jüngerian mobilization.[135] Virilio finds that it makes ironic sense for Mendelsohn to have designed the Einstein Observatory Tower (1919–1921) out of the ashes of the Great War—its plain concrete surface given life by an expressionistic, organically "grown" roundness of contour—in homage to the author of the 1905 essay "On the Electrodynamics of Moving Bodies," the very text that led to the splitting of the atom. Mendelsohn himself wrote in 1953 that his tower had been born of both Einstein's theory and "in the trenches, in the experience of war."[136] For Virilio, the subsequent nuclear application of the utopianism visible in such dynamic architecture gives, with hindsight, a rather different valuation to Mendelsohn's renown in Weimar commercial *Lichtarchitektur.*

Kracauer takes Mendelsohn's touch one step further when he describes how a train speeds along above the street on the overhead tracks and stops in the middle of the Friedrichstraße—except, he adds, no one notices it, for

Figure 30. Petersdorff textiles store in Breslau, designed by Erich Mendelsohn (1928).

there is already too much frenetically trainlike activity on all levels of the street.[137] Kracauer has a point about the Simmelesque indifference of Berliners to this elevated train. Evidently, denizens of the modern metropolis had every right to feel that shock was their definitive motif.[138] Only a few years after the dawn of radio, photos were being wired from one newspaper to another across the world, and the possibilities for television were already being researched.[139] Ernst Jünger published a popular series of voyeuristically gratifying photo albums celebrating the shock-sensations of modern life.[140] Berliners were reading newspaper articles dealing with such topics as "noise in the city" and the "nerves of the metropolitan."[141] Motion, it was attested in 1929, was Berlin's major charm: "There is no city in the world so restless as Berlin. Everything moves. The traffic lights change restlessly from red to gold and then to green. The lighted advertisements flash with the dramatic iteration of coastal lighthouses. The trams swing and jingle. The jaguar in the Zoo paces feverishly all night. . . . "[142] The multiangularity of traffic, overhead railway, and buildings, as seen in Robert Herlth's set-design sketch for the film *Asphalt* (1929), suggests precisely this sense of frantic tempo coming at urbanites from all directions (fig. 31). Le Corbusier's comment on modernity in New York City—"Manhattan is hot jazz in stone and steel"[143]—can just as easily be applied to Weimar Berlin.

Robert Musil, who resided in Berlin during the 1920s, writes of this modernity in *The Man Without Qualities* as a scene of frenetic motion: " . . . a kind of super-American city where everyone rushes about, or stands still, with a stop-watch in his hand. Air and earth form an ant-hill, veined by channels of traffic, rising storey upon storey. Overhead-trains, overground-trains, underground-trains, pneumatic express mails carrying consignments of human beings, chains of motor-vehicles all racing along horizontally, express lifts pumping crowds from one traffic-level to another. . . . "[144] Elsewhere, however, Musil—himself a psychotechnically trained former engineer—points to how a member of the public may well react to the above chaos by abusing the technologized vision inherent to modern life. In a short story entitled "The Monster AGOAG" (standing for the ironically named *Allgemein-geschätzte-Omnibus-Athleten-Gesellschaft*), the paltry little hero, a latter-day Underground Man, takes a short cut to becoming a pastiche of the Nietzschean *Übermensch* by sitting on the top front seat of an omnibus and pretending to shoot at people in the street as if through the viewfinder of a WWI-tank.[145]

We can contrast this eternally functioning and disruptive vision of the modern urban condition to the way in which, as geographer Mike Savage has stated, postmodern cities attempt to "cocoon visitors in safe spaces" in order to cut down on the shock effect.[146] Musil's imagery is clearly suggestive of Lang's *Metropolis,* whose skyscraper surface-city of lights is wholly dependent on the production of electric current from the hellish labyrinth below ground. Both Musil's prose and Lang's film drew their architectural inspiration from popular magazine illustrations from the first decades of the twentieth century depicting the city of the future, which was in metaphorical ways already the city of the present.[147] The representation of German modernity as riotous trauma is perhaps nowhere so clear as in George Grosz's fiery red city paintings, such as *Dedicated to Oskar Panizza* (*Widmung an Oskar Panizza,* 1917–1918). Grosz presents in this midwar funereal cortege a futurist hell of Bosch and Brueghel, with contorted human figures and building façades that buckle around the centrally depicted skeleton, who rides and drinks atop his coffin. Urban modernity, emerging as it did for Germans with the civil revolution at the end of

Figure 31. "S-Bahn Crossing." Sketch by Robert Herlth for *Asphalt* (dir. Joe May, 1929).

World War I, is experienced here as a psychosocial breakdown rather than as a breakthrough.[148]

But the "shock of the new"[149] cannot, by definition, last very long in its original shock-format—at least, not if sanity is to be maintained. Schivelbusch investigates what must lie beneath the "blasé" attitude of Simmel's city-dweller of modernity: in his interpretation of Freud's essay "Beyond the Pleasure Principle," Schivelbusch asserts that the development of a "stimulus shield" (*Reizschutz*) is mankind's natural defensive reaction to traumatic shock, and this skill is made all the more necessary in the neurasthenia of industrial modernity. As Schivelbusch relates, Freud takes up the example of a "vesicle" or small cell whose surface layer becomes deadened to further stimulation for the ultimate benefit of the organism itself. Freud states:

> The surface turned toward the external world will from its very situation be differentiated and will serve as an organ for receiving stimuli. . . . [A]s a result of the ceaseless impact of external stimuli on the surface of the vesicle, . . . [a] crust [Rinde] would thus be formed which would at last have been so thoroughly "baked through" ["durchgebrannt"] by stimulation that it would present the most favourable possible conditions for the reception of stimuli. . . . [The organism]

> would be killed by the stimulation emanating from . . . [the energies of the external world] if it were not provided with a protective shield against stimuli. It acquires the shield in this way: its outermost surface ceases to have the structure proper to living matter, becomes to some degree inorganic and thenceforward functions as a special envelope or membrane resistant to stimuli. . . . By its death, the outer layer has saved all the deeper ones from a similar fate—unless, that is to say, stimuli reach it which are so strong that they break through the protective shield.[150]

The shocks of modernity are subcutaneously "baked through" into the psychological skin of the city-dweller: this stimulus shield alters his or her consciousness forever, creating a new level of epigenous adaptability that actually seeks out a series of minor stimuli and shocks (as in, say, film-viewing) in order to better deal with major ones. Freud found, accordingly, that shell shock was less common among WWI veterans who had fixated repeatedly and anxiously on the potential horror of modern technological warfare prior to actually experiencing it in the trenches.

Following Benjamin's analysis in "On Some Motifs in Baudelaire" of Freud's above thesis, Schivelbusch casts this stimuli-raising process within the historic moment of the birth of "panoramic [i.e., filmic] vision" that train travel brought to its passengers.[151] Railway locomotion, compounded with the auditory and ocular onslaught of the city street, reconfigured passengers' apperception into a permanently "on" state that then required some sort of tranquilizing dosage. Likewise, the early-twentieth-century development of the cinematic "eye" extended ever further the extremities of the visually possible and impossible: what was physical danger could now be recast into the adventures of a filmic sublime (today's version of the same would be virtual reality). In this remapping of the subject, the panoramic gaze was both mobile and mobilized, and promised infinite, if illusory, powers of expansion to the participant.[152] Modernity's human *Reizschutz* was ready for the shock of pleasure and the pleasure of shock at every turn.

This model can, in turn, be situated within the shock or stimulation that Weimar advertising aimed to create in the mass spectator. Outdoor ads of the German 1920s took the apparently ingenuous, literal form of surface decoration; but they strategically aimed, via the techniques of montage stimulation and desire simulation, to break through the stimulus shield of the indifferent or distracted passer-by, and so remold the urban mass consciousness in their own image. As Susan Buck-Morss demonstrates in her readings of Benjamin reading Baudelaire and Freud, the "neurologically catastrophic, persistent repetition of shock" literally shatters the experience of urban *flânerie,* and exposes the "techno-aesthetics of the urban phantasmagoria" to be a "compensatory form"[153] wherein the "goal is manipulation of the synaesthetic system by control of environmental stimuli. It has the effect of anaesthetizing the organism, not through numbing, but through flooding the senses."[154] Also referring to Benjamin, Bolz writes in this context of the contemporary "Darwinism of the media," which play "games of stimulation" (*Reizspiele*) with us, and function like "metaphors" that "pre-structure the world that we perceive." At the end of the twentieth century, states Bolz, the average American eighteen-year-old has already seen 350,000 TV ads. These days, our "media skin" has become so thick that filmic/virtual reality *is* our reality; feelings of love and hate are felt more strongly in the cinema than in real life.[155]

This kind of mediated cognition was already occurring in the 1920s: electric advertising was deemed so effective that it could, potentially, outshine the product it was purportedly relating to the public, as Hans Kafka complained in the *Berliner Tageblatt* in 1928. In comparison to the display outside, the wares within could well amount for the consumer to a "superficial diminution . . . thus advertising often damages itself." But most people, Kafka concedes, are not so discerning. He proceeds to mock the "miracle"-work of electric advertising by telling a joke about a man who so utterly believed a huge advertisement at the Potsdamer Platz for shoe polish and foot plasters that he went straightaway to buy the advertised items; and even though both boxes were devoid of actual products, such was his faith in the light-display outside the store that lo, his shoes shone and his feet hurt no more.[156]

While the train traveler or film viewer of modernity (or the plane traveler or VR-rider today) could forget the dangers of motion thanks to his or her acquired thick skin, the viewer of Weimar advertising spectacle needed to transform the visually disturbing irritations of advertising into a pleasurably and memorably stimulative experience—or else the ad would fail. One artist drew an illustration for the *Seidels Reklame* advertising journal in 1925 of an imaginary fire at the premiere Ufa-Palast movie palace in Berlin: in this alarm-scenario of electric power as delectable danger-cum-pleasure, the fire itself is just one aspect among others of red and gold light (from the advertising on the cinema's roof, from its entrance, from the passing automobile's headlights) exploding forth onto the street. But in real life, not every location was appropriate for street stimulation. The tendency of effective street advertising to distract was the reason the Stuttgart city council had to reject an application in 1929 by a local businessman to introduce "pedestrian barriers" (*Gehbahn-Schranken*) at city crossroads; the barriers, ostensibly intended for controlling foot traffic so that people would be prevented from crossing in chaotic patterns into the path of turning traffic, were also proposed to serve, simultaneously and profitably, as advertising placards (fig. 32). Luckily for the traffic accident rate, the city council realized this would be a contradiction in terms.[157] Again, too much light in advertising would be equally self-destructive: while it was necessary, as Frankfurt chief architect May pointed out, for electric advertising to produce "strong stimulative methods" to match the "nerves of the modern city dweller," it was equally possible to wreck the intended effect by perceptual overkill. Broadway's light-spectacle, for example, had become so intense by 1928 that "the eye does not read any text here, does not distinguish any form here any more; one is only blinded here by a superabundance of flashing lights, by an excess of light fixtures that cancel out each other's effects."[158]

Thus, ironically, shock could occasionally be induced by the contrastive *deprivation* of advertising light. In Vicki Baum's best-selling novel of 1929, *Menschen im Hotel* (*Grand Hotel*), the identity of the hotel itself seems somehow temporarily imperiled when the floodlights on its façade go out one night—right at the very moment when Baron von Gaigern, the façade-climbing burglar (*Fassadenkletterer*), intends to hide behind the floodlights as they light up the street and blind passers-by to a man scaling the hotel wall behind them, rather like Lang's Dr. Mabuse with his hypnotic trick light effects in a magic show. A similar lights-out experience is described by Kracauer in his essay "Street Without Memory" ("Straße ohne Erinnerung"), a veritable light-parable written in 1932 about Weimar Germany's steep decline after the stock market crash. At first he finds the *Glanz* of the Ku-Damm café he is sitting in to be exaggerated: walking by, one is struck by the "light effects that the café sent out in wasteful abundance. The brighter the lights, the duller the public." The next time he goes by, however, it is gone, and in place of the light all he sees is a dark "glass abyss" for rent.[159] Despite the economic plight that this empty store indicated, a sense of relief at the failed omnipotence of Weimar light culture is tangible within Kracauer's terse prose.

Psychotechnician Friedlaender noted that electric street displays must make use of sudden contrastive changes in color, shape, and intensity, so that the stimulus shield of passers-by can be broken—here Friedlaender cites the rather gruesome cautionary tale of a Yale experiment wherein a frog, which had immediately jumped out when placed into a container of warm water, slowly boiled to death when placed into a container of cold water whose temperature was raised at an imperceptibly slow rate.[160] Not

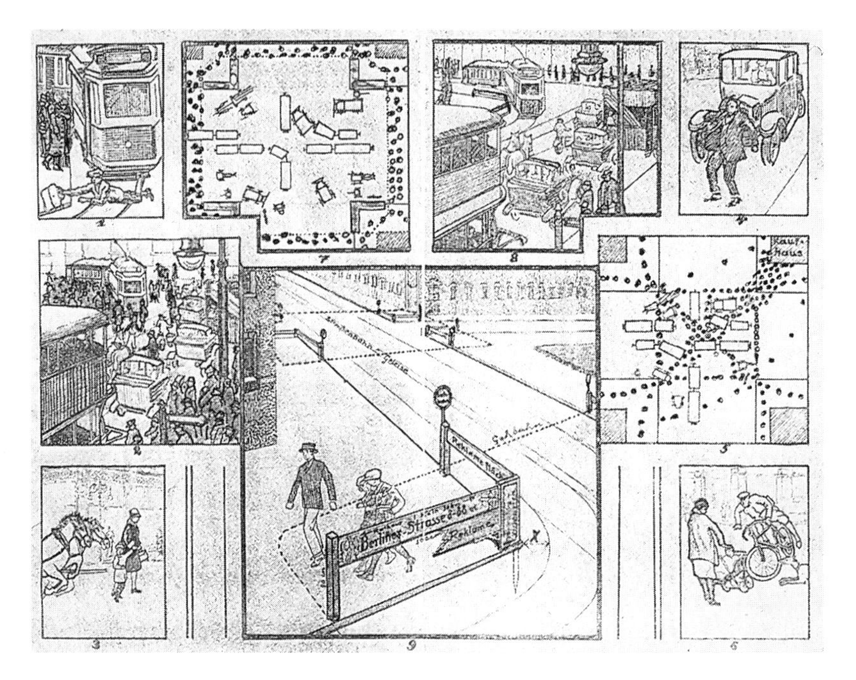

Figure 32. Proposal to install pedestrian barriers (*Gehbahn-Schranken*) bearing advertisements at street intersections in Stuttgart (1929).

all Weimar Germans, however, were thick-skinned to a perceptual boiling point, that is to say as well suited to the shock of modernity and its breaking-down of the humanist individual as were the survivor-protagonists of mid-Weimar literature—the "driver" types,[161] or what Helmut Lethen has defined as the "cold *personae*" fostered by New Objectivity[162]—like Kracauer's Ginster, Baum's Baron von Gaigern, Musil's Ulrich, Rudolf Braune's Erna, Erich Kästner's Fabian, or Ernst Jünger's Worker. When hapless Franz Biberkopf emerges in 1928 from Tegel after his four years of imprisonment for murder, he has to play catch-up with the advances of the New Objectivity years that have passed him by. His psychic shock in the initial chapter of Döblin's *Berlin Alexanderplatz* is a WWI trauma reactivated by the montage-effects experienced visually and aurally by the pedestrian and tram-traveler of Weimar Berlin's city streets; it is also a memorable literary acting-out of the modernist collapse of subjecthood and of transcendental representational beliefs.[163]

Biberkopf's tram journey can be contrasted with the ride, in F. W. Murnau's *Sunrise* (1927), that is shot from the trolleycar as it travels into the city: while the former deconstructs the mind of the out-of-synch traveler, the latter constructs and even conquers the entered city for the film-viewer. It is precisely because Biberkopf's own stimulus shield is shell-shocked (and hence insufficiently protective) that he gains a schizophrenic insight into the dead world beneath the surface of surface culture: "Outside everything moved, but—behind it all—was nothing! Nothing—was—alive!"[164] Through Biberkopf's eyes and ears we perceive the electrified condition of modernity as if through the mind of a time traveler, a Schreberian psychotic,[165] or through an antitechnological expressionist pen. If Biberkopf could reflect on the process of modernization he would most likely join Karl Thomas, protagonist in Toller's expressionist drama *Hoppla, wir leben!* in shouting that the world has become a madhouse[166]—but only for those who cannot keep up. "The Demons of the Cities," in Georg Heym's expressionist poem of the same name,[167] have by now, as vision has been traumatized by the *Materialschlacht,* been swallowed up by the commercialized face of *Lichtreklame,* and Biberkopf faces the ruthless ultimatum of adapting to the new rule of New Objectivity or perishing at the hands of Berlin, the "whore of Babylon."

We can find an oneiric corollary of Biberkopf's plight in Ernst Jünger's Weimar texts; as a fellow WWI veteran, Jünger displays an equally allergic sensitivity to the urban electricity all around him. For the Jüngerian narrative voice as for Döblin's protagonist, the modern metropolis functions as a memory-trigger of the assault of WWI technologies; Jünger finds, for example, that the neon lights of the metropolis lend to faces the "color of corpses."[168] But Jünger's path in German modernity follows the option of a total self-immersion within the (albeit diabolical) ocular forces unleashed in the city. In *Notes by Day and Night* (*Aufzeichnungen bei Tag und Nacht,* 1929), he sketches in his usual purple prose a waking nightmare induced by the "midnight light" of street advertising:

> We have dived into the flickering night of nonbelief, of which the hellish aspect of our cities sparkling in light is a terrible metaphor. The geometry of reason is a veil over a diabolical mosaic that at times becomes horrifyingly alive. . . . Electric advertising in its incandescently glistening red and ice-blue fascination, a modern bar, an American film comedy—all these are segments of the mighty Luciferian tumult, the sight of which fills the lonely viewer equally with both raging desire and overwhelming fear. . . . Hell itself could not be equipped with a more poisonous show of splendid lights.[169]

Behind the ubiquitous "coat of reality" that advertising paints over the metropolis there is for Jünger a new hell-fire born of modern rationality and Lucifer the light-bearer.

"LIGHT LURES PEOPLE"

Just as the traveler of train or airplane is subdued into neglecting the danger of suprahuman speed, so too is the audience of advertising lulled into a forgetful acceptance of this medium's ultimate aim: a synchronizing and possibly reifying or even mobilizing control. Ads themselves reflected this panopticism, to be exercised (in theory) by whoever bought into the electric vision of and over the globe. It became a Weimar truism that "light lures people" (*Licht lockt Leute*), as the Regi electric advertising company promised (fig. 33). The romantic artificial "lamp" of manmade genius had simply leaped over into capitalism's electric dreamworld, which declared the war on darkness finally over, now that man had become godlike enough to assert, in a 1926 trade ad for electrically lit-up posters: "Let there be light!" (*Es werde Licht!*).[170] Teichmüller's definition of light-architecture likewise proclaimed that "we must avoid adhering to the old rule of imitating the sun: we must be *better* than the sun."[171] Weimar Cultural Minister Redslob happily admits that light forces shabby people to tidy up their appearances so as to conform to the electric "*interrogative eye of our time,*" the new "*yardstick of things.*"[172] Light forces people to behave; not for nothing did the emergence of street lighting in the nineteenth century coincide with the rise of modern policing and the detective novel.[173] A tangential benefit of all the *Lichtarchitektur* was, it was hoped, fewer burglaries and automobile accidents at night.[174] Current plans to electrically renovate the Breitscheidplatz around the Kaiser Wilhelm Memorial Church stem from a similarly panoptic "light"-motif.

Part of the attraction that brought people to gaze upon modern advertising—for all its structural shock-tactics as a traumatic, dislocating experience that split open the unity of the subject—was, of course, an intense scopophilia. The visual pleasure of Weimar advertising occurred (then as now) within a sphere of sexually charged stimulation.[175] Kracauer understood well how to present the ethical ambiguity of this modern technologized *flânerie,* the rationalized street's intoxication, or *Rausch*-effect. In an essay of 1924, he describes how the urban wanderer's inner emptiness seeks a self-transferential surge into the distractions conveniently provided by electric advertising:

> In the evening one saunters through the streets, replete with an unfulfillment from which a fullness could sprout. Illuminated words glide by on the rooftops, and already one is banished from one's own emptiness into the alien advertisement. One's body takes root in the asphalt, and, together with the enlightening revelations of the illuminations, one's

Figure 33. "Light lures people." Advertisement for electrically lit posters made by the Regi company (1926).

> spirit—which is no longer one's own—roams ceaselessly out of the night and into the night. . . . Some sort of magic spurs that spirit relentlessly amid the thousand electric bulbs, out of which it constitutes and reconstitutes itself into glittering sentences.[176]

Kracauer's impressions of electric advertising are accentuated by those of the Communist Hermann Kesser, writing for *Die neue Rundschau* in 1929, who was appalled at what he perceived as a new dictatorship forged by electric consumerism and technology at the Potsdamer Platz, where one could see ". . . words of flames that roll along, glowing plays of color and light, and fantasies of golden rain. The façades look at you liberally and volubly . . . Every house is a glistening Christmas tree and partakes of the nightly business festival. The horizon is crowded with advertising. The sky is trade. The real stars are nowhere to be seen. They have fled out into interstellar space, not wanting to become rivals of artificial light. . . . We stand on the asphalt ground of the most up-to-date earth."[177] All that Kesser and Kracauer are evoking here is matched by the psychedelic color poster for Karl Grune's film *Die Straße,* from 1924 (fig. 34).The posthumanist subject is cloned into what capitalism wants to make of it; the individual is the experimental guinea pig in a rebirth of the surface-self out of the spirit of advertising. The imagination of the urban white-collar worker was thus emptied out and refilled by the stimulus shield induced first by the shocks of technological change, but then strengthened and maintained by the desires of the consumer industry.[178]

The pleasure afforded by these images, and their associated cult of idealized yet rationalized beauty, helped re-auratize (reenchant, retotalize) the apparently functionalist advertisement. *Lichtreklame* was considered a "holistic event" (*Totalereignis*) for passers-by, one that forced their emotions into a shared, Dionysian, buying-ready playfulness, as one commentator wrote: "The obtrusiveness with which this holistic decoration [*Totaldekoration*] is set in place affects the entire street: street life, street communication, and crowds, wherein the individual is enframed. . . . In the crowd, the holistic event grows for the single person into a collective intoxication, a release of feelings, in which people mutually enflame one another. The façade functions like a magnet that pulls people in and makes them buy."[179] This double-state of drunken formalism, or posthumanist re-auratization, was further amplified by the intense commodification of the (again, apparently functionalist) New Woman, whose Kracauerian mass ornamentation appeared not only in the Tiller Girls' dance troupe as collective body unit, in the display window as fashion mannequin, or on the silver screen as star, but also on the street outside as consumer in her various configurations, such as technologized housewife, pink-collar typist, sales assistant, or prostitute. Kracauer, in a lesser-known article of 1927, "Lichtreklame," clearly identifies the sex appeal latent within New Objective technologies, referring to electric advertisements as "fire-lusts that shiver with salable sensuality."[180] The lights project, he says, into a sky devoid of angels but which contains more than just business; advertising becomes a commercial form of "illumination" in the literal, sacred, and sexual sense. The aim here is semiotic fetishism: the creation of a consumerist drive.

In a similarly sensualized vein, Simmel was the first to explain, in an essay of 1896, "The Berlin Trade Exhibition," the inevitable, logical rise of

Figure 34. Poster for *Die Straße* (dir. Karl Grune, 1924).

advertising in the modern age of consumerism. He speaks here in favor of giving otherwise unnecessary products "a tempting exterior" (*eine verlockende Außenseite*) as the new surface aesthetic (the "stimulus of appearance") for the era: "Where competition no longer operates in matters of usefulness and intrinsic properties, the interest of the buyer has to be aroused by the external stimulus of the object, even in the manner of its presentation. . . . The striving to make the merely useful visually stimulating . . . comes from the struggle to render the graceless graceful for consumers."[181] Here, Simmel approaches the architectural-artistic stimulation of the merchandising event with far less moral distrust than, say, Adorno, who in his retrospective "Functionalism Today" essay of 1979 critiques advertising's engagement with both surface (ornament) and function (nonornament): "[A] self-mocking contradiction emerges in the omnipresence of advertisements. . . . If an advertisement were strictly functional, without ornamental surplus, it would no longer fulfil its purpose as advertisement."[182] But Simmel easily equates advertising's seductive veils with a new purchasing state of grace for consumers; his positive tone overflows with such sexual metaphoricity as the need for an "external stimulus of the object," so that the "visually stimulating" outfit of advertising can arouse purchasing lust. One can relate this to Freud's definition of the effect of the Medusa upon the little boy who looks upon his mother's genitalia: out of the initial condition of his shock and castration/petrification at the sight emerges the new condition of his pleasure and erection/arousal.[183] Even for the female consumer or the feminized mass audience of modernity,[184] the act of succumbing to the commodity or ad (to the "shop-window quality of things") was a voyeuristically charged moment full of imminent (pseudo-male) possession of the (pseudo-female) object of desire. In this respect, then, Simmel foresaw the path that strategic advertising would end up taking over the course of the twentieth century: a study conducted on trends in American advertisements from the 1910s to the 1980s documents the not-too-surprising fact that the frequency of purely "rational" ads has clearly diminished, while the number of "sensual" ads has continually increased.[185]

Light's attraction in advertising, the obvious panoptic potentiality of electricity's appeal, was also something that Nazi architect Albert Speer noticed and redirected away from mere consumerist enticement to the arenas of Nazi mass rallies. After spending a decade attacking outdoor advertising for its alleged role in helping Jewish retail to defeat the "little businessman" (declaring in Nuremberg, for example, a city tax against all exterior use of posters and electric ads),[186] the Nazis promptly co-opted the medium. Eight months after Hitler came to power a restriction law was passed, and all advertising activity was henceforth controlled by the office of the Werberat, whose decisions and judgments of a "moral nature" were distributed in a newsletter with the Germanic title of *Wirtschaftswerbung*.[187] Nonetheless, the use of electric advertising continued unabated up to World War II. Post-1933 changes in advertising were subtle rather than obvious: Jewish contributors and modern fonts were dropped from trade magazines like *Die Reklame,* but much of the proelectric tone remained the same. The Nazi government made its presence clear in such journals only in full-page pictures of Hitler telling advertising professionals of their new "duty" to "adapt advertising" to fit in with the "changed conditions" of Germany.[188]

While it is indeed true that floodlighting, so beloved of the Nazis, began in earnest on the façades of Weimar metropolitan streets, it would be going too far to chart any causal relation between the commercial use of light-architecture in the 1920s and the Nazi rallies' abuse of the same. As Buck-Morss states, "Fascism was not an alternative to commodity culture, but appropriated its most sophisticated techniques—while robbing them of material content."[189] Schivelbusch agrees, asking first if there can be both a "human" and an "inhuman" form of electric light, since it can serve both democracy and fascism so well, and finding instead that light is as neutral (and hence as flexible) as is language or technology.[190] This plasticity was first demonstrated on May 1, 1933, for Hitler's speech to the masses at Tempelhof in Berlin: the event was concluded by a monumental fireworks display that arguably enunciates a key bridge between Weimar electric advertising and the Nazi applications yet to come. "The light and color impressions," wrote an eyewitness, "were right at the point of what the human eye can even endure."[191] For a further instance of the Nazi manipulation of Weimar light-architecture, compare the Persil company's 1932 light-projection of the company's name into the night sky with Speer's subsequent "cathedral of light" (*Lichtdom*) of 1937, which consisted of 130 searchlights rising in ecstatic night-sky fusion above the Zeppelin field of the Reich Party Congress Grounds in Nuremberg.[192] Speer's creation exists both in its virtual form as "chimera" (Speer's own term) and as a mise-en-scène of Nazi aspirations orgiastically petrified for all time.[193] In Hitler and Speer's conception of the ten-thousand-year use of granite in Germania (Hitler's rebuilt Berlin), the monumental buildings along the north-south axis would constitute the ultimate stage of an eternity-seeking light-architecture. As Henri Lefebvre has suggested in *The Production of Space*, Nazism thus weighed down the façade that Weimar modernism had sought to lighten.[194] It was through this electrically inspired, never-ending ossification that Nazism reemphasized the opacity of the façade after the Bauhaus' translucent modernization of the same.[195]

REJECTING THE MODERN

Equating the immediacy of Nazi propaganda with the rise of producer-manipulated advertising and a general regression of modernity into psychotechnically controlled myth came naturally to Theodor W. Adorno during his Los Angeles exile, where he found in 1944 that the very "idiom or 'style' of the culture industry" has been permanently invaded by advertising techniques—a victory so total that modern stores, as "floodlit advertising turned to stone," do not require actual advertisements, such is the extent of the "enforced mimesis of consumers onto the cultural commodities," wanting what they (we) are told to want.[196] Indeed, the trenchant critiques of advertising and consumerism by postwar German intellectuals, as begun by Adorno in the Frankfurt School and continued by other left-wing writers in the 1970s,[197] have much to do with an understandable revulsion at the Nazi abuse of such techniques in propaganda and mass manipulation. German social theorists today continue to distrust advertising to a degree not found in British or American society—producing thereby an ongoing equivalent, so to speak, of New German Cinema's attack on the unspoken continuity of Nazi attitudes in postwar German society and film (*Papas Kino*).[198]

Efforts to curb outdoor advertising in Germany first began at the turn of the century, when billboards especially were at their most chaotic. In 1900, the Berlin police legislated against flashing electric lights because they were apparently causing traffic accidents.[199] Dresden and the Bavarian cities of Munich and Nuremberg banned electric advertising for their medieval centers before World War I, and controlled it severely afterwards. Building conservation task forces (*Baupflegekommissionen*) attempted during the Weimar years to protect the city street from excesses of the advertising industry—especially what was considered "disfigurement" (*Verunstaltung* or *Verunzierung*) by obtrusive, moving, on-off *Lichtreklame* in sensitive locations.[200] Such acts of resistance were extensions of the work of the conservative-conservationist reform groups (*Heimatschutz*) formed prior to World War I in the name of the environment, in response to the invasion of the street and countryside by outdoor advertising, whether billboard or electric.[201]

Nonetheless, after an initial elitist distrust of advertising as a foreign invasion from those philistine nations of *Zivilisation* that threatened their Teutonic brand of *Kultur,* interwar Germans began to literally see the light—that is, they began to see the connection between the art of advertising and the rebuilding of a tarnished postwar national image, rather than opposing advertising as something inherently un-German. The Prussian *Verunstaltungsgesetz* (antidisfigurement law) of 1902, which was still valid during the Weimar years, proved largely ineffectual in opposing this practical-cum-patriotic role for advertising as an "economic necessity" in Berlin, [202] while stronger municipal resistances to outdoor advertising were decreed in more conservative cities like Munich, Stuttgart, Nuremberg, and Hamburg, and the majority of the population supported stricter restrictions regarding domestic dwellings, rural settings, and historically or artistically valued buildings.[203] In 1930, Hamburg was host to a renewed debate over the pros and cons of allowing electric signs above one-storey height in its central Binnenalster area.[204] In Stuttgart, where Mendelsohn designed a Schocken department store, a lengthy struggle developed between Mendelsohn and the local building authorities over permission to have the letters "SCHOCKEN" be electrically displayed, one storey high, across the entire length of the building above the row of display windows.[205] When the store gained permission to do so, it literally advertised itself, and nothing more.

On the whole, however, the prewar influence of the *Heimatschutz* movements was transformed during the Weimar years into a pragmatic compromise effort, whereby German outdoor ads could be "ennobled" beyond the merely "slavish imitation" of "alien" (American) prototypes.[206] Many of the battles fought on local levels by *Heimatschutz* groups were less effective in that they were waged against the general sin of immorality, that is, against the purportedly degenerate effects of advertising on the public. By the mid-1920s, even the term *Heimatschutz* was beginning to be used by pragmatists in conjunction with, rather than in opposition to, advertising,[207] as the national and economic benefits of advertising became more widely understood. It became the job of the *Baupolizei* not so much to resist as to charge money: it was a truism among advertisers that "the higher the effect [of the electric advertisement], the higher you pay."[208]

Meanwhile, New York exercised far fewer controls over outdoor advertising in the 1920s than did Berlin.[209] Maria Leitner's popular novel *Hotel Amerika* (1930) is an all-too-German portrayal of the purportedly classless society of America as an exploitation of workers, hierarchically arranged in direct relation to the actual vertical height and depth of a Manhattan skyscraper (the site of the hotel). The story includes two magnates at war with each other over the (very German) issue of outdoor electric advertising. In Leitner's socialist depiction, not only is *Außenreklame* the "currency" of Herr Vandercock, but the power of this entire American industry is located in the latter figure. Resistance to this electric advertising comes from newspapers and from the pulpit; but Vandercock's canny response, which promptly shuts up his critics, is to give his service to churches, allowing them to spread even the Word via "electrically lit crosses and Bible sayings."[210]

THE EMBRACE OF THE AVANT-GARDE

The Weimar and European avant-garde, meanwhile, preferred to recognize in the new architectonics of light and the shock-techniques of advertising a parallel procedure for modernist art, and particularly for film. Consider, after all, their shared methodologies: like advertising, cubist, dada, and Bauhaus art forms engaged in radical contrast of tone, shape, and color, all accentuated by a carefully montaged organization of materials and movement (juxtaposition, alternation, repetition—both topographically serial and temporally sequential). Benjamin, in "The Work of Art in the Age of Mechanical Reproducibility" (1935)—his single clear-cut instance of praise for the Baudelairean "disintegration of the aura in the experience of shock"[211]—categorically states that film is (at least in its material technology and Brechtian promise) an affine of dadaism, with the same effect: "The work of art of the Dadaists became an instrument of ballistics. It hit the spectator like a bullet, it happened to him, thus acquiring a tactile quality. It promoted a demand for film, the distracting element of which is also primarily tactile, being based on changes of place and focus which periodically assail the spectator."[212] The emergence of film thus struck the viewer like "epistemological TNT," to use Anne Friedberg's comment.[213] This assessment of film's tactility is enhanced by Benjamin in his *One-Way Street* (*Einbahnstraße*, published in 1928), where he underlines the acute kinship in the perceptual power of advertising and cinema:

> Today the most real, the mercantile gaze into the heart of things is the advertisement. It tears down the stage upon which contemplation moved, and all but hits us between the eyes with things as a car, growing to gigantic proportions, careens at us out of a film screen. And just as the film does not present furniture and façades in completed forms for critical inspection, their insistent, jerky nearness alone being sensational, the genuine advertisement hurls things at us with the tempo of a good film.[214]

Advertising, like the experimental modernist films of Fernand Léger, Hans Richter, Dziga Vertov, and Walther Ruttmann, arose in the city-based, fragmented realm of *Erlebnis* (happening, event) instead of the community-based, holistic *Erfahrung* (experience)—to use Benjamin's terms (1936).[215] The shared methodology of these creations reflected the fact that the shocks of modern urban life continually upset the process of auratization in any sphere—art, religion, family, or community—and Benjamin was well aware of the "price" to be paid for this embrace.[216]

Advertising arenas so ideally suited to montage naturally attracted the Bauhaus school, which, by dint of its own endeavors to deconstruct the barriers between decorative and structural arts, fully promoted the new street art forms of functional "advertising theater" (*Werbetheater*).[217] It became recognized that in order to attract the public's attention to their art, artists now had to compete with the "enormous stage set of life" produced by industry and commerce, and specifically with the ongoing shocks of advertising on the street—as Léger saw in 1924:

> *There is the origin of the modern spectacle.* The shock of the surprise effect. To organize a spectacle based on these daily phenomena, the artists who want to distract the crowd must undergo a continual renewal. It is a hard profession, the hardest profession. . . . The intensity of the street shatters our nerves and drives us crazy. Let's tackle the problem in all its scope. Let's organize the exterior spectacle. This is nothing more or less than creating "polychromed architecture" from scratch, taking in all the manifestations of current advertising. . . . Let's organize exterior life in its domain: form, color, light.[218]

The most radically tactile experiment of this ilk would be perhaps Moholy-Nagy's film-text *Dynamics of the City* (*Dynamik der Groß-Stadt*, 1921–1922), with its purported (if literally intolerable) aim of maintaining the spectator in a constant state of visual and psychological assault that recreates metropolitan street life. The metonymic self-consciousness of Moholy-Nagy's unrealized and unrealizable film, with its open-ended montage principle, insists that the spatial as well as temporal surfaces of the reel's photographic and typographic reality repeatedly protrude from the page into the eye of the spectating reader.[219]

It is in *One-Way Street* that Benjamin offers an informed voice of doubt concerning the New Objective tide of praise for advertising's strengths. He recognizes the façade behind New Objectivity's claim of being façade-free. For of course advertising, like film, uses techniques that are highly emotionally charged, and nothing sells better than (American) "sentimentality," no matter how whitewashed the wall: "What, in the end, makes advertisements so superior to criticism? Not what the moving red neon sign says—but the fiery pool reflecting it in the asphalt."[220] He especially bemoans the demise of the book in the Weimar era of surface culture: these days, he waxes nostalgically, only the "prompt language" of advertising (or photojournalism, or montage) is capable of expressing the moment.[221] The visual sound bites of these new forms of expression with their various shock tactics are altering all written language in a wave as radical as the Gutenberg revolution, cautions Benjamin in a gloomy version of a McLuhan moment. Sharing Benjamin's insight but facing the new "phototype" era with glee instead of concern is Bauhaus photographer Johannes Molzahn, who, writing for *Das Kunstblatt* in 1928, predicts that "'Stop Reading! Look!' will be the guiding developmental principle of daily newspapers."[222] Bolz expounds on these insights in his phenomenological reading of Benjamin's (and, by implication, Molzahn's) perceptions of interface between the Gutenberg galaxy and the realm of the new media: "As the world becomes a commodity, it approaches pictorial writing"—a splintered "mosaic" supplied by advertising, photography, film, and now electronic media, where the word becomes information.[223]

Textuality is no longer what it was (while intertextuality is just beginning), thanks to the "new excentric figurativeness" induced by advertising,[224] as Benjamin declares:

> Script—having found, in the book, a refuge in which it can lead an autonomous existence—is pitilessly dragged out into the street by advertisements and subjected to the brutal heteronomies of economic chaos. . . . The newspaper is read more in the vertical than in the horizontal plane, while film and advertisement force the printed word entirely into the dictatorial perpendicular. And before a contemporary finds his way clear to opening a book, his eyes have been exposed to such a blizzard of changing, colorful, conflicting letters that the chances of his penetrating the archaic stillness of the book are slight. Locust swarms of print, which already eclipse the sun of what city dwellers take for intellect, will grow thicker with each succeeding year.[225]

Here Benjamin laments the astonishing rise of an exteriorized, syncopated information age for the masses, taking over, like a "blizzard" or "locust swarm," from the bourgeoisie's interiorized, horizontally read culture.[226] He noted that the new building forms made specifically to host outdoor advertising were, like film, affecting text as well, forcing a new "dictatorial verticality" of the written word, and, again like film, bringing objects closer not so much for critical inspection but for sensationalist "tempo."[227] And yet, at the same time, Benjamin favors the document form (of which advertisements are surely a member) over the traditional artwork, offering in *One-Way Street* satirical advice against auratism in art, whereby the document's focus on form and materiality serves as a corrective balance to the work of art's emphasis on content and idea.[228]

Benjamin's polemic against the new vertical surface-method of reading called forth by advertising can be read in conjunction with Mendelsohn's commercially applied proliferation of a dynamic horizontalism in design that signified the masses' parallel release from the hierarchical encasement by religion and class. It also signified their liberation through the new methods of transportation: Werner Hegemann, in *Berlin of Stone* (*Das steinerne Berlin,* 1930), proclaims that the "age of the railway can accept only horizontal expansion."[229] While the expressionist early 1920s were host to euphoric debates concerning "tower" design in Germany (and some stunning paper-architecture, like Bruno Taut's alpine cathedrals and "city crowns" [*Stadtkronen*], or Mies' magically avant-gardistic and alien glass skyscrapers),[230] Berlin's sandy soil precluded any actual emulation of the New York and Chicago skylines. The philosophy of *Neues Bauen* focused primarily on the efficient functioning of the city as a whole rather than isolated tower-achievements.[231] Likewise, Le Corbusier's ideal city, his *Ville Radieuse* first conceived during the 1920s, is arranged according to a Cartesian grid (understood by Rem Koolhaas to be the horizontal "positive" to New York's vertical "negative").[232] In a description of commuting needs, Le Corbusier praises "speed" and attacks the "vertical" city for impeding it (yet praises the better-spaced skyscrapers of a Hilberseimerian hue).[233] Both Hilberseimer and Le Corbusier wished to free the skyscraper from the dark vertical entrapment of Manhattan—the nightmare vision of which appeared in the vertically structured city-to-come of Lang's *Metropolis.*

Indeed, the most successful skyscrapers of the Weimar years were made of wood, board, and material (*scilicet:* film sets).[234] In contrast to the "star" skyline of Manhattan's skyscrapers, of which there were 188 by 1929, and which were intended to glorify their merely mortal capitalist creators, the more low-key New Objectivity in European architecture attempted to suggest not a business version of a Gothic cathedral or of Versailles but rather the productive, incessant, horizontal efficacy of the factory production line. Yet both architectural forms also hosted consumerism's growing demand to show off phantasmagoric products to the masses, in order to distract the new class of worker-purchasers into the desire to acquire; hence the instantaneous (vertical) logic of advertising began to emerge even on the new horizontal façades. One literal example of this occurred when a stunning row of vertical blue electric pillars was added at the end of the 1920s to the rooftop of the Grünfeld department store (replacing the "Protos-Corner" ad). This display-prototype of what has become the sound-bite mentality of our TV era suggests, for Benjamin, the danger of the "dictatorial perpendicular" that would preclude reflection beyond the cult of surface effects and sensationalist tempo.[235]

In the same breath, however, Benjamin predicts a day when artists and writers will be so adept in the new technological media of expression that they will have reconquered the ground they are currently losing. Benjamin is also using his own text as a training ground for such dadaesque adroitness, for *One-Way Street* is littered with section-headings emulating what one sees walking in the city (e.g., "THIS SPACE FOR RENT," "POST NO BILLS," "CLOSED FOR ALTERATIONS"); and the original book cover, designed by Sasha Stone, was a photomontage of duplicated street signs on a background of storefronts with advertising placards. Throughout his work, Benjamin both regrets and employs advertising's antimythic montage methods; for, as Buck-Morss has shown, what is his *Arcades Project* if not a written montage that inspires a visual calling-forth in the same style?[236]

Notwithstanding the above creative participation in commercial modernity (and lest I slide here into the all-too-familiar cultural studies chant of automatically praising an aspect of popular culture just because it is powerful, and just because it *is*), advertising remains, for Benjamin, part of the ultimate con of consumerist reenchantment that promptly arrives to fill the void formed by the Weberian disenchantment of modernity: advertising is, he says, the "cunning with which the dream imposed itself upon industry."[237] Advertising thus has a *split function*, a *divided discourse*. It both rudely awakens the architectural "dream consciousness of the collective" using all the shock methods already discussed, and yet sends the collective into a new slumber at the same time.[238]

POSTMODERNITY AND THE SPACE OF ADVERTISING

What, then, remains nowadays of the Weimar era's creative space of outdoor urban advertising? Critic Susan Stewart has noticed how "the twentieth century has signaled the appropriation of the sphere of the gigantic by a centralized mode of commercial advertising"; the "gigantic" mode of the urban modern (typified by the Weimar street) has been transferred over into an "abstract space of production."[239] Post-WWII advertising has, after all, taken what is probably an irreversible inward turn away from the on-site dependency of the street.

We can turn again to that incessant viewfinder of postmodern visual culture, namely Baudrillard, for a haunting vision of where advertising has ended up in relation to the postmodern condition. His remarks lend themselves well to some concluding remarks on our predicament: advertising, born of the era of the October Revolution and the market crash of 1929 (Baudrillard's birth year), has become today "not what brightens or decorates the walls, it is what effaces the walls, effaces the streets, the façades, and all the architecture, effaces any support and any depth"; "this liquidation, this reabsorption of everything into the surface" is our "empty and inescapable form of seduction."[240] His reading of contemporary advertising is one of nihilistic yet orgiastic self-loss in the realm of *total* surface, or simulation, that is our electronic era. Sign and reality now "shar[e] a single shroud."[241]

In Las Vegas, Baudrillard finds that advertising is still on the street—but on a strip that has become the hyperreal. There is no street as such, only advertising's prepackaged effects that create a street-effect. Indeed, Ada Louise Huxtable finds the latest electric advertising of 1990s Las Vegas to be too much for the walker, producing in him or her not so much the modern trauma of urban shock but a Baudrillardian "obscenity" of overexposure to the postmodern show:[242] "The dream of pedestrianism . . . has been aggressively neutralized; the social stroll has become a sensuous assault. In a [Jon] Jerde makeover, a 1,400-foot-long, 90-foot-high arched space frame spans Las Vegas's Fremont Street . . . wrapping the nighttime walker in a computer-generated sound and light show provided by 211 million lights and a 540,000-watt sound system."[243] The older billboarded and electrified Strip, the original "Glitter Gulch," that Venturi once rediscovered for postmodernists in the 1970s has been outdone by the new Las Vegas, which at the millennium is growing not just as a city but as a huge advertising site. The "linear urban theater" of the "Fremont Street Experience" is the extreme example of how material, outdoor locations for advertising have been dissolved into a new immaterial format that permits a single avatar—namely, advertising as itself—as the "only architecture" of today. As Baudrillard sums up the situation: "Advertising in its new version—which is no longer a more or less baroque, utopian or ecstatic scenario of objects and consumption, but the effect of an omnipresent visibility of enterprises, brands, social interlocutors and the social virtues of communication—advertising in its new dimension invades everything, as public space (the street, monument, market, scene) disappears."[244] This invasion of everything by advertising points up the major point of difference between modernity and postmodernity: while Weimar Germany oscillated over the tension-filled difference between depth and surface, dark and light, stasis and tempo, real text and advertising text, postmodernity no longer has any such point to argue. Baudrillard's vision of our postmodern advertising—as operating pointlessly now that reality has been "murdered"—is far beyond the realm of shock that so characterized modernity's embrace of this applied art. Small wonder, then, that Weimar modern advertising can strike us, if only nostalgically, as the shock of the new in ways that today's advertising never can.

3 Into the Mouth of the Moloch

Weimar Surface Culture Goes to the Movies

Une maison . . . est une machine à habiter.
Le Corbusier

Das Kino . . . ist eine Maschine zum Filmen.
Helmut Weihsmann

FROM 'CALIGARI'-EFFECT TO FILM-SET OMNIPOTENCE

The great age of German silent film, coinciding as it did with the emergence of New Objectivity out of the inverted spirit of expressionism, was experienced as an architectural event. In this conscious architecturalization of film, the 1920s German film industry excelled more than any other national cinema of any era; nowhere was the façadism of modern surface culture so excessively constituted in entertainment form. Weimar cinema was a technological façade that projected moving three-dimensional images about modernity to audiences sitting before a two-dimensional screen—just as the vision of city life shown to the protagonist of Karl Grune's 1924 film *The Street* (*Die Straße*) comes to him initially like a film projected on the wall of his room.[1] Evidently, the surfaces of film were, like the temptations of the city for Grune's protagonist, hard to resist: the cinema in 1920s Germany had become one of the largest industries in the country.[2] It is in the prefilmic stages of Weimar film, in its most literal "surface areas"—namely, film sets, studios, and movie palaces, particularly as critiqued by Kracauer—that the present chapter finds its focus. Here we find the most richly laden sites of how this industry signified film as apparatus, as the "motor of modernity,"[3] or, at the very least, as an instantaneous and inflammatory reflector of modernity's engine.

The crucial importance of film architecture during the German silent era was widely recognized at the time: "The entire filmwork can succeed or fail based on the milieu of the action, i.e., on film architecture with its character-giving and atmosphere [*Stimmung*]-creating nuances."[4] Film analyst Paul Rotha referred to German set design of the 1920s as an exegetically speaking "architecture of façades," a "tapestry" of "hieroglyphics."[5] Indeed, before the moving camera (*die entfesselte Kamera*), introduced by Karl Freund in 1924, could speak to the viewer of a "mobilization of space" such as that experienced outside the auditorium, the spatial language of film architecture was paramount.[6] Hermann Warm, who did the design along with Robert Herlth and Walter Röhrig for Robert Wiene's 1919 landmark expressionist film *The Cabinet of Dr. Caligari* (*Das Cabinet des Dr. Caligari*), claimed that this work initiated the new profession of film architect. Even though the film architecture used in *Caligari* was primarily two-dimensional painted sets, its organically "dynamic and daemonic" distortions of curves, lines, and angles succeeded in extending the observing perspective beyond the impression of flat surfaces, as the German art critic Hermann G. Scheffauer noted in 1920, "not only in flight from the spectator, that is, towards the background, but into and beyond the foreground, to overwhelm the spectator with it, to draw him into the trammels, the vortex of the action."[7] This is particularly the case with the prison-cell shot of the protagonist, where white arrowlike lines rise from the floor up the walls in concentric fashion, dragging the audience's gaze into the mental imprisonment of the inmate. *Caligari*'s architectural ability to thus involve the viewer so completely in the psychoses represented in the screen narrative follows entirely the direction, as noted by Anthony Vidler, of "light space" always already being invaded by the uncanny figure of "dark space," wherein the building, as "(negative) surface," doubles as the "death of the subject": "an architecture not only without real depth, but one that deliberately played on the ambiguities between absolute flatness and infinite depth."[8] It is a "filmic space" that was to be repeated, in New Objective format, in the double translucency of an onyx interior wall alongside a whole-wall picture window in Mies van der Rohe's Tugendhat House (1928–1930).[9]

In the wake of this painted *Caligari* effect, however, the massive and elaborate studios built just outside Berlin by the Universum Film Aktiengesellschaft (Ufa) offered a more prosaic approach to creating the chiaroscuro that so defined German silent cinema. By the mid-1920s, the huge "film-city" (*Filmstadt*) at Babelsberg near Potsdam dominated Berlin's twenty other film studios, and indeed came to represent, in its hegemony, something as important and fascinating as the actual filmic product. It was certainly "Babel"-esque, consisting of towers and tunnels over eighty-odd acres of artificially lit playgrounds;[10] moreover, its remote location outside Berlin and guaranteed financial backing offered limitless opportunities for the continued expansion of specially constructed indoor and outdoor scenes.[11] Germany's film studios had progressed from the pre-WWI *Glashaus,* via the post-WWI *Zeppelinhalle,* to the *Großatelier* of steel and iron. The former "glass houses" were gradually replaced with huge "exclusively artificial light ateliers" (*Nur-Kunstlicht-Ateliers*)—nine-tenths of all shots used artificial lighting in the Weimar years, as a result of Ufa's tradition of recreating entire cities within controlled lighting environments. Before these huge studios were built, Ufa made interim use of the former Zeppelin aerodrome at Staaken near Berlin, thereby creating overnight the largest atelier in the world (fig. 35); car and zoo exhibition halls and airplane hangars were also used. In 1926, Neubabelsberg opened the largest Nur-Kunstlicht-Atelier in Europe (today called the Metropolis-Halle), built specifically for the purpose: at 405 feet long, 185 feet wide, and 66 feet high, it had enough room for nine films to be directed at the same time.[12]

In this grand decade of silent film, the sets did far more than speak for the actors. The high experienced by visitors to the Ufa city evidently provided a surrogate feeling of filmic omnipotence—here in the words of a journalist who in 1925 accompanied Fritz Lang onto the famed set for *Metropolis* and experienced his own Babel-sublime by stepping momentarily into the shoes of the cameramen: "We walk further, and climb up a high tower made of powerful beams, to the position of the [camera] operators, from where Babelsberg lies deep down at our feet like a small city. To the point from which incredible optical effects are to be captured for the film."[13] In this way, the site of Babelsberg itself became a cinematic fetish for the public imagination—a concoction of film-cities within the film-city of Berlin proper.[14]

Ufa was founded during the years of the First World War as essentially part of the German propaganda machine. This inheritance is visible in the following quotation from an *Ufa-Programm* of 1925/1926, which effectively introduces (or advertises) the self-sufficiency of the studios as no less than a national powerhouse:

> The Neubabelsberg concern at Ufa is specifically made for outdoor shots. Here the skyscrapers and the lines of streets from *Metropolis,* city of the future, reach high up into the sky. . . . An amusement fair with carousels, swings, and rollercoasters—one of the sets for a scene in the film *Variété*—stretches far into the distance. . . . In addition to the detached buildings there are two large ateliers on the lot. Administration buildings and workshops are located in 22 massive buildings. Neu-

Figure 35. Postcard of the Zeppelin in its hangar, Berlin (1920s).

> babelsberg is an industrial concern that can produce its entire needs on site. A power plant translates a high-tension current of 10,000 volts in three transformers into normal direct current, and delivers enough power for about 15,000 amperes of light consumption. . . . Of special interest are the underground film chambers that provide extra protection against any explosions caused by spontaneous combustion. The best known blockbusters have been made in Babelsberg, from *The Golem* to *The Nibelungs* to *The Last Laugh,* and there are always new films being made here that create respect and status for German work far beyond Germany's borders.[15]

The site of cinematic production was thus glorified into a cradle of creative life force for the national collective. With such pragmatic sentiments about filmmaking technologies, Weimar cinema took up the tools of expressionist yearnings for a mythological rebirth for Germany in the wake of the defeat of World War I, and created thereby a neo-expressionist filmic monumentalism.

The rebuilding of Germany via film took place quite literally, since film offered the most lucrative and creative opportunities to underemployed architects—both in set-design and in constructing the new movie palaces. This need for employment dovetailed nicely with the theoretical desires of the then-expressionist architect Bruno Taut, who in a 1918 text entitled "A Program for Architecture" had already urgently desired an outdoor studio as a playground for architecture (and, by implication, for film production): " . . . a well-situated experimental site (e.g., in Berlin: the Tempelhofer Feld), on which architects can erect large-scale models of their ideas. Here . . . architectural effects (e.g., glass as a building material) shall be tried out, perfected, and exhibited to the masses in full-scale temporary constructions or individual parts of a building."[16] This wish was indirectly granted architects by the German film industry, but as part of a semiconscious commercial-cum-nationalistic design; it also satisfied the public's naive sensory intoxication with the new medium's plethora of imagery. The visual primacy and frenetic façadism of Weimar urbanism and modernization were given free rein in the realm of the moving image, with respect to which the following homily from a popular collector's film-still book of 1929, *Film Photos As Never Before* (*Film Photos wie noch nie*), was a typical outpouring:

> The image . . . [of film] governs all possibilities. The image is information. The image is a game. The image is fate. The image is chaos. The image is peace. The image can be everything, it can give everything, when it runs through the projector at thirty little pictures a second. This hellish tempo of the image is, after all, the reason why we convince ourselves we need to rush all the time and can't go slowly anymore. The image is to blame for everything. A narcotic. A drug. We want to see.[17]

As if in cued reaction to this kind of populist naiveté, critics from the left and the right voiced their grudging admiration regarding the new visual power of the medium. "What is film? Film is electricity," acknowledged Soviet author Ilya Ehrenburg in *The Dream Factory* (*Die Traumfabrik*, 1931)—his main aim therein being to uncover the prefilmic layers of the film industry's "cruel, devouring wasteland" and to reveal the goings-on below the surface of what he regards as its ruthlessly capitalistic production processes. Ehrenburg points to how the right-wing Ufa director Alfred Hugenberg's newsreel, the *Ufa-Wochenschau*, is so surface-oriented that it avoids giving the people any bad news: "They live very strangely, these two-dimensional people in the wide world and on the wide screen. They never work. They are occupied with higher things."[18] The conservative nationalist Hans Buchner resisted the emerging American involvement with the German film industry,[19] and derisively recounted how the average film-viewer "submits himself to the two-dimensional surface [of such American(ized) films] without a care, without criticism, without guidance, without enlightenment."[20] The constantly war-minded Ernst Jünger senses the stagnant yet sensationalist mindlessness of most films but wants instead to mobilize the propagandistic potentiality of the new medium for battle scenes, noting in 1930 that the mass vehicle of film is "of a character far from innocuous": cinema presents a "problem of power and [is] to be valued as such."[21]

KRACAUER VERSUS THE WEIMAR FILM-CITY

By far the greatest *Angst* about the intoxicating spectacles induced by the German film industry is voiced by Kracauer. A former—if mediocre—architect himself, now thoroughly disillusioned with monument-building,[22] Kracauer complains about the monumental film sets used by Ufa. His disengagement from (but insistent obsession with) the architectural profession and things architectural is on a par with Robert Musil's similar repugnance for, yet constant literary re-creation of, his own former training as an engineer. Kracauer had worked from 1909 to 1917 for Theodor Fischer, one of the most renowned architects of the day. Wolfgang Pehnt comments that Fischer's name was associated with "picturesque impressiveness" and overblown monumentalism[23]—no doubt a factor in Kracauer's subsequent low tolerance level for the same, whether on the street or on the screen.

In an article entitled "Calico-World: The Ufa City in Neubabelsberg" which was first broadcast as a Frankfurt radio feature on January 24, 1926, then published in the *Frankfurter Zeitung* a few days later, Kracauer asserts his retaliatory stance against the Weimar film-city. He complains about the literal façade culture of the Ufa-city film sets: "The things that rendezvous here do not belong to reality. They are copies and distortions that have been ripped out of time and jumbled together. They stand motionless, full of meaning from the front, while from the rear they are just empty nothingness. A bad dream about objects that has been forced into the corporeal realm."[24] He aligns the geographical and temporal arbitrariness of the film sets with the actors' custom-made facial masks hanging on the walls, for use by other actors as stand-ins. At any moment any or all may be disassembled or remetamorphosed, until "their plaster of paris shines through and they are junked."[25] Assigning to such fake (namely "calico," "material") façades a degree of worn-out metaphoricity in a way akin to that of Nietzsche's (as yet unpublished) extramoral diagnosis of language,[26] or even more akin to the longing expressed by Maurice Maeterlinck for the irretrievable treasures below the surface,[27] Kracauer complains: "Architectural constructions jut upward as if meant to be inhabited. But they represent only the external aspects of the prototypes, much the way language maintains façades of words whose original meaning has vanished."[28] Not coincidentally does he refer to F. W. Murnau's (and Ufa's) *Faust* of 1926 as a literal giant (*Riesenfilm*);[29] for it is the filmic enterprise itself, with its foundations of capitalism and nationalism, that he finds exaggeratedly Faustian and overblown. Babelsberg is, he warns, a disrespectful impersonation of the macrocosm, a "Noah's ark" of apparently realistic things made of "papier-mâché" that "rendezvous" here in a haphazard fashion, such as the "monstrous dragon" from Lang's epic *The Nibelungs.*[30] Its fault is not that it is not nature, but that it *poses as* nature: things here are but "copies and distortions" (*Abbilder und Fratzen*).[31] The industry has, in Kracauer's eyes, re-created the very thing Walter Benjamin (in the 1935 essay "The Work of Art in the Age of Mechanical Reproducibility") more naively hopes that film, as avant-gardistic art form, could and would destroy: namely the mimetically imbued *aura,* the voyeuristic-cinematic "fourth wall" in which absolute faith is invested.[32]

Why, indeed, does the film-city of façades present, for Kracauer, such a representational nightmare? His discomfort is first and foremost on behalf of the architectural profession: here he shares with postmodern architect Rem Koolhaas the regret that modernity's discovery of the formula "technology + cardboard (or any other flimsy material) = reality," has been haunting the production of architecture ever since.[33] Kracauer's evident unease amidst the "calico-world" is not merely due to the extravagance of the film sets, but also and moreover to "the things projected onto the screen":[34] that is, the camera's intrinsic power to transform this (of itself senseless) jumble of artifacts into an alternative, highly believable reality. For his readers, Kracauer repeatedly endeavors to dispel the apparatus's uncanny effect that visitors to Ufa (as to Universal Studios today) try to recreate in real time. Against this, he plays the role of cool, detached detective, a product of the antiornamental New Objectivity,[35] exposing the representational "crime" of the profilmic condition of the film sets and mercilessly exposing the technical sleight of hand involved in any mise-en-scène, but especially those effects that are fantastic and "supernatural."[36] He likes to undo the work of the camera and recreate the distance between actor and filmed environment. In a Brechtian manner he calls attention to the film-city's components as ahistorical and nondevelopmental, as new ruins that are not naturally fallen but a lawless set of artificial metamorphoses, a fragmented mixture of inorganic things soon to be dismantled. Only through what is for Kracauer a brigade of disconnected, cellular processes inherent to the entire filmmaking process (e.g., invisible mechanics, lighting, camera angle, editing) is the appearance of a unified whole created, and it is this he would like to remind his readers of. His ire is directed not only at this "pointillist" realm,[37] but moreover at the public's (particularly white-collar workers') naive consumption of the filmic product. As he scathingly comments in the 1927 essay "The Little Shopgirls Go to the Movies," the feminized masses fool themselves that the filmic product is created not in the surrealistically structured Ufa studios but out of their own existences: "Life is an invention of the haves, which the have-nots try to imitate [via film] to the best of their inability"[38]—hence Kracauer's need to send up the nonmimetic basis of the filmmaking process. We can, of course, only speculate on how Kracauer might have reacted to today's exaggeration of the mimetic influence spread by the electronic media to the point of supposed no return—a "classlessness" now shared by all, in that even the very rich follow the masses in following the media's lead in consumption and entertainment patterns.

What the spectator-subject of film *does not see* is revealed and derided by Kracauer as a manufactured, patently false, and potentially harmful art (or industry) of manipulation. Here Kracauer's complaint is rather reminiscent of Adolf Loos's derision of the Potemkin villages of board and canvas that were designed to deceive and delight Catherine the Great when she traveled through the Ukraine.[39] The illusion of monumentality, as told in *Metropolis* by the cautionary allegory of the Tower of Babel or the dizzying shots of the skyscraper city itself, is effectively cut down by Kracauer's critique to its miniature model-size. Many of the Weimar film sets were indeed gigantic, but some, like the workers' underground tower-blocks in *Metropolis,* were just bases, their height artificially reflected upwards using Eugen Schüfftan's famous mirror technique (a money-saving method that was, it is rumored, occasionally sabotaged by screen architects fearing for their future employment).[40] In point of fact, however, the forest in Lang's *Siegfried* was indeed a collection of huge (cement) trees. Or again, the rooftops in *Faust* were small models, while the Castle of Worms in *Siegfried* was truly massive. Kracauer's point is that the viewers—as merely passive recipients of the artistry of *"cinematic special effects"* (*Filmtricks*)—cannot know this.[41]

Kracauer appears to be conflating in his analysis here some distinct stylistic differences between the actual film architects: it was Erich Kettelhut, Otto Hunte, and Karl Vollbrecht who were essentially behind the gigantic stasis of the Lang sets, but Herlth, Röhrig, and Warm, among others, worked in tandem to effect a more sensually "flowing," milieu-based style for Murnau, and also for Lang's most expressionistic early film, *Destiny* (*Der müde Tod,* 1921).[42] But Kracauer's attack has certain merits with respect to *Metropolis.* In 1927, the year of *Metropolis*'s premiere and Kracauer's ensuing "Calico-World" article, the extent of Ufa's posturing by means of Lang's film would become even more apparent—not only in *Metropolis*'s mise-en-scène, nor in the allegorical tale of the tower of Babel, nor even the Harbouesque plot of the film, but simply in the fact that the film that had been fervently promoted for the entire previous year, cost more than five million Reichsmarks, lasted seven hours, and recovered only one-seventh of its production costs.[43] Since *Metropolis* only compounded Ufa's already rising debt and was not a success abroad, Ufa's most monumental effort to outdo Hollywood was a definitive financial failure. In this sense, then, Kracauer's attack on the Ufa artifice was vindicated.

How, then, are we to account for Kracauer's distrust and derision of architectural cinematics per se, of filmic staging in all its three-dimensionality? Remaining paramount is of course his socialist concern for the mass urban viewing public that is at the mercy of the new entertainment medium. In 1924, 40 million movie tickets were sold in Berlin alone, and approximately 500 million throughout Germany—the equivalent of every German seeing seventeen films per year.[44] For Kracauer, Weimar film gives cultish status to (that is, regressively impacts upon) modernity's prime product of commodification and technologized Fordist Taylorism: namely the "mass ornament" that turns the holistic entities of community and individual personality into a merely functioning "tiny piece of the mass."[45] Kracauer's comments in "The Mass Ornament" of 1927 evidently anticipate Horkheimer and Adorno's argument, in *The Dialectic of Enlightenment* (1944), against modern architecture's mass urban planning, for having enacted, like the Hollywood culture industry, a "mass deception" on its inhabitants/viewers.[46] Film—with its massifying production line, monumental film sets and manipulated spectators—constitutes for Kracauer just the most recent and striking phenomenon arising out of the ultimate *ir*rationality underlying the capitalist system of infinitely self-reproducing, self-perpetuating rationality.

This irrational base of filmic production was also noticed by another Weimar journalist, Alfred Polgar, who, writing for the *Berliner Tageblatt* in 1928, was similarly struck by this stark "incongruity" or gap between the huge expenditure in human, mechanical, and monetary terms needed to make a film, on the one hand, and the actual, apparently seamless filmic product, on the other: "The misunderstanding between the enormous expenditure of toil, money, nerves and muscle strength, of people, machines, skills and stupidity, patience, passion, energy of every kind, sweat from every source—and that which this effort brings forth. . . . It all looks grand, and small, too. Charming, and pathetic. Freshly built, and yet already there for a long time. A fossilized today! Spirits of millions of Rentenmarks hover around it, complaining."[47] Kracauer finds that the *ratio* of capitalism, like the mass ornament that is its "aesthetic reflex," knows no inner sense except to be an "end in itself."[48] The mass ornaments of film and other forms of Weimar popular entertainment arise as surface protrusions mirroring the functioning and fragmented subjectivities of a mechanized city in modern capitalism. Despite his warning cry, Kracauer is nonetheless the first to point out that the mass ornament remains a more genuine artistic production than any outdated high art form. Likewise, Kracauer's "Photography" essay (1927) demonstrates the author's mixed feelings toward the filmic/photographic medium as a contiguous stockpiler of exterior elements, not a creator of inner meaning through time by means of a reassortment of these elements: "In order for history to present itself, the mere surface coherence offered by photography must be destroyed."[49] But he thus willfully ignores the conscious surface *in*coherences of dadaist photomontage and Soviet-inspired avant-garde film. Kracauer remains ambiguous: not a reactionary Luddite, he is simply highly suspicious of the state of homogeneity for the working classes induced and encouraged by the German and American film industries' rival ambitions. His aim is not to smash the camera apparatus itself for being (as Jean-Louis Baudry would say)[50] a fatalistically predetermined instrument of Platonism, or a regressive recreator of the Lacanian mirror-stage, but rather, to de-auratize its monumentalist posturing in the name of social(ist) enlightenment.

Kracauer is specifically impatient with expressionist architects for crossing over to the film industry; he writes scathingly of Taut and Hans Poelzig for their desire to build great monumental projects, a desire witnessed by Taut's *Alpine Architecture* picture book of 1919—a visionary enterprise rather than a real one, since in the immediate post-WWI years actual building projects were hard to find. In Frankfurt a.M. in 1923, for example, Kracauer reports that only eight to ten of the fifty-four registered architects in the *Bund Deutscher Architekten* were gainfully employed.[51] In a 1921 article, "On Skyscrapers" (*Über Turmhäuser*), Kracauer states:

> The involuntary idleness that has been imposed for years now on German architects has not been able to stifle their desire for grand building projects. The impossibility of building in reality has driven artists like Poelzig to create expressionist movie palace architecture, while fanatics like Taut are dreaming up hazardous glass palaces and a utopian alpine architecture. But in the end even the most ingenious plaster-fantasies[52]

> will not suffice for the architect; he is driven to construct buildings and to invent works of permanence. . . . [53]

The vogue for lavish film-set design among German architects during the silent film era is indicative, for Kracauer, of their frustrated desire to create "towers" for posterity. He has in mind here Poelzig's set for the Gothic-stylized Jewish quarter of Prague in Paul Wegener's *Der Golem* (1920), as constructed life-size on the Tempelhofer Feld in Berlin. (Poelzig's original color designs for the film were in fact far more tower-oriented than the eventual set of labyrinthine streets and passages.) The origins of Kracauer's extreme realist stance vis-à-vis film after World War II are already visible in such reports as this from the 1920s—they inform his subsequent, somewhat obsessively psychologizing, character-based reading (in *From Caligari to Hitler* of 1946)[54] of the expressionist film decade as the dreamlike early "symptom" of a "disease" of which Nazism was a more advanced stage; his impatience with expressionist film sets is also echoed in 1934 by film theorist Rudolf Arnheim, who retrospectively finds them "painfully unreal" and "exposed" by the contrastive human actor.[55] Here in 1921, Kracauer sees the fantastical immortalities achieved in the monumentalist architectural substitutes of stage and screen as similarly unreal, as arising from an inability to build otherwise: in short, as born of a loss of societal applicability for professional skills that thus slide over, by default, into a misplaced art of seduction. Hence he was delighted when Taut was appointed Magdeburg's city planner in 1922—for this would, he accurately predicted, enable Taut to move on from his utopian paper-designs and on to "reality," like functionalist suburban housing projects.[56]

Hence, while Kracauer favors an authentic, posthumanist representation of modernity's distracted, uncontrolled "display of pure externality"[57]—rather like Irmgard Keun's protagonist Doris in her desire to become what Berlin is, sheer luster (*Glanz*)[58]—he protests the film industry's regressive mask over the same:

> The architectural setting tends to emphasize a dignity that used to inhabit the institutions of high culture. It favors the lofty and the *sacred* as if designed to accommodate works of eternal significance—just one step short of burning votive candles. . . . Distraction—which is meaningful only as improvisation, as a reflection of the uncontrolled anarchy of our world—is festooned with drapery and forced back into a unity that no longer exists.[59]

For this, then, one does not even require the ostentatiously monumentalist scenarios of Lang's silent films with their architecturally static, symmetrical mass scenes.[60] The "*reactionary* tendencies" of the filmic product are, in short, a side effect of the parent industry's preexisting ambitions and techniques.[61]

Here we can pause to extrapolate Kracauer's imagined reaction to the *Jurassic Park* syndrome: the current loss of set design altogether to computer imaging, wherein there is increasingly less and less need to build at all when filming—a trend due in no small part, as film architect Ken Adam (of Bond film fame) has noted, to television's "cutting" influence on cinema.[62] While, as the media event spawned by James Cameron's $220 million blockbuster *Titanic* (1997) demonstrates,[63] there is apparently still ongoing room for monumentalist excess at movie set-making, virtual reality is nonetheless ready to merge the old divide between the activities of architecture and film. As Vidler explains: "Where in the '20s and after, film and architecture were, in a fundamental sense, entirely different media utilizing their respective technologies, the one to simulate space, the other to build it, now, by contrast, the increasing digitalization of our world has rendered them if not the same, at least coterminous."[64] The new "virtual space" of film will be, continues Vidler, "neither flat nor deep; neither surveyed nor unsurveyed; neither changing nor unchanging," because it is self-generating, an "endless *mise-en-abyme*," where "no one is or could be at home." Kracauer's attack on the sacralization enacted by filmmaking in its illusion of "unity that no longer exists" can thus now be extended into concerns that film's virtual space, in the new electronic contiguity or even conflation of the architectural within the filmic, will not just mislead the viewer but recreate him/her in its own autocentric realm.

There is, however, an important subtext to Kracauer's noble attack (in addition, that is, to the irony of his own self-distancing from the mass film audiences toward whom he is supposedly sympathetic, revealed both in his tone and in the implied bourgeois readership of the *Frankfurter Zeitung*)—namely his own rivalry with a fellow Weimar cinematic hermeneut, Austria's most well-known film critic of the time, Béla Balázs. In *Visible Man or the Culture of Film* (*Der sichtbare Mensch oder die Kultur des Films*, 1924), the Hungarian Balázs categorically celebrates cinema qua narcissistic surface, and updates Goethe's aphorism for the cinema age: "Film is a *surface art* [*Flächenkunst*]"—what is "intrinsic" in film is always already "extrinsic" ("*was innen ist, ist außen*" *bei ihm*).[65] He sees that for silent film to escape its theatrical heritage, for film to become filmic, it had to become what it really was (to echo Nietzsche), namely surface, or both "nut and shell at the same time" ("*Kern und Schale mit einem Male*") whose edited parts proceed paratactically through time. He is not made uneasy by the notion of *Stimmung* as inherited from nineteenth-century art aesthetics, suggesting that without the application of such atmospheric qualities, silent film would produce only a bare, neutral description of an event or object, and actors would be made mute.[66] This enthusiastic validation by Balázs of atmosphere as an "objectified lyricism" directly supports filmic expressionism for producing a totalized environment.[67] *Stimmung,* according to Balázs, can be produced via intimate close-ups of the actors, but also by channeling audience perspective into the hero's own point of view. The methodology of producing this "subjective image of the world" via the camera lens is crucial:[68] he wants to invest as much organic status as possible in mass scenes,[69] and of course also in such mammoth structures as the Eiffel Tower, warehouses, factories, and railway stations, as well as in the photographic illusions of gigantic size, space, or height. These images of sublime, auratic "pathos" deserve more than just supporting roles in the all-important "reality-effect of greatness."[70] For Balázs there are rightly monumentalist scenes in film because of preexisting monumentalist scenes in our urban industrial lives. In Balázs's view, film's surface effect—its "monumentality of milieu"—is simply a positive term in the infinitely expanding field of fabrication and experience of film.[71] And it is certainly true that over the course of the twentieth century, the Hollywood film industry has followed this advice rather than Kracauer's more agonistic line.

Evidently this advocacy by Balázs of the sheer pictorial viewability or non-use inherent to an architecturalized cinema—whether on location in the city, on Babelsberg's terrain, or inside the Ufa movie palaces—is not dependent on any actual socioeconomic "culture" of film, and therefore runs counter to Kracauer's major concerns.[72] On the other hand, Kracauer's critique cannot account for the filmic-psychic notions of dream, distortion, and vision—indisputably important levels of expressivity in film and first explored by Balázs, in the wake of Hofmannsthal's dream-narratives. Moreover, Balázs is more at ease with stylizing techniques such as camera angles, the art of the cameraman, lighting, location, and actors' physiognomy; in other words, cinematic *Stimmung* deserves to be read as more artful and metaphorical, and less intent on mimetic illusionism, than Kracauer would have us believe. In response one could say, as Eisenstein in fact did in his 1926 essay "Béla Forgets about the Scissors," that the pro-*Stimmung* attitude of Balázs neglects the uses of alienation effects in film, especially montage.[73] More crucially, Balázs's work sees nothing problematic in the neo-expressionist shift during the later Weimar silent film era away from the painterly, stylized sets à la *Caligari* toward the macrocosmic construction of entire screen-worlds.[74] This is precisely what annoyed Kracauer the most—the fact that the film industry offered architects an all-too-tempting substitute for the building shortfalls of the crisis-ridden Weimar reality, a will to power facilitated by the very speed of on-set temporary construction and by the instant mass distribution of their works on screen—the will, that is, to create visual architectural effect for its own sake.[75]

CELEBRATORY FILM STREETS

But were Weimar filmgoers so wrong to obsess and fantasize about their self-renewing and ever self-rebuilding "film cities"? Perhaps Babelsberg et al represents, after all, the most truly modern, and even proto-postmodern, aspect of Weimar film. As the Swiss writer Walter Muschg more forgivingly remarked for the *Neue Zürcher Zeitung* in 1922, the forces at work in the Ufa film-city are still impressive by the very strength of their "conscious joy at the impossible."[76] There is within the multiworlded fake city a wholly *new* "fullness of life," as Muschg sees it, which imparts its dynamism in production and reproduction to the audiences at the receiving end of the film-item: it generates, in short, a highly credible "*popular-aesthetic behavior.*"[77] As Muschg describes the contradiction of Babelsberg, it is literally fake, cheap, dirty, and loud, and yet simultaneously wholly true to its own art form—namely, a pragmatics of production, tempo, and immediacy:

> Never before have I seen walls so covered with obscenities as in the film-city; never before have I received so strong an impression of how a culture must look where production springs from a real, fiercely driven need, where there are masters and succession, and where that which is accomplished is dragged out of the workshop right into the discussion. Here indeed the haste of production stands in reverse relation to the value and duration of the product.[78]

Nonetheless, Muschg reports that the medium Babelsberg serves does not live up to its potential, insofar as the *Nibelungs* type of pathos and the remedies for the postwar German spirit are full of "lazy magic" and "eternal yesterdays."[79]

While Babelsberg has experienced the violent transitions from its initial encoding as site of Weimar cinema to that of Nazi film production and, subsequently, site of East Germany's DEFA studios (before restaging itself as Babelsberg for postunification Germany), we can relate the vitalism of the (albeit short-lived) Weimar Babelsberg with Paul Virilio's account of the

Babelesque entity that Hollywood presents in its own twentieth-century shift from the modern to the postmodern. Hollywood, states Virilio, is

> . . . the city of living cinema where sets and reality, cadastral urban planning and cinematic footage planning, the living and the living dead merge to the point of delirium. Here, more than anywhere, advanced technologies have converged to create a synthetic space-time. The Babylon of film "derealization," the industrial zone of pretense, Hollywood built itself up neighborhood by neighborhood, avenue by avenue, upon the twilight of appearances, the success of illusions and the rise of spectacular productions (such as those of D. W. Griffith) while waiting for the megalomaniacal urbanizations of Disneyland, Disneyworld and Epcot Center.[80]

The irony is that Babelsberg today, in order to regain the life signs it needs to refunction fully as a major European film studio, and oblivious to Virilio's dread of Disneyland, has recreated itself as—a theme park.

One success story of the potential of the Weimar film-city was constructed for the set of the last silent film by Joe May in 1929: *Asphalt.* Just as Rochus Gliese built an entire modern city-set of glass and concrete at the Fox Studios for Murnau's *Sunrise* in 1927, so too was *Asphalt*'s "atelier street" set conceived by film architect Kettelhut (and originally also Herlth)[81] as a reflection of the entire city of Berlin. The studio street of *Asphalt* was so stunning that it merited being painted in and of itself (fig. 36). Kettelhut's challenge was to induce in the viewer through a series of panning shots a sense of the metropolitan street's commercialized tempo "the way the pedestrian views it," that is, via an "immensely mobile optics";[82] and indeed, the opening scenes of *Asphalt* succeed in bringing us this intensely peripatetic vision. But there was an extra agenda: for Ufa wished to show off its asphalted film street as a sign of the film company's reconstructed (literally re-surfaced) status after its recent bankruptcy.

Asphalt's street was "not just another piece of façade"[83] but a fully functioning three-dimensional set, with ten camera locations from which the newly invented mobile camera crane would move in all directions in order to capture Kettelhut's intended architectonics of mobility. "Real"-world brands such as Cords silk advertised themselves (for free) in the shop windows and the electric signs[84]—indeed, the film's fake *Schaufenster* street resembled nothing so much as the famed display-window street over the Alexandre III Bridge at the 1925 Exposition Internationale des Arts Décoratifs in Paris.[85] "Real" asphalt was laid on the 760-foot-long set; and the consumption of electricity on the asphalted street—its "sky" of

Figure 36. "A Street in the Atelier during Filming of *Asphalt*," by Rudi Feld (1929).

two thousand lamps amounting to the daily use of a medium-sized city—brought, when in operation, the rest of the film studios and almost the entire surrounding Babelsberg area to a complete standstill.[86] In an ironic gesture of reflexive self-engendering and conflation of the profilmic film-set "street" with the extrafilmic outside street, there is a scene in the film in which a movie palace (a copy of Erich Mendelsohn's Universum) is advertising a film called *Asphalt*.[87] The actual billboard advertisement that was made by Rudi Feld for *Asphalt*'s premiere at Berlin's Ufa-Palast am Zoo on February 18, 1929, bore, with its *Lichtreklame* simulacra and vehicular traffic in motion, a stunning resemblance to the film's own advertisement of itself (fig. 37). The entire "scene" was made even more memorable to people in the street by having two huge wooden "doors" periodically close over it, and upon the doors would then appear the flashing title of the film in huge letters.[88] In fact, as with *Metropolis*, one reviewer strongly

Figure 37. Façade for *Asphalt* at the Ufa-Palast am Zoo, by Rudi Feld (1929).

preferred the "vision of asphalt" contained within the film's opening shots, and especially in Feld's exterior design, to the moralizing love story of the film it was advertising.[89]

Not only the surfaces of the city but the figure of the Berliner as surface phenomenon is produced as a multiple—one might say *cloned*—in May's *Asphalt*. This occurs not only in the crowds on the film street, but also and more interestingly in the live shop-window model taking off her stockings for the voyeurs outside the shop (and those in the auditorium), or in the not-so-live wax figure effigies filling the double-decker buses. Moreover, the film's vamp, Else (played by Betty Amann), is the embodiment of conspicuous consumption: it is in her that the consequence of urban commodity excess is allegorized in the film as the ultimate act of surface-cloning. Else is a jewelry thief, the epitome of all male fears concerning the New Woman, who wears her wares on the outside, for she is nothing but surface (in the Nietzschean sense of antiessence and the realm of appearances being the greater truth for modernity). Like Lulu (Louise Brooks) in Pabst's *Pandora's Box* (*Die Büchse der Pandora,* 1929) or Lola (Marlene Dietrich) in Sternberg's *The Blue Angel* (*Der blaue Engel,* 1930),[90] Else is shown at key points in the film ruthlessly and destructively reflecting her own "surfaceness" to herself in a mirror. As a demonized, decadent, overblown, relatively late representation of the Weimar New Woman, Else the surface-clone is, moreover, the logical cinematic product of Weimar Berlin: her love affair with the policeman Holk (like the City Girl's affair with the Man from the country in *Sunrise*) draws him out of his world of apparent antisurface—in *Asphalt*'s case, of literally controlling the chaos of traffic, of guiding the exchange and circulation of the street. This deconstructive act of lovemaking forces Holk into an implied admission that his realm of depth (i.e., values, law and order) is ultimately no more than a prop of the (capitalist) system of infinite production and consumption, which ironically only Else, as thief and as surface-celebration, undermines—at least until her self-sacrificing resurrection at the film's end, when she turns herself in to save Holk from imprisonment.

The entire genre of the Weimar "street film" (*Straßenfilm*) of suprarealistically stylized sets may be said to symptomatically act out, with differing degrees of self-consciousness, the mobile surface culture of the German 1920s. As Anton Kaes states of this "dynamization of the setting" that *Asphalt* celebrates so masterfully, "the street [film] appears as the existential site of modernity, in which the individual is both the object of, and unwitting participant in, a series of incomprehensible and uncontrollable processes."[91] Indeed, when the otherwise anti-Babelsberg Kracauer *does* praise filmic surfaces as architectonically progressive, it is not the "pulp fiction"[92] May's film but rather relatively dadaesque, anti-illusionist, or Eisensteinian productions: one such film is Grune's *The Street*, precisely because it keeps the wound or "gap" open between actors and their filmic setting, and hence between filmic effect and audience. Their state of rupturedness is the opposite of that of "the shining film person" (*der glänzende Filmmensch*), Bloch's term for film actors and those who unthinkingly translate their glowing state of artificiality into reality.[93] Kracauer remarks in one of his reviews of Grune's film: "Instead of [the actors] living connected to the things [of the street], they sink down next to lifeless objects: like cars, rows of walls, electric advertisements that go light and dark, irrespective of time and yet in time. . . . "[94] Kracauer insists on *The Street*'s urban dissonance, wherein the "middle" ground between "film-picture and prophecy" remains necessarily empty and "unbuilt." In an earlier review, Kracauer praised the "technique of associations" in the film as one in which "an object takes a shape that only film can form, and in which possibilities are realized that are only ever possibilities in film."[95] The space of the city street in Grune's film is not a site in which identities are constructed: on the contrary, it is where "only figures come together, events happen and situations pile up blindly one upon another: all of this without continuity and consequence, an uncannily unreal togetherness of unreal people."[96] And yet these unreal film people are simultaneously endemic of the surface culture on the real Weimar street. Atomlike, they bump into one another and part again: "they are only exteriority, such as the street itself is. . . ."[97] Thus Grune's *Street* provides Kracauer with the bridge he needs between what he sees on the streets of "Berlin and elsewhere" and what could be achieved in the cinematic medium.

Kracauer's polemical writings on Babelsberg thus reveal the tension in the dual pull of his emotional attraction to, and political repulsion from, the Weimar film industry's effect-laden surfaces. We can, in particular, ask ourselves about Kracauer's evident fear of cinematic desire, or scopophilia (*Schaulust*).[98] He does not allow himself to partake (at least textually) of any Benjaminian, self-indulgent *flânerie* in the noisy silent film-city, even though this site so closely resembles his own excitedly allegorical and brilliantly cinematic city pictures of Weimar Berlin by night, as collected decades later for his volume *Streets in Berlin and Elsewhere* (*Straßen in Berlin und anderswo*). It is striking that Kracauer does not acknowledge the extent to which the same kind of alienation effect was likewise part of a visitor's experience of Babelsberg itself (even if one concurs that it was mostly excluded from the Weimar moviegoing experience).[99] The dynamic chaos of the densely populated, shifting-angled street that bespeaks both George Grosz's dada *Metropolis* (1917) and Fernand Léger's cubist *City* (1919), for example, came to be most accurately re-represented, so to speak, on the terrain of Weimar Berlin's film production. Even the lewd graffiti scrawled on or behind the scenery suggested an energy that the dadaists and cubists consciously had to recreate on their canvases: but Babelsberg came by all its own falsities naturally. All the mass ornaments that modern art embraced, Babelsberg, during the silent film years, already was: a total, shameless self-immersion in the fledgling culture industry. Its juxtaposed, lean-to sets formed a burlesque collage or incongruous series of overproduced images—a shrine of the new temporary art where several scenes could and would be built, filmed, or destroyed at any given moment. Again, it must be stressed that this posthumanist, creative condition does not refer to the bulk of the actual Weimar film products, which strove toward ever more bombastic monumentalism (whether in architecture or in sentimentality), but rather to the Babelesque body of the film-city that quite inadvertently gave it birth. It was an immense, intriguing, and labyrinthine corpus, the artifices of which linger in the mind long after the hyperbole of Kracauer's defensive, rather overly corrective stance toward the stagings and building strategies of the Weimar film industry.

This Kracauerian unease with film sets extended beyond Babelsberg itself to the general realm of urban entertainment. From the Old World point of view, the unreality of American mass entertainment only increased its threatening ability to convince audiences of its dictum, namely, that material surface mattered more than immaterial essence. Reporters like Hans Kafka wondered at what cost the Lunapark fairground, a Coney Island–inspired "piece of America" imported to Berlin, was entering the German psyche, and what would have to be given up in exchange.[100] Equally concerned with the masses' delight at this film-set version of the world, Kracauer offers an allegorical comment, in the essay "Rollercoaster" ("Berg- und Talbahn," 1928), about the two-dimensional painted background of a New York City skyscraper-scape that gave working-class Berliners a "city illusion" (*Stadtillusion*) on their Lunapark ride.[101] Kracauer was not keen on the bad "appearance architecture" (*Scheinarchitektur*) of New York City skyscrapers in the first place,[102] so it is hardly surprising that his Lunapark description reads like his mixed sentiments towards Babelsberg, and repeats his obsession with the pervasive influence of the new façade-style on everyday city life:

> The workers, the little people, the white-collar workers, oppressed during the working day by the city, now conquer on the aerial ride a supra-Berlinic New York. They are victors, the magically painted palaces lie at their feet. . . . A sharp bend, and the . . . glamour of the palaces is gone. The façades were only façades [*Die Fassaden sind nur Fassaden gewesen*], prefabricated pieces [*simple Versatzstücke*] that cover up a huge wooden construction at the back. Posts, props, beams: the kernel of the grand fronts is a scaffolding. Just now the wondrous city sparkled, and now the bare skeleton reveals itself. So that is New York—a painted surface [*eine angestrichene Fläche*] and behind it, nothing? The little couples are enchanted and disillusioned at the same time. . . . [T]hey see through the illusion, but the victory over the façades does not mean that much to them.[103]

The rollercoaster ride is the same one that is shown through the eye of Freund's speeding *entfesselte Kamera* as it rides at the head of the train in the opening scene of Ruttmann's *Berlin, Symphony of a City.* Kracauer's dictum of modern entertainment forms mirroring the mechanically determined speed of the metropolis is clearly reflected here; in a later scene in Ruttmann's film, however, shots of the orgiastic rollercoaster experience are intercut with spirals spinning and are annexed by a "staged" suicide of a woman jumping from a bridge, as if to indicate that the chaotic curvature of the ride's rise and fall cannot (like modern life itself) be tolerated by all urban denizens. In contrast to Ruttmann's vision, it is Kracauer's fervent hope that the Lunapark ride through the fake New York cityscape nonetheless permits people to see through the façade of the painted palatial skyscrapers; he wants to think the riders are relatively sophisticated readers of

Berlin's own city-façades in the more general sense. Thus he optimistically envisages here a moment of "double consciousness," as Miriam Hansen terms it,[104] one in which the passengers in the throes (or throws) of surface culture can see through their literal transport through the tempo of the age, and perceive—if only momentarily—that the Lunapark's rollercoaster backdrop of the 1928–1929 season was as false as so much of Weimar culture, and that the "façades were only façades."

Indeed, one can only hope for as much visionary self-empowerment for today's masses who go to the postmodern era's version of the Berlin Lunapark. Our ultimate rollercoaster is Las Vegas's Manhattan Express, which opened in 1997 at the New York–New York megahotel and casino complex, treating passengers to a ride (and a 67 mph, 144-foot dive) not against a screenic backdrop but around a *three*-dimensional skyscape of New York covering twenty acres: a supra-reality journey that has, in effect, lost its surface two-dimensionality, and is hence a backdrop no more.[105] Koolhaas's description of turn-of-the-century Coney Island as a "foetal Manhattan" is surely even more apt for Las Vegas's millennium experience of the Big Apple skyscrapers at one-third the size.[106] We may well wonder how Kracauer's persistent Brechtian faith in the sensible self-consciousness of the viewer can be maintained here at all, especially after the last century's tidal wave of technological development, one that moves unstoppably toward the totalizing absorption of the viewer's initial suspension of disbelief before the image.

It was due to the potential untrammeled infinity of such experiences that the scriptwriter Carl Mayer, in a pre-Debordian moment of antispectacle, took offense at Ruttmann's *Berlin* documentary for being nothing more than a negative-technical "surface configuration"[107]—that is, for concentrating on symphonic-machinic movement rather than exposing, for example, class differences and the sufferings of the actual people who live below the sheen of Weimar surface culture. The Ruttmann film (originally Mayer's idea, and with orchestrated music especially composed by *Potemkin*'s composer, Edmund Meisel) is indeed an aesthetics of pure surface, and for all its parallels to Vertov, taking film out of the studio and onto the street itself, it lacks the pointedly moral dialectic of (say) Murnau's *The Last Laugh* (*Der letzte Mann*) between light and dark, surface and depth, high and low, or rich and poor. As Sabine Hake states, Ruttmann's "structuring principle was simulation, not representation; his ultimate goal was visual pleasure, not critical analysis. . . . *Berlin* brings to perfection the fetishization of spectacle and specularity but does so without critical awareness."[108] Kracauer's argument against *Berlin* is that it is precisely a film of surface forms rather than political content: "Ruttmann leaves the thousands of details unconnected, one next to the other."[109] *Berlin* signifies for Kracauer's socialist sensibilities nothing more than a symphonic void: "It is just as blind to reality as any other feature film."[110] For all this, however, Ruttmann's montage-work still counts as a landmark achievement not just of the silent film era but of the entire first full century of film. In this low-budget film, funded by American money, Berliners loved to see their capital reflected as the "world-city" it had so recently become, and it was precisely *Berlin*'s ordered harmonies and contrapuntal reflections (that is to say, all the things that Kracauer found fault with) that proved so flattering and self-promotional to Weimar audiences fixated on surface culture.[111]

THE WEIMAR MOVIE PALACES: FAÇADES ON FAÇADES

Along with the surface irrealities of the film-set experience, Kracauer's second and equally crucial major target in the Weimar film industry, in the essay "Cult of Distraction" ("Kult der Zerstreuung"), appearing one month after "Calico-World" in the *Frankfurter Zeitung* in 1926, is the actual cinematic event staged by the newly built premiere movie palaces, particularly in Berlin, as they emerged out of cinema's lowly origins in the show booth (*Schaubude*).[112] No surface phenomenon was better suited to house and to project these collective fantasies than the grand film palaces, which were the most significant and most numerous public building enterprises of the entire Weimar Republic, particularly during the relative prosperity of the stabilization period of 1924 to 1929.[113] Never before or since in the history of cinema has there existed such a joint offensive of, as Kracauer so aptly phrases it, "atmospheric bombardment" (*Stimmungs-Kanonaden*),[114] launched by the movie palace's architecture at the unsuspecting viewing public.[115] Indeed, for Kracauer at least the same philosophy of "*surface splendor*" (*Prunk der Oberfläche*) informed and designed both the Babelsberg film sets and the cinema buildings' exteriors and interiors.[116] This was the cult of distraction that the new urban masses of modernity demanded and enjoyed nightly. The Ufa "film palaces" (*Filmpaläste*) or "light-play houses" (*Lichtspielhäuser*) were the Weimar mass equivalent of Wagner's Wilhelmine Bayreuth Festspielhaus, with such corresponding, often neoclassical names as Marmorhaus, Universum, Titania-Palast, Gloria-Palast, Mercedes-Palast, Capitol, and Babylon.[117] Their names were echoed in the movie palaces built across the country. These movie palaces (at one to seven RM a ticket, compared with seven-tenths to two RM for the smaller theaters)[118] helped create a mythology of the cinemagoing experience that warranted for Kracauer the abusive epithet of a schematized *"effect-ridden total work of art"* (a neo-Wagnerian *Gesamtkunstwerk der Effekte*), or "pseudo-totality" (*Scheintotalität*).[119]

Yet today we are in a position to look back at the innovative effects of the now-lost era of the Weimar movie palaces with fascination rather than Kracauerian distrust. First, it is worth stressing the sheer power indicated by the nighttime moviegoing experience of Weimar Berliners, which can be likened to the scene, from Lang's *Metropolis,* of the gigantic underground power plant. When the machine explodes, Freder's hallucination reconfigures its façade into a Moloch, the child-swallowing Old Testament god of the Ammonites and the Phoenicians, monstrously devouring its sacrificial workers. The scene is also clearly a reference to the Gods' entrance into Valhalla in Wagner's *Das Rheingold.*[120] Just as Kracauer pointed out that in the age of the mass ornament workers would inevitably seek out those media of entertainment which most closely resembled their work environments, so too the mouth of the devouring Moloch-machine into which workers are led parallels the electrically lit entrance of the movie palace, into which the new white-collar employees would stream, blissfully unaware, in their leisure time (fig. 38).

The threshold of the lure, or filmic attraction, was the actual façade constituted by the entrance to the movie theater. The façade of the building that housed the filmic product was promoted to the status of film itself.[121] As Curt Moreck remarked in 1926, the public needed something spectacular to lift them from the working life and into the entertainment realm; it was natural that the visual street language spoken by the movie theater, with its huge posters and electrically lit titles, would correspond to this need: "The street is the real world of the man from the masses, and the movie theater belongs to the street. . . . You enter it directly like a shop in which there are goods for sale, you enter it with aroused nerves from the tumult of the street, with eyes blinded by the glaring ads, with a soul made dull and heavy from everyday life."[122] For Kracauer, the lure of the *Kino,* for poor and rich alike, is based on the prerequisite of the public's bored idleness.[123] In the essay "Boredom" ("Langeweile," 1924), Kracauer grudgingly acknowledges the power of filmic advertising on the exterior walls of the film palaces to satiate the void of the modern human spirit:

> How could . . . [the spirit] resist these metamorphoses [of the movie theater]? The posters swoop into the empty space that the spirit itself would not mind pervading; they drag it in front of the silver screen, which is as barren as an emptied-out palazzo. And once the images

Figure 38. AEG advertisement for cinema apparatus (1923).

> begin to emerge one after another, there is nothing left in the world besides their evanescence. One forgets oneself in the process of gawking, and the huge dark hole is animated with the illusion of a life that belongs to no one and exhausts everyone.[124]

In this reflex response to an unconscious call to fill the spiritual "empty space" created by the very crowdedness of modern city living, the Weimar film industry followed its American partners and began to recognize cinema advertising (*Kinoreklame*) as a serious business. In the art of advertising on the movie palaces' façades, the general urge was to make a display window of the theater's façade, or a department store out of the body of the building: in short, to commodify and fetishize the film product at the site of its reception.[125] The use of electricity, of technologized movement, of as much glitz and glamour as possible, proved the most effective means of enticing the passers-by. Rudi Feld's Ufa-Palast façade design for the popular revue film *Das Girl von der Revue* (dir. Richard Eichberg, 1928) was one such "moving poster" (*Bewegungsplakat*) that far outdid any American counterpart of the day: the giant-sized legs of the Tiller Girls moved mechanically over the heads of passers-by (fig. 39).[126] Film advertising on the façades of the premiere theaters thus went beyond billboarded posters to reproduce wherever possible the technologized movement of the film images within.

Electrically enhanced film-façades were the most powerful and immediate means available of selling the film to the public. Light, after all, could transform the most lowly of small provincial cinemas, or it could make the audiences forget the fact that Ufa had gone bankrupt in 1926 and had had to be bailed out by Hollywood. "Harsh lights pull one across the street," comments Döblin of small, working-class movie houses.[127] In suburban or provincial areas with plainer cinema-fronts, electrically lit posters alone would do the trick: the massification technique, with a huge close-up of a New Woman star on twenty posters serially arranged above the entrance of the theater, could effectively create a "glowing façade" to draw the passer-by inside.[128] There were even plans to create a minifilm or advertising trailer showing excerpts from the film in display window areas of movie theaters, such was the realization that the filmic product was a commodity like any other on the Weimar street and had to be presented as such.[129] *Kinematograph*, a trade journal for movie theater owners, proclaimed in 1927: "Film is movement! . . . Our 'wares' are living images, which no one else except us can offer. That is why reproductions of these images are the only things that belong in our 'display windows': a sophisticated selection of living individual scenes, ones that are suggestive and make you curious, without betraying too much."[130] The highest commandment, explained the architectural trade journal *Deutsche Bauzeitung* in 1929, was to achieve the subliminal act of *Blickfangwerbung* (capturing the gaze) so that people would decide there and then (or return later) to see the movie.[131]

As was the re-auratizing case with the neon lights of advertising signs being placed directly over the New Objective façades of Weimar city buildings, it is somewhat ironic that at the very same time the overdone ornamental façades of the Wilhelmine era were being shed, the propagandized art of architectural advertising on the exteriors of movie theaters called for increased levels of complexity in design, particularly for the grand first-run movie theaters. For the much-hyped national premiere of *Metropolis* in January 1927 at the Ufa-Pavillon am Nollendorfplatz (Germany's first

Figure 39. Façade for *Das Girl von der Revue* at the Ufa-Palast am Zoo, by Rudi Feld (1929).

purpose-built cinema, designed by Oskar Kaufmann in 1912 and originally called Cines), the surfaces of the building's exterior and interior walls were spray-painted bright silver and lit up glowingly by night (fig. 40).[132] The gong from the film (from the labyrinthine city below the glittering city-world of Metropolis) was placed above the entrance to the theater. This celebratory event represented a constant tendency among the very best Weimar film-façade designs—namely, bringing the illusionary three-dimensionality of the film image's projected surface out onto the street in real three-dimensional format. As Kaes states of *Metropolis*'s premiere, the "public space" of the movie theater thus "became an extension of the movie set."[133]

Indeed, it is in the performance art of movie palace decoration (rather than in, say, its rather disappointing plot) that *Metropolis* truly corresponded to the sensational vision of the futuristic city contained in its sets and to the original inspiration of its director, who was stunned by the lights of Times Square when he visited Manhattan in 1923. Thus Lang's *Überfilm* succeeded far more in its surface-effects—its architectural cautionary message of the vertical city, its year-long build-up, its opening night attended by the president himself, and above all in its streetside presentation—than as story. Kaes's comment is that "*Metropolis,* the event, clearly overshadowed *Metropolis,* the film."[134] This discrepancy was immediately picked up on by Weimar Germans: a "profound lack of inner form" was the complaint voiced by Willy Haas in his initial review.[135] The

Figure 40. The silver-painted exterior for the premiere of *Metropolis* at the Ufa-Pavillon am Nollendorfplatz (January 1927).

general critical opinion was that *Metropolis* certainly represented surface culture—but not as it had intended. Its storyline was perceived to be an overly ornate, long-winded, moldy old "potboiler" (*Schinken*), as overblown and heavy as the old Wilhelmine "façade culture" (*Fassadenkultur*) that was being torn down from buildings in German cities.[136] Nonetheless, the care paid to its surface movie-palace presentation was deemed very much part of the ongoing "revolution" in the public presentation and reception of films.[137]

An important impetus in this revolutionary transformation of Weimar film qua surface was Rudi Feld. No one could "dress" a Weimar movie palace better than he.[138] Trained as a graphic designer, Feld single-handedly developed the art form of the technologized Berlin film-façade before he was obliged, as a Jew, to leave for Hollywood in 1933. In 1926, Feld was appointed supervising art director (or "propaganda" head) at Ufa, and became a seminal influence in Weimar film-premiere advertising for both the exterior and interior lobby of the grandest Berlin movie theaters.[139] Feld's film-façades obtrusively redecorated the surface of the movie theater. His ornamentation of exterior surface was not so much a contradiction of the Weimar age of deornamentalization as it was the film industry's logical extension of the way *Lichtreklame* was refurbishing the same surface area. Feld brought thereby an unabashed celebration of the cinematic viewing experience out onto the street, in order to entice people to see the film. It was optimistically claimed that in ninety out of one hundred cases, his "gaze-capturing" façades that so aptly reflected the Americanization of the age would inspire those walking by to buy a ticket.[140]

Feld's designs for the front of the Ufa-Palast for the premiere of Lang's *Woman in the Moon* (*Die Frau im Mond*) in October 1929 definitely count among the ultimate in modern visual culture's celebration of film as surface. In this famous film-façade, which rivaled the (rather disappointing) film itself, Feld displayed a sculpted rocket being launched from a three-dimensional skyscraper city that jutted out from the wall of the theater on the lower right side and traveling diagonally up to the moon on the upper left and back down to the city again (fig. 41). A contemporary observer admired in particular Feld's "skyscraper city, whose buildings are lit up from inside; this city, however, is built as a crater, so that a shining rocket can shoot out of it and later return into it."[141] Approximately one thousand twinkling electric stars (light bulbs) illuminated the dark blue backdrop.

Feld's theater façade decorations were at once innovative and yet inconceivable without a preabsorption of the rationale of Weimar *Lichtarchitektur;* he also remained wholly indebted to his era's focus on perceptual psychology (*Wahrnehmungspsychologie*) in architectural design. He boasted, for example, that his three basic construction materials—light, color, and movement—were succeeding if they resulted in causing a traffic jam, with people stopping as urgently as a train driver would break for a wrongly colored light on the tracks.[142] He knew that people would inevitably watch a moving display through to the completion of its program.[143] He could create a unified fantasy design for the theater, based on the images evoked in the film's title; he also recognized when to depend more simply on the single effect of the film's title in monumental electric letters outside the theater, as with *Asphalt.*[144] Creating decorations that reflected the *Stimmung* and regenerated a stylized version of the film itself, Feld saw to it that his displays brought forth an "intoxication" of [electric] color" (*Farbenrausch*) and functioned as a latter-day stained glass window in a church, that is to say, as a post-sacramental, technologically enhanced "sublime."[145] At the premiere of the animal adventure film *Chang,* a four-foot-tall sculpture of a tiger's head glowered with electric green eyes and red jaws above the street entrance to the Ufa-Pavillon am Nollendorfplatz.[146] For the adventure film *F.P.1 Does Not Answer* (*F.P.1 antwortet nicht,* dir. Karl Hartl, 1932), the entire façade of the Ufa-Palast am Zoo was transformed into an airplane hangar; and for the Paramount WWI film *Wings* (dir. William Wellmann, 1929), a sculpted life-size airplane appeared above the movie palace entrance, as if arrested in its fall out of the sky (fig. 42).

Figure 41. Façade for *Die Frau im Mond* at the Ufa-Palast am Zoo, by Rudi Feld (1929).

In a 1930 lecture at an Ufa convention, Feld compared the impressionable mind of his public to a visual wax record—the stronger (newer, more innovative) the film-façade, the stronger the needle's imprint of the image onto the surface of the record (i.e., the human brain). It is a matter, he proclaims, of creating an atmosphere of charged excitement: "Our advertising must make a deep imprint on the wax surface. . . . Before our inner eye there appears, as I term it, an inner photomontage [of the film, suggested by the advertisement]. . . . The public rushing by can only be chained to us if we succeed in projecting the . . . material [of the film] onto the outside world."[147] Like the best display-window designers of the era, Feld understood the nature of the relationship of the life of the street to the façade of the (movie theater or shop) building: "Our public races past our theaters of an evening with a motorized intensity. The same old even lights won't get noticed after a while.—Tonight is a premiere, and so everything is (say) green. We are screening a jungle film. All eyeballs are sensitive to new entities; the cerebral cortexes give the order to stop. Because of the unu-

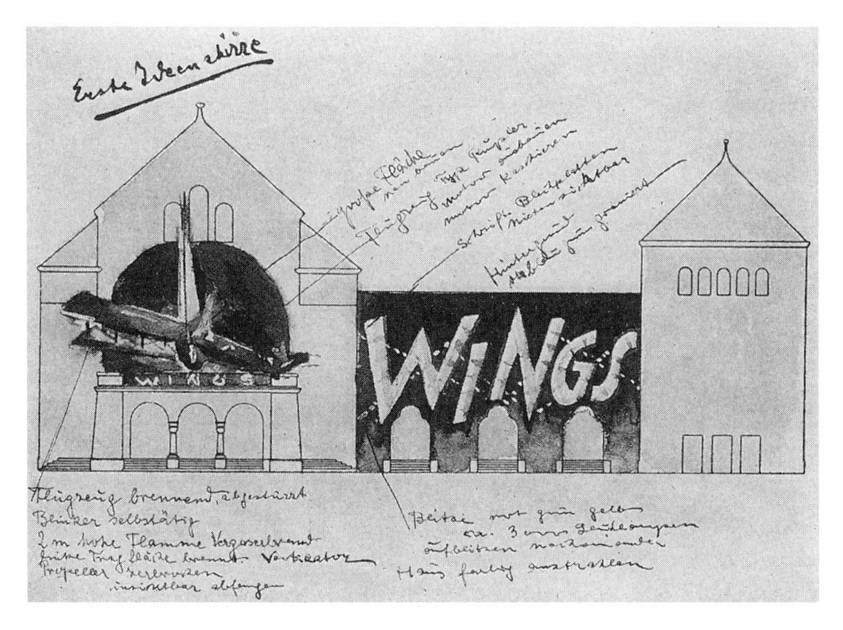

Figure 42. Sketch for the façade advertisement of *Wings* at the Ufa-Palast am Zoo, by Rudi Feld (1929).

sual, curiosity sets in."[148] Asserting that the origin of his art finds its affine in the medieval world of church design, specifically in the grand hourly displays of exterior church clocks in Strasbourg, Prague, or Lübeck, Feld reaffirms the Weimar advertising refrain of *Licht lockt Leute* ("light lures people") and the faith in electricity's ability to create movement in street advertisements, since "curiosity . . . is the angle-worm of our advertising hook."[149] Accordingly, for Lang's film *Spies* (*Spione*, 1928), Feld placed moving panoptic searchlights across the street from a huge eye and the film's title, mounted on the front of the Ufa-Palast am Zoo.

Feld's mesmerizing work amplified the actual architectural style of cinema buildings (termed at the time the "architecture of pleasure," or *Vergnügungsbauten*), which was, in turn, propagandized to more skillfully serve the end-effects of film. Benno, a Berlin film producer in the popular novel of 1930 by Heinrich Eduard Jacob, *Blood and Celluloid* (*Blut und Zelluloid*, 1930), relishes this engulfing intent: as he strolls by the movie theaters clustered around the Kaiser Wilhelm Gedächtniskirche near the Kurfürstendamm, Benno is wholly aware of their propagandistic, technological power, which seems but a continuation of the *Materialschlacht* of World War I by other, entertainment-based means:

> It was from the huge film palaces that the power of the era shot forth into the streets. . . . There the great movie theaters stood temptingly with their fountains of light that danced on their façades. Into their opened sluices they swallowed up the stream of people. . . .
>
> What a phenomenon, never before attained by any theater of any previous age—this pouring in of regiments, of divisions, of armies! Did they come voluntarily? What was will power? Advertising had installed itself into their bodies and souls like gas. . . .
>
> And so they flowed into the palaces, scooped up and in by the tentacles of light, posters, and newspapers. To be pushed before the great gunfire of the projectors. Before the rushing ribbon of celluloid. . . . Their brains were shot through, wounded, and mended again by celluloid cartridges.[150]

"THE TOTAL ARTWORK OF EFFECTS"

Of what, then, was this perceptual onslaught of Weimar filmic surfaces constituted? Beyond Feld's movie palace advertisements, what was the architectural ambience within which the viewing public was destined to absorb the cinematic product? In 1920, there were 218 movie theaters in Berlin; by 1927, the number had risen to more than 350;[151] and by 1928, there were 387, including 33 *Großkinos* (i.e., more than 1000 seats), 31 with 750–1000 seats, and 57 with 500–750 seats[152]—a trend which came at the direct expense of the number of theaters offering only stage drama (*Sprechtheater*). Of 55,000 movie theaters worldwide, 3,600 were located in Weimar Germany. The film palaces occupied a realm of conscious luxury for the masses: Berlin's Ufa-Palast had an orchestra of seventy, while the Tauentzien-Palast had the largest organ in Europe, and both enjoyed air conditioning that blew eau de cologne into the auditorium (a nice touch to round off the *Gesamtkunstwerk* experience).[153] The *Großkinos* belonged mostly to Berlin-West, from the Nollendorfplatz to the Gedächtniskirche (a total of eight cinemas with 7,650 seats), although many poorer Berliners attended the cheaper, unappealing, rather sordid *Lokale* that Kracauer describes in "Cinema in the Münzstrasse" ("Kino in der Münzstrasse"),[154] like the one Döblin's Biberkopf goes to in the Alexanderplatz area of the working-class, Jewish Scheunenviertel after being released from prison. The largest cinema in Weimar Germany was eventually built not in Berlin but in Hamburg: the Ufa-Palast opened with a mountain film in the midst of 1929's depression blues, offering the public 2,667 seats, as well as restaurants, bars, and 150,000 square feet of office space. With such gargantuan dimensions, it is not surprising that the theater was openly marketed as an accomplishment fit to inspire national confidence at a time of crisis.[155]

At their apogee, Weimar movie palaces realized a new level of New Objective architectural attainment. Indeed, it may be said that given the industry housed within and the ability of the Weimar film industry to consider the physical environment of the film's reception as an inherent part of the film's success or failure, the new movie palace type of building was in many ways inevitable.[156] As Paul Zucker and G. Otto Stindt stated in their 1931 analysis of movie palace architecture in Germany and abroad, only in Germany had the "building duty" of form following function (i.e., of actually making the cinema *look* like a cinema) been realized.[157] Part of this functionality was bringing the motion of the city without into the auditorium within: reinforced concrete for interior surfaces permitted heretofore impossible angles and sweeps of plain surfaces, as in Poelzig's gallery for the auditorium of his Deli cinema in Breslau, which dramatically swept along the walls all the way down to ground-floor level.[158]

The Weimar film palace was heralded as the only building form inherently predestined for electric advertising—not just of the film, but of itself qua building.[159] Some of the most spectacular examples of cinematic *Lichtarchitektur* were built in Berlin's suburbs: the horizontally lit Roxy-Palast in Schöneberg (1929), for example, or the Lichtburg (1929), which was appended to a Wedding housing project with an illuminated tower of revolving searchlights. The Titania-Palast in the middle-class borough of Steglitz (1927) possessed a thirty-foot-high tower whose twenty-seven red and pink horizontal bands of light provided a self-referencing index finger pointing to the movie palace entrance below (fig. 43). Poelzig's Babylon cinema (1927), part of a larger housing project to spruce up the Scheunenviertel, was strikingly accentuated by a vertical, star-topped flashing neon sign bearing the cinema's name (fig. 44). All these cinemas demonstrated the by-then-accepted duty of the Weimar film theater architect, namely to create for the benefit of the "very spoiled" city dwellers not just an interesting outer façade for the movie theater, but also "architectonic light effects" by night that could "arouse the curiosity of the passers-by on the street."[160] Accordingly, the ideal movie palace was pure façade, without other preexisting ornamental distractions—a façade that ideally lent itself to the full range of electric transformation. Even provincial cities engaged in this New Objectification of the movie palace experience, as in Wilhelm Kreis's cleansed, yet beckoning, square look for the entrance to the Gloria-Lichtspiele in Bielefeld, built in 1927, with clinker brick and 33 windowpanes.[161] Thus the new pure façade style, in tandem with electricity, liber-

Figure 43. Nighttime view of Titania-Palast, Berlin-Steglitz (1927).

ated the movie palace from its mimetic "poor relation" status vis-à-vis the stage.[162]

Mendelsohn's U-shaped Universum movie palace, which opened in 1928 on Berlin's Kurfürstendamm, most obviously fulfills these tenets. (Rebuilt in the 1980s after war damage, it operates today as a stage theater, the Schaubühne.) The trademark indicators of Mendelsohn's Weimar building style (namely, functionalism with neo-expressionist verve, or *Schwung*) are in full evidence here. Vachel Lindsay's call of 1915 for film to be an "architecture-in-motion"[163] is reflected in the Universum's literal position as a freestanding building on all four sides: its frontal curvature gave the impression of being what it contained, namely (a) motion (picture), rather in the manner of a train, Zeppelin airship, or the *Bremen* ocean liner. "It can and should only be a cinema!" exclaimed the Weimar critic Günther Herkt, because its various parts "are woven together with convincing clarity to an architectonic organic whole."[164] The exterior building (with its smooth walls fit for film advertising, and money-making rented shops along the first-floor level) appeared to the press to be pulled over the auditorium like a second "skin."[165] At the Universum's opening ceremony, Mendelsohn even presented a litany to the pure (but not "dry")

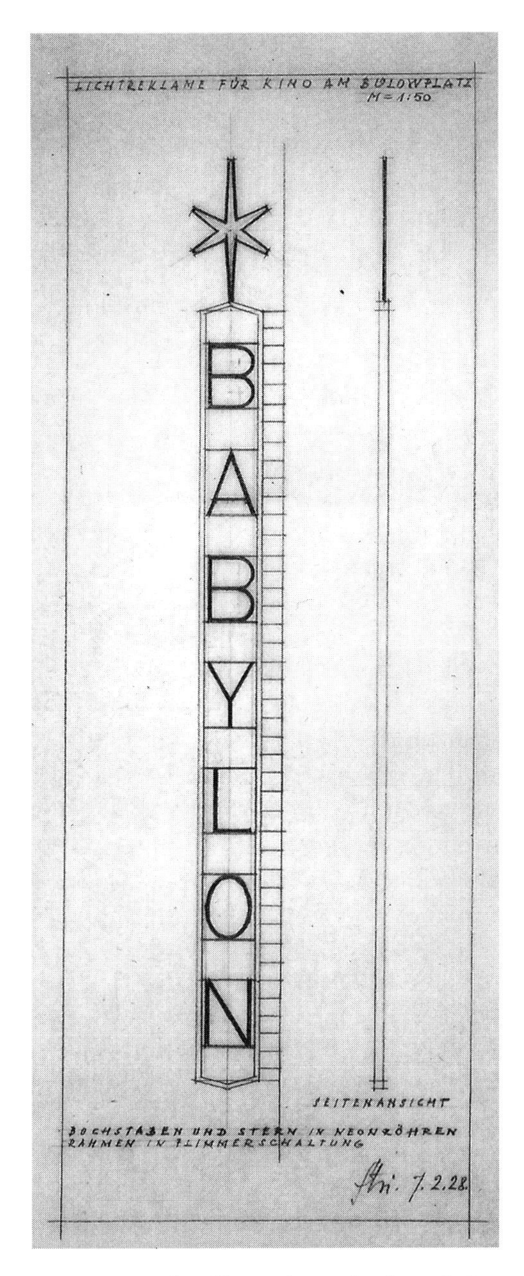

Figure 44. *Lichtreklame*-design for the Babylon movie palace, Berlin, by Hans Poelzig (1928).

functionalism of his building, which was such a true reflection of film as a "theater of movement," designed both to house film and to attract people inside.[166] The "curving ring" of the entrance-cum-lobby, said Mendelsohn in this prose poem, was a (Molochlike) "mouth" that was "gaping wide with floods of light and displays of splendor." But the *Sachlichkeit* of this wholly functional movie theater, was not, he assured people, about to cause "spatial anxiety" (*Raumangst*) in its visitors. Outside, the long line of second-storey windows followed the plain convex curvature of the building; inside, the balcony scooped in concave scimitar fashion, following the same architectonic dynamism but from the other side of the looking glass. Particularly stunning was the use of strong directional lines of indirect lighting (*Lichtrollen*) in the auditorium, which followed the principles of camera technology, guiding the spectator's gaze onward along the (ivory-painted) walls and (blue-lit) ceiling toward the screen at the front, in the same way that flower petals have lines to guide the honeybee to the pollen. As Herkt states of this spatial reconfiguration: "The space itself and every theme of the wall and ceiling apportionment concentrate the eye of the spectator toward the picture surface or stage just as a photographic camera does."[167] It was as if the "process of film projection" had been transferred into the shaping of the building and was taking place in the auditorium before the actual film began.[168]

In this way, the idea of the movie palaces constituting a new purity of building-as-façade extended to the interior as well, for the premier Weimar movie palaces were arenas of absolute functionality that could simultaneously be playfully engaged in what Mendelsohn referred to above as *Phantasie.* Their special position thus liberated them, above all Weimar building forms (even department stores), into a realm of sheer surface projection. By the time the Weimar Berlin spectator entered the lobby and then the auditorium, he or she had already anticipated the film itself in a three-dimensional way, due to the façade on the exterior and the general architecture of light by night that beckoned one inside.

Indirect lighting and the harmonic interrelationship of acoustics with design had been pioneered by Poelzig in 1919, in the Großes Schauspielhaus in Berlin for Max Reinhardt's mass drama productions of *Totaltheater* (i.e., the triple dramatic staging of circus, amphitheater, and cinematically oriented horseshoe theater).[169] With 3,200 seats, it was the largest theater in Europe, with fantastically arranged expressionist vaults and curves, and a sunset-colored ceiling (known as the "stalactite cave" [*Tropfsteinhöhle*]) rising to a dome in the middle above the stage.[170] The techniques Poelzig gained from his experience with this Friedrichstraße building helped mold his subsequent insistence that the interior must promote lighting, color, and acoustics.[171] As Schivelbusch points out, the only problem with the Großes Schauspielhaus was what made it a masterpiece: for its architecture of active, even interfering production (*Inszenierung*), created while Poelzig was designing his *Golem* film sets, was more filmic than dramatic. It was, then, already a movie theater, a "light-play-house" (*Lichtspielhaus*) of intoxicating illusion, without need of a screen. In his subsequent movie palace designs, Poelzig stressed the need for artificial light to be "space-creating" (*raumschaffend*)[172]—something achieved in his Capitol (1925), a film palace whose auditorium thematized how the body of the movie theater containing the "light-play" of film is the belly of the beast into which the spectator must first be lured. The Capitol's interior, which Schivelbusch considers the most "sacred" of Weimar auditoriums,[173] earned the nickname the "green cavern": the only decoration was in the dramatic vertical fluting of the octagonal dome ceiling, which was illuminated by a cover of ninety shooting-star lights. Poelzig realized here his obsession with creating a "sky in architectonic form" over people's heads.[174] It was a process of sensual entrapment via surface means.

The neo-expressionist sacrality of Poelzig's auditorium was, as Schivelbusch indicates,[175] upstaged by a different sort of sacrality, namely the functionalism of the later Weimar years. Schivelbusch also refers to the remarkable altar effect of the Titania-Palast's immense, parabolically undulating half-circles of light around the organ beneath the screen as an "arc of light and sound . . . a light-organ transformed into architecture" (fig. 45).[176] Even the New Objective movie auditorium was thus still a pseudo-church, but that which was to be worshipped was no longer an otherworldly dream-atmosphere, like the fairy-tale themes concurrently found in 1920s American movie palaces,[177] but was instead on a par with the outdoor reality of the busy, technologized city street.

Movie palaces in 1920s America, unaffected by German functionalism, sought predominantly to fantasize and sublate, not reflect and enhance, the metropolis. Ornament was worshipped rather than rejected.[178] Cubist painter Fernand Léger, himself the director of the purely object-focused avant-garde film *Ballet mécanique* (1923–1924), was nonetheless able to rave about New York's escapist movie theaters built in "an unbelievable accumulation of every European and Asian style, chaos on a colossal scale. . . . Hugeness in the game of 'I'm richer than you.' . . . I adore this overloaded spectacle, all that unrestrained vitality, the virulence that is there, even in mistakes."[179] By the early 1930s, the world's largest cinemas were Belloc's Gaumont Palace in Paris, crowned by a famed "light-

Figure 45. Auditorium of the Titania-Palast, Berlin-Steglitz (1928).

fountain,"[180] and the Roxy in Manhattan, which opened in 1927 with 6,200 seats.[181] While Los Angeles and Hollywood boasted G. Albert Lansburgh's fairy-tale palaces, such as the Shrine Auditorium (1925) and the Warner Bros. Western (1931), or Meyer and Holler's Egyptian Theater (1921), it was only in Weimar Germany that the movie palace first emerged as an architectural site that reached far beyond the nineteenth-century stylistic pastiches of world's fair, vaudeville, and stage theater. Kiesler's Film Guild Cinema in New York, or the New Victoria movie theater in London (1930), were examples of German design abroad, but they were the exception, not the rule, to an otherwise motley crew of decorative palaces on Anglo-American soil.[182] Belated art deco versions of the German New Objective innovations of the 1920s would not appear on Anglo-American soil until the 1930s and 1940s, during the years of cross-over influence from German-Jewish exiles; this was especially true as far as movie palace design was concerned.[183]

The German subjective arrangement of use-oriented space, however, its new combination of functionalism and myth, was something that Kracauer could not accept. The all-too-evident power of the interiors of the Berlin movie palaces galvanized him into resuming his antisurface tirade: indeed, movie palace interiors were worthy of both Kracauer's greatest attention and greatest suspicion. His well-known complaint in his "Cult of Distraction" essay, written in the wake of the 1925 openings of the Gloria-Palast and the Capitol, is that these interiors fill the minds of spectators with a false sense of unity and wholeness that is not well suited to the fragmented social and industrial reality outside. This is why he distrusts the "glittering, revue-like creature [that] has crawled out of the movies—*the total artwork [Gesamtkunstwerk] of effects.*"[184] As Nietzsche had complained in *The Case of Wagner,* the actual value of art was put aside in the frenzy of all the special formal effects aimed at the senses. Increasingly, Kracauer sounds like Nietzsche attacking the nationalistic, feminizing,[185] theatrical art inherent in the Wagner cult;[186] both share a repugnance at the downside to the effects of mass art. Kracauer is indicating here just how easily architectural effects may take over from function and structure, which were the components of the Bauhaus's parallel credo for a building as a "total work of art." Kracauer finds this entire visual support system to be based on the repressive delusions of Socratic rationalization, combined with the decadence of Wagnerian excessive display. Audience addiction to the entire movie palace infrastructure is for Kracauer an Apollonian coverup for the underlying Dionysian darkness, or void, of modernity: "The interior design of movie theaters serves one sole purpose: to rivet the viewers' attention to the peripheral, so that they will not sink into the abyss."[187] When the "white surface descends" and the film begins, the spatial film ends: "The events of the three-dimensional stage blend imperceptibly into two-dimensional illusions."[188]

Hence Kracauer, neo-Kantian and *Mündigkeit*-oriented,[189] is, in a fundamental way that anticipates his post-WWII stringent realist stance, profilm but anti-*Kino:* film "should be wrested from every three-dimensional surrounding, or it will fail as an illusion."[190] But, as with his critique of Weimar's mass ornament, Kracauer is not so much targeting the "display of pure externality" (*Entfaltung der puren Äußerlichkeit*)[191] in the auditorium—for this remains his accurate representation of the Weimar age—as he is attacking the false sense of wholeness and the sacral that is being recreated within these walls, indicating socially reactionary forces at work in the reception of film. He finds it only fitting that those most in need of distraction, the masses of Berlin, must relieve their workday "tension" and that "this need can be articulated only in terms of the same surface sphere [*Oberflächensphäre*] that imposed the lack in the first place."[192]

Moreover, while it is undeniable that a New Objective version of the *Gesamtkunstwerk* was underway in Weimar Germany's combined acme of movie palace exteriors and interiors and their concomitant product, silent film—even in their most functionalist examples—it is by no means automatically also the case that this act of visual intoxication and superficiality was inherently evil or protofascistic. Kracauer's assertion that the interior design of the new movie theaters necessarily led to "*reactionary* tendencies" is less than fully convincing.[193] His argument certainly works best when applied to the baroque interiors of the Gloria-Palast, for example, or the Piccadilly, and less well when applied to the sheer celebration of dynamic motion in the interiors of the Capitol, the Universum, and the Titania-Palast, which were truly Lindsayesque "architecture-in-motion." They did not detract from the film, as Kracauer complained; rather, the cinematic effect was intensified by the fiercely directional "light architecture" within, which drove the spectator's gaze constantly toward the destination of the film's projection, namely the screen. Even as the spectator arrived, say, in the foyer of the grand Mercedes-Palast in Berlin's working-class Neukölln suburb, he or she would be led in by the smooth curvature of the walls and the starlike lighting to the stars on the screen within. Moreover, the dynamic, functionalist style within accurately mirrored the streamlined façades of the street without, a facet demonstrated by the auditorium of the Gloria-Lichtspiele in Bielefeld, with its brown walls that lightened as they ascended into a domed ceiling of red and blue.[194] Indeed, Weimar film became a "total work of art" but in a manner true to the new surface culture, not contradicting it toward a prior state of wholeness as Kracauer would have us believe.

The single-feature film screening, along with its varieté acts during the silent film era, was thus couched in a setting that was equally and vitally a part of its production and distribution; indeed, as Kracauer complains, the film-text itself was but part of a "larger whole."[195] The whole was a multimedia event incorporating strobe lighting and a literally "orchestrated" musical anticipation of emotional response. Beyond the actual architectural event of the film's presentation were yet more features aimed at enhancing the illusion but occluding self-awareness: the movie palaces' advertising façades on the building exteriors and further gimmicks in the foyers, the film industry's star cult (in such manifestations as photos of the stars on collectible stamps, to be put in fans' albums), souvenir film programs that laboriously explained the entire narrative of the film and much of what went into the making of it, prerelease press hype in film trade magazines, and the mass distribution of film stills in the popular illustrated magazines for mostly female readers.[196] The age of the *Großfilm* had thus given birth to its three-dimensional equivalent, the systematic and rival presentation of the same by the movie theater as a *Großkino*.

It is precisely this architectonic systematization of mass entertainment that so alarms Kracauer.[197] His comments on the Berlin Lunapark, as a parallel Babelesque site of organized entertainment for the masses, go so far as to invoke military motifs of crowd control: the Lunapark is a place where searchlights are aimed—luckily—"not at enemy aeroplanes" but at the attractions; the marching rhythm of the military music accompanying the light shows "inwardly illuminates" the audience; and the trapeze artist is "caught in the crossfire" of the white beams of the searchlight. The inspiring *Stimmung* of the film auditoriums or the Lunapark, where entertainment could literally conquer all, spread equally to Potsdamer Platz, where Kempinski's Haus Vaterland on Stresemann Straße, known as "Germany's largest coffee-house" with its myriad theme restaurants and movie theater, could transport its willing customers to multiple fantasy realms. One commentator described an American visitor to Berlin as "beaming like a movie theater façade on Broadway" when told that Haus Vaterland contained the famed Rhine Terrace restaurant, which had a filmic panorama of the Rhein appearing at the back of the room every hour, to the accompanying crashes and flashes of thunder and lightning effects.[198]

CINEMA AND THE SECULARIZATION OF RITUAL

An undeniable social tension arising from the new architectural presence of the Weimar movie palaces was felt nowhere more strongly than in the area surrounding Berlin's Kaiser Wilhelm Memorial Church. Preceding the movie palaces as competitors with the Gedächtniskirche were the grand Wilhelmine department stores nearby, especially the Kaufhaus des Westens on the Wittenbergplatz, the fame of which helped confirm the elegant Ku-Damm as the most cosmopolitan shopping area of Berlin-West. In a rivalry unknown to the New York Broadway scene, the Gedächtniskirche became increasingly surrounded by and thus marooned amidst the nation's premier cinemas (Ufa-Palast am Zoo, Capitol, Marmorhaus, Tauentzien-Palast) and other prominent new commercial buildings. Together this secular collection formed a New Objective generation of Tautian "city crowns" (Kracauer referred to them facing off like "proud castles of the Dardanelles"),[199] coming into direct competition with the church's traditional role of housing the collective soul. Indeed, when Kettelhut drew a draft of the cathedral dwarfed by skyscrapers for the *Metropolis* film set, he may well have been replicating this tension between the Gedächtniskirche and its surroundings. Proponents of surface culture wanted to make this part of the city into the "Broadway of Europe"[200]—in his book *The-*

aters and Movie Palaces (*Theater und Lichtspielhäuser,* 1926), Paul Zucker praised the opening of Poelzig's Capitol that same year as the "superlative of our citified life, pulsing with our rhythm, the truest expression of our time"[201]—but opponents hated the yellow exterior ("the yellow peril" [*die gelbe Gefahr*])[202] of the Haus am Zoo that housed the cinema itself, and favored the Tiergarten's trees over what they despised as the "superfluous stone boxes" of commercial architecture.[203] The owners of the Capitol complained that the city's strict regulations (based on the 1920 cinema law [*Lichtspielgesetz*] requiring local governmental permission for outdoor advertising on movie theaters)[204] prevented them from using advertisements as they wanted to on the building's front, thereby rendering the "entire shape of the façade . . . *useless*" and destroying its entire "purpose" for existence, which was to bear *Lichtreklame.*[205] Even Poelzig himself was drawn into the fray, bemoaning how such restrictions could bring about the loss of his Capitol's intended "unified façade" of electric light.[206] Despite these compromises, the Capitol succeeded in stepping forth from its relatively camouflaged position onto the more noticeable street front of unified electric architecture alongside the Gedächtniskirche.

Of all the cinemas around this church, however, the Gloria-Palast was the site of the greatest controversy, due to its location just opposite the church's main entrance and its own preexisting "Mozart" architectural style.[207] Opened as a cinema in 1926 after being remodeled from Wilhelmine luxury apartments in 1925, the Gloria was publicly heralded as Germany's post-Bayreuth *Festspielhaus* for the modern age, and rather than the New Objectivity style of most of the new premier film palaces, its auditorium was remodeled in full prefunctionalist splendor so as to be less offensive to the neo-Gothic church across the street. Accordingly, the Gloria was expressly forbidden to change any exterior stones in the neobaroque exterior or decorate the façade with pictorial or textual advertisements. Nonetheless, Ufa tried many times to repeal this decision, asserting in its letters to the local building code enforcers[208] that the Gloria ought to strive to keep up with Berlin-West's international "world-city image," and not interrupt the continuity of the electric façade flow all around the church.[209] While Ufa's plans to create an enlarged, multistorey front window for electric advertising were adamantly rejected by the "building police" (*Baupolizei*), the latter did reluctantly allow lettering on the rooftop and in the twelve (unaltered) front windows, where the twelve letters of the theater's name were permitted to appear (fig. 46). The Gloria's architects complained vociferously (but in vain) to the city that while the neigh-

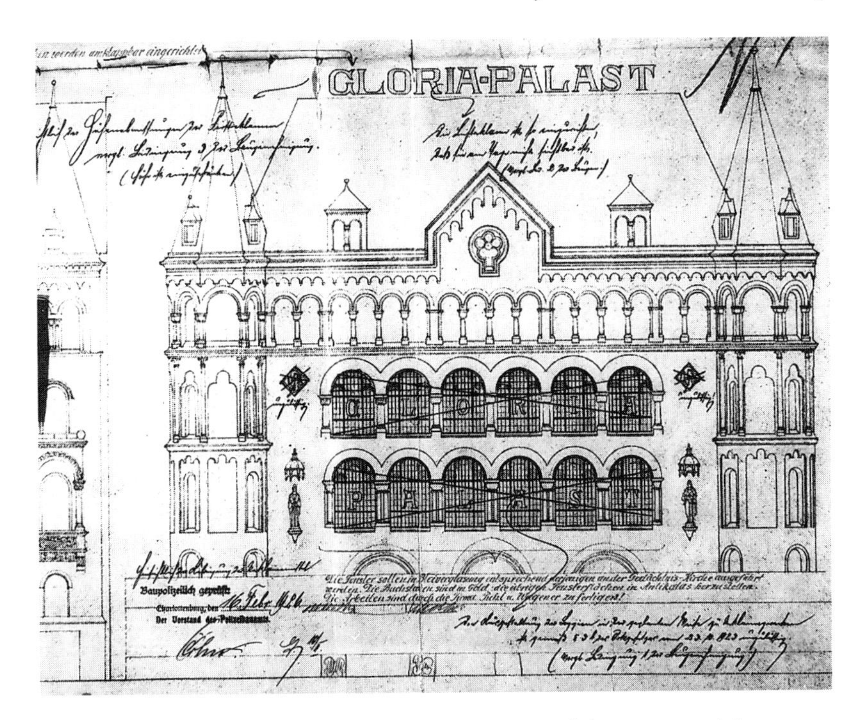

Figure 46. Architectural plans for the modernization of the exterior of the Gloria-Palast, Berlin (1926).

boring premier theaters Ufa-Palast am Zoo, Marmorhaus, and Capitol had all been allowed to use "enormous advertisements" with multicolored, flashing, moving light displays, the Gloria had been singled out for the most conservative of controls.[210]

The Gedächtniskirche as a lonely island, with the streets all around it unified through the electrification of façades—indeed, the entire sociotopographical rivalry between movie palaces and conservative controls—became the subject of commentaries across the political spectrum. Josef Goebbels's text of 1928, "Around the Kaiser Wilhelm Memorial Church" ("Rund um die Gedächtniskirche"), is an obvious Nazi manifesto against the bright lights of Weimar modernity, setting up the Gedächtniskirche as a pillar of morality that mourns what the noisy corruption of Berlin-West has destroyed, and railing against the "spirit of the asphalt democracy" and the "most repulsive pseudoculture"—a surface world that is populated, he says (unsurprisingly), by Jews.[211] Here Goebbels is exaggerating the traditional conservative fear that our understanding of aesthetics itself would be undone by the street's "invidious" new forms of commercial beauty, as Henry James wrote in 1904 of the emergent bidding war between churches and display windows in Manhattan.[212] The journalist Hermann Kesser, writing for the *Berliner Tageblatt* in the same year as Goebbels, likewise points to the architectonic demise of the glow of religious faith at the hands of the more powerful (and hence godly, Faustian) man-made light:

> Between electric advertising, dancing, beer, silks, and delicatessens stands the Gedächtniskirche: bare, speechless, and faded. Tossed around by the carousel-path of the mob of automobiles. A silent pale old man, the church stands beneath the moon's crescent.
>
> The eye of God stares at it. Not from the heavens but from a theater façade. It's a real godly eye, a monstrous eye, triangular, like the ritual eye in Christian imagery. It throws huge beams of light to all sides. It shines on the façade of a film palace. With captivating light it twinkles into the rows of streets.[213]

Kracauer, on the other hand, in an essay called "Picture Postcard," finds a subtle, unspoken victory in the church's nonparticipation in the surface game. His text parallels those of Kesser and Goebbels to the extent that he also portrays an isolated Gedächtniskirche under a veritable siege from the cinema lights, but he promotes instead the gentle atmosphere created by the church's *own* secretive light as an unintentional reaction to the competition all around:

> The secretive glow [of the Gedächtniskirche] is in reality a reflex. Reflex of the light façades that, from the Ufa-Palast to the Capitol, make night into day. . . . The house-high glass columns of light, the bright overlit surfaces of the movie palace posters, and the hubbub behind the mirrors of gleaming neon together undertake a campaign . . . against the emptiness. . . . [The lights] roar, they drum, they hammer against the crowd with the brutality of madmen. An unrestrained flashing by no means serving advertising alone, but which is over and above that an end in itself.[214]

He finds in the church's emitted *Glanz* (a luster variously described as faint, secretive, and mild) a "reflex" of, or counteractive "reflection" to, the harsh *Glanz* of the light façades on the movie palaces all around it—a sheen that is as unrelenting as that of Mies' glass skyscraper. Like the excess functioning of the Tiller Girls as mass ornament, the palaces' spectacle of light has gone beyond the profit-margin of advertising to being an "end in itself" (*Selbstzweck*); while the gently sparkling glow from the church serves neither of these, but is instead a "protest against the darkness of our existence."

Here the disingenuousness of Kracauer's nostalgic antimodern position against the spectacle of commodified light becomes increasingly transparent. After all, as Kracauer noticed, it was the movie palaces, "those optical fairylands," that were "shaping the face of Berlin" more than any other buildings.[215] In "Street Without Memory," he both dislikes and yet finds himself drawn to the tasteless, overly bright lights of a café on the Kurfürstendamm that is there one night and gone the next due to the economic instability of the times.[216] While his Weimar writings are generally beholden to the *Glanz* of Berlin-by-night, as he iterates in the essay "Seen from the Window,"[217] his "Picture Postcard" piece offers an auratized image of the Gedächtniskirche as sole remnant of a different source and function of light as indicator of interiority (versus the excess light-as-exteriority all around it). As Hansen states of Kracauer's account of the lonesome Gedächtniskirche as "waste product," the "luminous façade of the obsolescent site of interiority becomes a surface for remembering (Kracauer puns on the name of the church), a public screen or, less grandiose, a picture postcard inviting us to project what is being eclipsed, however undefined and unspectacular."[218] Yet what is most indicative here of Kracauer's blind spot is that he does not consider the innate correlation of the Gedächtniskirche's light-induced *Stimmung* in the city turmoil to the worshipful strategies employed by the cinema auditoriums (strategies that he himself examines in "Cult of Distraction").[219] He supports worship-inducing light when applied as unction to the city street, but condemns the same when used in the movie palaces, which are de facto churches for a desanctified age.

Kracauer's emphasis on the godless sacrality of communality induced by the movie palace, its emptying-out of religious ritual yet parading of its outer vestiges in order to fill the metropolitan void, is echoed in his insistent allegorical positioning of the Weimar luxury hotel (like the Hotel Adlon on Unter den Linden). In "The Hotel Lobby" (part of the posthumously published work *The Detective Novel,* written between 1922 and 1925), he writes extremely negatively about the surface spatiality of hotels and their effects on their denizens.[220] He critiques the hotel lobby for being the decentered topos of surface, for being a "negative church" of distraction—thus, by implication, very much like the movie palaces in their stand-off with the Gedächtniskirche, but even more exaggeratedly so, for the only ritual performance in a hotel lobby is the one in which all spectators continually participate as both actors and spectators in real time. In parallel step with the function of the cinema for the masses, the hotel lobby is the spectacular "setting" (*Schauplatz*) allowing the rich and those who feed off or attend to the rich to ride the wave of surface culture in vitro.[221]

A hotel lobby, states Kracauer, houses not individuals but mass ciphers who come and go, who unreflectively enjoy their status as "marionettes of *ratio*," even in their state of idleness:[222]

> Remnants of individuals slip into the nirvana of relaxation, faces disappear behind newspapers, and the artificial continuous light illuminates nothing but mannequins. It is the coming and going of unfamiliar people who have become empty forms [*Leerform*] because they have lost their password, and who now file by as ungraspable flat ghosts [*plane Gespenster*]. If they possessed an interior, it would have no windows at all, and they would perish aware of their endless abandonment, instead of knowing of their homeland as the congregation does. But as pure exterior [*bloßes Außen*], they escape themselves and express their nonbeing through the false aesthetic affirmation of the estrangement that has been installed between them. The presentation of the surface [*Darbietung der Oberfläche*] strikes them as an attraction. . . . they allow themselves to be bounced off a proximity that they themselves have conjured up: their monological fantasy attaches designations to the masks, designations that use the person facing them as a toy.[223]

These strong words are a more philosophically informed version of Dr. Otternschlag's depressive recognition of the hotel lobby's soulless emptiness in Vicki Baum's bestselling novel of 1929, *Grand Hotel* (*Menschen im Hotel*).[224] They demonstrate Kracauer's emotional resistance to the surface-play afforded by the hotel lobby and movie palace auditorium alike: an essentially nonludic yet infinitely autotelic vortex, a spatial aporia producing only the empty nihilism of infinite self-representation. Since the environment of the hotel fosters, like a greenhouse, hermetic "pseudo-life," mere ersatz supplements for the world outside, Kracauer adduces that he cannot lend his support to such a "false aesthetic situation."[225] At the site of the hotel lobby, surface culture adumbrates only itself, and for this Kracauer cannot forgive it: "The aesthetic that has become an end in itself pulls up its own roots; it obscures the higher level toward which it should refer and signifies only its own emptiness."[226] In the 1928 essay "In the Luxury Hotel" ("Im Luxushotel"), he sardonically reflects on the nonboundary between glamorized film versions of hotel guests and their real, yet surface-bound, counterparts: "The question is merely whether they have emerged from the screen to enjoy a fleeting existence, or whether the films are created after their image. It almost seems as if they live only by the grace of an imaginary director."[227]

Small wonder, then, that Kracauer thought so highly of Murnau's *Kammerspielfilm*, *The Last Laugh* (*Der letzte Mann*), which takes up the topography of the hotel (qua movie palace) as an illustration of the over-valorization of Weimar society's surfaces at the expense of inner-directed beliefs and practices. A huge poster of the film's antihero, an aging hotel doorman played by Emil Jannings, was hung on the exterior of the Zoo movie palace (fig. 47): ironically, this advertisement depicts the film's own last man as much, much larger than life, certainly more imposing than the tiny, real-life last man left standing before the poster. In a key scene shot from behind an interior glass wall of the hotel, as if to signify the public nature of his humiliation, the elderly doorman is demoted by the manager from his usual proud position, standing by the glass lobby doors of the luxury hotel Atlantic, to the lowly job of restroom attendant, hidden away in the basement. But his entire life had been focused on his former position, both in his actual positionality in the hotel and more obviously in his glamorous military-style doorman's uniform.

Where Jannings's character was happiest was standing at the energy-center of the hotel—by the iconic revolving door that separates lobby from street, and through which the camera boldly tracks.[228] The beginning of the film tirelessly stresses the location of the revolving glass door as gateway to the vibrant surface culture both of the street without and of the wealthy hotel denizens within, just as Baum's *Grand Hotel* ends on the note of the hotel door's continual revolving motion, so as to indicate how the door takes symbolic precedence over any merely human events. As doorman, Jannings's protagonist proudly guards and conducts this scene of entry and exit. Karl Freund's camera reflects this surface-synergy as it takes pleasure, as Lotte Eisner first remarked, "in opalescent surfaces streaming with reflections, rain, or light: car windows, the glazed leaves of the revolving door reflecting the silhouette of the doorman dressed in a gleaming black waterproof, the dark mass of houses with lighted windows, wet pavements and shimmering puddles."[229]

The luxury hotel entrance in *The Last Laugh* is posited as a self-reflexive reference to the movie theater lobby—the equivalent luxury building for the white-collar workers watching this film. The doorman, in his uniform, is empowered to stand at the point of entry to this world of fantasy. The Berlin movie palaces, like the hotel in this film or like Haus Vaterland, offered the Weimar viewing public only an illusory splendor. This splendor is of course the lure of the movies per se, but it is all the more poignant in a film based on the collective anxiety of a "lowest/last man" after the German defeat in World War I and the inflation crisis of November 1923, dressed as he is in a uniform that is a Wilhelmine throwback. He stands as the harbinger or literal embodiment of urban surface splendor, of the lure

Figure 47. Movie palace façade for *Der letzte Mann* (dir. F. W. Murnau, 1924).

of the movie palace. And this is what he is forced to lose when he must hand in his hotel uniform and work in the hotel's basement lavatory (with its own, rather more humble, swinging doors),[230] then return symbolically naked, without the loan of surface in his public role, to the labyrinthine depths of his private existence in the working-class tenement building.

This "last man's" schizoid division between hotel and tenement calls to mind Kracauer's critique of a department store publication that boasts that the environment of the store actually improves the chances of its employees climbing the social ladder—especially the store's lighting, in the form of a trickle-down or torrent effect (*Lichtflut*) on the employees who live in dark, dingy apartments. But Kracauer thinks the rationalized lighting is more likely to befuddle the employees' judgment: "The light blinds rather than illuminates."[231] Hence the hotel porter's theft of the uniform to wear for his daughter's wedding, and his subsequent ridicule at the hands of family and neighbors after he is found out as a man pretending to the role of glamorized surface after he has lost it. Only producer Erich Pommer could reinstate him (for the sake of the film's export to American audiences),[232] in an unbelievable ending of Surface Regained, as the fluke recipient of a millionaire's fortune.

The two nightmare sequences of *The Last Laugh,* both masterful uses of the then-new subjective camera, are suggestive in their parallel shifting of the architectural perspectival ground that had previously provided the doorman with his diurnal position in Weimar surface culture. As if to clearly state that the stability of his world has now gone, he has a guilty vision of the massive hotel's façade moving threateningly toward him (and us, the viewers) as he creeps away down the street after having stolen his own former coat—an effect achieved by the camera at low angle. Also, in a drunken vision, he dreams that his (private) tenement block and (public) hotel façade blend into one distorted structure, wherein the hotel's revolving door rises to gigantic (again, threatening) stature: this time, however, the dream permits him to exist as a tiny cog within the logic of the massive doorway. Here the dream corresponds to the film's spatial dialectic: it was noticed right away in 1924 that these two massive structures, both of which were built actual-size on the set by Murnau's architects, Herlth and Röhrig, were inversely related social spaces (*heterotopia,* to use Foucault's term)—the tenement is the "interior façade" of the doorman's life to which the hotel provides the exterior, hence it is only logical that the two become sublated in his moment of intoxicated stupor.[233] Through these interspliced spatial discourses, then, Murnau's film provides us with a vital illustration of the incessant feedback loop of Weimar cinema as it narcissistically represented itself in all visual stages of public unveiling, and as the key player in the era's cult of surface distractions. The entire culture of Weimar film production and reception was modeled around this same conceptual notion.

This chapter has sought to present evidence that when Weimar surface culture went to the movies, it produced a visual excess that in key experiential ways far outdid our own contemporary film culture. We share today an acute sense of having lost an era of cinema when the film itself was but one player in a whole host of visual signifiers, all connected to the experiences of evening *flânerie* and urban distraction.[234] The death of this optically celebratory era occurred on several levels: the introduction of sound film at the end of the 1920s; the redirection of collective architecture toward serving only the Nazi state in the early 1930s; the literal destruction of the movie palaces in the bombing of German cities during World War II; the subsequent tearing down or closure in the 1950s and 1960s of most of those movie palaces that remained from the Weimar era; the postwar electronic fragmentation of movie reception into TV, video, and home viewing; and, ultimately, in Europe and even more in the U.S., the advent of suburban movie theaters, and the increasing loss of the downtown street and its promenading public as the nexus of the urban experience.

There is nonetheless some recent indication that today's multiplex cinemas are in fact seeking to reinvent the Molochlike lure of the Weimar movie palaces of old—or at the very least, movie theater chains are now cognizant of the public's reemerging desire to enter the world of film through the very grandest of big-screen formats. The Austrian architectural firm Coop Himmelb(l)au's glass-façaded "open body" concept of 1994 for the UFA Cinema Center in Dresden,[235] for example, bears an uncanny resemblance to Gropius's Bauhaus design for the Total Theater: amidst an emancipation of enclosed space, the spectator outside is constantly invited thereby to become a spectator *in*side, where he or she first enters a transparent (hotel-like) lobby before finally sitting within the opaque inner "skin" of the actual film auditorium. In the U.S. (especially in Southern California and Las Vegas), multiscreen theaters, now increasingly located in shopping malls, clearly emphasize the theme-park nature of the experience by including virtual-reality game rooms, roller-skating tracks, and Disneyesque restaurants in their floor plans; they even recreate in their designs the Egyptian, art deco, and Chinese styles of American movie palace architectural excess from the 1930s.[236] Post-Wall Germany is following the American example and currently undergoing a massive building program of multiplex cinemas—that is, many auditoriums housed under one roof, such as at the new Potsdamer Platz—as if consciously remodeling the communal collective experience forged by the *Lichtspielhäuser* of the 1920s. This time around, however, the new boxlike structures are a far cry from Kracauer's palaces of architectonic distraction, appealing to the masses through the technological luxuries of filmic reception, namely high-tech sound and projection systems.[237] It would seem that Rudolf Klar's question of 1928, whether the "ideal movie theater" could ever be built,[238] whether the ultimate filmic mass ornament could ever be fashioned, is now being resurrected for the twenty-first century.

4 The Display Window

Designs and Desires of Weimar Consumerism

Kniefrei und Sportfrisur
Radio und Film
Auto und Flugzeug
Bananenspezialhaus und Warenhauskonzern.
Denk nicht das sind Äußerlichkeiten.
Die Innerlichkeiten stehen dahinter.
Erich Mendelsohn

THE PHANTASMAGORIA OF SELLING

"For now we see through a glass, darkly; but then face to face: now I know in part; but then shall I know even as also I am known."[1] It has been a Platonic-monotheistic article of faith that our material lives are spent in the realm of mediated shadows, removed from beholding the incorporeal immediacy of essential truth.[2] This structure of epistemological dispossession clearly originates in an age Before Consumerism. For industrial modernity transformed human perception; the growth of capitalism has been predicated on creating at least the promise of a definitive self-empowerment for the consumer, who simply has to consume in order to attain insight. In order to combat such surface intoxication, Karl Marx sought to redefine the production process away from the magical, emancipatory fiat implied by the commodity fetishism of glass-covered display. In the hope of deconstructing the aestheticized field of vision, Marx applied the metaphor of phantasmagoria—a term invoking both feverish, fantastic, associative dreams as well as the magic-lantern sequences of the beginning of the nineteenth century, which hid the technique of their art using back projection—to represent consumerism's hold over us in our cavelike "mist-enveloped regions of the religious world."[3]

Marx's analysis of the "fetishism of commodities" in *Capital* (1867) refers to how, under capitalism, commodities are made mysterious and their use value, or origins of production, are obscured by their exchange value.[4] This act of phantasmagorical veiling-over constitutes for Marx an act of fraud: the surface cult of commodities thus distorts the way people understand social relations and working conditions behind the production of objects. In fetishizing (masking) the commodity by means of advertising and display, capitalism gives the consumer the impression that the existing social conditions are unchangeable. Accordingly, commodity aesthetics are by nature a fraud, or con (following the sense of *consumption* as "to destroy, to use up, to waste, to exhaust");[5] mass consumption is a front created to cover up the pitfall of overproduction. Worse yet, this facilitates for Marx only a false consciousness in the alienated worker and the consuming public.

This phantasmagorical world of commodities finds its musical correlate, as Theodor W. Adorno suggested, in the Wagnerian *Gesamtkunstwerk:* both give out a surface impression of wholeness wherein the alienated and commodified "dreamer encounters his [her] own image impotently."[6] Adorno shares Marx's focus, which permits no interest in any active fantasy or autonomous play on the part of the consumer standing before and relishing the goods on display precisely *for* their exchange value—as Benjamin does, in contrast, in his acknowledgment of the strength of this signifying dreamworld in his *Arcades* analysis of modernity.[7] One might compare Marx's missionary stance concerning the power of commodities with Sigmund Freud's explanation of totemism in *Totem and Taboo* (1912–1913): here, Freud deems the animistic relationship to things to be mentally ill, manic, and narcissistic: by extension, then, goods on display come alive at the expense of the humans observing them.[8] Benjamin is more susceptible to consumerism's totemic powers: in *One-Way Street* he cites Baudelaire in an epigraph: "I never pass by a wooden fetish, a gilded Buddha, a Mexican idol without reflecting: perhaps it is the true God."[9]

The strictly Marxist viewpoint does not wish to appreciate how the late nineteenth century, the first era that celebrated industrial display, also effectively brought about a proletarization of commodity desire: for the first time, all classes were encouraged to enter the department store,[10] to attend the world trade fair, to gaze at the display windows. As Balzac wrote: "The Human Comedy gave way before the comedy of cashmeres."[11] For Marx this would amount to no more than a surface freedom in the inauthentic culture generated by capitalism, since all consumers are passive before the cannibalesque spectacle. Marx's resistance notwithstanding, there is today also the notion of capitalism producing active possibilities of carnivalesque festival in the distribution of goods. Social theorists Colin Campbell[12] and Mike Featherstone believe in such an "aestheticization of everyday life,"[13] one which is active, hedonistic, even transgressive in its ways of consuming postmodern culture, rather than being consumed by it; in short, there is and can be such a thing as a dandyism or *flânerie* for the masses. According to this more affirming view of consumerism, suggestive of an infinite circle of Nietzschean self-creation via an aestheticization of everyday life, goods offer themselves as artworks not just for sale but also for use in people's fantasies, in the production of a lifestyle.[14]

Marx's lost bid is the gain of the unknown photographer who appears reflected near the bottom center of his 1929 photograph of a display window (*Schaufenster*) on the Kurfürstendamm in Berlin (fig. 48). The interrelated reflections in this photograph suggest a self-conscious celebration of the workings of the phantasmagoria—the very opposite to any fixed limitations on human visuality in the world of material goods. In addition to the auteurial tripod, the window also shows a striking reflection of one of Berlin's most elegant movie theaters across the street, the Gloria-Palast. The silhouette of the well-known Gloria, its baroque style remodeled from grand Wilhelmine apartments to an even grander "light-play-house" (*Lichtspielhaus*) in 1925, is shown in the center of the window and is framed by theatrical curtains, suggesting that the building opposite and the films it presents are as much a commodity to be possessed by the gaze as are the cascading silks and laces in the window itself. Beyond the transparent pane of glass, a buddhalike feminine model, from whom all the luxurious cloths emanate at rhythmically varied, curving angles, appears as if she were part of the reflected façade of the Gloria-Palast, or even a player in one of its films. All the spectators of this scene—the moviegoer and the window-shopper, like the photographer and the viewer of the photo—are knowing parties to the two viewing systems of desire projected by the glass, that of the cinema and that of the storefront objects. Parallel in time to the new exhibitionism of the technologized art work of film came the historical rise of the display window exhibiting its wares. Neither cinema nor *Schaufenster* existed to distance themselves from the viewing public or to be shrouded in secrecy—they were there, as Benjamin stated, to be seen and understood by the masses.[15]

This kinship is neatly demonstrated in the fact that for the premiere of the popular film *Casanova* of 1927, the Gloria-Palast itself became a display window of sorts, when Rudi Feld, head of advertising for the Ufa film company, decorated its foyer and auditorium with draped silks, soft lighting, pearls, and perfume, all distributed to emulate the film's romantic atmosphere (*Stimmung*). Like a window showing off its wares, the movie palace's decoration was intended as a direct lure, as a "luxurious casket holding within a valuable jewel" (i.e., the film itself).[16] It was the strategy

Figure 48. Display window opposite Gloria-Palast movie palace, Berlin (1929).

of Weimar consumerism to lead people far (in their imaginations, at least) from their prior realm of blind shadows and into a world of light-play, where purchasing desire equaled consumer insight when the purchase occurred. According to the logic of modern advertising, that which lies projected behind the glass pane or on the film screen was not to be understood as a mirror of empty illusionism, but as modernity's legitimization of the masses' right to democratic self-expression via the plays of specular spectacle.

The layerings of surface upon and within surface, as featured in this photograph's artful doubling-effect of goods displayed both behind and in front of the window,[17] invite a series of reflections not only about Plato's cave,[18] but also about consumerism in the interwar German metropolis. Weimar display, as in the Latin root for the term (*displicare*), was an act of unfolding, spreading out, in the sense of constantly calling attention to itself as the Kracauerian epithet of "surface glamour" (*Oberflächen-glanz*).[19] The act of buying, based as it was on the display art of selling, became a prime arena of the surface condition, as K. Michael Hays realizes in his study of modern architecture's relation to twentieth-century modern and postmodern aesthetics: "As consumers we are dispersed outward across the exteriority of the fields of signs or aesthetic surfaces (what Walter Benjamin called wish-images) that are the immediate result of collective modes of production, of which the individual subject, like the individual article of consumption, is a *decentered effect*, and to which bourgeois individualism, illusionism, and interiority cannot lay claim."[20] Moreover, as Peter Wollen has emphasized, visual display pays attention to the "other side of spectacle"—the exhibitionist realm of production, designer, and agent—rather than to the purely scopophilic realm of reception, viewer, and patient. The narcissistic strategies of (self-)presentation within which visual display encodes itself should be understood, as Wollen indicates, not just "in terms of the image, but in terms of the symptom" as well.[21] With these points in mind, what follows in this chapter is a reconnoitering of the designs and projected desires of modern German consumerism as they were played out to the utmost in the setting of the display window. In the Weimar display window, the distinction that Lefebvre draws between the spatial metaphors of the "space of representation" (that of department stores) and "representational space" (that of advertising) merges into one.[22]

The build-up to the Weimar *Schaufenster* era was predicted in 1896 by Georg Simmel, when he noticed the "shop-window quality of things," "a new synthesis between the principles of external stimulus and the practical functions of objects," promoted by the nineteenth century's series of world trade fairs.[23] Simmel's confident account of the new ennobling of products according to their surface aesthetics is an apt precursor to the American retail analyst Paul Mazur's influential book *American Prosperity* (1928), which announced that goods were good, and that consumption equaled emancipation, the American Dream, and the "satisfaction of desires."[24] And Marx, especially, was aware of the very special sheen lent to goods in the new display culture of capitalism: "The busiest streets of

London are crowded with shops whose show cases display all the riches of the world: Indian shawls, American revolvers, Chinese porcelain, Parisian corsets, furs from Russia and spices from the tropics; but all of these worldly things bear odious white paper labels with Arabian numerals and the laconic symbols LSD [pounds, shillings, pence]. This is how commodities are presented in circulation."[25] In these observations, not just Mazur but also Simmel and Marx are themselves "products" of the (French) nineteenth century's fundamental transformation of the identity of the urban consumer from the old elite to the new masses: Martin Jay notes how, at this time, the "ocularcentric spectacle of desire" based on the royal court was transposed away from Versailles to the bourgeois commodified zone of the Paris city street.[26] To denote this shift, Benjamin quotes Victor Fournel's Haussmannization-era remark on the degradation of the Parisian *flâneur* into the *badaud,* the deindividualized gawker or gaper who is wholly of the masses,[27] and who is by implication predicated on a recasting of the consumer from male to female.[28]

In order to fully enter into the consumerist sphere of the Weimar Republic, we must first suspend awareness of our post-Fordist, postmodern condition of "overconsumptionism," to use Mike Davis's term.[29] It is Jean Baudrillard who, resting on Guy Debord's antispectacle hyperbole while simultaneously dispensing with its revolutionary capacity, effectively deconstructs the major activist tenet behind the Marxist critique of commodity fetishism, namely that the distortion of the original use value of goods by their capitalist exchange value can be overcome.[30] Whereas for Marx, in the age of industrial modernity, commodity aesthetics is a transparently fake system of representation to be defeated in favor of the truth of the opaque object, for Baudrillard in the postmodern age the only thing that still exists is the exchange value of the commodity form (Baudrillard terms it "sign value"), a medium that perpetuates itself in an obscenely totalizing hegemony in Euro-American nations and beyond.[31] Unlike Marx and other pious "'alienists' of consumption,"[32] Baudrillard, extending Debord's emphasis on spectacle as the "social relationship between people that is mediated by images,"[33] argues that in late capitalism the sole accurate measure has become the mediation of these images: it is how goods *signify* (or *play*) in the spectacular play of exchange that they acquire meaning, and in no other way can consumerism be understood: "In this way a washing machine *serves* as an equipment and *plays* as an element of comfort, or of prestige, etc. It is the field of play that is specifically the field of consumption."[34] Or again, as Baudrillard asks in *The System of*

Objects, his Barthesian first book (1968): "How is the 'language' of objects spoken?"[35] Commodities thus acquire a completely stylized identity that is more immediate and all-determining than any original use value might have ever been. In a "reality that is absent" and a hyperreality that is overpresent, consumption increases and goods multiply without limit, in order to compensate, Apollonian-style, for the terrible "*lack*" of truth beneath the surface.[36] It is precisely this conspicuous, overly fecund presentation of signifying commodities that Baudrillard targets: "Those are our Valleys of Canaan where flows, instead of milk and honey, streams of neon on ketchup and plastic."[37]

What Baudrillard does not consider, however, is the important space of Weimar modernity, which arose between Marx's time and his (our) own as a space in which the first grand era of a truly mass-oriented consumerism was already being born. Already in the 1920s and hence before the rise of postwar electronic mass media, that which Celia Lury terms the aesthetic "stylization of consumption" (i.e., the creation of a popular lifestyle via consumable goods) was firmly in place.[38] Thus we begin to suspect that the "society of the spectacle" condemned by Debord in 1967 (a spectacle since deemed by Baudrillard to be abolished)[39] began much earlier—in the 1920s,[40] in fact, when exchange value's triumph over Marx's sacred cow, use value, became so definitive in the U.S. and in Europe's most Americanized counterpart, Weimar Germany, that its insignia swiftly became the leading denominators of sociocultural meaning for the masses. In 1923 the Marxist critic Georg Lukács belatedly warned against the consuming public's spiritual entrapment, or reification (*Verdinglichung*), by the phantasmagorical fraud that commodity fetishism could enact on them;[41] by then, viewers of the urban spectacle were already convinced they were full participants in advertising's transparency for all.

Indeed, in the stabilization years, 1924 to 1929, Weimar commodity display was at its zenith, both in its relation to avant-garde design and in its ability to engender the desire to buy in the passing consumer. The display window became recognized as a major direct-marketing lure, in many ways outdoing even the print medium;[42] city workers window-shopped when they could—in the evening—and most purchases made by women occurred after work, between the hours of four and seven o'clock.[43] The store window, in particular, as the primary mise-en-scène of the designs and desires of Weimar consumerism, was host to the daily (and especially nightly) acts of seduction that occurred on the city street. Display window architects like Frederick Kiesler recognized that window design was the major location in which the "invigorating stimulus" of the medieval bazaar could be re-created for the modern urban era that had lost its open market places.[44]

But the window's power is a power now lost—or at best, reminisced over. Today, even if we are city-dwellers, most of us no longer have a street-based field of reference for the visual power that the display window once occupied as a vital emblem of Western modernity's own cult of surface. As a recent *Tagesspiegel* article complains, Berlin's celebrated culture of the display window was lost not so much to the bombs of the Second World War as to economic shifts in the ways of presenting of consumer goods; and besides, the social problems of the contemporary inner city work against the inviting, lingering, after-hours principle of display windows and their arcades.[45] Virilio, in *Open Sky*, denotes the window as "long since replaced by the telesurveillance screen," and even the latter is now being ousted by the "*gateway*" of cyberspace.[46] Occasionally, perhaps, we can catch a glimpse of modernity's show window as a once-heady locus of design: in the summer of 1995, for example, during Berlin's heady weeks of Christo and Jeanne-Claude's Wrapped Reichstag—a thoroughly postmodern artwork that yet celebrated surface in a way that harkened back to the more perambulatory nature of the modern city experience—the display windows of the Ka De We department store became, just as temporarily as Christo's effect on the city of Berlin itself, a pale shadow of their former Weimar selves when they humorously reflected the surface artist's efforts with mannequins and boxes wrapped in Ka De We's own matching silver material.[47]

THROUGH THE LOOKING GLASS

It was the age of vitrification, the new glass culture, that fully unleashed capitalistic display as such and permitted exchange value to signify itself freely to the consuming public. As Benjamin writes in the *Arcades Project*, the second half of the nineteenth century became the era of glass architecture and its allegorical amplification of light and display.[48] He stresses the era of the great department stores, which, with their rows of display windows and grand "light-courts" full of ready-to-wear and mass produced items, brought about an innovative totalization of the labyrinthine space of the older glass-roofed arcades with their small shops.[49] Paris's *grands magasins*, reports Benjamin, were the "last coup for the *flâneur*"—before his demise at the *flâneuses* of consumption—and heralded the emergence of a generally feminized state of *flânerie*.[50] Emile Zola, in his novel *Ladies' Paradise* (*Au bonheur des dames*, 1883), tells how Mouret, the capitalist owner of the actual Magasin au bon Marché, has enslaved women consumers in his department store, and is in turn enslaved by his love for a *vendeuse* in his own store, namely Denise.[51] It is Denise's female/poor "victory" over the male/rich domain of the machinery of modern consumption (which otherwise, at least in Zola's naturalist logic, subjugates women, the poor, the bourgeoisie, and the nobility alike as addicts of the surface-cult of consumption)[52] that is suggestive of how the department store itself, as the new social space of shopping, was from the outset acknowledged as a site of fluid opportunity for all.[53] Joining in Zola's victorious tone, Benjamin saw in these Mammon-temples of Baudelairean urban *ivresse*[54] the birth of the crowd as subject: "For the first time in history," he writes, "with the founding of the department store consumers begin to experience themselves as a mass. . . . In this way the magical and spectacular element of trade rises quite incredibly."[55]

The highest rate of department store openings in Germany occurred during the 1890s, several decades after equivalent growth spurts in France, England, and the United States—a fact reflective of Imperial Germany's belated accession to the new organizational structure of the retail trade.[56] The 1897 Wertheim department store on the Leipziger Platz, designed by Alfred Messel, grew to be the largest in Europe (after its remodeling in 1927, it measured over a million square feet on a ground surface of approximately 270,200 square feet, which was twice the area covered by the Reichstag)[57] until its destruction in World War II. Wertheim had an outer façade of about 1090 feet on the Leipziger Straße, a line defined by massive granite pillars and windows which facilitated a view inside the store from the street. Architectural critic Adolf Behne pointed out how the play of transparent glass surfaces was the essential key to the new spatiality invoked for whoever entered the Wertheim store—not only in its multistorey display windows and its grand street entrances, but most effectively in the light-court or light-well (*Lichthof*), designed by Messel in 1904, reaching five storeys to a glass roof:

> But here . . . there arose a new type [of store], a bold, light frame of pillars, between which enormous glass walls captured a sea of light. The inner light-court is clear, transparent in its simple organicity, and of lovely living brightness in all aspects. A severely oppressive weighty structure has been done away with overnight, and an original form, a totality, can breathe. The magical healing has a charming effect, as does the bold opening of the wall, which has still had only a corrupted connotation in contemporary design, having being identified simply with "façade."[58]

The light-court, initially introduced in Paris to combat the fire hazard of gas interior lighting,[59] gave consumers a sublime respite from congested urban conditions, replicating for modernity in the same way as did Paxton's Crystal Palace the emotional effects of the interior of a vaulted "pseudo-cathedral."[60] Messel's light-court was regarded as a supreme advertisement of Wilhelmine capitalism—to be rivaled, in turn, by the Tietz department store at Alexanderplatz (designed by Cremer and Wolffenstein in 1912), the light-court of which was deemed so vital that it invaded the space of the street with its exposed curvature.[61] The light-court was thus deemed the "representational space" of any modern department store.[62]

The art and industry of display windows emerged out of these new areas of light-design with increasing confidence.[63] Already by the 1880s, huge plate-glass windows had been introduced to American department stores, all the better to reflect the demands of mass merchandising to show off phantasmagorical products to passers-by.[64] Such massification in window-design was introduced to Germany by the Tietz store on the Leipziger Straße in Berlin (1900), which had a huge double window-façade, designed by Bernard Sehring, at the store's main entrance—it was four storeys high and measured sixteen windows across (58 by 86 feet). Major department stores boasted up to forty display windows each. Competition was rife and frantic between major stores for top display-window designs.[65] Turn-of-the-century stores asserted their status and reputation according to the size of their display windows: in 1901, Hans Schliepmann critiqued the current opinion that measured stores' creditworthiness by their degree of "glass luxury."[66] Amidst great protest during the first decade of the twentieth century, Germany dropped its churchgoing prescription that store window displays must be covered on Sundays.[67]

Concomitant with the deployment of window design was the emergence of a new professional identity, the *Schaufensterdekorateur* (today: *Schauwerber*), or the French *étalagiste,* both of which imply a certain intended artistic dignity (one thinks here of the German silent film industry's term for set designers, *Filmarchitekt*).[68] Compare this to the 1920s American term, "window trimmer"! In 1907, the German Werkbund organized a conference on "The Decoration of Shop Fronts"; by the same year, there were three schools for "window trimmers" in New York and Chicago. From 1909 onwards (save for a hiatus during World War I) there were annual display window contests organized by the Berlin retail organization (Verein Berliner Kaufleute und Industrieller). Various associations of display window decorators were formed in Germany, reflecting the fact that practitioners received higher pay than in any other employee branch of retail: Verband künstlerischer Schaufensterdekorateure (1913), Verband der Schaufensterdekorateure Deutschlands (1919), Verein Berliner Schaufensterdekorateure (1920). Display artist Elisabeth von Stephani-Hahn is credited with developing the art for Wertheim at the turn of the century, and she wrote the first book on the subject in 1919.[69] In 1925, the national organization of window dressers (Bund der Schaufensterdekorateure Deutschlands) was founded, and by 1930 two-thirds of Germany's six thousand window dressers were members.[70] 1928 witnessed the first international congress of window dressers, in Leipzig.

The Weimar display window was immediately understood as a vital, interactive, spatial membrane along the newly streamlined façades of metropolitan buildings.[71] Alongside other strata of urban display, like *Lichtreklame* on building façades, the *Schaufenster* was ideally situated as a powerful point of interconnection between product and potential buyer. Because it alone provided a literal link between the wares inside and the consumers outside, the display window of a department store (or of the first floor of an office block) became during the functionally obsessed mid-1920s the defining motif of the entire building: the expositional interface between inside and outside now commanded the logic of structure.[72] Already in 1913, one duly impressed German commentator stated: "At the boldness of the architectural thought of making the display window in this way into the major motif of an entire building and giving glass the character of a monumental material, one should have the greatest respect." It amounts to a "complete sublation of the wall" (*vollständige Auflösung der Wand*).[73] Not just the wall, indeed: expressionist Paul Scheerbart's prediction was that the end of the window as it was then known was nigh in the coming age of glass architecture.[74]

Most striking is the comment by Benjamin that the huge pane of glass of the display window with its insistent electric lighting can have no "aura," no "secret": it could be, in short, only pure surface.[75] Here, the modernist drive to rationalize architecture and cleanse culture of old, inauthentic decoration ironically entered a revolving-door scenario: for glass architecture was from its outset, in the world of Parisian *grands magasins*, an advertisement (and hence a future ornament) waiting to happen. Glass culture brought with it the potential for a new re-auratization, reenchantment, or monumentalization of the art work—an insight shared by Benjamin, the expressionists,[76] and Baudrillard,[77] alike. One thinks here of Bruno Taut's expressionist design of 1919, the fantasy glass "Monument of the New Law,"[78] which functions inadvertently like a film or display window and hence as an apposite pre-site of Weimar exhibitionism: Taut's glass tower, with its revolving, Zarathustran-inscribed tablets of sheer glass, lit by night in bright colors, is designed to entertain and edify the public walking outside it.

Evidently, the impetus behind the surface renovations of modern architecture was in many respects a desire to have buildings fulfill machinic principles and a will to harness the power of technology in architectural form. Taut's image of a heavily guided public gaze through the looking glass intersects nicely with a trade advertisement of 1929, "The Display Window—The Key to Success," for a window display marketing firm, Wezel & Naumann (fig. 49): according to the promotional logic of this ad, it is the *raison d'être* of the *Schaufenster* to facilitate the public's "natural desire to see the goods" and awaken not just "buying desire" (*Kauflust*) but actual purchases from those who gaze upon (but apparently not through) it. This potentially panoptic and disciplinary applicability of glass's crystalline qualities[79] (even if utilized only in the direction of advertising) can be situated in tandem with Michel Foucault's ultimately bleak assessment of Jean-Jacques Rousseau's and Jeremy Bentham's shared universal "dream of a transparent society, visible and legible in each of its parts, the dream of there no longer existing any zones of darkness."[80] It has been noted of London's Crystal Palace that it gave people precisely what they wanted: a combination of surveillance with spectacle, an airy reversal of the panoptic principle whereby everyone could see (the commodities) rather than be seen.[81]

Likewise, Scheerbart's utopian expressionist manifestos and imaginary architecture promote a severe purification of space and a new social hygiene through light: to wit, Scheerbart claimed that in the glass houses of the future no (Kafkaesque) "vermin" (*Ungeziefer*) will be possible once the "bacillus of brick" has been superseded.[82] Such a comment triggers an alternative contemplation of Kafka's "Metamorphosis" as a vision of an already panopticized and bureaucratized culture, one that the protagonist resists by becoming vermin and literally leaving his "traces" across the floor, ceiling, and walls of his bedroom.[83] Indeed, Hitler himself was inclined to believe in the totalitarian applicability of the *Schaufenster:* he made a speech in the first year of his regime about the "cultural mission" of German commercialism, a call which was duly interpreted by Paul Mahlberg, architect of Berlin Tempelhof airport, to mean that the educational duty for all teutonically true store windows was to mobilize the consumers' gaze into a collective, always cheerful "vigor" (*Tatkraft*).[84]

Nonetheless, glass also causes any implicit agenda of mass surveillance to somehow slip up, because glass, as an ostensibly nonauratic agency,

Figure 49. "The display window—the key to success." Advertisement for display windows made by Wezel & Naumann (1929).

causes a condition of spectatorial reenchantment, and continues to engender reactions that consistently go beyond the uniquely rational sphere. As Wolfgang Schivelbusch has iterated, the re-auratizing *Glanz* of glass tends to interfere with (even as it is harnessed to serve) mass suggestion; as a gateway between interior(ity) and exterior(ity), it possesses the ability to reflect an unreality beyond its material existence.[85] In this way, consumerism's imagination-oriented dictum of the incitement to buy, as paraded in window design, gave to the new glass culture of retail the very thing that both Benjamin and Kracauer[86] found missing from modern architecture's attempted transformation of the domestic living space—namely, a certain warmth, imagination, and desire of occupancy that yet did not return to the old surplus ornamentation of the Wilhelmine era. Rather, consumerism harnessed glass as a key medium of the Weimar modern.

Such acceptance of what may be termed the display window principle was certainly lacking in the 1935 retrospective on Weimar culture penned by Weberian philosopher Ernst Bloch, *Heritage of Our Times* (*Erbschaft dieser Zeit*). Here Bloch attacks the requisite "*emptiness*" and "*deceit*" within New Objectivity, specifically the "voiding of the soul, the commodification [*das zur Ware-Werden*] of human beings and things,"[87] and doubts the existence of *any* ultimate value of this reveal-all kind of "'New Objective' façade of nickel and glass. Nothing is behind it except dirty laundry: but precisely this is to be covered up with glassy openness (in the way that much light only serves an increase of darkness)."[88] An advertising trade journal, *Die Auslage,* unwittingly makes Bloch's point in its own illustrated cover design of 1928 (fig. 50): here we see the massification of people as commodified items according to the ad's four tenets of display window decoration, namely organization, advertising, sales techniques, and display window decoration (*Organisation—Reklame—Verkaufspraxis—Schaufenster-Dekoration*), which are listed beneath the four transparently walled storeys of the building's façade. The illustration strongly suggests that the success of the department store of the lower storeys and the office of the upper is wholly dependent upon the totalizing, symmetrical organization and visible display of everyone's position and movement, be they consumers or workers. For Bloch, who remained a staunch minority supporter of expressionism even when such architects as Taut or Mendelsohn had transformed their expressionist desires into New Objective functionalism, this kind of arrangement is a front showing only the "honesty of the foreground."[89] He abhors how the puritanical "light," "brightness," and "clarity" of this façade culture "denote the part for the whole, the display window for the store" itself.[90]

Yet it is the Weimar era's "glassy openness" so detested by Bloch, this factual opening-up of interiority, that most closely depicts Friedrich Nietzsche's preferred way of representing the modern material world, a world where (Dionysian) depth is released precisely within the playful arrangements of its (Apollonian) surfaces, illusions, and lies;[91] it also best depicts Kracauer's stated technique of reading depth into a given era by means of the culture's inconspicuous "surface-level expressions" (*Oberflächenäußerungen*).[92] The advertising magi of the Weimar Republic knew just how to heed the viewing desire of the public, the onlookers of modern glass culture, for more than just a voided-out machinic space; in this way, the newly deornamentalized façades were *re*decorated with the new ornaments that

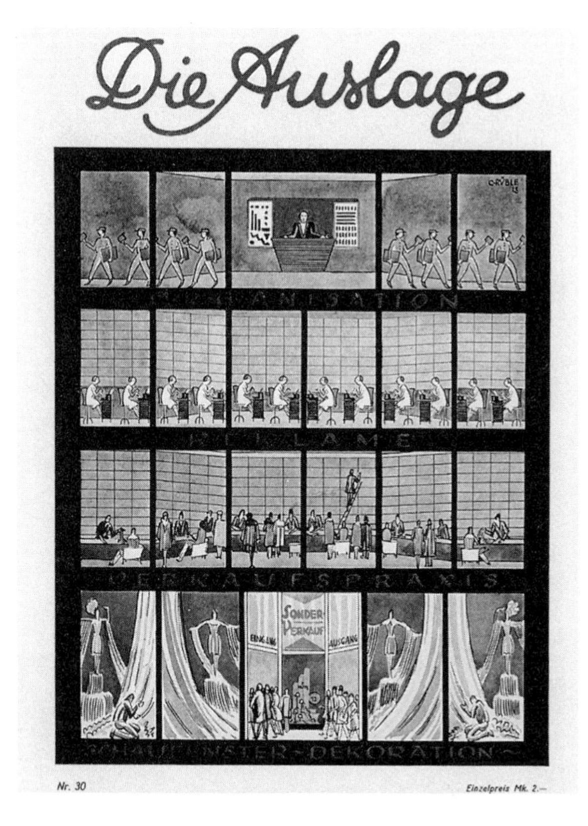

Figure 50. "Organization—Advertising—Sales Techniques—Display Window Decoration." Front cover design for *Die Auslage* (1928).

best fit the functionalism of the Weimar age. The gravity and transparency of the new glass culture were duly leavened with the special (yet organized) effects of electric advertising, billboards, posters—and above all, display windows. The effect, then, of paring down all the elements of the building according to functionalist minimalism was, in the case of the display window, to focus attention more absolutely on the commodity itself. During the Berlin in Light week of 1928, the breakdown between inside and outside was such that the Ka De We store dissolved any distinction between window design and façade decoration on the building's outer wall, with huge electric ladders and electric dolls rising up from street level, showing people the (literal) way to the display of dolls (the results of a public competition from the previous summer) on the third storey (fig. 51).[93] The window itself thus became the space in which such surface-play

Figure 51. Façade decoration for a doll show at the Ka De We (Kaufhaus des Westens) department store, Berlin, during the Berlin in Light week (October 1928).

could occur—the creative arrangement of its contents signaling the "climbing out of the glass," the "fleshing out" of the glass room by the human element, as called for by an angst-ridden Kracauer.[94]

In addition to the liberal critics' misgivings about the new glass culture, there were some stronger resistances to the Weimar display-era's overt commercialization of the gaze. The Nazis were especially swift to assign to Jews the relevant blame for the morally degenerating aspects of mass consumerism. A constant anti-Semitic theme of Nazi publications during the Weimar years was that department stores were an "oriental bazaar," a hegemonic swindle run in tandem with large banks by Jews.[95] The non-Jewish head of the national department store association, Althoff, was derided as a *Reklamegoj*.[96] Even as early as 1903, one of Oscar Tietz's major reasons for founding the Verband Deutscher Waren- und Kauf-

Figure 52. "Every new department store—a thousand destroyed existences." Anti-semitic caricature in *Der Angriff* (1928).

häuser e.V.[97] was self-protection for department stores, not just against taxes and the rigid antifire measures of the building code enforcers (*Baupolizei*), but against anti-Semitism. The racist reaction of small retailers asserted itself officially in 1932, before the end of the Weimar Republic: the association founded by Tietz was forced out of the national trade organization after Hindenburg signed a law in March of the same year to protect small businesses against department stores.[98] And in 1934 a law (the *Verordnung zur Durchführung des Gesetzes zum Schutze des Einzelhandels*) was passed to prevent any new building of (the by-now synchronized, or *gleichgeschaltet*) department stores in Nazi Germany. Indeed, Hitler's sixteenth point in his 1920 NSDAP manifesto already demands the "immediate communalization" of department stores.[99]

All this is not surprising if one examines 1920s Nazi caricatures of the purported Jewish control of large-scale retail: "Every new department store—a thousand destroyed existences," announced a cartoon in the Nazi newspaper *Der Angriff* in 1928 (fig. 52). Here the Jewish department store owner stands before the entrance to his store (Tietz-Wertheim-Karstadt combined, but mostly resembling the main entrance to the 1905 Tietz store at Alexanderplatz), his monstrous body having gorged itself on the consumption habits of the masses, and displays this self-enrichment in architectural display, for the Jew of the Nazi social imaginary has become synonymous with the front entrance to the building, which pulls the people in to their ultimate doom and then regurgitates them back onto the street whence they came.

THE OPENING IN THE WALL

The Nazis' obsession with the very modernity of Weimar consumerism highlights the fact that 1920s America was nowhere near Germany in innovations in display window design: the U.S. retail scene had, for all the concomitant *Amerikanismus* influence on the German industrial and cultural imagination, as yet no parallel concept of "less-is-more,"[100] no attempt to use the window to transform the relation of the building to the street, no link to avant-garde abstract art or to the new design media, Bauhaus rationalism, expressionist film, Taylorist streamlining, or the machine.[101] Even though Americans used 120 million square feet of plate glass in 1925 for their windows,[102] it was the show windows of Berlin that were most renowned worldwide until the gradual decline in innovation during the 1930s with the onset of Nazism.[103] Display windows were the dominant feature of a plethora of Weimar trade journals, such as *Architektur und Schaufenster, Die Auslage, Das Schaufenster* (in Berlin and Vienna editions), *Schaufenster-Kunst und -Technik, Neue Dekoration, Licht und Lampe,* and *Farbe und Form.* Show windows in Paris, Amsterdam, and Prague came closest on the modernist inventiveness scale to those of Germany, while London and New York simply trailed behind.

The influence that finally crossed the Atlantic to the U.S. was the more decorative French art deco style (deplored by Austrian-trained architect Frederick Kiesler in his influential 1930 book *Contemporary Art Applied to the Store and Its Display*),[104] with its visible links to the earlier windows of the Wiener Werkstätte rather than to the more startlingly functionalist, machinic Weimar modern. Modernist window display hit America only after the 1925 Paris Exposition des Arts Décoratifs (featuring a specially built "street" of firms' display windows)[105] had traveled from France to the U.S., and after the 1927 Macy's exposition of modernist interior design and furniture was held in conjunction with the Metropolitan Museum of Art.[106] In 1926 the American journal of show window advertising, *Display World,* finally began to notice the art deco display aesthetics of its European counterparts; and in 1928 Kiesler designed a series of modernist window displays for Saks Fifth Avenue by removing the interior panels between the fourteen windows and thus creating a "free rhythmic background throughout."[107] By the 1930s, there were even surrealist designs in Manhattan store windows by Salvador Dalí and Marcel Duchamp.

The design of the actual window, as the façade's expositional interface between inside and outside, began to command in the Weimar era the structural logic of the entire building, and wholly reflected the shifts in modern urban planning.[108] This trend began in Austria when the Wiener Werkstätte, founded in 1903, began the focus on geometrically simple designs that concentrated the gaze on the display window itself.[109] By 1922, essayist Gustav Brandes was welcoming the trend of eliminating or sublating the entire first-story façade of a department store or office block into a unified *Schaufenster* of glass and iron.[110] The actual storefronts were renovated and rebuilt along the metamorphosis logic of Weimar façade renewal: the aim was to "make the window look like an entrance and the entrance like a window,"[111] often with rounded window corners at the street corner or the doorway, so as to "suck" the customer along the display and into the shop. Kiesler advocated the use of "funnel" doorways to bring in customers step by step as they went from one window display to the next in the doorway of the store. Likewise, Mendelsohn's entrances for the Nuremberg Schocken department store and the Cohen & Epstein store in Duisburg produced the absolute in the functionalist integration of window and doorway. Mendelsohn noted in a lecture entitled "The Shop and the Department Store" that individual shop owners were slow to realize the "dissonance" between their modern commodities inside and the "out-of-touch façade on the exterior" of their buildings, and equally slow to catch on to the long-term benefits of modernizing the window front along the new lines of "functionality" (*Zweckmäßigkeit*).[112]

The praise lavished on the functional display window by the Berlin publisher Ernst Pollak in 1929 underscores the centrality of the role it was understood to play in modern building design:

> Today the shop window is no longer an opening in the wall, like the remaining windows in the building. . . . [It] open[s] up the back rooms and allows the contents as it were to spill out onto the pavement.
>
> Nor does it compete with any other openings in the building. It has become a weighty, powerful aspect of the building [*Ein gewichtiges, eigenmächtiges Gebilde*], and this must be realized when the building as a whole is erected. It must be the most imposing aspect [*dessen eindruckvollster Teil*], for the crowds that flood along the streets of the big

> city do not have the time to cast their eyes over a four-storied façade. They only see what is there at ground level, shops and their fronts. . . . Whereas in the past it was often necessary to break through old façades to create shops, the modern architect frequently designs rows of shops so that the entire building appears to stand on stilts [*so, daß dieser auf Stelzen zu stehen scheint*] and the shops nestle under their canopy, as entirely independent beings.[113]

Pollak notes that the display window has to be "assertive" amid the "obtrusive noise and colorful muddle of the street," so as to "attract the stream of people rushing by." This logic of self-assertion was enhanced further by the Krupp-Nirosta firm's introduction in 1927 of stainless steel for window frames (fig. 53), the aim of which was to increase the *Glanz* of the display windows' general "physiognomy," not simply in encouraging a stronger profile for the window, which could now protrude into the street without fear of rain damage (as Paul Mahlberg, who designed the frames, explained, "the surface of the material is so hard that nothing adheres to it"), but also in promoting a ballast-shedding deconstruction of interior and exterior boundaries through the use of the same unifying material within and without, so that the spatial sense of bringing the "interior to the fore" could be further reinforced: "The more adventurous aspect is the fact that the façade structure can be lighter [*das Frontbild-tragende Gerüst noch schmaler zu halten*] and is, as a result, more functional [*es noch mehr durchzutrainieren*], so that the shop itself will be lighter, with a more open view, where the interior landscape is more visible and the image of the shop in general becomes more an image of our time."[114] Transformations in window design continued through the 1920s: a new lengthening of the window, for example, was introduced at the 1929 Advertising Exhibition (*Reklameschau*) in Berlin, in response to the growing awareness that automobile passengers did not have enough time to survey the window's contents: thus began window designs that incorporated the eye "in transit" (*eine wandernde Schaufensterdekoration*).[115]

This new interrelation of display window and building as a whole is best demonstrated in Mendelsohn's successful series of buildings for Weimar German commercial life. His Herpich building (1924), a store for the fur dealer Herpich on Berlin's Leipziger Straße, initially provoked a strong negative reaction[116] against its strikingly plain façade of almost all glass, with strong horizontal bands of concealed lighting between the storeys to accentuate the nighttime display of the windows below. The whole building seemed built to project only one thing, the interconnectedness of its

Figure 53. Stainless steel frames for display window of Krupp-Nirosta store, Düsseldorf, designed by Paul Mahlberg (1928).

windows and façade lines—a dynamic horizontalism that authentically reflected the motion and direction of the traffic flow below. In the ensuing years it was realized that Mendelsohn was right to refrain from recreating pointless display windows in the upper storeys and instead to use this surface to push open new possibilities for the façade.

Mendelsohn's characteristic technique of using the entire façade as a "horizontal" outgrowth rising above the row of display windows below is taken to the limit by the eighty-foot-high glass stairwell tower at the corner of his Schocken department store in Stuttgart (1926–1928), which burst out onto the street in a controlled curvature of sheer façade energy (fig. 54). The glass stairwell tower adds an electrically charged twist to the stasis of its groundbreaking predecessor, Gropius's glass-encased spiral staircase for the 1914 Cologne Werkbund exhibition. The sense of machinic control exuded by the Schocken building is effected by the multiple horizontal bands that underline each level of glass around the tower; these bands function contrapuntally, accentuating by contrast the verticality of the building and forcing the building, as it were, into a fixed position, like an animalistic coil ready to spring.[117] The narrow band height of these lines (far more than the actual number of floors) promotes a sense that the structure is taller than it actually is. Until its razing in the 1970s, the Stuttgart

Figure 54. Schocken department store, Stuttgart, designed by Erich Mendelsohn (1928).

Schocken offered in its multiple surface effects (or "poster-architecture")[118] a culmination of Mendelsohn's skilled commercial-propagandistic application of the scopic drive. It was emulated more modestly in Mendelsohn's renovation of the interior and outer façade of the Deukon House (1928) for a textile magazine publisher in the Berlin garment industry area, near the Potsdamer Platz. Even though the Deukon's new glass and bronze façade remained a more intrinsic "part of the [Wilhelmine] street," its stairwell reflected the Stuttgart store's multiplication of storeys.[119]

Another dramatic opening-up of the wall, this time for the interior of a store, was used by the architect Otto Firle in his late-Weimar design of a glass and chrome metal elevator shaft for the Grünfeld drapery shop on the Ku-Damm (fig. 55). Here the elevator shaft functions as a technologized encapsulation of the grand *Lichthof* of the fin-de-siècle department store (and as a presaging of the multistorey, hermetically sealed spiral of glass at the center of the post-Wall Galeries Lafayette store by Jean Nouvel, part of the intriguing conglomeration of the Friedrichstadtpassagen's indoor mall with outdoor stores on the Friedrichstraße). The person walking up or down Firle's stairs can see through the glass walls of the elevator

Figure 55. Elevator shaft for the Grünfeld department store, Kurfürstendamm, Berlin, designed by Otto Firle (c. 1928).

shaft in the middle and between the spherically rotating chrome bannisters that continue around the shaft, to the multiple floors of the store. Lighting serves to amplify the reflection of these surfaces off one another. The view from within the glass shaft offers a cylindrically contracting perspective both above and below, suggestive of a continual rotating motion.

In this way, then, new department stores and office blocks built during the Weimar years, as well as old Wilhelmine ones whose decorative façades were stripped off and modernized, billed themselves as purpose-built monumentalities geared toward what became in fact this century's most architecturally unified spectacle of modern commercial advertising. New Objectivity's influence on department store design amounted, most significantly, to the introduction of the store as a "commodity container."[120] Mia Klein, a Weimar advertising expert, supported this shift from the decorative palace of the Wilhelmine era's Wertheim store on the Leipziger Straße to the functional box-design of the 1929 Karstadt store built above the Hermannplatz U-Bahn station in the working-class area of Berlin-Neukölln (fig. 56): she asserted that the qualification for a good store in the late 1920s was to correspond architecturally to New Objectivity and to the general new image of the city, in order to overcome the old "kitschy" façades.[121]

Designed by Philipp Schäfer (who continued to build under the Nazis—for example, Berlin's Fehrbelliner Platz buildings of 1935–1936), the Karstadt store was always intended to have nighttime illumination for its massive twin towers.[122] While its palatial dimensions caused an outcry in the Nazi press,[123] in the general media of Berlin its sixteen-month construction was greeted with admiration and hailed as a "unique spectacle of modern construction acrobatics."[124] Karstadt company literature proclaimed that by night the store became the embodiment of "utopian worlds of technology" à la Jules Verne or H. G. Wells.[125] It boasted three interior light-courts, 720,000 square feet, up to 4,000 employees, a restaurant, a lounge, and every fixture reflective of the store's self-billing as "metropolitan marvel" (*Großstadtwunder*). Due to the vertical effect of its limestone façade, which emphasized its seven storeys in the manner of a Manhattan skyscraper, the building was deemed "American" in its Gothic-machinic style.[126] A rooftop garden of 40,000 square feet was its crowning glory—a celebration of its own monumentalism, offering an unparalleled view of the capital.

Efforts like Karstadt toward the creation of consumerist architecture offered a degree of comfort and efficiency for Weimar consumers that the contemporary suburban mall is still seeking to provide, offering post offices, winter gardens, child care, restaurants, reading rooms, tea rooms, special events, musical entertainment, travel agencies, libraries, ticket kiosks for theater and concerts—and, in 1927, even a cinema.[127] Such a trend toward totalization led Kracauer to mock a Berlin-Ost department store for artistic pretensions amidst its "wonderful mechanism" of commerce, when in 1930 the store invited Heinrich Mann to give a public reading of his latest novel in its dining hall to customers having their "five o'clock tea."[128]

These stores' new monumentality of commerce may well have come later to Germany than to France, the U.S., or England—but when it did, its growth was astounding. This phenomenal expansion evidently satisfied Germany's interwar self-image more than the actual economy. By 1929, there were sixty-five department stores in Berlin, and seven-hundred-odd across all of Germany;[129] twelve of the world's twenty-nine largest retail concerns were German, with Karstadt, Tietz, Wertheim, and Schocken at the top.[130] All this

Figure 56. Karstadt department store in Neukölln, Berlin (1929).

despite the fact that Weimar German shoppers continued to lag behind their French, English, and U.S. counterparts in terms of actual sales originating in department stores.[131] With three-quarters of the working population of Germany earning less than 125 RM a month in 1929, and over 50 percent of the average budget being spent on food,[132] it is no wonder that the 1928 rate of trade in German department stores was half that of the U.S.[133]

WINDOW TECHNIQUES

What went on inside the window was akin to what was going on outside in the advertising images that passers-by would see on building façades, posters, or magazines. That which was on display was temporary; its short life span prodded the art of window display to be more daring, exaggerated, and self-prostituting, in order to cause a disruption in potential consumers' fields of vision. Despite the window's evident need to be noticed by potential consumers, its designs were predicated on a holistic, "symphonic" performance.[134] This occurred in the wares themselves with as few appendages as possible; beauty lay in the geometrical yet musical "rhythm" of unbroken lines and curves, and in the clarity of form.[135] Thus even the human touch was subservient to New Objective doctrine. Nothing was left to chance effect, and every element of the window's display was subjected to analysis: floor height, depth, width, height of ceiling, general style of architecture, color of the walls, construction materials used.[136] Psychotechnical experiments were conducted on how best to achieve an eye-catcher (*Blickfang*),[137] measuring which areas of the window were most frequently looked at by passers-by (the center and lower half), or whether windows with item-prices on display sold more than those without (they did).[138] Different strategies for color and form were used in window dressing for the slower tempo of provincial towns, or for the changing seasons.[139] The intended purity of the window matched the machine- and Bauhaus-inspired tenet of form equaling function, in which "ornament, arabesque, everything 'not useful' is useless."[140] Paramount was the serial reproduction of the commodity, as in the *Stapelfenster.* This particular window type developed from its turn-of-the-century origins in stockpiling into machinic, paratactic repetitions of goods—a modern (symmetrical) version, indeed, of the postmodern (asymmetrical) updates in the artwork of Andy Warhol, a former window dresser himself.

The aim was to move, incite, be electric, or simply impress by the rationalized repetition of mass-produced goods. The Schocken department store chain even numbered its display windows so as to help customers explain to sales assistants which item they wanted to examine; and, presaging much of postwar retail advertising, Schocken centralized its display window designs so as to promote a sense of recognizable style for all Schocken stores across Germany.[141] Not surprisingly, there was an intense religiosity in window-dressing hype: "absolute objectivity" in the display is attainable if one "learns how to think oneself into the commodity" and its function, claimed a teacher at Berlin's respected Reimann School for window design.[142]

As part of the constant campaign to ensure that the phantasmagoria remain in consumers' consciousness, the single-theme *Spezialschaufenster* was deemed more effective than one with mixed contents.[143] The window often shamelessly encouraged certain buying responses, even by downright (self-)mockery: playwright-poet-politician Sergei Tretiakov, for example, praises a humorous Ka De We window that featured female mannequins as simulations of female buyers, caught in the act of falling over each other to get to items on sale inside the store (fig. 57).[144] A certain "pea-window" was the talk of the town in Berlin in 1925: the Charlottenburg Sports Club launched a competition to guess the number of peas in a huge bottle, displayed in a window at the Wertheim department store on the Leipziger Straße. First prize was a sports car, a piano, and an apartment: needless to say, a veritable guessing frenzy arose.[145]

Another popular type, the neo-expressionist *Szenenschaufenster*, was a stage for narrative "living pictures" that promoted wished-for lifestyles of work and home, adapting and transforming images of high culture or wealthy leisure activities for the masses.[146] The mechanics of these displays occasionally overshot the mark: the "staged" effect could be so unusual that it distracted from the products themselves.[147] In 1925, for example, Berlin staged a "Then and Now" (*Einst und Jetzt*) show in its display windows: all major department stores participated, and even Dr. Erwin Redslob, the cultural minister (*Reichskunstwart*), gave a speech. Each store showed comparative scenes of "Then" and "Now" with such items as bridal wear, office furniture, the baby's bedroom, and types of machinery—the "Now" window being much simpler and less ornamental than the "Then" of a hundred years before. One window may well have been the source of then-Berliner Billy Wilder's subsequent direction of Marilyn Monroe's famous skirt scene.[148] But there were complaints that this particular competition was overly decorative, that is, not functional enough and neglectful of the basic "publicity purpose" (*Werbezweck*) of the display window, which was to sell.[149]

Small wonder, then, that Kracauer felt driven to satirize the apparent design overkill of the display window: he describes how a particular "sales temple" in Berlin, with its semicircular window of glass, gold, metal, and perfect illumination, is in effect "no advertisement, it's a prophecy that is being promulgated to the profane passers-by"—so much so that they dare not even enter to buy the elegant toiletries on show within, and the shop remains deserted.[150] Indeed, Kracauer's complaint about the Ku-Damm, Berlin's most famous street for display windows, was that this surface-celebration resulted in a masquerade of "rootlessness" and "transitoriness," with shopfronts that did not even bother to look like real businesses; they could give only the "impression of improvising."[151] Elsewhere among his many reviews for the *Frankfurter Zeitung* during the Weimar years, he

Figure 57. Ka De We (Kaufhaus des Westens) display window (1932).

gently mocks the consuming masses for being made over by the *Schaufenster's* power of suggestion into an army of recruits—in one instance, for letting themselves be persuaded by window displays of holiday destinations to indeed go on vacation.[152] Kracauer forces home the mobilization metaphor with his comment that the names of these foreign cities now emblazoned on department store façades are like place-names of WWI battles. Here Kracauer implies his awareness that for a nation stripped of its dignities in the Versailles treaty, advances in advertising and trade fairs served as a vital new guarantor of a new, economically based international prestige during the Weimar years.

Illustrating such pragmatism, between 1926 and 1927, in true German organizational style, the newly founded Head Office of German Display Window Lighting (Zentrale der Deutschen Schaufenster-Lichtwerbung) mobilized in the course of a single year the installation of electric lighting in 70 percent of window displays in forty-six German cities.[153] As a result, daytime advertising was completely eclipsed by the night, when Kracauer's employees or little shop girls would be wandering the streets in search of distraction. Weimar window dressers became, after their three years of apprenticeship, experts in the effects of lighting, arranging their scenes as carefully as film technicians, and generally adhering to the tenet that the

Figure 58. Advertisement for Zeiss Spiegellicht lighting for window displays (1927).

brighter the light (carefully guided so as not to blind), the more people drawn to the window and the goods therein.[154]

It was generally acknowledged that the most powerful tool used to transform the space of the window into a target of spectatorial desire was electricity, according to the logic of "more light, more buyers," as proudly proclaimed in a trade advertisement for the Zeiss lighting company (fig. 58). In this ad, the "real" people on the street stand as mere reflected shadows who behold before them the light-filled realm of display-window Platonic essence. Even though the electric technology of the window announces a visual empowerment to consumers such that they no longer need look "through a glass, darkly" but instead can attain (at a price) that which lies beyond in the land of transparency, it is nonetheless the crowd's own opaque materiality on the other side of the window that remains emphasized before the commodity's now brighter-than-daylight glow. Sometimes, the message from the bright window is even threatening: in one passage in Döblin's *Berlin Alexanderplatz*, the window techniques of a "well-lit butcher's shop" are reviewed in a factual manner that appears to be taken directly from a trade journal in the field—but this New Objective parallel tendency of Döblin's is used as an effective contrast with the novel's other Biblical-mythical discourse about Biberkopf's personal, yet prototypical, relation to slaughter and suffering in the modern city.[155]

There were, however, no such hints of shadowy human limitations for the second Bauhaus leader, Hannes Meyer, who in his 1926 "The New World" (a veritable communist manifesto for the modern design age) proudly announced that lighting in store windows best exhibited the "constructivist principle" driving Weimar Germany as a representative of the new collective society: "In the new display window, lighting is used to exploit the tensions of modern materials to psychological ends. Display window organization instead of display window decoration."[156] Yet beyond all these functional reasons for constant use of electricity was an aimless, mystical desire to shine for shining's sake. After all, lighting is, as Baudrillard quips, the "least rare commodity, without which merchandise would merely be what it is."[157] Praise for the bright lights of consumer display culture was forthcoming even from communist corners: the Soviet Tretiakov wrote that the lover of Berlin's display windows must be a "light alcoholic" (*Lichtalkoholiker*);[158] their design was so good that it could be applied to communist display windows, to be used purely for exhibition purposes and without the capitalist "Buy! Buy!" refrain/demand of Berlin's department stores.[159]

THE DISPLAY WINDOW AS MECHANICAL-AGE ARTWORK

Buying-propaganda aside, it is certainly the case that the exhibitionist streak of the Weimar display window sought to entertain the urban public in much the same way as Tom Gunning has suggested was operational in the "cinema of attractions" of the early film years (the visual display of circus, fairground, and amusement park).[160] Coming on the heels of cinema's shift during World War I from spectacle to narrative, window display placed attention back on spectacle, and found a panoramic-perambulatory zone[161] in which modern art, Fordist-Bauhaus function principles, and popular culture all successfully converged.[162] The changed perception skills of the city-dweller, fully adapted to what Benjamin has called modernity's shock-effects, could find in the *Schaufenster* a new form of beauty more befitting the urban lifestyle than traditional art forms.

Tretiakov, for one, was obsessed with Weimar Berlin's "electric pantomime" window scenes, neither film nor theater and yet both.[163] He would have been pleased that slide projectors were sold for display window use.[164] In the same vein, Kiesler, who had done stage designs for Piscator as well as for Karel Capek's robot drama *R.U.R.* (1923), defined filmic kinetics as the life of the window: "The evolution of the show window is due to one fact: speed. For this reason the show window is a modern method of communication."[165] Actual movement in the window that mirrored the circulating movement in the city street outside was understood to be a key factor in arousing pedestrians' buying desire.[166] Focal points of motion in the window often included mechanical toys, as in Ruttmann's film *Berlin, Symphony of a City* (*Berlin, Sinfonie der Großstadt*) of 1927, where robotic dolls in the windows serve as ironic images of contrast or of consequence with the cross-cut scenes of real Berliners. Another focalizing aspect of the display window was the employment of contrastive color, something the 1920s film industry could not use, except in the light-architecture of its movie palaces.

Evidently, the entire relation of the Weimar window to the street (of inside to outside) and the organization of its commodities can be examined (and was understood at the time to behave) as a microcosmically cinematic device. Kiesler predicted the day beyond cinema when the display window would be used as a "Window Daily" of televised news and events for passers-by.[167] For the modern city street, however, the display window served as the urbanite's very own cinema screen.[168] There were even film screenings in the windows themselves, as when the Tietz department store in 1927 showed a humorous advertising film for Dornbusch shirt collars.[169] Mia Klein recognized that the dozens of display windows along the exterior of a department store could easily create an instant filmic *Schaulust* with their pictorial focus.[170] For the great advantage of display window advertising is, in short, that it is not experienced *as* advertising. While Anne Friedberg, in her illuminating study *Window Shopping,* views this filmic connection of spectator/passer-by to be one of a noncommittal "speculative regard" or "distanced contemplation,"[171] modernity's store window and silver screen share perhaps not so much a calm process of seeing and deciding, as enthrallment: both consumer and filmgoer are captivated by the image behind the transparent pane—ultimately driven to suspend disbelief enough to feel a need for the product, or an identification with the filmic protagonist.

A (de)constructive act of joining with the other arts was hence occurring in the Weimar display window—not only with its closest affine, film, but also with its older cousin, the theater.[172] The *Schaufenster* was a theatrical stage, with all the requisite props, mannequin actors, and scenery, creating a "pictorial effect" (*Bildwirkung*) as in the theater.[173] The commodity window simultaneously opened itself to other art formats: painting, photography, architecture, textiles, sculpture, the art gallery, and the museum. It caused the lines separating the conventions of high versus low, and autonomous versus applied, cultural output to become increasingly blurred. For modernist aesthetics was, as Bolz indicates, "no longer oriented at art, but at communication."[174] And not just in functionalist Germany—since the 1900s, Eugène Atget had been using photography to record and portray Parisian store windows, thereby challenging both the medium and the subject of what was deemed art; avant-gardistic French film sets, meanwhile, were in their staged simulations tantamount to both art deco window displays and the latest in interior design.[175]

As for the contents of the modern (and especially Weimar) display window itself, the art of antimimetic dadaist montage or of Picasso's or Braque's "flat" collage was now employed in the service of consumerism, both in the window and reflected without.[176] The geometric collage of the New Objective window was not chaotic or off-the-canvas, but highly framed and ordered: this is where the Bauhaus came in with its functionalist philosophy of art following function, not disfunction. Bauhaus designers, as leaders in the international avant-garde scene of the 1920s, sincerely believed in their ability to influence and contribute to advertising and production design for the benefit of their own cultural mission; however, as with pre-Stalinist Soviet constructivism and with the futurist art movement,[177] this proved to be but a short-lived coexistence and cooperation of avant-garde and industry.

But the impact of such mixed practices was lasting: there was no longer any fixed boundary between the aesthetics of painting and popular culture, and no more autonomy for creative artists unrelated to the needs of industry. Artists who were aware of this new Bloomian anxiety of influence included the cubist Fernand Léger, who himself engaged in show window design for the 1925 Paris exposition as he sought to redefine the role of art in a mechanized, urban society.[178] As Jean-Paul Bouillon has asked: "Which triumphed, then, the shop window or the painting?"[179] In the same way that art let itself be molded, or de-classified,[180] by the show window, so window dressers rather understandably wished to be seen as display artists, and their creations as a new art form.[181] Kiesler refers to the profession of "display manager" as the "modern Cagliostro," very much a "product of our century."[182] Gaston Derys, a French art critic of the 1920s, called the display window the "museum of the people," and the window dresser the creator of *tableaux*.[183] In 1929, the question arose in Germany whether copyright was necessary to protect display window designs as works of art, so as to protect individual firms' ideas.[184] Stephani-Hahn promoted the individual artist-identities of window designers in her book *Schaufenster-Kunst*.[185] Ironically, keen resistance to such a "profanization of art"[186] came mostly from business people themselves, who were far from ashamed of the show-window aesthetic as a "means to an end."[187]

Certainly, by the Kantian yardstick of disinterestedness in aesthetic taste, the advertising arts fail if measured as art[188]—and yet the twentieth century has shown that art has, instead, come over to the applied side, not just in advertising but in other worse (ideological) uses instead. Even as applied art, however, there nonetheless emerged during the Weimar Republic a strong sense of the *Schaufenster*'s culturally significant status; as Mike Featherstone has noted, window dressers are "cultural intermediaries" who transmit the latest aesthetic styles in terms understandable by the mass viewing public.[189] One trade article of 1929 boasted: "Our modern economy today is inconceivable today without display decoration. By means of display window decoration within the framework of *display window architecture*, the entire image of the city is amplified with *an enlivening, seductive, and culturally valuable element*. In this way a single display window decoration rises far beyond its factual economic relevance."[190] Thus the modern metropolitan individual, and even local and national economic health, were all reflected and amplified by what went on in the window of the commercial street. The store window was, as Kiesler noted, a "silent loud speaker" of the age.[191]

TRANSPARENCIES OF TRUTH AND LIE

But what of the other side of the spectacle, where the spectator stands in a state of scopophilic distraction? One's gaze can penetrate the glass but one cannot touch the commodities or mannequins within. The question arises as to how much "light alcoholism" or consumer addiction goes on, whether in Weimar or in contemporary culture—an ongoing conundrum, indeed, for theorists of consumerism.[192] The illusion of society blissfully united through consumption is quite definitely, for Debord, the spectacle's "opium war" against the masses.[193] The early Baudrillard agrees, reminding us that the capitalist system of production invades even the apparently private realm of the subject's reception of the commodity. Baudrillard's rather acerbic summation, in his essay "Consumer Society," of how desire operates in consumerism, denies the myth of individual liminal pleasure in the act of purchasing, and suggests instead a chilling systematization of desire into something mindlessly obligatory for all:

> Consumer behavior, which appears to be focused and directed at the object and at pleasure, in fact, responds to quite different objectives: the metaphoric or displaced expression of desire, and the production of a code of social values through the use of differentiating signs. . . . The truth about consumption is that it is a *function of production* and not a function of pleasure, and therefore, like material production, is not an individual function but one that is *directly and totally* collective. . . . [M]an-as-consumer considers the *experience of pleasure an obligation*, like an *enterprise of pleasure and satisfaction:* one is obliged to be happy, to be in love, to be adulating/adulated, seducing/seduced, participating, euphoric, and dynamic.[194]

This "fun-system, or the constraint of desires," continues Baudrillard bleakly, amounts to a rationalization of consumption on a par with the nineteenth century's socialization of the rural workforce into citified industrial labor; as consumers, then, we are effectively panopticized in our wants and longings, and are constantly encouraged to participate, in order to be "content to consume."[195] Here the early Baudrillard's assessment is in tandem with Adorno's even darker reading of apparent individualism and freedom of choice in the culture industry as a reifying system of wholly programmable reactions, wishes, and drives for the masses.[196]

Yet these judgments remain totally at odds with the creative voyeurism suggested by the display window as art form, according to what Baudelaire noticed in the gaze of the passer-by: "What one can see in the light of day is always less interesting that what happens behind a pane of glass. In this black or lustrous pit lives life."[197] Even the Soviet observer Tretiakov sowed a seed of doubt into the absolutism of the antispectacular Marxist position. "There are display windows," he noted on a trip to Berlin, "before which people ceaselessly stand and laugh, as if it was not a display at all but the opened page of a well-done satirical journal."[198] Confessions such as this serve to deflate somewhat the pro forma Marxist view of advertising manipulating the mindless masses. Or again, there was a positive response from the general public to the kind of window design that you, the passer-by, could activate, such as a shoe store's electric button on the street for people to press in order to light up the display.

Weimar modern display culture certainly billed itself as the very opposite to the Baudrillardian scenario, concentrating instead on promulgating a scopic empowerment (rather than panoptic entrapment) for the viewer. Parallel to the spectatorial pleasure-vehicle of the retail window was Le Corbusier's long picture window for the domestic dwelling that opened up the entire wall of the living room: devoid of any interfering (sheltering) shutter or alcove, the intended effect of the free façade was, as Beatriz Colomina relates, to let daylight unremittingly in, to "turn . . . the outside world into an image to be consumed by those inside the house."[199] By symptomatic inversion, the same process occurs in the glass panorama of the display window, which ostensibly changes the direction of the consuming gaze, making the scene within one of voyeuristic desire espied from the street without.

However, both these transformations of home and retail spaces had side effects that undermined the epiphenomenon of an emancipated clarity of vision for the dweller/consumer of modernity: it soon became apparent that those who lived in the new glass-walled houses felt they were more on display for those who walked by than vice versa (Colomina terms this the "publicity of the private").[200] Benjamin's vision of the first display window streets, the Parisian arcades of the nineteenth century, suggests that the power of the commodities was so great that it was they, the objects in the window, that performed the most powerful act of looking: "Pedestrians in the arcades are so to speak inhabitants of a panorama. . . . They are observed from the windows but they themselves cannot see in." Benjamin's rather unsettling suggestion here is that truth (*das Wahre*) cannot reside in windows at all, only in their absence, in a "*windowless* house."[201]

Regarding the contentious issue of whether the display window is by definition a misrepresentation, a lie, a bloated façade over social reality,[202] we come to the problem of class. Already in Weimar Germany, glass certainly belied class distinctions, and there was often a distinct gap between the display window's ability to arouse consumer desire and the consumer's corresponding ability to buy. The historian William Leach has referred to this condition as the windows' simultaneous democratization of desire and *de*democratization of actual access to the commodities shown.[203] Stores accentuated this disjunction in their employment of window-gawkers (*Schaufenster-Gaffer*), outdoor human mannequins who were paid to encourage others to look into the windows.[204] Only the very rich could afford to distance themselves from the excesses of display: a rather overaestheticized strategy for dealing with commodity fetishism is given by

Clemens, the philologist-observer of life in Franz Hessel's novel *Heimliches Berlin* (1927), who advises young Wendelin to love commodities and people only from afar, to be a Baudelairean ego-less *flâneur* rather than a Weimarean consumer.[205] This piece of advice appears somewhat unrealistic and out of "tempo" with the Weimar mass culture all around, and it is also divorced from the situation of the masses. Exclusion from the spectacle soon became the worst form of punishment—just as working-class women would put on their Sunday best just to go shopping, so the titular narrator of Erich Kästner's novel of late Weimar cynicism, *Fabian,* notes how unemployed men dressed up like wealthy, voluntarily idle *flâneurs,* ready to stroll the Ku-Damm. In order to even observe display, one must give the appearance of being already part of the display oneself.

There was and still is little room for class consciousness in consumerist viewing desire: only *glass* consciousness is permitted. Writing for *Vorwärts* in 1923, Joseph Roth declared that glass is a material that controls the world, since it slices up people into those who live "*behind*" the display window (i.e., in possession of the goods), and those who must remain "*in front*" of it, unable to purchase what they see. Roth finds himself astounded that more people don't just smash the glass: "[The pane] paralyzes ten thousand greedy fists daily, and guards the goods entrusted to it better than a wall."[206] (In fact, it was not uncommon for this antinomy to be translated into consumer debt, or actual theft: usually the windows smashed in were the ones with the brightest lights and the most valuable items, such as fur coats.)[207] But the paralysis of the poor majority during the Weimar German years, which had to look but never buy, is connected to consumerism's key role in persuading the worker-consumer to identify with the product and its producer—to "partake in the luster of capital," as Eric Alliez and Michel Feher have written of the new, decidedly *non*revolutionary, credit-card-laden *homo economicus.*[208] Debord finds that in the facticity of the spectacle's courtship of employees, a pseudo-need is created as soon as they become consumers at the end of the working day: "Once work is over, they are treated like grown-ups, with a great show of solicitude and politeness, in their new role as consumers."[209] It was Henry Ford, after all, who is said to have declared: our workers should also be our customers.

The rules of "U" and "non-U," to apply Nancy Mitford's terms to the arena of consumerist vision, are echoed in the early Baudrillard's assessment of glass as it functions prophylactically in display windows. In *The System of Objects* (1968), Baudrillard focuses on the medium's dual nature of inclusion and exclusion:

> [Glass] is at once proximity and distance, intimacy and the refusal of intimacy, communication and non-communication. Whether as packaging, window or partition, glass is the basis of a transparency without transition; we see, but cannot touch. . . . A shop window is at once magical and frustrating—the strategy of advertising in epitome. . . . Glass works exactly like atmosphere in that it allows nothing but the *sign* of its content to emerge . . . [210]

The price paid by the consumer of average means (or worse) who believes in the promises of prestige and delight held out by these transparencies is indeed a steep one, as Baudrillard indicates: in the culture of glass hygiene, credit is hyped as a consumer right or "freedom" when in fact it is but a postmodern version of feudalistic "subjection."[211] In this way, the "*consumption [of objects] precedes their production.*"[212] This false magic is illustrated in Erich Maria Remarque's late Weimar novel *The Three Comrades* (*Die Drei Kameraden*), in which the *Schaufenster*-lit displays of fur coats or even food in Berlin-by-night act as signifiers of all that is forever materially unattainable for Robert, the narrator. The novel is full of references to surface glamour (*Glanz*), a nonsubstance that has nothing to do with people's lives, their socioeconomic and psychological (post-WWI) misery. Kracauer refers to these nonparticipatory outsiders, particularly the unemployed, as "Zille figures."[213]

Similar left-wing sympathy with the plight of the dispossessed within Weimar display culture is expressed by Hans Fallada in his novel of 1932, *Little Man, What Now?* (*Kleiner Mann—Was nun?*), in which the working-class protagonist bankrupts himself due to *Schaufenster* addiction. Pinneberg, the little man struggling to survive as a department store assistant in the latter years of the Weimar Republic, stupidly spends almost his entire first month's wages on a vanity mirror and dresser for his bride—a purchase brought on by a month of staring at such items in display windows throughout Berlin and finally succumbing to the glamour of their "magical illusion."[214] After Pinneberg has been forced to join the ranks of the long-term unemployed, his deepest moment of alienation is felt when a policeman forces him away from even looking into the display window of a store where he would like to buy butter for his toddler son. When he sees his shabby appearance reflected in the store window, Pinneberg realizes that in the eyes of the public he is rightfully excluded and does not deserve to be part of the glamorous surface culture of Berlin. By the close of the novel, however, when Weimar surface culture has come to the end of its life span amongst the populace, a new beginning (or ending) is sensed: it is precisely the ("Jewish") display windows that the Nazis are beginning to smash in.

MANNEQUINS ON BOTH SIDES OF THE GLASS

It would appear, then, that the visual pleasure contained in commodity fetishism is a controlled, atomizing desire: human-to-human contact is not encouraged, but human-to-object contact is.[215] In 1924, Alfred Döblin perceives this objectifying, amoral side to the "technical spirit" of the display process and gives a clear sign that he is ready to use the same techniques for his own literary discourse, as in fact proved to be the case in his 1929 novel *Berlin Alexanderplatz:*

> Nothing compares to the challenge and shamelessness of the city shops, display windows, and department stores. Any private citizen can without bother set up shops, entire department stores and display his wares. Here there is no censorship as there is in the much less dangerous (because conservative) intellectual areas of literature and art. The insignificant tradesman can decorate his wares, light them up, arrange them suggestively. One glance shows what is going on here: needs are satisfied and new needs are bred. The job being done on humans here is intensely practical. The technical spirit goes through the streets, stirs things up and fashions things.[216]

Window shopping was, as such, a voyeuristic, noncontact sport for the modern age.[217] Likewise, in the parodic photomontage text *Germany Germany Over Everything* (*Deutschland Deutschland über alles,* 1929), Kurt Tucholsky mocked the morals of those who pretended to be shocked by the exhibition of female (wax) bosoms on display in Berlin's store windows.[218]

The source of this hygienically contained and "paned" viewing desire was the female body as wax mannequin, both clothed and unclothed. Woman as mannequin epitomized the general trend of modernity toward composing the body as surface, as Kracauer notes: "The *body* has come to the surface and not only the body, but everything that is in and around it—the entire person from head to toe."[219] Indeed, Benjamin's portrait of the posthumanistic mannequin, of modern woman-as-surface, verges on the grotesque: "The wax figure is in fact the scene where the appearance of humanity capsizes. That is to say, human surface, complexion and color are expressed in her so completely and unsurpassably that this reproduction of its appearance outdoes itself, so that now the mannequin represents nothing but a dreadful, artful mediation between entrails and costume."[220] Le Corbusier's rating of display window mannequins in New York City as versions of the *Überfrau* is hardly more comforting.[221] Yet clearly, the way in which the store mannequin showed off her body and her wares to the women outside provided them with a flattering mirror of selfhood: mannequins thus lent the consumer a new surface-self that was born of identificatory visual pleasure.[222]

Wax models, originating in the late seventeenth and early eighteenth centuries,[223] melted at first under the electric lights of turn-of-the-century display windows, until more satisfactory materials were found for their production.[224] Zola's designation of the headless shop dummies with exaggerated bustlines and hips (and, in the Wilhelmine case, real hair) as the shapely, realistic "beautiful women for sale"[225] gave way to the leaner, elongated body lines of the 1920s woman, as well as to the far more abstract forms introduced during under the influence of German New Objectivity and the 1925 Paris Exposition des Arts Décoratifs.[226] The Weimar years featured both androgynous-realistic *and* androgynous-abstract automatons that were compliant with *Neue Sachlichkeit.* Bauhaus artist Oskar Schlemmer's new formations of the abstracted, machinic body were a driving force in these latter compositions, such as mannequin designs by Rudolf Belling or Alexander Gummitsch.[227] In its mannequin form, the body could be sectioned up into highly suggestive, salable parts like the legs, as in a photomontage by Hanna Höch or a close-up of Marlene Dietrich's legs.[228] This antimimetic direction sought to reproduce not so much the actual female body but an "intensified rhythm" of the same, "expressed in line, color, and form."[229] At the same time there were also mannequins that had wholly naturalistic aims, with individualized eyes and expressions, such as child figures by Käthe Kruse, or adult figures like those designed by the Erdmannsdorfer Büstenfabrik in Berlin, which were practically indistinguishable from those walking by on the other side of the glass.

It was predominantly the female gender that appeared on both sides of the Weimar glass window (as mannequins, as sales assistants, as a rising proportion of the more highly paid window dressers, and, ultimately, as customers), and who thus played the most significant role in the merchandising of goods and in anchoring the gaze into the window. She is depicted as the majority shopper in the Karstadt store's illustration of its new subway entrance (fig. 59). As Zola's Mouret summarizes the system of modern commerce: "It was woman whom the stores fought over in their rivalry, woman whom they kept on taking hostage in their sales, after having overcome her with their display windows."[230] Kracauer, in "The Sales Temple," treats a mannequin he has observed as if she were human, a bored little shop girl: "Doubtless she is aware of her duty to decorate. With carefully stylized grace she maintains the symmetry, visible from afar, and conscientiously fulfills her charge of being the meeting point of various

Figure 59. Entrance to the Hermannplatz U-Bahn station underneath the Karstadt department store, Berlin (1929).

spatial lines."[231] But perhaps her most significant *renommé* is as prostitute. This is a position of distracted display: the age-old whoring/waiting game. Benjamin continues the tradition of blaming women for the modern condition in his acerbic remark about the feminized masses who are in the Kracauerian sense the bearers of surface culture: "The mob, impelled by a frenetic hatred of the life of the mind, . . . forms ranks and advances in marching order to the department store. No one sees further than the back before him . . . the march of penury, standing in line, is the invention of women."[232] Ruttmann's film confirms Benjamin's analysis of what Baudelaire first allegorized as the link of women's "commodity-characteristic" to the rise of prostitution:[233] in one scene of *Berlin* a female prostitute picks up a male passer-by, literally through the right angle of a corner store's two windows.

Nonetheless, this massified act of self-prostitution was a controlled, sexless, androgynous act of and for the New Woman's body; the caption to a photo of a naked female mannequin in the trade magazine *Die Auslage* in 1928 (fig. 60) stressed how the "anatomy of this body sculpture is unobjectionable. Any hint of eroticism has been avoided here. The effect of the body stands in direct connection to the goods on offer."[234] Thus any scopophilia remains hygienically separate. But there were definite instances of crossing-over. The practice, as shown in Joe May's 1929 silent film *Asphalt*, of having

Figure 60. Mannequin for display window (1928).

live women in display windows "demonstrate" clothing like stockings is an indication of a parallel valorization of the performances of both woman and mannequin. If women could be mannequins, then mannequins could be women—or rather, the Weimar New Woman was construed (by a majority of trade advertisements at least) as a mannequin-masquerade. She also literally stopped traffic: in 1928 a lingerie shop-owner in Hamburg was fined when his live *Schaufenster* model caused a traffic jam of voyeurs in front of the store.[235] While actual women, as well as black people, were often used in "live" shop windows from the 1890s onwards and were still visible in Weimar Germany,[236] by World War I this was beginning to be thought of as a circus sideshow (although it has, ironically, gravitated upwards to the rank of performance art today).

Weimar mannequins, whether realistic or abstract, were absolute window versions of surface culture's "mass ornament," as Kracauer dubbed the Tiller Girls' dance revue. In this system of regimented desire, women consumers beheld their own reflected ornamentation in the window and obeyed the command held out to them. Already in August Macke's expressionist paintings of 1913–1914, there is a colorful celebration of the optical stimulation of the urban display window, showing women's mirrorlike relation to the clothes behind the glass: the women outside are already wearing what is on display inside, but their bodies incline toward more.[237] Marketing research of the 1920s recognized the central role played by women consumers in Weimar advertising strategy.[238] Women, who surveys found read fewer newspapers than men and were hence less responsive to newspaper advertising, were also discovered in tests to look at objects displayed in store windows for an average of two seconds longer than did their male counterparts, as well as to outnumber them in this act of sheer, undisguised street *Schaulust* by a factor of four to three.[239] That which Emilie Altenloh reported in 1914 as women's greater kinetic sensibility as cinemagoers finds its correlate in the discoveries of Weimar psychotechnicians measuring women's seduction by the lure of the *Schaufenster.* Weimar author Richard Huelsenbeck remarked in 1929 that "advertisements tell anyone who knows how to listen that woman as consumer is more important than man" (who nonetheless gets to keep his role as producer of goods, albeit a role now diminished in the age of the machine).[240]

Female propensity or sensitivity to Weimar consumerism was explained in 1928 in terms of Eve and the serpent by Elisabeth von Stephani-Hahn, self-proclaimed "reformer of display window decoration." The serpent of street advertising was unrelenting in its ferocious demands that women fully engage themselves in the cult of appearances: "Not only nighttime tells us of such Eve-paradises: even by the clear light of day the serpent of infatuation cries to us from the display windows: 'You must—you must—you must come along, enjoy, my little dear [*Froufrou*]—you must appear [*scheinen*]—I'll help you seem as if you could, as if you were—even if you can't, or have nothing, or are nothing.'"[241] Nonetheless, despite the apparent parallel here with the *Fabian*esque Weimar cynicism analyzed by Sloterdijk, Stephani-Hahn's critique of a show-window society that breeds the "lie of deceit" or mere "bluff" is insistent on the ultimate higher purpose of commodity display.[242] As a proponent of the radical truth and goodness of streamlined purity in modern design over the lie of "decorative façades" (*Schmuckfassaden*), Stephani-Hahn is confident that the New Objective presentation of goods can be "ennobled" to show off the "heart" of the commodity for consumers; for her it is a style that can speak a "rich language of forms" and not just an "empty language of lines."[243] Woman, then, as the embodiment of mass culture, is the commodity, but she buys it/buys into it, too.

Clearly, however, modernity's new disciplinarity for woman as she-who-consumes contains a convenient omission of female fields of productivity, as Susan Stewart has noticed: "The conception of woman as consumer is no less fantastic or violent than its literalization in the *vagina dentata* myth, for it is a conception which functions to erase the true labor, the true productivity, of women. Yet this erasure forms the very possibility of the cycle of exchange."[244] The very act of consumption remains open to multiple positionalities, as Jane Gaines asks: "Does 'consuming' mean buying, having, or using?"[245] This issue of whether women consumers are using or being used, having or being had, buying or being bought (off), is relevant to the recent critical debate over the attainability of a true *flânerie* for women in the face of its original male paradigm.[246] Moreover, the question regarding the Weimar New Woman's relation to consumerism and commodity display thus remains: if the New Woman existed only as a sham or masquerade of advertising, is she to be regarded only as a reifying constraint, or can she be simultaneously understood as an emancipatory figure? Even if one cannot buy one's way to freedom, as the images generated of the New Woman indicated that one in fact could and should, is it still possible to utilize this surface illusionism to feminist ends? In short, is the icon of the New Woman, for all her androgynous naiveté, still one of the best images the twentieth century has had to offer of a self-liberating woman? If so, the New Woman may constitute a clear example of how feminism may yet hijack Weimar surface culture, adjusting the course of consumerism's conditioning of woman in a direction better suited to women's own advantage.[247] Even if all one reaches through advertising's imagery is the "shortest way to another image," as Baudrillard indicates,[248] this does not preclude adopting the visual power of this realm. Such a possibility is entirely in tandem with Nietzsche's celebration of the feminine as Apollonian surface, as the creative lie that defeats uncreative truth.

THE MURDERER AT THE WINDOW

So are Weimar consumers consumed like the workers by the Moloch of Fritz Lang's *Metropolis* (1927), or are they liberated by the visual feast of window shopping? Certainly they are on occasion represented as fodder before the seductive motions of the display window, which, in Karl Grune's film *Die Straße* (1923), projects a spectacle-shop sign of enormous "eyes" that light up and frighten the protagonist walking underneath as he is being entranced by the woman of the street[249]—a scene which gives literal credence to John Wanamaker's faith in store windows as "eyes to meet eyes."[250] And yet, despite the inequalities of class and gender that the window ruthlessly played into, it played a crucial role as a central, innovating stage for the spectacle that Weimar urban culture produced. For all its transparent illusions, the Weimar display window managed to signify much of what virtual reality aims to deliver to its expectant consumers: namely, disruption, danger, dream-displacement, and an ephemeral intensification of the urban experience, as memorable yet fleeting as the London Crystal Palace or Christo's Reichstag.

A last hermeneutic uncovering of the surfaces in Weimar visual display can best be found in the "Murderers among Us!" (*Mörder unter uns!*), to quote Fritz Lang's draft title for his film about the psychopathic consumer of *Schaufenster* contents and of little girls—namely, Peter Lorre's character in *M* (1931), as he meanders around the street scenes of Berlin constructed by Lang's film architect, Emil Hasler. Indeed, this film, which came out during the severe economic depression resulting from the stock market crash of October 25, 1929, repeatedly suggests an intimate relationship between the display window and sex crimes—murders that are in fact dependent on visual codes of glass transparency and the consumer gaze (tellingly, another draft title for the film was "Your Murderer Is Looking at You" [*Dein Mörder sieht dich an*]). During this crisis period at the end of the Weimar Republic, these codes could no longer offer the success and solace they once did. Lang's film serves, then, as an epilogue to the New Objectivity years, showing us the collapse of the value system of Weimar visual culture from within a killer's mind. The Nazis thought that the film's original title was meant to implicate them (indeed, Goebbels had it banned in 1934).

At a key point in the film, when a detective is unwittingly in the child murderer's rented room, there is a cut to Beckert himself ("M," the murderer), who is seen buying fruit from a street vendor and then walking past a J. A. Henckels shop, a well-known metalware brand. M stops, attracted by the sheer numbers of knives displayed in the window, in a collection of glistening metallic surface in various shapes and designs. He is framed not only by the shop window frame but by the car wheels at each side of the image. Then we see a medium shot of M the murderer, with the camera located within the shop window; our perspective is now situated in the knives looking out at him looking in (fig. 61). Most striking here is how the

Figure 61. The murderer at the display window of knives in *M* (dir. Fritz Lang, 1931).

display of the knives (M's weapon of choice) is reflected in the glass against his body—the lower half of a diamond shape is reflected against his chest, and a circle of knives are reflected against his groin.

As M stands before the window, devouring both the apple and the knives in a literal and visual sense, respectively, we are reminded how fundamentally the command of advertising on our psyches is based on the promise of gratification. The early Baudrillard proposes a "Father Christmas" theory of advertising's collusion. The consumer manages to suspend disbelief when faced with advertising:

> Even though we may be getting better and better at resisting advertising in the imperative, we are at the same time becoming ever more susceptible to advertising in the indicative—that is, to its actual existence as a product to be consumed at a secondary level, and as the clear expression of a culture. . . . Without "believing" in the product, therefore, we believe in the advertising that tries to get us to believe in it. . . . [The individual] thus no more "believes" in advertising than the

> child believes in Father Christmas, but this in no way impedes his capacity to embrace an internalized infantile situation, and to act accordingly.[251]

Baudrillard considers advertising to be effective insofar as it follows a "logic of belief and regression," with tactics of solicitous "warmth," "protection and gratification": "If the object loves me, then shall I be saved."[252] In this eroticized system of *Werbung*—the German word for both advertising and courtship—"society" "puts itself on display and consumes its own image."[253] This intoxicating spectacle can, at best, satisfy the imagination of the one who spectates by providing him or her with a series of possible ideal images of self worth striving for. At worst (as in the case of Lang's M), it can reify the individual in a childlike condition of play that brings the opposite of active cognitive agency. M is located at the extreme end of the spectrum of consumers for whom advertising transmits, states Baudrillard, "transient images of hypnagogic states."[254]

Suddenly we are given M's view, looking at the window, of a little girl, who is reflected in the mirror inside the diamond-shaped knife display. She, like M, is mesmerized by the vast collection of sheer bright surface. Also like M, she is a reflection in the window, only more dangerously so (for her). After this point the scene is no longer one of aimless window-shopping, but of fixed excitement and desire: it is no coincidence that at this moment, in Lang's first sound film, the soundtrack of street noise diminishes almost completely so as to encourage the viewer to visually "listen" to the protagonist's inner turmoil. Until now, M had been merely "walking in the city" in Michel de Certeau's sense[255]—but now his meandering has gained a panoptic directionality toward (childish/sexual) possession.[256] As early as 1913 it was recognized that "I must own you" was the thought pattern inspired by the successful display window: "The whole breathes the atmosphere that a child feels before the curtain that is to reveal the world of dreams to him for the first time."[257] It is strongly implied here that the *Schaufenster* brings M literally to the kill, or brings the kill (the item to be consumed) to him. The film cuts back to the reverse shot of M looking in at the window, whereupon his gesture of wiping sudden perspiration from his lip and licking his finger indicate to us his sexual loss of control at what he has just seen. We are given another shot of the reflected girl from his point of view, and then back to the display window's view of M, who is forced to lean against the window for support, eyes bulging. The next time the camera cuts back to the little girl, it is to show her walking off to the left. A medium shot of M from the sidewalk follows, as he looks left after the girl: to his right is the diamond-shaped mirror showing the street space where the girl had just stood; in her stead is the reflection of a car wheel, top, and what appears to be a rectangular bike stand, below. The geometric display patterns of the knives that had been reflected on M's body as a rectangle above a circle are now inverted as a circle above a rectangle. In this shot, M begins his infamous *Peer Gynt* whistle and his eyes go into shadow as he starts to stalk the girl, leaving the space of the window of knives.

At this point the spectator may well have become aware of a complicitous visual involvement in what is going on: the frequent to-and-fro of the subjective shots serves to implicate us in the heightening of sexual desire via the heightening of commodified desire that the display window promotes.[258] Our vantage point is both the window and the pursuing M; we are wholly part of the consumerist-sexual spatial practice of voyeurism in operation here. Indeed, just in case we were to consider Lang's images of *Schaufenster* arousal to be somewhat exaggerated beyond Weimar business actuality, we can turn to the insistence of a trade journal article of 1929: "With a display window, stimulation is everything!"[259] Further cross-references to Weimar advertising reality are provided, rather uncannily, by a psychotechnical experiment conducted by Rudolf Seyffert, business professor at the University of Cologne, as described in his *Allgemeine Werbelehre* (1929), in which he timed the length of the gaze of passers-by at various store windows.[260] Not only does Seyffert's "candid-camera" photograph of men staring into a gun shop resemble to a remarkable degree of psychological-topographical proximity the shot just described of M at the knife store, but there is also a strong cinematic resemblance between Seyffert's photograph of children gazing at toy butterflies in a window display (fig. 62) and another scene in *M*, where the child murderer is leading on a potential victim by bringing her before the fascinations of a toy store window.[261] M the adult, standing before the window of knives, shares the rapturous gaze of these seduced children standing before their windows of toys. It is, moreover, far from coincidental that the moment of M's betrayal occurs at the window: the little girl points out the "M" that has been chalked onto his shoulder, and he espies it himself in the shop entrance's mirror.

The *Schaufenster* motif does not leave the scene of sexual entrapment for a moment. Following the knife store scene, the little girl is next seen walking by a new store selling books and prints. Strangely compelling for her vision and for our understanding of M's psychosis are the two moving signs in the display (fig. 63), the (phallic/controlled) vertical arrow bobbing

Figure 62. Candid-camera photograph of children watching moving toy butterflies in a display window, by Rudolf Seyffert, Berlin (1929).

up and down and, to its right, the (vaginal/chaotic) disc spiraling inward, two popular mechanical displays in Weimar display windows.[262] The symbols are made abundantly clear as the camera tracks the girl moving to the right and we perceive the shadow of the arrow moving incessantly up and down over the hypnotic spiral. As viewers we do not yet know where M is standing, but the camera implicates us again in his vision as we track the girl like prey. The girl meets her mother at the street corner by the continuous display window, and they walk back to the left, past M, who is left hovering in the shop entrance with his back to them. The camera then closes in to show M walking out to the sidewalk and rubbing his nervous, frustrated hands, his desire negated by the arrival of the mother. The whistling of his desire (heard against a background of uncanny silence) has been broken by the conversation of the girl with her mother (at which point the normal sounds from the street traffic start up again). To his left we still see, however, the moving circle, the female as commodity, with the insistent shadow of the phallic arrow shifting back and forth over it in a sexual motion.

Lang, the master of mise-en-scène, has provided us here with several key indications of the *Schaufenster*'s role in the Weimar metropolis. First, M, the slayer of little girls, falls prey himself to the sexual combination of

Figure 63. *M* (dir. Fritz Lang, 1931).

male and female geometric configurations that the display window has to offer. Second, the film makes a heavy-handed commentary on the role the big city plays in creating perverse scenarios of harmful sexual desire—and in this scene, the visual rules set up by the display window only exacerbate M's longing. The *Schaufenster* entices him to it, and literally "frames" the little girl in its mirror of knives for him to espy and pursue. Third, all three of M's seduction scenes in this film depend on surface and consumerism in order to succeed. M uses the techniques of the *Schaufenster*, but he is himself caught up within its visual codes. He is as much a childlike, window-shopping little girl as his prey[263]—and so, by extension, are the Weimar shopping masses. This film artfully suggests that Weimar surface culture has produced, by the bankruptcy of the Republic's last years, not only dreamlike images for the masses in the *Schaufenster*, but also an aggressive drive to consume at any cost: here, a murderer who is both prey to consumerist fantasy structures and an assailant of unsuspecting consumers (personified by the virginal innocence of little girls). In the last gasps of Weimar surface, window-shopping has become a dangerous thing to do.

POST-WALL RE-CREATIONS

After the violent death throes of window culture announced in late Weimar's *M*, the window's subsequent synchronization under Nazism, and its final submergence within the pervasive realm of televisual display, is the *Schaufenster* doomed, then, to remain a closed chapter, for all its once-powerful role as a major space of modern consumerism? Virilio and Baudrillard's electronic pessimism notwithstanding, we find that, hearteningly, as part of the new German capital's ongoing efforts, new department stores are, in fact, reapplying window culture as part of their self-conscious focus on urbanism as walked experience.

Several examples of this critical reconstruction urge of the post-Wall era in Berlin are—while postmodern in conceptualization—evidently bent on recreating the city's pre-WWII glory as display window center of the modern era. They include the Salamander shoe store, rebuilt on its own corner site on the Tauentzienstraße, which offers a simple yet effective sheltered glass arcade, composed of internal as well as external display windows on the ground floor; the Galeria department store in Berlin Steglitz, with its wall of sheer glass revealing people, goods on sale, a glass elevator, and escalators alike to the passers-by below; and the Stilwerk building of furniture and interior design stores on the Kantstraße in Charlottenburg, with its rounded glass corner eye-catchingly reminiscent of Mendelsohnian consumerist architecture.[264] These recent architectural recreations of glass display culture, predicated as they are on people walking outside in order to entice those walkers to enter the scene of buying inside, are indications of postmodern urbanism's increasing recognition of the need to reconstitute spaces of streetwise consumption. They also signify the most interesting underbelly of post-Wall Berlin's reconstruction craze, amidst its obvious ongoing need to recreate itself as the metaphorical extension of a new nationhood. These new city windows reflect an impossible wish: the desire to recapture the Berlin of the 1920s. It is an eternal return that can seek but never arrive at a continually reminisced Weimar identity.

APPENDIX

Selected Weimar Periodicals and Newspapers

AEG-Mitteilungen
Der Angriff
Architektur und Schaufenster
Die Auslage. Dekoration, Reklame, Verkaufspraxis, Organisation. Deutsches Fachorgan für Ladeninhaber, Schaufensterdekorateure sowie für alle Ladenbau- und Ladenausstattungsbranchen
Berlin. Berliner Wochenspiegel für Leben, Wirtschaft und Verkehr der Reichshauptstadt
Berliner Illustrirte Zeitung
Berliner Lokal-Anzeiger
Berliner Morgen-Zeitung
Berliner Stadtblatt
Berliner Tageblatt
Berliner Wochenschau
Blau-Rot
City
Die Dame
Die Damenkonfektion
Deutsche Bauzeitung
Deutsche Schokoladen-Zeitung. Das unabhängige wirtschaftliche Fachblatt für das gesamte Süßwarengewerbe
Dixi Magazin
Farbe und Form. Monatsschrift für Kunst und Kunstgewerbe
Die farbige Stadt (Stadtbaukunst)
Der Film. Zeitschrift für das Gesamt-Interessen der Kinematographie
Film-Express (export periodical for *Licht-Bild-Bühne*)
Film-Kurier
Die Filmwoche

Die Form. Monatsschrift für gestaltende Arbeit
Frankfurter Zeitung
Freie Presse (Leipzig)
Germania
Die Grüne Post
Hamburger Anzeiger
Hamburger Echo
Hamburger Fremdenblatt
Hamburger Tageblatt
Hamburgischer Correspondent
Haushalt—Wirtschaft—Lebensführung
Illustrierter Film-Kurier
Illustrierte Film-Woche
Der Kinematograph
Die Koralle. Magazin für alle Freunde von Natur und Technik
Kritische Berliner Illustrirte Woche
Das Kunstblatt
Das Licht. Zeitschrift für praktische Leucht- und Beleuchtungs-Aufgaben
Licht-Bild-Bühne. Die Wochenzeitung der Film-Industrie
Licht und Lampe. Rundschau für die Beleuchtungsindustrie und Installation
Die Mode (Moden-Beilag der Textil-Woche)
Mode und Heim
Das neue Frankfurt. Monatsschrift für die Fragen der Großstadtgestaltung
Neue Frauenkleidung und Frauenkultur. Zeitschrift für persönliche künstlerische Kleidung, Körperkultur und Kunsthandwerk
Die neue Linie
Das Plakat
Die Propaganda (before 1927: *Reklamekunst. Ratgeber für das gesamte Werbewesen*)
Der Querschnitt
Reichsfilmblatt. Offizielles Organ des Reichsverbandes Deutscher Lichtspiel-Theaterbesitzer e.V. (Berlin)
Die Reklame. Fachblatt für das gesamte Werbewesen
Das Schaufenster. Offizielles Organ des Bundes Österreichischer Schaufenster-Dekorateure (after 1929: *Schaufenster und Dekoration*)
Das Schaufenster. Ständige Beilage für Schaufenster und Innendekoration
Schaufenster-Kunst und -Technik
Seidels Reklame. Das Blatt für Werbewesen und Verkaufstechnik
Siemens-Zeitschrift
Styl. Blätter für Mode und die angenehmen Dinge des Lebens
Der Tag
Uhu
Vorwärts

Vossische Zeitung
Der Weg der Frau
Die Weltbühne
Die Woche
Zeitschrift für Waren- und Kaufhäuser. Offizielles Organ des Verbandes Deutscher Waren- und Kaufhäuser

Notes

INTRODUCTION: MODERN SURFACE AND POSTMODERN SIMULATION

1. The word *surface,* like *superficies,* is derived from the Latin *super* (above) and *facies* (face, form, figure, appearance, visage).

2. See Anne Friedberg's thesis of the "mobilized 'virtual' gaze" of postmodernity, in her *Window Shopping: Cinema and the Postmodern* (Berkeley: University of California Press, 1993), 2. A case in point: while Theodor W. Adorno during his Weimar years was a contributor to *The Headlight (Der Scheinwerfer),* a magazine dedicated to the latest in New Objectivity commentary, these days there is a journal of cultural critique called *Surfaces* that exists, in accordance with the Baudrillardian hyperreality thesis, in electronic format only.

3. Fredric Jameson, *Postmodernism, or, The Cultural Logic of Late Capitalism* (Durham: Duke University Press, 1995), 1.

4. Jean Baudrillard, "The Precession of Simulacra," in *Simulacra and Simulation,* trans. Sheila Faria Glaser (Ann Arbor: University of Michigan Press, 1994), 1–42. See also Arthur Kroker, "Baudrillard's Marx," *Theory, Culture and Society* 2.3 (1985): 80.

5. Henri Lefebvre, *The Production of Space* (1974), trans. Donald Nicholson-Smith (Cambridge, Mass.: Basil Blackwell, 1991). Lefebvre brings together the philosophy and the geography of neocapitalistic space by charting a "spatial 'code,'" a spatial "language common to practice and theory" (64).

6. Baudrillard, "The Ecstasy of Communication," in *The Anti-Aesthetic: Essays on Postmodern Culture,* ed. Hal Foster (Port Townsend, Wash.: Bay Press, 1983), 133.

7. David Harvey offers a succinct summary of how postmodernism is regarded as a step beyond the limitations of modernist surface culture: "Atten-

tion to surfaces has, of course, always been important to modernist thought and practice (particularly since the cubists), but it has always been paralleled by the kind of question that [J.] Raban [in *Soft City*, 1974] posed about urban life: how can we build, represent, and attend to these surfaces with the requisite sympathy and seriousness in order to get behind them and identify essential meanings? Postmodernism, with its resignation to bottomless fragmentation and ephemerality, generally refuses to contemplate that question." Harvey, *The Condition of Postmodernity: An Enquiry into the Origins of Cultural Change* (Cambridge: Blackwell, 1989), 58–59.

8. This is Ann Douglas's phrase. In her study of Manhattan, Douglas offers the following assessment of modernity's ongoing connection to the present: "The pace of change had not only accelerated but *peaked* in the 1920s: the consequent transformation of American culture was not followed by any cultural change so wide or drastic. The modern world as we know it today, all the phenomena that to our minds spell the contemporary, from athletic bodies and sexual freedom for women to airplanes, radios, skyscrapers, chain stores, and the culture of credit, arrived on the scene then, and although these phenomena have been extended and vastly empowered in the decades since, they have not fundamentally altered. Only the computer, developed in the 1940s from the electric calculator, can claim a revolutionary effect comparable to those brought about in the first decades of the twentieth century." Ann Douglas, *Terrible Honesty: Mongrel Manhattan in the 1920s* (New York: Farrar, Straus and Giroux, 1995), 192.

9. See Jonathan Crary, "Spectacle, Attention, Counter-Memory," *October* 50 (1989): 100.

10. See Thomas F. McDonough's summary of recent French assessments of Debord and the S.I. in "Rereading Debord, Rereading the Situationists," *October* 79 (1997): 3, 5.

11. Michel Foucault, *Discipline and Punish*, trans. Alan Sheridan (New York, 1977), 217.

12. See Jonathan Crary's bridging discussion of Debord and Foucault in *Techniques of the Observer: On Vision and Modernity in the Nineteenth Century* (Cambridge: MIT Press, 1990), 17–19.

13. Guy Debord, *The Society of the Spectacle*, trans. Donald Nicholson-Smith (New York: Zone Books, 1994), 24, 29. See Martin Jay, *Downcast Eyes: The Denigration of Vision in Twentieth-Century French Thought* (Berkeley: University of California Press, 1993), 416–34 for a discussion of Debord's and the Situationists' anti-ocular theory.

14. Debord, *The Society of the Spectacle*, 13.

15. Debord, *The Society of the Spectacle*, 12.

16. Debord, *The Society of the Spectacle*, 14. Emphasis in original.

17. See Baudrillard, *The Gulf War Did Not Take Place*, trans. Paul Patton (Sydney: Power Publications, 1995).

18. Baudrillard, *Simulacra and Simulation*, 56.

19. Jameson, *Postmodernism*, 9, 12.

20. Baudrillard, "The Ecstasy of Communication," 130.

21. Baudrillard, "The Ecstasy of Communication," 132.

22. Baudrillard, "The Ecstasy of Communication," 131. Critics like Neil Leach have noticed Baudrillard's "'fatal strategy' of pushing his analyses to an extreme, so that his work becomes less a representation of reality than a transcendence of it"; Leach, *Rethinking Architecture: A Reader in Cultural Theory,* ed. Neil Leach (New York: Routledge, 1997), 209. Andreas Huyssen critiques the "black hole" at the end of Baudrillard's search for apocalyptic transcendence; see "In the Shadow of McLuhan: Baudrillard's Theory of Simulation," in Huyssen, *Twilight Memories: Marking Time in a Culture of Amnesia* (New York: Routledge, 1995), 190.

23. See Ernst Bloch, *Heritage of Our Times* (1934), trans. Neville and Stephen Plaice (Berkeley: University of California Press, 1991), 97–103; and Bloch, "Nonsynchronism and Dialectics," *New German Critique* 11 (1977): 22–38. See also Jameson, *Postmodernism,* 302–13.

24. See Detlev Peukert, *Die Weimarer Republik. Krisenjahre der Klassischen Moderne* (Frankfurt a.M.: Suhrkamp, 1987), translated by Richard Deveson as *The Weimar Republic: The Crisis of Classical Modernity* (New York: Hill & Wang, 1992); and Peter Fritzsche, "Landscape of Danger, Landscape of Design: Crisis and Modernism in Weimar Germany," in *Dancing on the Volcano: Essays on the Culture of the Weimar Republic,* ed. Thomas W. Kniesche and Stephen Brockmann (New York: Camden House, 1994), 29–46.

25. See Jameson, "Postmodernism and Consumer Society," in *The Anti-Aesthetic,* ed. Foster, 113–14.

26. Norbert Bolz, "Design des Immateriellen," in *Sehsucht. Über die Veränderung der visuellen Wahrnehmung,* Schriftenreihe Forum vol. 4, ed. Kunst- und Ausstellungshalle der Bundesrepublik Deutschland GmbH (Göttingen: Steidl Verlag, 1995), 160. All translations are my own unless otherwise noted.

27. Marshall McLuhan's famed categorization of technological change from the modern (hot, detribalized, passive, visual, auratic, electric) to the postmodern (cool, retribalized, interactive, postvisual, postauratic, electronic) has not worked out quite as he planned, since visuality is not in decline. See Marshall McLuhan, *Understanding Media: The Extensions of Man* (New York: McGraw-Hill, 1964), 46, 172; and Huyssen, "In the Shadow of McLuhan," 175–91.

28. Mike Featherstone, *Consumer Culture and Postmodernism* (London: Sage, 1991), x. Emphasis in original.

29. Instances of this transmodernity do not necessarily flatter the inherited picture of modernity: Peter Sloterdijk, for example, has christened the dark side to surface-oriented Weimar modernity as a symptomatic "cynicism," an "*enlightened false consciousness*" that connects well with what he terms the postmodern neocynical attitude. Sloterdijk, *Critique of Cynical Reason,* trans. Michael Eldred (Minneapolis: Minnesota University Press, 1987), 546.

30. Susan Buck-Morss, *The Dialectics of Seeing: Walter Benjamin and the Arcades Project* (Cambridge: MIT Press, 1989), 359.

31. Jürgen Habermas, "Modernity—An Incomplete Project," in *The Anti-Aesthetic,* ed. Foster, 13.

32. Jacques Derrida, "Architecture Where the Desire May Live," interview with Eva Meyer, *Domus* 671 (1986); repr. in *Rethinking Architecture,* 323.

33. Miriam Bratu Hansen, "America, Paris, the Alps: Kracauer (and Benjamin) on Cinema and Modernity," in *Cinema and the Invention of Modern Life,* ed. Leo Charney and Vanessa R. Schwartz (Berkeley: University of California Press, 1995), 364.

34. Hansen, "America, Paris, the Alps," 365.

35. See also Martin Jay, "Den Blick erwidern. Die amerikanische Antwort auf die französische Kritik am Okularzentrismus," in *Privileg Blick. Kritik der visuellen Kultur,* ed. Christian Kravagna (Berlin: Edition ID-Archiv, 1997), 154–74.

36. W. J. T. Mitchell, *Picture Theory* (Chicago: University of Chicago Press, 1994).

37. See Anton Kaes, "Filmgeschichte als Kulturgeschichte. Reflexionen zum Kino der Weimarer Republik," in *Filmkultur zur Zeit der Weimarer Republik,* ed. Uli Jung and Walter Schatzberg (New York/Munich: K. G. Saur, 1992), 58.

38. Jean Starobinski, *L'Oeil vivant: Essais* (Paris: Gallimard, 1961), 26. See also Jay in *Downcast Eyes,* 19.

39. On the transition from Fordism to post-Keynesian neo-Fordism, see Eric Alliez and Michel Feher, "The Luster of Capital," trans. Alyson Waters, *Zone* 1/2 (1986): 315–59; Harvey, *The Condition of Postmodernity,* 141–97; and Peter Wollen, "Modern Times: Cinema/Americanism/The Robot," in Wollen, *Raiding the Icebox: Reflections on Twentieth-Century Culture* (Bloomington: Indiana University Press, 1993), 35–71.

40. David Harvey, "The Geopolitics of Capitalism," in *Social Relations and Spatial Structures,* ed. Derek Gregory and John Urry (New York: St. Martin's Press, 1985), 150. Harvey's point is discussed by Edward W. Soja in *Postmodern Geographies: The Reassertion of Space in Critical Social Theory* (New York: Verso, 1989), 157. As Soja amplifies, it is, despite many other heterogeneous influences, a "persistently capitalist landscape" which emerges under capital and which remains the "crude and restless *auteur*" (158, 157).

41. For the major cultural histories on Weimar Germany, see Peter Gay, *Weimar Culture: The Outsider as Insider* (New York: Harper & Row, 1968); Walter Laqueur, *Weimar: A Cultural History 1918–1933* (New York: G. P. Putnam's Sons, 1974); John Willett, *Art and Politics in the Weimar Period: The New Sobriety 1917–1933* (New York: Pantheon, 1978); Jost Hermand and Frank Trommler, *Die Kultur der Weimarer Republik* (Frankfurt a.M.: Fischer, 1989); Peukert, *The Weimar Republic,* and Sander Gilman and Claudia Schmölders, *Gesichter der Weimarer Republik. Eine physiognomische Kulturgeschichte* (Cologne: Dumont, 2000). See also the edited collections *Culture and Society in the Weimar Republic,* ed. Keith Bullivant (Manchester: Manchester University Press, 1977), and *Dancing on the Volcano,* ed. Kniesche and Brockmann.

42. *Neue Sachlichkeit* caught on as a term after being featured as the title of a contemporary art exhibition in Mannheim in 1925 (an exhibition that was restaged there in 1995). For origins, connotations, successes, and limitations of the term itself, see Franz Roh, "Post-Expressionist Schema" (1925), in *The Weimar Republic Sourcebook,* ed. Anton Kaes, Martin Jay, and Edward Dimendberg (Berkeley: University of California Press, 1994), 493; Helmut Lethen, *Neue Sachlichkeit 1924–1932. Studien zur Literatur des "weissen Sozialismus"* (Stuttgart: J. B. Metzler, 1970), 1–12; Jost Hermand, "Unity within Diversity? The Origins of the Concept 'Neue Sachlichkeit,'" trans. Peter and Margaret Lincoln, in *Culture and Society in the Weimar Republic,* ed. Bullivant, 166–82; Willett, *Art and Politics in the Weimar Period,* 111–17; Hermand and Trommler, *Die Kultur der Weimarer Republik,* 116–20, 385–421; and Martin Lindner, *Leben in der Krise. Zeitromane der Neuen Sachlichkeit und die intellektuelle Mentalität der klassischen Moderne* (Stuttgart: J. B. Metzler, 1994), 157–62.

43. Weimar Berlin profited from the extreme pace of industrialization during the Wilhelmine Empire: as the economist Werner Sombart noted, from 1882 to 1907 German industrial production doubled in size. Cited by Massimo Cacciari, *Architecture and Nihilism: On the Philosophy of Modern Architecture,* trans. Stephen Sartarelli (New Haven: Yale University Press, 1993), 33.

44. *Berlin Handbuch. Das Lexikon der Bundeshauptstadt,* ed. Horst Ulrich and Uwe Prell (Berlin: FAB Verlag, 1992), 238.

45. Franz Grüger, "Die Wirtschaft Deutschlands als Grundlage der Werbetätigkeit," *Die Reklame* 22.1 (1929): 526.

46. See Clifford Geertz, *The Interpretation of Cultures: Selected Essays* (New York: Basic Books, 1973); and Geertz, *Local Knowledge: Further Essays in Interpretive Anthropology* (New York: Basic Books, 1983).

47. For a parallel study of the visual culture of American modernity (albeit with a greater focus on Fordist labor), see Terry Smith, *Making the Modern: Industry, Art, and Design in America* (Chicago: University of Chicago Press, 1993).

48. Hermand and Trommler, *Die Kultur der Weimarer Republik,* 52; see also 54–56.

49. See *Berlin wirbt! Metropolenwerbung zwischen Verkehrsreklame und Stadtmarketing, 1920–1995* (Berlin: FAB Verlag, 1995), 14.

50. Clement Greenberg, "On the Role of Nature in Modernist Painting," in *Art and Culture: Critical Essays* (Boston: Beacon Press, 1965), 172; cited and discussed by Jay, *Downcast Eyes,* 160. As an instance of this, Jay points to how the linguistic cacaphony in the midst of Marcel Duchamp's "fetishism of sight" operates as a vibrant self-critique within the apparently more dominant ocular metaphor (164). Mark C. Taylor also senses this double exposure in his discussion of Greenberg's theory: modern art's "valorization of flatness . . . can be understood either as the culmination of the erasure of ornament or as the transformation of *l'oeuvre d'art* as such into nothing but ornament." Taylor, *Hiding* (Chicago: University of Chicago Press, 1997), 107.

51. Jay, *Downcast Eyes*, 181.

52. Saskia Sassen, *The Global City: New York, London, Tokyo* (Princeton: Princeton University Press, 1991); and Sassen, *Cities in a World Economy* (Thousand Oaks, Calif.: Pine Forge Press, 1994).

53. Sociologist Werner Schiffauer has noted how the ascendance of the "local" (whereby the new provincial areas like Silicon Valley or Research Triangle in North Carolina have assumed economic and political clout previously reserved only for urban centers) corresponds fully, in fact, to the rise of the "global." Schiffauer, "Zur Logik von kulturellen Strömungen in Großstädten," in *Fremde in der Stadt. Zehn Essays über Kultur und Differenz* (Frankfurt a.M.: Suhrkamp, 1997), 101.

54. Paul Virilio, "The Overexposed City," trans. Astrid Hustvedt from *L'Espace critique* (1984), *Zone 1/2* (1986): 20.

55. Virilio, "The Overexposed City," 17, 18. For a recent study on electronic communication in the postmodern city, see J. Mitchell, *City of Bits: Space, Place, and the Infobahn* (Cambridge: MIT Press, 1996).

56. Virilio, "The Overexposed City," 18, 20.

57. Baudrillard, "The Ecstasy of Communication," 127, 126.

58. Baudrillard, *America*, trans. Chris Turner (London: Verso, 1988), 56.

59. Virilio, "The Overexposed City," 18.

60. Virilio, "The Overexposed City," 23, 20.

61. Virilio, "The Overexposed City," 30–31.

62. See Andreas Huyssen, "Mass Culture as Woman: Modernism's Other," in *After the Great Divide: Modernism, Mass Culture, Postmodernism* (Bloomington: Indiana University Press, 1986), 44–62.

63. Le Corbusier, *The City of Tomorrow* (1929), trans. Frederick Etchells (London: The Architectural Press, 1947), 143.

64. Walter Benjamin, *Gesammelte Schriften*, ed. Rolf Tiedemann and Hermann Schweppenhäuser, 7 vols. (Frankfurt a.M.: Suhrkamp, 1972), 5.2:1051.

65. This filmic juxtaposition formed the basis of Anton Kaes's keynote speech at the 1995 Conference on Literature & Film (Tallahassee, Florida). See also Hanno Möbius and Guntram Vogt, *Drehort Stadt. Das Thema "Großstadt" im deutschen Film* (Marburg: Hitzeroth, 1990), 17.

66. Michel de Certeau, *The Practice of Everyday Life*, trans. Steven Rendall (Berkeley: University of California Press, 1984), 97.

67. See the contested pronouncement of Hans Stimman, city building director, that "we must bring this [inner] city back . . . Berlin must look like Berlin." Paul Goldberger, "Reimagining Berlin," *The New York Times Magazine* (February 5, 1995).

68. Eberhard H. Zeidler complains that nowadays, as mall shopping is increasingly becoming a Disney type of experience, the display of goods is not enough in itself and "has to be concealed behind an 'entertainment' façade." *Architektur für den Handel/Architecture for the Retail Trade*, ed. Wolfgang Hocquél, Friedel Kellermann, et al. (Berlin: Birkhäuser Verlag, 1996), 11.

69. Friedberg, *Window Shopping*, 110, 113.

70. Baudrillard, *Simulacra and Simulation,* 12, 13; emphasis in original.

71. Eco, "The City of Robots," in *Travels in Hyperreality,* trans. William Weaver (London: Pan Books, 1987); repr. in *Postmodernism: A Reader,* ed. Thomas Docherty (New York: Columbia University Press, 1993), 202.

72. See Mark Taylor on the "cinemascape" of the new Strip in Las Vegas, in *Hiding,* 255, 261.

73. Friedberg, *Window Shopping,* 182. On the loss of *flânerie,* see also Keith Tester's introduction to *The Flâneur,* ed. Tester (New York: Routledge, 1994), 13–17. For resurrective studies on Benjamin- and Hessel-inspired *flânerie* in the Weimar and contemporary eras respectively, see Anke Gleber, *The Art of Taking a Walk: Flânerie, Literature, and Film in Weimar Culture* (Princeton: Princeton University Press, 1999); and Günter Kunert, *Da sind noch ein paar Menschen in Berlin* (Munich: Bucher-Verlag, 1999).

74. See Margaret Leslie Davis, *Bullocks Wilshire* (Los Angeles: Balcony Press, 1996), 10, 33, 41, 50–51.

75. See Bertolt Brecht, "Hollywood-Elegien," in *Gedichte für Städtebewohner,* ed. Franco Buono (Frankfurt a.M.: Suhrkamp, 1980), 124–25.

76. Bruno Taut, in his *Stadtkrone* (Jena: Eugen Diederichs, 1919), proposes a reformation of the metropolis into the "garden city," but (unlike L.A.) one nonetheless with an urban centerpiece or "city crown."

77. Mike Davis, *City of Quartz: Excavating the Future in Los Angeles* (New York: Vintage Books, 1992), 23, 47, 21. As Davis continues: "The American city . . . is being systematically turned inside out—or rather, outside in" (226). On Los Angeles, see also Soja, *Postmodern Geographies,* 190–248.

78. Erich Maria Remarque, *Shadows in Paradise,* cited in *Deutsche Exilliteratur seit 1933. Teil 1: Kalifornien,* ed. J. M. Spalek and J. Strekla (Bern: Francke, 1976), 595; discussed by Davis, *City of Quartz,* 50.

79. Anton Wagner, *Los Angeles: Werden, Leben und Gestalt der Zweimillionenstadt in Südkalifornien* (Kiel: Universität Kiel [Geographisches Institut], 1935), 156; cited by Davis, *City of Quartz,* 49.

80. Max Horkheimer and Theodor W. Adorno, *Dialektik der Aufklärung. Philosophische Fragmente* (Frankfurt a.M.: Fischer, 1988), 128; discussed by Davis, *City of Quartz,* 48–49.

81. Davis, *City of Quartz,* 223, 231.

82. Even though Baudrillard refers to Beaubourg as a "monument to total disconnection, to hyperreality, and to the implosion of culture," he also remarks that it is precisely its tactility that draws the masses. Baudrillard, *Simulacra and Simulation,* 63, 70.

83. See Herbert Muschamp, "The Miracle in Bilbao," *The New York Times Magazine* (September 7, 1997): 54–59, 72, 82.

84. See Michael Rutschky, "Art on Buildings: The Flaneur as the Self-Sufficient Person," *Daidalos* 49 (1993): 82–87.

85. Cited by Petra Kipphoff, "Verweile nicht! Du bist so schön!" *Die Zeit* (June 30, 1995): 43.

86. Kipphoff, "Verweile nicht!" 44.

87. Martin Heidegger, "The Origin of the Work of Art" (1935), in Heidegger, *Basic Writings,* ed. David Farrell Krell (New York: Harper & Row, 1977), 180.

88. See Michael S. Cullen, *Der Reichstag. Parlament, Denkmal, Symbol* (Berlin: be.bra verlag, 1995), 284–311.

89. See Peter-Klaus Schuster, "Impressionismus als Denkbild," *Der Tagesspiegel* (July 5, 1995): 19.

90. See, for example, the articles by Heiner Bastian, Tilmann Buddensieg, Alexander Demandt, and Franz-Joachim Verspohl in *project wrapped reichstag—unwrapped,* a special issue of *Copernicus—Ansichten aus Wissenschaft, Politik, Kunst* (Berlin: Markus Braun Verlag, 1995).

91. Andreas Huyssen, "Monumental Seduction," *New German Critique* 69 (1996): 198.

92. On the age of the great exhibitions, see Siegfried Giedion, *Space, Time, and Architecture: The Growth of a New Tradition,* 4th ed. (Cambridge: Harvard University Press, 1962), 241–75; and Giedion, *Bauen in Frankreich, Bauen in Eisen, Bauen in Eisenbeton* (Leipzig: Klinkhardt & Biermann, 1928), 120–42. See also Tony Bennett, "The Exhibitionary Complex," in *Thinking About Exhibitions,* ed. Reesa Greenberg, Bruce W. Ferguson, and Sandy Nairne (New York: Routledge, 1996), 81–112.

93. Georg Simmel, "Berliner Gewerbeausstellung," *Die Zeit* (Vienna) 7.91 (July 25, 1896). Translated by Sam Whimster as "The Berlin Trade Exhibition," *Theory, Culture & Society* 8 (1991): here, 122. I thank Anton Kaes for referring me to this essay.

94. Simmel, "The Berlin Trade Exhibition," 121.

95. See Friedberg's comment on this aspect: "The World Exhibition was a monumental site for the conflation of the *mobilized* gaze of shopping and tourism with the *virtual* gaze of the *faux-real*" of commodity fetishism. Friedberg, *Window Shopping,* 82.

96. Buck-Morss, *Dialectics of Seeing,* 85; citing Benjamin, *Gesammelte Schriften,* 5.1:267, citing Giedion. Giedion, in *Bauen in Frankreich,* remarks that exhibitions were the "birthplace of today's *advertising*" (121).

97. Eco, "How an Exposition Exposes Itself," in *Travels in Hyperreality;* repr. in *Rethinking Architecture,* ed. Leach, 204.

98. Siegfried Kracauer, *Orpheus in Paris: Offenbach and the Paris of His Time,* trans. Gwenda David and Eric Mosbacher (New York: Alfred A. Knopf, 1938), 140–41; a translation of *Jacques Offenbach und das Paris seiner Zeit* (Frankfurt a.M.: Suhrkamp, 1976), 145.

99. Benjamin, *Gesammelte Schriften,* 5.1:50.

100. Benjamin, *Gesammelte Schriften,* 5.1:238; citing Giedion, *Bauen in Frankreich,* 121, 37. See also Giedion, *Space, Time and Architecture,* 242.

101. Benjamin, *Gesammelte Schriften,* 5.1:448.

102. Daniel H. Burnham and Edward H. Bennett, *Plan of Chicago,* ed. Charles Moore (New York: Princeton Architectural Press, 1993), 6.

103. Lewis Mumford, *Sticks and Stones: A Study of American Architecture and Civilization* (New York: Boni & Liveright, 1924), 150, 148. Cited by

Neil Harris, "Memory and the White City," in *Grand Illusions: Chicago's World Fair of 1893*, ed. Neil Harris et al. (Chicago: Chicago Historical Society, 1993), 17.

104. Giedion, *Space, Time and Architecture*, 273.

105. Stuart Ewen and Elizabeth Ewen, *Channels of Desire: Mass Images and the Shaping of American Consciousness* (New York: McGraw-Hill, 1982), 199.

106. See Harris, "Memory and the White City," 23–29.

107. See Curtus M. Hinsley, "Strolling through the Colonies," in *Walter Benjamin and the Demands of History*, ed. Michael P. Steinberg (Ithaca: Cornell University Press, 1996), 119–40.

108. See Lawrence Biemüller's essay on the 1996 Olympics, "Notes from Academe," *The Chronicle of Higher Education* (April 19, 1996): A67.

109. Robert Venturi, Denise Scott Brown, and Steven Izenour, *Learning from Las Vegas: The Forgotten Symbolism of Architectural Form* (Cambridge: MIT Press, 1977), 87.

110. Ada Louise Huxtable, "Living with the Fake, and Liking It," *The New York Times* (March 30, 1997): sec. 2, p. 1. Excerpted from Huxtable, *The Unreal America: Architecture and Illusion* (New York: New Press, 1997).

111. See Mark C. Taylor's discussion of the Luxor hotel as "cinematic space," *Hiding*, 242–48. See also Taylor's CD-ROM, *The Real: Las Vegas, NV*, Williams College Museum of Art and the Massachusetts Museum of Contemporary Art (Chicago: University of Chicago Press, 1997).

112. Richard Wolkomir, "Las Vegas Meets La-La Land," *Smithsonian* (October 1995): 57, 58.

113. Friedrich Nietzsche, *Sämtliche Werke: Kritische Studienausgabe*, ed. Giorgio Colli and Mazzino Montinari, 15 vols. (New York: de Gruyter, 1967–1977), 1:880–81.

114. For Nietzsche's treatment of surface, see *Sämtliche Werke: Daybreak*, 3:52; *The Birth of Tragedy Out of the Spirit of Music*, 1:64–65; *Beyond Good and Evil*, 5:41; *The Gay Science*, 3:500; *On The Advantage and Disadvantage of History for Life*, 1:250.

115. Nietzsche, *Sämtliche Werke*, 9:309.

116. Bolz has amplified Nietzsche's perceptual philosophy thus: "Today we know that perceiving is a form of scanning that does not present the things of the world, rather it examines relations and on the basis of this examination computes pictures in the interior world-space [*Weltinnenraum*] of the brain. . . . Perception has therefore nothing to do with the truth of the world. . . . There is no mimesis." Bolz, "Design des Immateriellen," 155, 156.

117. Nietzsche, *Sämtliche Werke*, 5:517; *The Gay Science*, trans. Walter Kaufmann (New York: Vintage, 1974), 217.

118. Nietzsche, *Sämtliche Werke*, 3:352; *The Gay Science*, 38. Emphasis in original.

119. Nietzsche, *Sämtliche Werke*, 6:37, 27.

120. Nietzsche, *Sämtliche Werke*, 2:675–76.

121. See, for example, Geoff Waite, *Nietzsche's Corps/e: Aesthetics: Politics, Prophecy, or, The Spectacular Technoculture of Everyday Life* (Durham: Duke University Press, 1996).

122. Nietzsche, *Sämtliche Werke,* 7:817. Discussed by David Frisby, *Fragments of Modernity: Theories of Modernity in the Work of Simmel, Kracauer and Benjamin* (Cambridge: MIT Press, 1986), 31.

123. Nietzsche, *Sämtliche Werke,* 7:817.

124. See Massimo Cacciari's discussion of Nietzsche's disdain for the metropolis in *Thus Spake Zarathustra,* in *Architecture and Nihilism: On the Philosophy of Modern Architecture* (New Haven: Yale University Press, 1993), 24–29.

125. Jürgen Habermas, "Georg Simmel on Philosophy and Culture: Postscript to a Collection of Essays," trans. Mathieu Deflem, *Critical Inquiry* 22 (1996): 406.

126. Georg Simmel, "The Metropolis and Mental Life," trans. H. H. Gerth with C. Wright Mills, in *Classic Essays on the Culture of Cities,* ed. Richard Sennett (Englewood Cliffs, N.J.: Prentice-Hall, 1969), 59.

127. Simmel, "The Metropolis and Mental Life," 51, 48. The term *blasé* was in use at the turn of the century to denote the big-city mentality: see, for example, Upton Sinclair, *The Metropolis* (New York: Moffat, Yard, & Co., 1908), 120.

128. Simmel, "The Berlin Trade Exhibition," 122.

129. Simmel, "Das Geld in der modernen Kultur" (1896), in *Schriften zur Soziologie. Eine Auswahl,* ed. Heinz-Jürgen Dahme and Ottheim Rammstedt (Frankfurt a.M.: Suhrkamp, 1983), 89. See also Simmel's *Philosophie des Geldes* (1900), ed. David P. Frisby and Klaus Christian Köhnke (Frankfurt a.M.: Suhrkamp, 1989).

130. Simmel, "The Metropolis and Mental Life," 52.

131. See Gianfranco Poggi, *Money and the Modern Mind: Georg Simmel's* Philosophy of Money (Berkeley: University of California Press, 1993), 95–101, 134–36.

132. See Poggi's comparison of Marx's and Simmel's notions of alienation. Poggi, *Money and the Modern Mind,* 185–212.

133. Benjamin, *Gesammelte Schriften,* 5.1:576. See also chapter 3 of Graeme Gilloch, *Myth and Metropolis. Walter Benjamin and the City* (Cambridge, Mass.: Blackwell, 1996).

134. See Friedberg's history of the arcade, in *Window Shopping,* 68–76.

135. Benjamin, *Gesammelte Schriften,* 5.1:494; emphasis in original. Benjamin wrote to Giedion in 1929, praising *Building in France* and Giedion's ability to "illuminate, or rather to uncover, the tradition by observing the present." See Sokratis Georgiadis's introduction to *Building in France: Building in Iron, Building in Ferroconcrete,* trans. J. Duncan Freyas (Santa Monica: The Getty Center for the History of Art & the Humanities, 1995), 53, 87.

136. Benjamin, *Gesammelte Schriften,* 5.1:45, 55.

137. Benjamin, *Gesammelte Schriften,* 5.1:93.

138. Benjamin, *Gesammelte Schriften,* 5.1:511, 513.

139. Benjamin, *Gesammelte Schriften,* 5.1:135.

140. Benjamin, *Gesammelte Schriften,* 5.1:223.

141. Benjamin, *Gesammelte Schriften,* 5.1:560.

142. Max Weber, *Wissenschaft als Beruf* (Berlin: Duncker & Humblot, 1992), 17; emphasis in original.

143. Buck-Morss, *The Dialectics of Seeing,* 254; citing Benjamin, *Gesammelte Schriften,* 5.1:96.

144. See Buck-Morss's definition of Benjamin's text as a "materialist history that disenchants the new nature in order to free it from the spell of capitalism, and yet rescues all the power of enchantment for the purpose of social transformation." Buck-Morss, *The Dialectics of Seeing,* 275.

145. Benjamin, *Gesammelte Schriften,* 4.1:93; *Selected Writings,* ed. Marcus Bullock, Howard Eiland, Michael W. Jennings, and Gary Smith (Cambridge: Belknap Press, 1996), 449, 450.

146. Benjamin, *Gesammelte Schriften,* 4.1:93; *Selected Writings,* 450.

147. De Certeau, *The Practice of Everyday Life,* 31.

148. Edward Said, *Culture and Imperialism* (New York: Vintage, 1993), xii. On the connections between urban European surface culture and Orientalism/colonialism, see Rolf J. Goebel, "Japanese Urban Space and the Citation of Western Signs," *Comparative Literature* 35.2 (1998): 93–106.

149. Benjamin, *Gesammelte Schriften,* 4.1:101; *Selected Writings,* 454.

150. Kracauer studied architecture in Darmstadt, Berlin, and Munich from 1906 to 1914 and practiced architecture in Frankfurt a.M. from 1915 to 1917 before being enlisted, whereupon he worked for the Osnabrück city planning office from 1917 to 1918. See Gerwin Zohlen, "Schmugglerpfad. Siegfried Kracauer, Architekt und Schriftsteller," in *Siegfried Kracauer. Neue Interpretationen,* ed. Michael Kessler and Thomas Y. Levin (Tübingen: Stauffenberg Verlag, 1990), 325–44.

151. Theodor W. Adorno, "The Curious Realist: On Siegfried Kracauer," trans. Shierry Weber Nicholsen, *New German Critique* 54 (1991): 163.

152. Kracauer, "Über Arbeitsnachweise" (1930), repr. in *Straßen in Berlin und anderswo* (Berlin: Das Arsenal, 1987), 52.

153. Kracauer, *The Mass Ornament: Weimar Essays,* trans. and ed. Thomas Y. Levin (Cambridge: Harvard University Press, 1995), 234.

154. Kracauer, *The Mass Ornament,* 253.

155. See, e.g., Alexandra Warwick and Dani Cavallaro's *Fashioning the Frame: Boundaries, Dress and Body* (New York: Berg, 1998).

156. Kracauer, *The Mass Ornament,* 75; Kracauer, *Das Ornament der Masse. Essays* (Frankfurt a.M.: Suhrkamp, 1963), 50.

157. Chris Jenks points out how Lévi-Strauss recommends an excavation of cultural phenomena as the "surface appearances or manifestations of underlying patterns at the deeper level, both within time, the 'synchronic,' and through time, the 'diachronic.'" Jenks, *Culture* (New York: Routledge, 1993), 127.

158. Michel Foucault, *The Archaeology of Knowledge,* trans. A. M. Sheridan Smith (New York: Pantheon, 1972), 131.

159. Foucault, "The Discourse on Language," in *The Archaeology of Knowledge,* 229, 231, 229.

160. See Levin, "Der enthüllte Kracauer," in *Siegfried Kracauer,* ed. Kessler and Levin, 236.

161. See Inka Mülder-Bach, "Der Umschlag der Negativität. Zur Verschränkung von Phänomenologie, Geschichtsphilosophie und Filmästhetik in Siegfried Kracauers Metaphorik der 'Oberfläche,'" *Deutsche Vierteljahrsschrift* 61.2 (1987): 359–73; and Inka Mülder, *Siegfried Kracauer—Grenzgänger zwischen Theorie und Literatur. Seine frühen Schriften 1913–1933* (Stuttgart: Metzler, 1985), 86–95. See also Miriam Hansen on Mülder-Bach's thesis of a perspectival shift in Kracauer's understanding of surface, around 1925, from negative to positive, from *Oberfläche* to *Fläche,* with a diminishing need for a reality underneath, and a rising acceptance of the transformative value of material realities. Hansen, "Decentric Perspectives: Kracauer's Early Writings on Film and Mass Culture," *New German Critique* 54 (1991): 51.

162. Kracauer, *Straßen in Berlin,* 29.

163. Kracauer, "Der neue Alexanderplatz," *Frankfurter Zeitung* (November 18, 1932). Repr. in *Glänzender Asphalt. Berlin im Feuilleton der Weimarer Republik,* ed. Christian Jäger and Erhard Schütz (Berlin: Fannei & Walz, 1994), 182, 183.

164. Kracauer, "Am Paradies vorbei," *Frankfurter Zeitung* 75.865 (November 20, 1930).

165. See Heide Schlüppmann, "Die nebensächliche Frau. Geschlechterdifferenz in Siegfried Kracauers Essayistik der zwanziger Jahre," *Feministische Studien* 11.1 (1993): 38–47.

166. Walther G. Hoffmann, *Das Wachstum der deutschen Wirtschaft seit der Mitte des 19. Jahrhunderts* (Berlin: Springer-Verlag, 1965), 214. Cited by Dirk Reinhardt, *Von der Reklame zum Marketing. Geschichte der Wirtschaftswerbung in Deutschland* (Berlin: Akademie Verlag, 1993), 443.

167. Benjamin, "On Some Motifs in Baudelaire" (1939), in Benjamin, *Illuminations: Essays and Reflections,* ed. Hannah Arendt, trans. Harry Zohn (New York: Shocken, 1968), 176.

168. Kracauer, "Organisiertes Glück. Zur Wiedereröffnung des Lunaparks," *Frankfurter Zeitung* 338 (May 8, 1930).

169. Alfred Döblin, "Der Geist des naturalistischen Zeitalters," *Die neue Rundschau* 35.2 (1924). Repr. in Döblin, *Schriften zu Ästhetik, Poetik und Literatur,* ed. Erich Kleinschmidt (Olten: Walter-Verlag, 1989), 179, 190.

170. See Alfred Polgar, "Girls," *Prager Tageblatt* (November 4, 1926). Repr. in *Glänzender Asphalt,* ed. Jäger and Schütz, 238.

171. Joseph Roth, "Die 'Girls,'" *Frankfurter Zeitung* (April 28, 1925), repr. in Roth, *Werke,* ed. Hermann Kesten (Kiepenheuer & Witsch, 1975), 4:547.

172. Kracauer, "The Mass Ornament," in *The Mass Ornament,* 77. For a likely influence on Kracauer, see Fritz Giese's account of the "collective person"

depicted by such Tilleresque "girl-technics" in *Girlkultur. Vergleich zwischen amerikanischem und europäischem Rhythmus und Lebensgefühl* (Munich: Delphin-Verlag, 1925), 13–36, 86–87. For commentaries on Kracauer's essay, see Sabine Hake, "Girls and Crisis: The Other Side of Diversion," *New German Critique* 40 (1987); and Wollen, "Modern Times," in *Raiding the Icebox*, 54–56.

173. Kracauer, "Girls und Krise," *Frankfurter Zeitung* (May 26, 1931); repr. in *Glänzender Asphalt*, ed. Jäger and Schütz, 241. Emphasis in original.

174. Kracauer, *The Mass Ornament*, 79.

175. Kracauer, *The Mass Ornament*, 326; *Das Ornament der Masse*, 315.

176. Kracauer, *The Mass Ornament*, 76; *Das Ornament der Masse*, 52.

177. Kracauer, *The Mass Ornament*, 83. On this point, see also Gerhard Menz, *Irrationales in der Rationalisierung. Mensch und Maschine* (Breslau: M. & H. Marcus, 1928).

178. Kracauer, *The Mass Ornament*, 327.

179. Kracauer, *The Mass Ornament*, 324.

180. Kracauer, *Die Angestellten. Aus dem neuesten Deutschland* (1930), in Kracauer, *Schriften 1*, ed. Karsten Witte (Frankfurt a.M.: Suhrkamp, 1971), 99. Partially translated in *The Weimar Republic Sourcebook*, ed. Kaes, Jay, and Dimendberg, 191.

181. Kracauer, *Die Angestellten*, 91.

182. Kracauer, *Die Angestellten*, 11.

183. Kracauer, "Asyle für Obdachlose," in *Straßen in Berlin*, 16.

184. See Kracauer, *Orpheus in Paris*, 68–78.

185. Stefan Zweig, "Die Monotonisierung der Welt," *Berliner Börsen-Courier* (February 1, 1925); repr. in *The Weimar Republic Sourcebook*, ed. Kaes, Jay, and Dimendberg, 399, 397, 398.

186. See Mark M. Anderson, *Kafka's Clothes: Ornament and Aestheticism in the Habsburg Fin de Siècle* (New York: Oxford University Press, 1992).

187. For an analysis of Kafka's writing as a unique blend of Marxist and Freudian discourses that literally internalize the modern condition of human alienation, see Walter H. Sokel, "Kafka at the End of the Century: Kafka and the Twentieth Century: Its Discourses in His Work," *The Journal of the Kafka Society of America* 19.1–2 (1995).

188. Léon Daudet, "Deutsche Kultur," cited by Traugott Schalcher in *Die Auslage* 26 (1928): 10.

189. Gertrud Bäumler, *Die Frau in der Krisis der Kultur* (Berlin: F. A. Herbig, 1926), 3.

190. Bäumer, *Die Frau in der Krisis der Kultur*, 4, 5, 9.

191. Friedrich Schönemann, *Die Kunst der Massenbeeinflussung in den Vereinigten Staaten von America* (Berlin: Deutsche Verlags-Anstalt, 1924).

192. Georg Lukács, "Reification and the Consciousness of the Proletariat" (1922), in *History and Class Consciousness*, trans. Rodney Livingstone (Cambridge: MIT Press, 1971), 208.

193. Lukács, "Reification and the Consciousness of the Proletariat," 208.

194. Lukács, *Studies in European Realism* (New York: Grosset & Dunlap, 1964); cited by Jay, *Downcast Eyes,* 173.

195. Lukács, "Reification and the Consciousness of the Proletariat," 197; emphasis in original.

196. Kracauer, *The Mass Ornament,* 327; emphasis in original.

197. Ernst Toller, *Hoppla, wir leben! Ein Vorspiel und fünf Akte* (Stuttgart: Reclam, 1962, 1980), 105.

198. Erich Kästner, *Fabian* (Zürich: Atrium Verlag/dtv, 1985), 148–49.

199. Stössinger, "Die verwandelte Tauentzien," in *Glänzender Asphalt,* ed. Jäger and Schütz, 107–11.

200. Fritz Wertheim, *Die Reklame des Warenhauses* (diss., University of Cologne, 1933), 73.

201. Oskar Maurus Fontana, "Berlin ist zu vermieten. Die Meinung eines Passanten," *Berliner Tageblatt* (April 23, 1930). Repr. in *Glänzender Asphalt,* ed. Jäger and Schütz, 317, 319.

202. Kracauer, "Unter der Oberfläche," *Frankfurter Zeitung* 75.510 (July 11, 1931).

203. Debord, *The Society of the Spectacle,* 14.

204. Terry Eagleton, *The Illusions of Postmodernism* (Cambridge, Mass.: Blackwell, 1996), 15, 17.

205. Bill Readings, *The University in Ruins* (Cambridge: Harvard University Press, 1996), 121.

206. Pierre Bourdieu, *Distinction: A Social Critique of the Judgement of Taste,* trans. R. Nice (New York: Routledge, 1984), 53, 54. See also Bourdieu's *Homo Academicus,* trans. Peter Collier (Stanford: Stanford University Press, 1988).

207. W. J. T. Mitchell, "What Do Pictures *Really* Want?" *October* 77 (1996): 74.

208. Baudrillard, "The Ecstasy of Communication," 130.

209. Benjamin, "Theses on the Philosophy of History," in *Illuminations,* 255, 261.

CHAPTER 1. FUNCTIONALIST FAÇADES

1. Adolf Behne, *Der moderne Zweckbau* (Munich: Drei Masken Verlag, 1925), 12.

2. H. M. Geiger, "Das Stadtbild der Zukunft und seine Schaufenster," *Schaufenster-Kunst und -Technik* (March-April 1926): 17. Cited by Tilman Osterwold, *Schaufenster—Die Kulturgeschichte eines Massenmediums* (Stuttgart: Württembergischer Kunstverein, 1974), 41.

3. Topes, "Ecken von gestern und heute," *Berliner Zeitung* 58.153 (March 31, 1929).

4. Ottomar Starke, "Fassaden," *Der Querschnitt* 9.11 (1929): 775.

5. See Mark Wigley's comment on modern architectural surface as verb-form: "It is this exhibition of the subordinated surface, rather than an exhibi-

tion of the new means of production, that renders architecture modern. . . . Its surfaces are not simply cleansed of ornament, the structure stripped of clothing, the layers of representation scraped off to expose the abstract forms of modern life, and so on. Rather, the surfaces are trained to represent the very process of cleansing, stripping, and scraping." Mark Wigley, *White Walls, Designer Dresses: The Fashioning of Modern Architecture* (Cambridge: MIT Press, 1995), 39.

6. See Wolfgang Schivelbusch, *Licht Schein und Wahn. Auftritte der elektrischen Beleuchtung im 20. Jahrhundert* (Berlin: Ernst & Sohn, 1992), 14.

7. Geiger, "Das Stadtbild der Zukunft und seine Schaufenster," 17.

8. Martin Wagner and Adolf Behne, eds., *Das neue Berlin. Großstadtprobleme,* twelve issues (Berlin: Deutsche Bauzeitung, 1929); repr. with an introduction by Julius Posener (Boston: Birkhäuser Verlag, 1988), 1.

9. Martin Wagner and Adolf Behne, "Einfachheit ist höchste Konzentration," *Architektur und Schaufenster* 25 (January 1928): 7; emphasis in original.

10. Maximilian Sladek, "Unsere Schau," in Erik Charell, *An Alle* (Program Notes, 1924); trans. as "Our Show," in *The Weimar Republic Sourcebook,* ed. Kaes, Jay, and Dimendberg, 556.

11. See "Tietz in Schöneberg," *Berliner Tageblatt* 58.93 (February 23, 1929).

12. See P. Morton Shand's study of Weimar movie palace design, *The Architecture of Pleasure: Modern Theatres and Cinemas* (London: B. T. Batsford, 1930), 22, 25.

13. Behne and Wagner, *Das neue Berlin,* 5. Emphasis in original.

14. Max Osborn, Adolph Donath, and Franz M. Feldhaus, *Berlins Aufstieg zur Weltstadt* (Berlin: Verlag von Reimar Hobbing, 1929), 212–13.

15. See Kracauer's essay "Sendestation: Das Haus," *Frankfurter Zeitung* (January 23, 1931); repr. in *Hans Poelzig. Haus des Rundfunks,* ed. Sender Freies Berlin (Berlin: Ars Nicolai, 1994), 11–13.

16. The first season of fairs in 1925 was launched with articles like "Berlin, the Town of the Special Trade Fairs and Exhibitions," *Berlin. Berliner Wochenspiegel für Leben, Wirtschaft und Verkehr der Reichshauptstadt* 7 (August 1–7, 1925): 17–22; see also *Berlin wirbt! Metropolenwerbung zwischen Verkehrsreklame und Stadtmarketing, 1920–1995* (Berlin: FAB Verlag, 1995), 11, 13.

17. J. Herle, "Positive Ausstellungspolitik," in the Deutsche Ausstellungs- und Messe-Amt's *Neudeutsche Ausstellungspolitik* 4 (1928): 17, 6; emphasis in original.

18. Appendix 2, *Neudeutsche Ausstellungspolitik,* 86–89.

19. Ernst Jäckh, "Neudeutsche Ausstellungspolitik," in *Neudeutsche Ausstellungspolitik* 4 (1928): 49, 61.

20. Jäckh, "Neudeutsche Ausstellungspolitik," 57.

21. "Die internationale Werkbund-Ausstellung 1932 in Köln und am Rhein," *Die Form* 3.1 (1928): 194.

22. Otto Neurath, "'Die Neue Zeit,' Köln 1932," *Die Form* 4.21 (1929): 588.

23. Mies van der Rohe, "Zum Thema: Ausstellungen," *Die Form* 4.1 (1928): 121.

24. Rem Koolhaas, *Delirious New York: A Retroactive Manifesto for Manhattan* (New York: Oxford University Press, 1978), 7.

25. I am indebted here to Thomas Brockelman, "Collage City / Event City: Architectural Urbanism and the Contemporary Avant-Garde," unpublished paper presented at the conference of the International Association of Philosophy and Literature, University of California at Irvine, 1998.

26. Karl Jaspers, *Die geistige Situation der Zeit* (New York: de Gruyter, 1978), 160, 43.

27. Cited by Karsten Harries, *The Ethical Function of Architecture* (Cambridge: MIT Press, 1997), 8.

28. Philip Johson's "Modern Architecture: International Exhibition," featuring Gropius, Mies van der Rohe, Le Corbusier, Wright, et al., was held at the Museum of Modern Art in 1932 and travelled across the U.S. for seven years, being shown in department stores in areas without museums. See Beatriz Colomina, *Privacy and Publicity: Modern Architecture as Mass Media* (Cambridge: MIT Press, 1994), 201–12, 366n1.

29. Charles Jencks defines thus the end of streamlined functionalism and the beginning of postmodern hybridity in architecture. See Jencks, *The Language of Post-Modern Architecture* (New York: Rizzoli, 1977), 9.

30. See David Harvey's discussion of Moore's Piazza d'Italia in *The Condition of Postmodernity*, 93–97. Harries refers to this kind of postmodern pastiche architecture as engaging in "metasymbols," in *The Ethical Function of Architecture*, 132.

31. Named after the "Long Island Duckling" cited by Venturi. See Venturi, Brown, and Izenour, *Learning from Las Vegas*, 87, 162.

32. The following quotation from Ulf Jonak distinguishing postmodern from modern surfaces is a typical downplaying of Weimar architecture's inclusion of, for example, electric advertising as an ever-changing scribble on its surfaces. For Jonak, postmodern architecture's "increasing significance of the outer skins" is due to our era's total loss of idealism, whereas modernism still downplayed the "skin": "This is what is new about postmodern architecture: there is a consistent recharging of surfaces. In its best materialisations the façade is no longer a backdrop, but a medium which bears information, traversed by currents, filled with pulsating energy, producer and filter in one. . . . Whereas in modernism the outer wall was, speaking in non-material terms, reduced into a two-dimensional membrane, it now became the transport area for countless events which penetrate it and glide over it, an apparatus of substance, initially certainly comparable with a model railway which has been stood up on end." Jonak, "The Discovery of Deception: Immateriality and Postmodernism," *Daidalos* 52 (June 1994): 135.

33. See Harries's deconstruction of Venturi's "duck/decorated shed" dichotomy as catachresis, in *The Ethical Function of Architecture*, 72–81.

34. Harries, *The Ethical Function of Architecture*, 53.

35. Harries, *The Ethical Function of Architecture,* 9.

36. Harries, *The Ethical Function of Architecture,* 132.

37. Harries, "Mask and Veil—Reflections on the Superficiality of Ornament," paper presented at the Einstein Forum symposium "On Ornament," Potsdam (June 1998); forthcoming in the symposium proceedings *Die Rhetorik des Ornaments,* ed. Isabelle Frank and Freia Hartung (Munich: Fink, 2000).

38. Harries, *The Ethical Function of Architecture,* 125.

39. Hans-Georg Gadamer, "The Ontological Foundation of the Occasional and the Decorative," in *Truth and Method,* trans. William Glen-Doepel (London: Sheed and Ward, 1979); repr. in *Rethinking Architecture,* ed. Leach, 136.

40. Frederick Kiesler, *Contemporary Art Applied to the Store and Its Display* (New York: Brentano's, 1930), 40.

41. Kiesler, foreword to *Contemporary Art Applied to the Store and Its Display;* emphasis in original.

42. Erich Mendelsohn, "Warum diese Architektur?" repr. in Renate Palmer, *Der Stuttgarter Schocken-Bau von Erich Mendelsohn. Die Geschichte eines Kaufhauses und seiner Architektur* (Stuttgart: Silberburg-Verlag, 1995), 8; trans. in *The Weimar Republic Sourcebook,* ed. Kaes, Jay, and Dimendberg, 452.

43. Walter Riezler, "Zum Geleit," *Die Form* 1.1 (1922): 1.

44. These are K. Michael Hays's terms with regard to Hannes Meyer, in Hays's *Modernism and the Posthumanist Subject: The Architecture of Hannes Meyer and Ludwig Hilberseimer* (Cambridge: MIT Press, 1992), 168, 159.

45. Ludwig Hilberseimer, "Der Wille zur Architektur," *Das Kunstblatt* 5 (1923): 134, 136, 133.

46. Sigfried Giedion, *Space, Time and Architecture,* 458. Discussed by Wigley, *White Walls, Designer Dresses,* 42, 113.

47. See Giedion, *Space, Time and Architecture,* 510–11.

48. Jürgen Habermas, "Modern and Postmodern Architecture," trans. Helen Tsoskounglou, *9H* 4 (1982); repr. in *Rethinking Architecture,* ed. Leach, 228.

49. All cited in Kristiana Hartmann, ed., *trotzdem modern. Die wichtigsten Texte zur Architektur in Deutschland 1919–1933,* (Braunschweig: Vieweg, 1994), 133, 156, 233, respectively.

50. Frederick Kiesler, in a 1925 article written for the De Stijl magazine, repr. in *Contemporary Art Applied to the Store and Its Display,* 49.

51. Hermann Muthesius, *Stilarchitektur und Baukunst* (Mülheim a.d. Ruhr: K. Schimmelpfeng, 1902). Translated as *Style-Architecture and Building-Art* by Stanford Anderson (Santa Monica: The Getty Center for the History of Art & the Humanities, 1995), 79.

52. See Louis Sullivan, "Ornament in Architecture" (1892), in *Kindergarten Chats and Other Writings* (New York: Wittenborn Art Books, 1947); and Giedion, *Space, Time and Architecture,* 408.

53. As Hays points out, both in dadaist photomontages and in the modern architecture of Hannes Meyer or Ludwig Hilberseimer there occurred a key

"shifting" of architectural meaning "*to the outside,*" that is, to "public, cultural space." Hays, *Modernism and the Posthumanist Subject*, 159.

54. Kracauer, "Deutsche Bauausstellung," *Frankfurter Zeitung* 75.348 (May 11, 1931).

55. Frederick Kiesler, *Contemporary Art Applied to the Store and Its Display*, 39.

56. Alois Riegl, *Problems of Style: Foundations for a History of Ornament*, trans. Evelyn Kain (Princton: Princeton University Press, 1992); and Riegl, *Historische Grammatik der bildenden Künste*, ed. Karl M. Swoboda and Otto Pacht (Graz: Bohlau, 1966).

57. See Giedion, *Space, Time and Architecture*, 316.

58. Adolf Loos, "The Principle of Cladding" (1898), in *Spoken into the Void: Collected Essays 1897–1900*, trans. Jane O. Newman and John H. Smith (Cambridge: MIT Press, 1982), 66.

59. Beatriz Colomina sees in Loos a gender distinction of space, where the exterior of the building is conceptualized as masculine and the interior as feminine; however, since the wall between inside and outside is being eroded by Loos' theory and practice, so is this gender distinction. See Colomina, "The Split Wall: Domestic Voyeurism," in *Sexuality and Space*, ed. Colomina (New York: Princeton Architectural Press, 1992), 93.

60. See Colomina's discussion of the Baker house as "all surface; it does not have an interior." Colomina, *Privacy and Publicity*, 281; see also 260–64, 276.

61. See Colomina, *Privacy and Publicity*, 43; and Harries, *The Ethical Function of Architecture*, 32–43. See also Christoph Asendorf, *Batteries of Life: On the History of Things and Their Perception in Modernity*, trans. Don Reneau (Berkeley: University of California Press, 1993), 186; Asendorf notes that the word "ornament" is derived from both *ordinare* and *adornare*—a sense of phantasmagorical, reunifying world-order in miniature.

62. In *Architecture and Nihilism: On the Philosophy of Modern Architecture*, trans. Stephen Sartarelli (New Haven: Yale University Press, 1993), 173, Massimo Mazziari comments that the "exterior is neither a mirror image of the 'truth' contained in the interior (the modern exterior that reveals the structure), nor a mere fiction or veil that hides a place otherwise unanalyzable."

63. Loos, *Spoken into the Void*, 102.

64. Colomina, *Privacy and Publicity*, 38.

65. Wigley points out that Loos got the inspiration for his "Ornament and Crime" essay from Louis Sullivan's "Ornament in Architecture" of 1892 (*White Walls*, 61).

66. See Anderson, *Kafka's Clothes*, 180–81.

67. See Harries's discussion of Nietzsche, *The Ethical Function of Architecture*, 55, 65.

68. Loos, "Ornament and Crime," in *The Architecture of Adolf Loos*, ed. Yehuda Safran and Wilfried Wang (London: Arts Council of Great Britain,

1985), 100, 103 (emphasis in original). Translation of Loos's texts by Wilfried Wang, with Rosamund Diamond and Robert Godsill. See also Mark C. Taylor's chapter on tattooing in *Hiding*, 77–145.

69. See Loos, "The Plumber," in *Spoken into the Void*, 45–49.

70. Hannes Meyer, "Die neue Welt," *Das Werk* 13.7 (1926); transl. as "The New World," in *The Weimar Republic Sourcebook*, ed. Kaes, Jay, and Dimendberg, 446, 447. See also Meyer, "Building," in *Programs and Manifestoes on 20th-Century Architecture*, ed. Ulrich Conrads, trans. Michael Bullock (Cambridge: MIT Press, 1975); discussed by Harries, *The Ethical Function of Architecture*, 142–44.

71. Paul Westheim, "The Aesthetics of the Flat Roof" (with Adolf Behne), in *The Weimar Republic Sourcebook*, ed. Kaes, Jay, and Dimendberg, 450, 449. Orig. "Zur Ästhetik des flachen Daches," *Das neue Frankfurt* 7 (1926–1927): 163–64.

72. Le Corbusier, *L'Art décoratif d'aujourd'hui* (Paris: Edition G. Crès, 1925). Translated as *The Decorative Art of Today* by James I. Dunnett (Cambridge: MIT Press, 1987), 134.

73. Le Corbusier, *Vers une Architecture* (Paris: Editions Crès, 1923); translated by Frederick Etchells as *Towards a New Architecture* (London: The Architectural Press, 1927), 21.

74. Le Corbusier, *The Decorative Art of Today*, xxi; Le Corbusier, *Towards a New Architecture*, 10, 89.

75. See Mark C. Taylor, *Disfiguring: Art, Architecture, Religion* (Chicago: University of Chicago Press, 1992), 113.

76. Le Corbusier, *The Decorative Art of Today*, 135.

77. Kracauer, *Der Detektiv-Roman. Ein philosophischer Traktat* (Frankfurt a.M.: Suhrkamp, 1971), 53.

78. Le Corbusier, *Towards a New Architecture*, 8, 11, 37. See also Ludwig Hilberseimer, *Großstadtbauten* (Hannover: Aposs-Verlag, 1925), 6: "The architect will in future do without beautifying buildings' exteriors or lending them a mask that is meant to be monumental. . . . A better example for him than the decorational schema of any style is the economy of an express train carriage or an ocean liner."

79. See Behne, *Neues Wohnen—Neues Bauen* (Leipzig: Hesse & Becker Verlag, 1927); and also Benno Franz Moebus, "Der neue Geist in der Wohnnung," *Der Tag* (October 26, 1928).

80. Le Corbusier, "Fünf Punkte zu einer neuen Architektur," *Die Form* 2.8 (1927): 273; and "Wo beginnt die Architektur?" *Die Form* 4.7 (April 1, 1929): 181. See also Giedion, *Space, Time and Architecture*, 514.

81. "The façade loses its customary, visible, supportive function, and becomes freely shapeable—a free surface of projection, since the support, a skeleton of pillars in grid-formation and false ceilings, has taken up residence in the interior. . . . " Vrääth Öhner and Marc Ries, "Bildbau," in *Cinetecture: Film. Architektur. Moderne*, ed. Helmut Weihsmann (Vienna: PVS Verleger, 1995), 35–36.

82. See *Die Form* 2.8 (1927), a special issue on the Weissenhof houses.

83. Stadtarchiv Stuttgart CIV A 12 Bd. 46 Nr. 116 (Bauregistratur), Weissenhof: städt. Wohnhausbau, Siedlung 1925/1929.

84. Paul Bonatz, "Noch einmal die Werkbundsiedlung," *Schwäbische Merkur* 206 (May 5, 1926). Stadtarchiv Stuttgart CIV A 12 Bd. 46 Nr. 116 (Bauregistratur), Weissenhof: städt. Wohnhausbau, Siedlung 1925/1929: 69.

85. Kracauer, "Das neue Bauen. Zur Stuttgarter Werkbund-Ausstellung: 'Die Wohnung,'" *Frankfurter Zeitung* 72.561 (July 31, 1927).

86. See Michael Z. Wise, *Capital Dilemma: Germany's Search for a New Architecture of Democracy* (Princeton, N.J.: Princeton University Press, 1998), 25.

87. See Vidler's discussion of transparency in *The Architectural Uncanny: Essays in the Modern Unhomely* (Cambridge: MIT Press, 1992), 220, 218.

88. Gottlieb Wilhelm Bötticher was the first nineteenth-century voice in the call for iron construction in new building types like railway stations. See Georgiadis's introduction to Giedion, *Building in France*, 4–44.

89. Buck-Morss, "The City as Dreamworld and Catastrophe," *October* 73 (1995): 6.

90. For analyses of the powerful glass effects of the Crystal Palace, see Julius Lessing, "Das halbe Jahrhundert der Weltausstellungen," *Volkswirthschaftliche Zeitfragen* 22.6 (1900): 6–10; Giedion, *Space, Time and Architecture*, 249; Asendorf, *Batteries of Life*, 26–29; Thomas A. Markus, *Buildings and Power: Freedom and Control in the Origin of Modern Building Types* (New York: Routledge, 1993), 219–28; and Heinz W. Kreiwinkel, "145 Jahre Glasarchitektur. Vom Kristallpalast bis zum Schloß Juval," *Deutsche Bauzeitung* 4 (1997): 43–47.

91. Habermas, "Modern and Postmodern Architecture," in Leach, ed., *Rethinking Architecture*, 229.

92. See Giedion, *Space, Time and Architecture*, 255.

93. Giedion, *Space, Time and Architecture*, 269. The same interpenetration of outer and inner space, states Giedion (282), is achieved in the pedestrian experience of descending the ironwork of the Eiffel Tower.

94. Benjamin notes that the Parisian arcades were built somewhat prematurely, since the architectural techniques of the midnineteenth century were not yet able to fully realize the potential of glass and iron (a potential that was not fully realized until Benjamin's own day): "That is why the daylight shining down through the panes between their iron supports was so dirty and gloomy." Benjamin, *Gesammelte Schriften*, 5.1:212.

95. Praise for Scheerbart forms the basis of Ludwig Hilberseimer's article "Glasarchitektur," in *Die Form* 4.19 (1929): 521–22.

96. Gerschom Scholem, *Walter Benjamin: The Story of a Friendship* (New York: Schocken, 1981), 38.

97. Paul Scheerbart, *Lesabéndio. Ein Asteroidenroman* (Kehl: SWAN Buch-Vertrieb, 1994), 28–29.

98. Paul Scheerbart, *Glasarchitektur* (Berlin: Verlag Der Sturm, 1914), 89, 90.

99. Scheerbart, *Glasarchitektur*, 48; see also 57.

100. Bruno Taut, *Alpine Architektur* (Hagen: Folkwang-Verlag G.M.B.H., 1919).

101. Taut, "Zur Bauplastik," *Die Form* 2.2 (1927): 60; see also *Die neue Baukunst in Europa und Amerika*, 2d ed. (Stuttgart: Julius Hoffmann Verlag, 1979), 2.

102. Karl Scheffler, "Wie sieht der Potsdamer Platz in 25 Jahren aus? Ein Gespräch," *Vossische Zeitung* (August 29, 1920). Repr. in *Glänzender Asphalt*, ed. Jäger and Schütz, 119.

103. Bruno Taut, *Die Galoschen des Glücks*, Akademie der Künste: Bruno Taut D5.61.1 Gläserne Kette. Trans. by Pellegrino d'Acierno and Robert Connolly as *The Galoshes of Fortune*, in Manfredo Tafuri, *The Sphere and the Labyrinth: Avant-Gardes and Architecture from Piranesi to the 1970s* (Cambridge: MIT Press, 1987), 112–17.

104. See Cacciari, *Architecture and Nihilism*, 187–90. In 1934, Lukács linked expressionist monumentalist fantasies to the rise of Nazism: see Lukács, "'Grösse und Verfall' des Expressionismus," *Internationale Literatur* 1 (1934), 153–73. Trans. by David Temback as "Expressionism: Its Significance and Decline" in *Georg Lukács: Essays on Realism*, ed. Rodney Livingstone (Cambridge: MIT Press, 1980).

105. See Angelika Thiekötter, et al., eds., *Kristallisationen, Splitterungen. Bruno Tauts Glashaus* (Boston: Birkhäuser Verlag, 1993).

106. "Ohne einen Glaspalast / Ist das Leben eine Last." Paul Scheerbart, *Frühlicht* 3 (1920); translated in Asendorf, *Batteries of Life*, 24. See Matthias Schirren, "Ironie und Bewegung. Die Sprüche Paul Scheerbarts," in *Kristallisationen*, ed. Thiekötter et al., 89–91; see also 167.

107. See Peter Behrens's 1910 description of his AEG Turbine Factory in Tilman Buddensieg and Henning Rogge, eds., *Industriekultur: Peter Behrens and the AEG, 1907–1914*, trans. Iain Boyd White (Cambridge: MIT Press, 1984), 210–11.

108. Bruno Taut, *Die neue Baukunst in Europa und Amerika*, 2d ed. (Stuttgart: Julius Hoffmann Verlag, 1979), 6.

109. Max Landsberg, "Die Kulturmission des Glases," *Deutsche Bauzeitung* 8 (January 26, 1929): 89–94.

110. Giedion, *Space, Time and Architecture*, 264.

111. Walter Gropius, ed., *Internationale Architektur* (Munich: Albert Langen, 1925), 6.

112. See Giedion, *Space, Time, and Architecure*, 478–79.

113. See Harmen Thies, "Glass Corners," *Daidalos* 33 (1989): 110–19.

114. Giedion, *Space, Time, and Architecture*, 491. See also Hilberseimer's "Glasarchitektur," *Die Form* 4.19 (1929): 521–22.

115. Lefebvre, *The Production of Space*, 125. Emphasis in original.

116. Walter Gropius, *The New Architecture and the Bauhaus*, trans. P. Morton Shand (Cambridge: MIT Press, 1989), 43–44.

117. Gropius, *The New Architecture and the Bauhaus*, 29.

118. Taylor, *Disfiguring*, 124.

119. The dynamism of machinic movement is not directly transferable onto architecture, cautions Mendelsohn, nor is dynamism unique to the modern era. "But if you want to understand dynamism as the logical motional expression of the strengths inherent to building materials, and the building therefore as nothing other than the expression of the actual conditions *and* these strengths, then it seems to me that—in contrast to the machine—a completely unequivocal image will emerge for "movement," extended to the Absolute, precisely the same image as for *all* original epochs of construction." Mendelsohn, *Erich Mendelsohn. Das Gesamtschaffen des Architekten. Skizzen, Entwürfe, Bauten* (Berlin: Rudolf Mosse Verlag, 1930), 26–27.

120. Mendelsohn, "Die internationale Übereinstimmung des neuen Baugedankens oder Dynamik und Funktion," *Architectura* (Amsterdam, February 2 & 9, 1924); repr. in *Erich Mendelsohn*, 22–34.

121. The real estate company that purchased this East Berlin building from the Mosse family after the fall of the Wall has had this corner renovated (by the architectural firms of Bernd Kemper and Fissler-Ernst) in the style of Mendelsohn's original; unfortunately, the rounding of the original glass panes has not been reproduced, producing a "staccato" curve.

122. Erich Mendelsohn, *Das Gesamtschaffen des Architekten*, 28. Cited by Schivelbusch, *Licht Schein und Wahn*, 74.

123. Behne, *Der moderne Zweckbau*, 67.

124. Ludwig Hilberseimer, "Glasarchitektur," *Die Form* 4.19 (October 1, 1929): 522.

125. Mies van der Rohe stated in the essay "Hochhaus Projekt für Bahnhof Friedrichstrasse in Berlin," *Frühlicht* 1 (1922): 122: "My efforts with an actual glass model helped me to recognize that the most important thing about using glass is not the effects of light and shadow, but the rich play of reflection." Cited by Hays in *Modernism and the Posthumanist Subject* (314n1). See also Jochen Meyer's analysis of Mies's "Kennwort: Wabe" in *Der Schrei nach dem Turmhaus. Der Ideenwettbewerb Hochhaus am Bahnhof Friedrichstraße. Berlin 1921/22*, ed. Florian Zimmerman et al. (Berlin: Argon, 1988), 106.

126. Le Corbusier envisages a Miesian glass skyscraper for his "gridiron" City of To-Morrow that depends upon a self-reflexive light-play: "The skyscrapers raise immense geometrical façades all of glass, and in them is reflected the blue glory of the sky. An overwhelming sensation. Immense but radiant prisms. . . . It is a spectacle organized by an Architecture which uses plastic resources for the modulation of forms seen in light." Le Corbusier, *The City of To-Morrow and Its Planning* (a translation of his *Urbanisme* of 1924), trans. Frederick Etchells (London: The Architectural Press, 1947), 190.

127. Kurt W. Forster remarks of Mies' Seagram building (built in New York from 1954 to 1958 and with a glass curtain wall that is a clear offshoot of the Friedrichstraße skyscraper project) that it radiates at night nothing "but its own emptiness." Forster, "Mies van der Rohes Seagram Building," in *Die nützlichen Künste*, ed. Tilmann Buddensieg and Henning Rogge (Berlin,

1981), 368; cited by Asendorf, *Batteries of Life*, 28. See also Hays, *Modernism and the Posthumanist Subject*, 189.

128. Manfredo Tafuri, *The Sphere and the Labyrinth*, 177. If we compare, however, this inclusive ideal of the expressionist skyscraper discourse to the postmodern skyscraper of today, we find a glaring dissonance in the application of glass. This is specifically the case in the exclusionary use of the "reflective glass skin" on the Westin Bonaventure Hotel in Los Angeles, which, for Fredric Jameson (as for Baudrillard), achieves a self-blinding "dissociation" of the building from the neighborhood by showing not itself but only the "distorted images of everything that surrounds it." The building's façade points up an "alarming disjunction between the body and its built environment," which Jameson refers to as "postmodern hyperspace." Jameson, *Postmodernism*, 42, 44. Baudrillard says the same thing about this hotel, designed by John Portman (*America*, 60): "Blocks like the Bonaventure building . . . cut themselves off from the city more than they interact with it. They stop seeing it. They refract it like a dark surface. . . . All around, the tinted glass façades of the buildings are like faces: frosted surfaces. It is as though there were no one inside the buildings, as if there were no one behind the faces. And there *really* is no one. This is what the ideal city is like."

129. Adorno, "Functionalism Today" (1965), *Oppositions* 17 (1979), trans. Jane Newman and John Smith; repr. in *Rethinking Architecture*, ed. Leach, 8. See also Friedensreich Hundertwasser's prodecorative attack on postwar functionalism, "Verschimmelungs-Manifest gegen den Rationalismus in der Architektur" (1958); repr. in *Programme und Manifeste zur Architektur des 20. Jahrhunderts*, ed. Ulrich Conrads (Berlin: Gütersloh, 1971), 149–52.

130. Adolf Loos, "Ornament und Erziehung" (1924), in *Trotzdem*; repr. in *Sämtliche Schriften*, ed. Franz Glück (Vienna: Verlag Herold, 1962), 393.

131. Hermann Muthesius, "Kunst und Modeströmungen," *Wasmuths Monatshefte für Baukunst* 11 (1927): 498. See Wigley, *White Walls*, 177–78.

132. Hans Eckstein, introduction to *Neue Wohnbauten. Ein Querschnitt durch die Wohnarchitektur in Deutschland* (Munich, 1932); cited in "Vorbehalte der Moderne," *Daidalos* 52 (1994): 74.

133. Ernst Pollak, *Moderne Ladenbauten* (Berlin: Ernst Pollak Verlag, 1928), vi. Reprinted as "Modern Shop Constructions" in *Interior Design 1929. Vom Opp-Laden in die Kakadu-Bar / From Opp Shop to Cockatoo Bar*, ed. Martina Düttmann, trans. M. M. Barkei (Berlin: Birkhäuser Verlag, 1989, a selected reprint of *Moderne Ladenbauten* and *Moderne Cafés, Restaurants und Vergnügungsstätten* (Berlin: Ernst Pollak Verlag, 1928).

134. Siegfried Kracauer, *Die Angestellten. Aus dem neuesten Deutschland* (1930), in Kracauer, *Schriften 1*, 96.

135. Kracauer, *Straßen in Berlin*, 18.

136. Ludwig Hilberseimer, *Groszstadtarchitektur* (Stuttgart: Verlag Julius Hoffmann, 1927), 98.

137. Wagner, "Das Formproblem eines Weltstadtplatzes. Wettbewerb der Verkehrs-A.G. für eine Umbauung des Alexanderplatzes," in *Das neue Berlin*,

ed. Wagner and Behne, 37. See also Le Corbusier's comment: *"A city made for speed is made for success."* Le Corbusier, *The City of To-Morrow,* 191; emphasis in original.

138. Kracauer, *Straßen in Berlin,* 23.

139. Kracauer, "Das neue Bauen. Zur Stuttgarter Werkbund-Ausstellung: 'Die Wohnung,'" *Frankfurter Zeitung* 72.561 (July 31, 1927).

140. See the parodic essay by Friedrich Sieburg, "Anbetung der Fahrstühlen," *Die literarische Welt* 2.30 (1926): 8; trans. as "Worshipping Elevators," in *The Weimar Republic Sourcebook,* ed. Kaes, Jay, and Dimendberg, 402–4.

141. Bloch, *Erbschaft dieser Zeit* (Frankfurt a.M.: Suhrkamp, 1962), 217.

142. Bloch, *Erbschaft dieser Zeit,* 212. By 1962, in a radio conversation, Bloch has amended his term for the Weimar years to a "hollow space with sparks" (*ein Hohlraum mit Funken*); see "Gespräch über die Zwanziger Jahre," *Bloch-Almanach* 2 (1982): 16.

143. Theodor W. Adorno, "Jene zwanziger Jahre," *Merkur* 16.1 (1962): 48.

144. Adolf Behne, "Glasarchitektur," *Die Wiederkehr der Kunst* (Leipzig: Kurt Wolff Verlag, 1919); repr. in Ulrich Conrads and Hans G. Sperlich, *The Architecture of Fantasy: Utopian Building and Planning in Modern Times,* trans. Christine Crasemann Collins and George R. Collins (New York: Frederick A. Praeger, 1962), 134.

145. Hilberseimer, *Groszstadtarchitektur,* 18. See Hugo Häring's gentle critique of Hilberseimer's and Le Corbusier's ordered cities: "Zwei Städte," *Die Form* 1.7 (1926): 172–75; and Hays's reading of Hilberseimer's "paranoid" *Groszstadtarchitektur* in *Modernism and the Posthumanist Subject,* 240–77.

146. See Ayn Rand's novel of 1943, *The Fountainhead* (New York: Plume, 1994).

147. Benjamin, "Der destruktive Character," *Frankfurter Zeitung* (November 20, 1931); repr. in "Denkbilder," in *Gesammelte Schriften,* 4.1:397–98; trans. as "The Destructive Character," in Benjamin, *Reflections: Essays, Aphorisms, Autobiographical Writings,* ed. Peter Demetz, trans. Edmund Jephcott (New York: Harcourt Brace Jovanovich, 1978), 301–2.

148. See also Baudrillard's anatomy of the collector in *The System of Objects,* 85–106.

149. Benjamin, *Gesammelte Schriften,* 4.1:428; see also 2.1:217.

150. Nietzsche, *Sämtliche Werke,* 1:270.

151. Scheerbart, *Glasarchitektur,* 125. See Pierre Missac's discussion of Benjamin's reading of Scheerbart, in Missac, *Walter Benjamin's Passages,* trans. Shierry Weber Nicholsen (Cambridge: MIT Press, 1995), 147–72.

152. Benjamin, *Illuminationen. Ausgewählte Schriften I,* (Frankfurt a.M.: Suhrkamp, 1974), 294. See also Detlef Mertins, "The Enticing and Threatening Face of Prehistory: Walter Benjamin and the Utopia of Glass," *Assemblage* 29 (1996): 6–23.

153. The "glass man" (possessing veins and arteries, but no genitalia) is on permanent display at the German Historical Museum (Zeughaus), Berlin.

154. Le Corbusier, *The City of To-Morrow,* 256. Lefebvre refers to Le Corbusier's vision of the totally planned City of Tomorrow as a "disarticulation of external space" and more—a "disordering of elements" that tears apart the urban fabric; Lefebvre, *The Production of Space,* 303. Koolhaas, in *Delirious New York* (199–233), mocks Le Corbusier's potentate-plans for refashioning the happily unwieldy Manhattan. See also Hays's reading of Ludwig Hilberseimer's architectural work as an ultimately paranoid "process of negation" (*Modernism and the Posthumanist Subject,* 185–210).

155. Speech given by Mendelsohn in 1923; repr. in *Der Mendelsohn-Bau am Lehniner Platz. Erich Mendelsohn und Berlin* (Berlin: Schaubühne am Lehniner Platz, 1981), 39.

156. See Gerhard Weiss, "Krach im Hinterhaus. Die Berliner Mietskaserne als soziologisches Phänomen und literarischer Ort," paper presented at the 1996 German Studies Association conference.

157. Alfred Döblin, "Berlin, die unsichtbare Stadt," foreword to *Berlin 1928. Das Gesicht der Stadt,* ed. Mario von Bucovich (orig. 1928; repr. Berlin: Nicolaische Verlagshandlung, 1992), 6.

158. Bruno Taut, *Bauen. Der neue Wohnbau* (Leipzig & Berlin: Klinkhardt & Biermann, 1927), 2.

159. Werner Hegemann, *Das steinerne Berlin* (1930); cited by Hermand and Trommler, *Die Kultur der Weimarer Republik,* 418.

160. Taut, *Bauen,* 9.

161. See Barbara Miller Lane, *Architecture and Politics in Germany, 1918–1933* (Cambridge: Harvard University Press, 1968), 103.

162. Ernst May, "Das flache Dach," special issue of *Das neue Frankfurt. Monatsschrift für die Fragen der Großstadtgestaltung* 1.7 (1927): 150, 151.

163. Taut, *Bauen,* 57.

164. For a discussion of the debate, see Landesdenkmalamt Berlin, ed., *Denkmaltopographie Bundesrepublik Deutschland. Baudenkmale in Berlin: Bezirk Zehlendorf, Ortsteil Zehlendorf* (Berlin: Nicolaische Verlagsbuchhandlung Beuermann GmbH, 1995), 47–48, 201–11.

165. Taut, *Bauen,* 46. See also Manfredo Tafuri's discussion of Taut's Horseshoe colony and the *Trabantenprinzip* that it incorporates, namely the "idea of a city divided into semiautonomous nuclei," in *The Sphere and the Labyrinth,* 206. Tafuri does not find in these rationalized living spaces a training ground for Nazism; rather he finds the latter to be located in the mass rites of the Social Democrats and Communists. (208).

166. Bruno Taut, *Die neue Wohnung. Die Frau als Schöpferin,* 2d ed. (Leipzig: Verlag von Klinkhardt & Biermann, 1924), 9.

167. Ludwig Hilberseimer, "Über die Typisierung des Mietshauses," *Die Form* 1.15 (1926): 339, 340. See also *Uhu* 3.1 (1926): 26.

168. Sigfried Giedion, *Befreites Wohnen,* ed. Emil Schaeffer (Zürich: O. Füssli, 1929).

169. Mark Peach finds that the New Woman's radical housecleaning acts were linked, inevitably, to assisting the productivity needs of the New Man. See

Peach, "'Der Architekt Denkt, Die Hausfrau Lenkt': German Modern Architecture and the Modern Woman," *German Studies Review* 18.3 (1995): 441–63.

170. Paul Scheerbart, *Die Auflösung der Städte; oder, Die Erde eine gute Wohnung; oder auch, Der Weg zur Alpinen Architektur* (Hagen: Folkwang Verlag, 1920); cited by Taut, *Die neue Wohnung,* 92.

171. Taut, *Die neue Wohnung,* 95.

172. See Taut, *Die neue Wohnung,* 28–29.

173. Erna Meyer, *Der neue Haushalt. Ein Wegweiser zu wirtschaftlicher Hausführung,* 33d ed. (Stuttgart: Franckh'sche Verlagshandlung, 1928), 1.

174. Meyer, *Der neue Haushalt,* 4.

175. Meyer, *Der neue Haushalt,* 185, 6.

176. On the advantages inherent in the electrification of the Weimar home, see "Die elektrische Küche," *AEG-Mitteilungen* 21.6 (1925): 199–201; "Elektrizität im Haushalt," *Die Form* 2.10 (1927): 313–15; and *Die Weite Welt,* special issue "Elektrizität im Haushalt," 43 (October 21, 1938). The representational bond between women and electricity was a longstanding one: Schivelbusch finds, for example, iconic similarities between advertisments for turn-of-the-century American dancer Loie Fuller, famous for her dancing style of embracing beams of light, and advertisements of similiarly cultic women with vacuum cleaners during the 1920s and 1930s. Schivelbusch, *Licht Schein und Wahn,* 19.

177. Meyer, *Der neue Haushalt,* 63; emphasis in original. Helmut Lethen discusses how refrigerators became a metaphor long before their middle-class availability in Germany; see Lethen, "Refrigerators of Intelligence," trans. Gail Wise and Thomas Ketron, in *Qui parle* 5.2 (1992): 84–85. See also Giedion on household mechanization: *Mechanization Takes Command: A Contribution to Anonymous History* (New York: Oxford University Press, 1948).

178. Atina Grossmann, "*Girlkultur* or Thoroughly Rationalized Female: A New Woman in Weimar Germany?" in *Women in Culture and Politics: A Century of Change,* ed. Judith Friedlander (Bloomington: Indiana University Press, 1986), 71.

179. See W. Lakomy's design for a home for professional women in "So wohnt die Junggesellin!" *Neue Frauenkleidung und Frauenkultur* 27.3 (1930): 66.

180. Clothing design was not included in the Bauhaus "total work of art" conception. See Wigley, *White Walls,* 98–99.

181. While proclaiming the Bauhaus the home of sexual equality, Gropius demonstrated an overtly masculinist approach to all artwork with his announcement in 1919 that his pupils should be "artisans," not the makers of "sweet little salon pictures." See Anja Baumhoff, "Die 'moderne Frau' und ihre Stellung in der Bauhaus-Avantgarde," in *Die Neue Frau. Herausforderung für die Bildmedien der Zwanziger Jahre,* ed. Katharina Sykora, Annette Dorgerloh, Doris Noell-Rumpeltes, Ada Raev 84, 91–92.

182. Lydia, "Die grosse Heerschau der Frauen," *Deutsche Bauausstellung Berlin 1931. Blätter für den Redakteur* 11 (April 1931): 2. Geheimes Staatsarchiv: Rep. 120 E XVI.2 Nr. 13.

183. Wilhelm Westecker, "Die Kunst in der Bauausstellung," *Berliner Börsen-Zeitung* 230 (May 20, 1931). Geheimes Staatsarchiv: Rep. 120 E XVI.2 Nr. 13.

184. Meyer, *Der neue Haushalt*, 102.

185. See Adelheid v. Saldern, "Neues Wohnen. Wohnverhältnisse und Wohnverhalten in Grosswohnanlagen der 20er Jahre," in *Massenwohnung und Eigenheim. Wohnungsbau und Wohnen in der Großstadt seit dem Ersten Weltkrieg*, ed. Axel Schildt and Arnold Sywottek (New York: Campus Verlag, 1988), 205. See also Vollmer-Heitmann's discussion of the "working kitchen" (in Schmidt and Sywottek, 148–53).

186. Lethen, "Refrigerators of Intelligence," trans. Wise and Ketron, *Qui parle* 5.2 (1992): 97. See also Lethen's reading of Brecht's parodic tale of Bauhaus functionalism in the home, "Nordseekrabben" (1926), in Lethen, *Verhaltenslehren der Kälte. Lebensversuche zwischen den Kriegen* (Frankfurt a.M.: Suhrkamp, 1994), 163–70; forthcoming in translation by Don Reneau as *Cool Conduct: The Culture of Distance in Weimar Germany* (Berkeley: University of California Press, 2001).

187. Meyer, *Der neue Haushalt*, 80, 90.

188. Meyer, *Der neue Haushalt*, 90.

189. Ilse Reicke, "Neue Sachlichkeit jenseits der Ostsee," *Haushalt—Wirtschaft—Lebensführung* (September 1930): 11. Geheimes Staatsarchiv: Rep. 120 E XVI.2 Nr. 13.

190. Le Corbusier, *The Decorative Art of Today*, 188. Wigley terms Le Corbusier's white walls a "hygiene of vision," a "cleaning agent" (*White Walls*, 5, 8; see also xvi–xvii.

191. Ford proclaims: "Without cleanliness, no morality either." Cited by Adolf Behne, *Der moderne Zweckbau*, 25.

192. On Taut's use of bold colors in his interior and exterior functionalist design, see Bettina Zöller-Stock, *Bruno Taut. Die Innenraumentwürfe des Berliner Architekten* (Stuttgart: Deutsche Verlags-Anstalt, 1993), 94–95. The Klee-Kandinsky double "master house," one of four designed by Gropius for the Dessau Bauhaus, was restored in 2000 to its original color scheme of 1932, the last year that Klee, Kandinsky, and their wives lived in the house. See *Das Meisterhaus Kandinsky-Klee in Dessau*, ed. Gilbert von Lupfer, Norbert Michel, Regina Prange, et al. (Leipzig: E. A. Seemann, 2000).

193. Oswald Flamm, "Sieg des Staubsaugerprinzips in der Welt," *Berliner Zeitung* 58.153 (March 31, 1929).

194. See "Der Staubsauger 'Vampyr' als Insektenfänger," *AEG-Mitteilungen* 22.3 (1927): 150.

195. Taut, *Die neue Wohnung*, 9; see also 86.

196. Meyer, *Der neue Haushalt*, 137.

197. Meyer, *Der neue Haushalt*, 81–82.

198. Kracauer, *Die Angestellten*, 287.

199. "Dresden 1930. Die Dame auf der Hygiene-Ausstellung," *Die neue Linie* (June 1930).

200. M. A. Brünner, "Die Bedeutung der Hygieneausstellung für die Frau," *Neue Frauenkleidung und Frauenkultur* 17.14 (1931): 366.

201. In her recent study *Fast Cars, Clean Bodies: Decolonization and the Reordering of French Culture* (Cambridge: MIT Press, 1995), Kristin Ross refers to postwar Americanized France as an "object-world" (147). See also Roland Barthes's 1956 analysis of daily French life for reflections on France's prehistory of postmodernism: *Mythologies*, trans. Annette Lavers (New York: Hill & Wang, 1972).

202. See Ross, *Fast Cars, Clean Bodies*, 73.

203. Georg Simmel, "Die Mode" (1911), repr. in *Die Listen der Mode*, ed. Silvia Bovenschen (Frankfurt a.M.: Suhrkamp, 1986), 181.

204. See the special issue of *Die Form* 1.5 (1922) dedicated to the evolution of women's fashion in accordance with modern architectural values.

205. See Wigley, *White Walls*, 119.

206. Vidler discusses the connection between face and façade in his reading of the decentered front for James Stirling's Staatsgalerie Stuttgart in *The Architectural Uncanny*, 85–99.

207. See, for example, ads for Eva hair-removal cream, *Die Reklame* 38.30 (July 28, 1932): 1348; and for the facial Creme Mouson, *Berliner Illustrirte Zeitung* 38.41 (October 13, 1929): 1832, respectively.

208. Wigley, *White Walls*, 153.

209. On the rise of the New Woman and her concomitant visual mythologization, see the study by Weimar author Elsa Herrmann, *So ist die Neue Frau* (Berlin: Avalun Verlag, 1929). See also Katharina Sykora, "Die Neue Frau. Ein Alltagsmythos der Zwanziger Jahre," in *Die Neue Frau*, ed. Sykora et al. (Berlin: Jonas Verlag, 1993), 9–24.

210. See, in particular, Patrice Petro's analysis of the representation of female identity in *Die Dame*, in her *Joyless Streets: Women and Melodramatic Representation in Weimar Germany* (Princeton: Princeton University Press, 1989), 110–27.

211. Atina Grossmann refers to Jessica Benjamin on the Weberian notion of instrumental rationality (*Zweckrationalität*): the New Woman fits this metaphor of modern labor, and, as such, upsets the old association of woman with the irrational. See Grossmann, "*Girlkultur* or Thoroughly Rationalized Female?" 75, citing Jessica Benjamin, "Authority and the Family Revisited: Or, A World Without Fathers?" *New German Critique* 13 (1978): 36–37.

212. See Rudolf Braune's socialistically inspired *Das Mädchen an der Orga Privat. Ein kleiner Roman aus Berlin* (Frankfurt a.M.: Societäts-Verlag, 1930); and the far bleaker novel by Christa Anita Brück, *Schicksal hinter Schreibmaschinen* (Berlin: Sieben-Stäbe-Verlag, 1930).

213. Robert Musil, "Die Frau gestern und morgen," in *Die Frau von morgen wie wir sie wünschen*, ed. Friedrich M. Huebner (Leipzig: Verlag E. A. Seemann, 1929), 86.

214. Irmgard Keun, *Das kunstseidene Mädchen* (Munich: Deutscher Taschenbuch Verlag, 1991). See Katharina von Ankum, "Gendered Urban

Spaces in Irmgard Keun's *Das kunstseidene Mädchen,*" in *Women in the Metropolis: Gender and Modernity in Weimar Culture,* ed. Ankum (Berkeley: University of California Press, 1997), 162–84.

215. See Jeffrey T. Schnapp's essay on rayon and Italian modernity, "The Fabric of Modern Times," *Critical Inquiry* 24 (1997): 191–245.

216. Dr. Berthold, *Volkswirtschaft in Zahlen und Bildern. Eine Erinnerung an die Ausstellung im Herbst 1929. Was, wie, wo kauft die Hausfrau?* (Berlin: Reichsverband Deutscher Hausfrauenvereine e.V., 1930), 1, 4. Geheimes Staatsarchiv, Berlin: Rep. 120 E. XVI.2 Nr. 13.

217. Stössinger, "Die verwandelte Tauentzien," 108.

218. Economist Werner Sombart in 1902, citing Schopenhauer, notes the democratization process of fashion: silk stockings, once the purview of queens, had become (in the nineteenth century) commonplace items in a prostitute's wardrobe. Sombart, *Wirtschaft und Mode. Ein Beitrag zur Theorie der modernen Bedarfsgestaltung,* partially repr. in *Die Listen der Mode,* ed. Bovenschen, 81. See Ulrike Thoms, "Dünn und dick, schön und häßlich. Schönheitsideal und Körpersilhouette in der Werbung 1850–1950," in *Bilderwelt des Alltags. Werbung in der Konsumgesellschaft des 19. und 20. Jahrhunderts,* ed. Peter Borscheid and Clemens Wischermann (Stuttgart: Steiner, 1995), 258–60.

219. Petra Bock warns against reducing the New Woman to the Kracauerian passivity of little typists (*Tippmädels*) and shop girls (*Ladenmädchen*). Bock, "Zwischen den Zeiten—Neue Frauen und die Weimarer Republik," in *Neue Frauen zwischen den Zeiten,* ed. Petra Bock and Katja Koblitz (Berlin: Edition Hentrich, 1995), 15.

220. Pierre Bourdieu states of the "schemes of the habitus": "Taste is a practical mastery of distributions which makes it possible to sense or intuit what is likely (or unlikely) to befall—and therefore to befit—an individual occupying a given position in social space." Bourdieu, *Distinction,* 466.

221. Simone de Beauvoir, *The Second Sex,* trans. H. M. Parshley (New York: Knopf, 1953), 529.

222. Grossmann, "*Girlkultur* or Thoroughly Rationalized Female?" 64.

223. See Susanne Meyer-Büser, *"Das schönste deutsche Frauenporträt". Tendenzen der Bildnismalerei in der Weimarer Republik* (Berlin: Reimer, 1994), 45–47. Commentators at the time were not blind to how the woman in the winning painting resembled the hypernormal women depicted in Elida advertisements; commodity aesthetics thus made its pact with art history official. See Topas, "Sei schön durch Willy Jäckel," *Berliner Tageblatt* 57.541 (November 15, 1928); repr. in Meyer-Büser, ed., *Das schönste deutsche Frauenporträt,* 80.

224. See Emmy Schoch-Leimbach, "Die 'neue Sachlichkeit' im Kleide," *Neue Frauenkleidung und Frauenkultur* 23.8 (1927): 214–17.

225. Else Rasch, "Die Beeinflussung des weiblichen Körpers durch Körperkultur und Sport," in *Der weibliche Körper und seine Beeinflussung durch Mode und Sport,* ed. R. Arringer et al. (Leipzig: Verlag für Kultur und Menschenkunde, 1931), 104.

226. Fritz Giese, *Girl-Kultur* (Munich 1925), 39.

227. Giese, *Girl-Kultur,* 49, 68, 113.

228. Giese, *Girl-Kultur,* 137.

229. Future Nazi architect Paul Schultze-Naumburg's 1903 book *Die Kultur des weiblichen Körpers als Grundlage der Frauenkleidung* (Jena: Eugen Diederichs, 1922) sought to provide an enlightenment-text against the corset's deformations of the spine (and hence also the female body of the Germanic race). On the effects of corsetry, see Ewen and Ewen, *Channels of Desire,* 141–42. See also Wigley's remarkable discussion of the dress reform movement, in his *White Walls,* 128–87.

230. Wollen, *Raiding the Icebox,* 20.

231. Alice Rühle-Gerstel, *Das Frauenproblem der Gegenwart. Eine psychologische Bilanz* (Leipzig: Verlag von S. Hirzel, 1932), repr. as *Die Frau und der Kapitalismus. Eine psychologische Bilanz* (Frankfurt a.M.: Verlag Neue Kritik KG, 1972), 78.

232. See "Die Vermännlichung in der Baderobe," *Die Mode* 5 (April 30, 1926).

233. Alfred Döblin, "Sexualität als Sport?" (1931), *Berlin im "Querschnitt,"* ed. Rolf-Peter Baacke (Berlin: Fannei & Walz, 1990), 135.

234. "Who is the man and who is the woman?" *Berliner Morgenzeitung* (May 11, 1924). See also Sabine Hake's discussion of the transgressions of dressing via the *garçonne* in "The Mirror of Fashion," in *Women in the Metropolis,* ed. Ankum, 195–96.

235. See "Die beschnittene Frau," *Er und Sie* 2.1 (1925): 11; and "Die Welt in 40 Jahren," *Berliner Illustrirte Zeitung* 35.1 (January 3, 1926): 5.

236. Emil Lucka, "Verwandlung der Frau," in *Die Frau von morgen,* ed. Huebner, 77–78.

237. Lucka, "Verwandlung der Frau," 77.

238. See Janet Lungstrum (now Ward), "Nietzsche Writing Woman / Woman Writing Nietzsche. The Sexual Dialectic of Palingenesis," in *Nietzsche and the Feminine,* ed. Peter J. Burgard (Charlottesville: University of Virginia Press, 1994): 135–57.

239. Joan Rivière, "Womanliness as a Masquerade," *The International Journal of Psychoanalysis* 10 (1929); repr. in *Formations of Fantasy,* ed. Victor Burgin, James Donald, and Cora Kaplan (New York: Methuen, 1986), 35–44.

240. Petro, *Joyless Streets,* 118. The "feminism of fashion" and "masculinization of women" were the keywords referred to in *Die Dame* (March 1927); repr. in *Die Dame. Ein deutsches Journal für den verwöhnten Geschmack. 1912 bis 1943,* ed. Christian Ferber (Berlin: Ullstein, 1980), 172; see also J. W. Samson, "Die Frauenmode der Gegenwart. Eine medizinisch-psychologische Studie," *Zeitschrift für Sexualwissenschaft* 14 (1927); Rudolf Bosselt, "Zur Psychologie der gegenwärtigen Mode," *Neue Frauenkleidung und Frauenkultur* 23.3 (1927): 58–60; and Werner Suhr, "Amerikanismus der Seele," *Neue Frauenkleidung und Frauenkultur* 24.5 (1928): 177.

241. Jünger, *Aufzeichnungen bei Tag und Nacht* (first version of *Das abenteuerliche Herz*), in *Sämtliche Werke: Essays III* (Stuttgart: Klett-Cotta, 1979), 9:78.

242. "Die 'neue Sachlichkeit' im Schaufenster," *Architektur und Schaufenster* 25 (1928): 11.

243. Erich Kästner, *Fabian*, 91.

244. Bäumer, *Die Frau in der Krisis der Kultur*, 34.

245. Bäumer continues this thesis in *Woman in the New Living Space*, finding in the New Woman's "emancipation of the flesh" signs of a neo-Dionysian degeneration. Bäumer, *Die Frau im neuen Lebensraum* (Berlin: F. A. Herbig, 1931), 19. See also Claudia Koonz's explanation of how the term *Lebensraum* had a pre-Nazi connotation of a separate living sphere for women in society. Koonz, "The Competition for a Women's *Lebensraum*, 1928–1934," in *When Biology Became Destiny: Women in Weimar and Nazi Germany*, ed. Renate Bridenthal, Atina Grossmann, and Marion Kaplan (New York: Monthly Review Press, 1984), 200–201.

246. Kracauer, *Die Angestellten*, 23, 24.

247. Kracauer, *Die Angestellten*, 51.

248. Kracauer, *Die Angestellten*, 25, 24.

249. Rühle-Gerstel, *Das Frauenproblem der Gegenwart*, 295.

250. Rühle-Gerstel, *Das Frauenproblem der Gegenwart*, 300.

251. Gabriele Tergit, "Die Frauen-Tribüne," *Die Frauen Tribüne* 1.1–2 (January 1933): 3. Cited by Petra Bock, "Zwischen den Zeiten," 14.

252. Phrase used in a 1933 poem, "Mode: Herzlichkeit," by Hertra Pauli, published in *Die Frauen Tribüne* 1.4 (1933): 13. Cited by Bock, "Zwischen den Zeiten," 34.

253. Lucka, "Verwandlung der Frau," 83.

254. Marieluise Fleisser, "Die Vision des Schneiderleins," *Berliner Tageblatt* 374 (August 10, 1929); special issue, "Reklame und Publikum."

255. See Thomas Schubauer, "Die Neue Frau und die radikale Frauenbewegung," in *Neue Frauen zwischen den Zeiten*, ed. Bock and Koblitz, 38–60.

256. Charles Baudelaire, "The Painter of Modern Life" (1863), in *The Painter of Modern Life and Other Essays*, trans. Jonathan Mayne (London: Phaidon Press, 1964), 5.

257. Baudelaire, "The Painter of Modern Life," 13.

258. Gilles Lipovetsky, *The Empire of Fashion: Dressing Modern Democracy*, trans. Catherine Porter (Princeton: Princeton University Press, 1994), 10.

259. Lipovetsky, *The Empire of Fashion*, 9.

CHAPTER 2. ELECTRIC STIMULATIONS

1. See C. H. von Hartungen, *Psychologie der Reklame*, 2d ed. (Stuttgart: C. E. Poeschel Verlag, 1926), vi–vii. In adopting the French term, Weimar advertising abandoned the WWI hysteria against using foreign (French) words

in advertising (such as *Parfümerie*); see, e.g., Staatsarchiv Hamburg 324–4 Baupflegekommission 127.

2. Walter Benjamin, *Gesammelte Schriften,* 5.1:51. Advertising as such has been in existence at least since Pompeii, where a wall was found that had been covered in political campaign graffiti. See Sandra Uhrig, "Werbung im Stadtbild," in *Die Kunst zu werben. Das Jahrhundert der Reklame,* ed. Susanne Bäumler (Munich: Münchner Stadtmuseum/Dumont, 1996), 50.

3. See P. D. Glennie's and N. J. Thrift's article "Modernity, Urbanism, and Modern Consumption," *Environment and Planning. D, Society and Space* 10 (1992): 434. Glennie and Thrift underplay the impact of the electric media in modern advertising in their study of consumer habits in industrial and postindustrial societies.

4. For an account of the German Werkbund's role in advertising, see Dirk Reinhardt, *Von der Reklame zum Marketing. Geschichte der Wirtschaftswerbung in Deutschland* (Berlin: Akademie Verlag, 1993), 69–76.

5. On the relationship of modern art and industry, see Peter-Klaus Schuster, "Zur Ästhetik des Alltages. Über Kunst, Werbung und Geschmack," in *Die Kunst zu werben,* ed. Bäumler, 268–72.

6. *Essentials of Outdoor Advertising* (New York: Association of National Advertisers, Inc., 1958), 46, 32.

7. Ernst Litfaß was the inventor of the first advertising columns for posters in Berlin in 1855 (see Uhrig, "Werbung im Stadtbild," in *Die Kunst zu werben,* ed. Bäumler, 52–56). By 1929 there were 3,200 such pillars in Berlin alone, excluding the electrically lit *Normaluhren*—a figure almost three times greater than that of Munich, and far exceeding the 600 in each of Frankfurt a.M., Cologne, and Leipzig. See also Reinhardt, *Von der Reklame zum Marketing,* 253.

8. Bruno Taut, "Die Reklame als Schmuck des Straßenbildes," *Freie Presse* (February 18, 1922); Bundesarchiv Koblenz R32/180 Reklamewesen.

9. For a study of pre-WWI advertising that sought to introduce American tactics to German speakers, see Viktor Mataja, *Die Reklame* (Leipzig: Duncker & Humblot, 1910).

10. See Reinhardt, *Von der Reklame zum Marketing,* 441.

11. See Bundesarchiv Koblenz R32/164 Postreklame.

12. Reinhardt, *Von der Reklame zum Marketing,* 442.

13. See Max Riesebrodt, "Advertising Groups and Associations," *Die Reklame* 22.1 (1929): 524.

14. See Daniel Pope's *The Making of Modern Advertising* (New York: Basic Books, 1983).

15. Hans Rolffsen, "Aufgaben der Außenreklame," sent to editor of *Die Reklame* in September 1924. Staatsarchiv Hamburg 324–4 Baupflegekommission 116.

16. Speech by Julius Hirsch, as cited by Wertheim in *Die Reklame des Warenhauses,* 15–16. In 1924, German firms spent 1,026,000,000 RM on advertising, while American companies spent $1,304,000,000; cited by Rudolf Seyffert, *Allgemeine Werbelehre* (Stuttgart: C. E. Poeschel Verlag, 1929), 664.

17. See Hugo Münsterberg, *Psychologie und Wirtschaftsleben. Ein Beitrag zur angewandten Experimental-Psychologie,* 3d ed. (Leipzig: Johann Ambrosius Barth, 1916).

18. See, for example, "Der Angestellte im Warenhaus," *Zeitschrift für Waren- und Kaufhäuser* 26.33 (August 12, 1928): 42; Georg Villwock, "Zwei psychologische Proben für Warenhausangestellte," *Zeitschrift für Waren- und Kaufhäuser* 23.52 (August 9, 1925): 1–2; and M. Waldau, "Psychotechnische Eignungsprüfung von Facharbeiterinnen für die Elektroindustrie," *Siemens-Zeitschrift* 1.11 (1921): 393–402.

19. Reinhardt, *Von der Reklame zum Marketing,* 92.

20. Kracauer, "Heißer Abend," *Frankfurter Zeitung* 439 (June 15, 1932). See also Mazziari, *Architecture and Nihilism,* 16–17.

21. This is essentially the view of advertising's socializing role within modernization proposed by Stuart Ewen in *Captains of Consciousness: Advertising and the Social Roots of the Consumer Culture* (New York: McGraw-Hill, 1976).

22. Social theorists today often miss out on how "lifestyle" ads were already in existence in the German 1920s. See William Leiss, Stephen Kline, and Sut Jhally, *Social Communications in Advertising: Persons, Products and Images of Well-Being* (London: Methuen, 1985).

23. Alfred Döblin, "Reklame und Literatur," in *Reklame und Publikum,* a special issue of the *Berliner Tageblatt* 374 (August 10, 1929).

24. Alfred Döblin, *Berlin Alexanderplatz. Die Geschichte von Franz Biberkopf* (Olten: Walter-Verlag [dtv], 1961), 105–6.

25. Albert Renger-Patzsch, *Die Welt ist schön. Einhundert photographische Aufnahmen von Albert Renger-Patzsch* (Munich: K. Wolff, 1928). Discussed in *The Weimar Republic Sourcebook,* ed. Kaes, Jay, and Dimendberg, 643.

26. Seyffert, *Allgemeine Werbelehre,* 8; emphasis in original.

27. Seyffert, *Allgemeine Werbelehre,* 654–55, 663–64, 675–80.

28. Daniel Starch, *Principles of Advertising* (Chicago: A. W. Shaw, 1923).

29. See Seyffert, *Allgemeine Werbelehre,* 140–55, 390–391, 596–97, 421–51.

30. Karl Marbe, *Psychologie der Werbung* (Stuttgart: C. E. Poeschel, 1927), 34, 36, 35.

31. Kurt Th. Friedlaender, *Der Weg zum Käufer. Theorie der praktischen Reklame,* 2d ed. (Berlin: Verlag von Julius Springer, 1926).

32. Von Hartungen, *Psychologie der Reklame,* 86.

33. Von Hartungen, *Psychologie der Reklame,* 313.

34. Mia Klein, *Die Reklame des Warenhauses* (Coburg: Tageblatt-Haus, 1931), 9.

35. Klein, *Die Reklame des Warenhauses,* 10.

36. Klein, *Die Reklame des Warenhauses,* 39.

37. "Moderne Reklame," *Berliner Tageblatt* 400 (August 25, 1929); Geheimes Staatsarchiv: Rep. 120 E XVI.2 Nr. 13.

38. See Wolf Zucker, "Kunst und Reklame. Zum Weltreklamekongreß in Berlin," *Die literarische Welt* 5.32 (August 1929): 1; repr. in *Weimarer Republik. Manifeste und Dokumente zur deutschen Literatur 1918–1933,* ed. Anton Kaes (Stuttgart: Metzler, 1983), 262.

39. Reinhardt, *Von der Reklame zum Marketing,* 97.

40. Reinhardt quotes the 1933 report of the *Bund Deutscher Gebrauchsgraphiker,* which boasts of its association's Nazi takeover as having been "absolutely frictionless" (*Von der Reklame zum Marketing,* 87).

41. Kracauer, *The Mass Ornament,* 151.

42. See Edward Bernays, *Propaganda* (New York: H. Liveright, 1928), and *Biography of an Idea: Memoirs of Public Relations Counsel Edward L. Bernays* (New York: Simon & Schuster, 1965). In 1928, Bernays set up a Viennese office with the Schicht advertising company. See *Seidels Reklame* 9.10 (1925): 500; repr. in Meyer-Büser, *Das schönste deutsche Frauenporträt,* 157.

43. "Be It So, Electrical Advertising Has Only Begun," *Signs of the Times* (December 1912). Cited by William Leach, *Land of Desire: Merchants, Power, and the Rise of a New American Culture* (New York: Vintage, 1993), 47.

44. Discussed by Carola Jüllig, "'Wo nachts keine Lichter brennen, ist finstere Provinz.' Neue Werbung in Berlin," in *Die Kunst zu werben,* ed. Bäumler, 67–68.

45. See Reinhardt, *Von der Reklame zum Marketing,* 318–20; and Uhrig, "Lichter der Großstadt," in *Die Kunst zu werben,* ed. Bäumler, 78.

46. Hans Ostwald, *Sittengeschichte der Inflation. Ein Kulturdokument aus den Jahren des Marktsturzes* (Berlin: Neufeld & Henius, 1931), 280.

47. See Eugen R. Haberfeld, "Die Lichtwerbung und ihre Technik," in *Licht und Beleuchtung. Lichttechnische Fragen unter Berücksichtigung der Bedürfnisse der Architektur,* ed. Wilhelm Lotz et al. (Berlin: Verlag Hermann Reckendorf, 1928), 48.

48. Ernst Pollak, "Modern Shop Constructions," in *Interior Design 1929.* One can contrast this free-market attitude with current Chancellor Schröder's deference to post-WWII Germany's *Ladenschlußgesetz,* the law that strictly regulates retail opening hours.

49. Noted by Amédée Ozenfant, "Weekend Berlin" (1931), in *Berlin im "Querschnitt,"* 42.

50. See L. Hamel, "Berlin im Licht, seine Aufgaben und Ziele," *Die Reklame* 16 (1928). Cited by Jüllig, "Wo nachts keine Lichter brennen," in *Die Kunst zu werben,* ed. Bäumler, 66.

51. Muthesius, "Lichtreklame-Architektur," *Seidels Reklame* 9.5 (1925): 206.

52. See Peter Fritzsche's thesis of how Weimar German experimentation in, for example, architecture and engineering arose as a spirit of necessity out of the country's defeat in WWI. Fritzsche, "Landscape of Danger, Landscape of Design," 29–46.

53. For a demonstration of a unified approach, see Robert Hosel's announcement of 1925 as a "jubilee year" for the German "power of advertising,"

thanks to which a more "genuine truce" has been forged than in 1914. Hosel, "Zur Jahreswende," *Seidels Reklame* 9.1 (1925): 2–3.

54. Hermann Kircher, *Das Licht in der Werbung* (Frankfurt a.M.: University of Frankfurt, 1930), 6.

55. Kurt Rose, "Werbung durch Licht," *Berliner Tageblatt* (April 30, 1928); cited in *Licht und Beleuchtung. Lichttechnische Fragen unter Berücksichtigung der Bedürfnisse der Architektur,* ed. Wilhelm Lotz et al. (Berlin: Verlag Hermann Reckendorf, 1928), 60.

56. Paul Scheerbart, *Glasarchitektur*, 58, 97.

57. See "Der Wettbewerb für das Messe- und Ausstellungsgelände in Berlin," *Deutsche Bauzeitung* 20 (March 10, 1926): 1.

58. *Kleine Presse* 1 (November 11, 1891): 2. Cited in *"Eine neue Zeit . . . !" Die internationale Elektrotechnische Ausstellung 1891,* ed. Jürgen Steen (Frankfurt a.M.: Historisches Museum Frankfurt am Main, 1991), 389.

59. See Schivelbusch, *Licht Schein und Wahn,* 9–20. In *The Railway Journey: The Industrialization of Time and Space in the 19th Century* (Berkeley: University of California Press, 1986), 49. Schivelbusch sees a source of impressionism's breakthrough in nineteenth-century exhibitions' new architectural arrangements of light.

60. For a history of the AEG, see Henning Rogge, "A Motor Must Look Like a Birthday Present," in *Industriekultur,* ed. Buddensieg and Rogge, 96–123.

61. Reinhardt, *Von der Reklame zum Marketing,* 323.

62. See Reinhardt, *Von der Reklame zum Marketing,* 320.

63. Jüllig, "Wo nachts keine Lichter brennen," in *Die Kunst zu werben,* ed. Bäumler, 73. See also C. Hunger, "Neon-Leuchtröhren," *Seidels Reklame* 10.8 (1926): 361.

64. Giedion's term for this is *indi-leuchten* ("a new light—a new space"), to express what he saw going on around him. Sigfried Giedion, "Konstruktion und Chaos," in *Zur Entstehung des heutigen Menschen* (unpublished, 1929–1938). Cited by Sokratis Georgiadis, "Giedion and the 'Third Factor,'" *Daidalos* 27 (1988): 63, 64.

65. See Reinhardt, *Von der Reklame zum Marketing,* 451, 325–29.

66. Schivelbusch, *Licht Schein und Wahn,* 67.

67. Mark C. Taylor, lecture at the University of Colorado at Boulder (April 24, 1998).

68. Benjamin, *Gesammelte Schriften,* 5.2:698, 700.

69. See Christoph Asendorf, *Batteries of Life,* 165–66.

70. Cited in *Der Hang zum Gesamtkunstwerk. Europäische Utopien seit 1800,* ed. Harald Szeemann (Aarau: Verlag Sauerländer, 1983).

71. See Janet Lungstrum (now Ward), "*Metropolis* and the Technosexual Woman of German Modernity," in *Women in the Metropolis,* ed. Ankum, 128–44.

72. Ludwig Meidner, "Anleitung zum Malen von Großstadtbildern," *Kunst und Künstler* 12.6 (1914), 312–14. Cited by Jüllig, "Wo nachts keine Lichter brennen," in *Die Kunst zu werben,* ed. Bäumler, 66.

73. Jay explains how an entire interwar generation lived with the recent memory of trench warfare and its extreme visual disorientation of "lightning flashes of blinding intensity" and "phantasmagoric, often gas-induced haze." Jay, *Downcast Eyes,* 212. See also Buck-Morss, "Aesthetics and Anaesthetics: Walter Benjamin's Artwork Essay Reconsidered," *October* 62 (1992): 16–18; and Douglas, *Terrible Honesty,* 202–16.

74. Gertrude Stein, *Picasso* (Boston: Beacon Press, 1959), 11; see also Stephen Kern, *The Culture of Time and Space, 1880–1918* (Cambridge: Harvard University Press, 1983), 288; and Jay, *Downcast Eyes,* 213.

75. See David Cook, *History of Narrative Film* (New York: W. W. Norton, 1981), 11.

76. See Jay, *Downcast Eyes,* 214–15; and also his discussion of Georges Bataille's post-WWI self-retrenchment from visuality (216–36).

77. In *Um uns die Stadt. Eine Anthologie neuer Großstadtdichtung,* ed. Robert Seitz and Heinz Zucker (Berlin: Sieben-Stäbe Verlag, 1931; repr. Braunschweig: Friedr. Vieweg & Sohn, 1986), 173.

78. Eugen R. Haberfeld, "Die Lichtwerbung und ihre Technik," in *Licht und Beleuchtung,* ed. Lotz, 52–53.

79. Walter Riezler, "Licht und Architektur," in *Licht und Beleuchtung,* ed. Lotz, 43.

80. Kracauer, *Straßen in Berlin,* 41.

81. Ernst Bloch, "Gespräch über die Zwanziger Jahre," *Bloch-Almanach* 2 (1982): 11. Somewhat less emphatic but equally doubtful was the comment of Le Corbusier, who was not quite taken in by the "incandescent path" of Broadway of the 1930s: "Electricity reigns, but it is dynamic here, exploding, moving, sparkling, with lights turning white, blue, red, green, yellow. The things behind it are disappointing. These close-range constellations, this Milky Way in which you are carried along, lead to objects of enjoyment which are often mediocre." Le Corbusier, *When the Cathedrals Were White: A Journey to the Country of Timid People,* trans. Francis E. Hyslop, Jr. (New York: Reynal & Hitchcock, 1947), 102.

82. Hans Erasmus Fischer, "Eine Fahrt durch Berlin im Licht," *Berliner Lokal-Anzeiger* (October 13, 1928). See also "Das Programm des Berliner Lichtfestes," *Berliner Lokal-Anzeiger* (October 10, 1928). I would like to thank Christian Rogowski for first bringing the Berlin Light Week to my attention.

83. Ingrid Scheib-Rotbart, personal communication, March 1995.

84. "Der Warenhausbrand bei Tietz," *Berliner Morgen-Zeitung* (October 12, 1928).

85. See Wladimir Koschewnikoff's "Die Stadt im Licht" (published in the conservative *Germania* 489 [October 1928]), a poem that posits the night hidden behind the Light Week as the bearer of truth and reflection. See also the jokey poem "Berlin im Licht," about Berliners and their dogs wearing light bulbs (*Berliner Morgen-Zeitung* [October 18, 1928]).

86. A recording can be found on Teresa Stratas, *The Unknown Kurt Weill* (Elektra/Asylum/Nonesuch Records, 1981).

87. See *Die Weite Welt,* special issue "Elektrizität im Haushalt," 43 (October 21, 1938).

88. Nietzsche, *Sämtliche Werke,* 3:356; *The Gay Science,* 45.

89. On the Berlin Light Week's relation to the darker, poorer sides of Berlin, see Bärbel Schrader and Jürgen Schebera, *Kunstmetropole Berlin 1918–1933: Die Kunststadt in der Novemberrevolution. Die "goldenen" Zwanziger. Die Kunststadt in der Krise* (Berlin: Aufbau-Verlag, 1987), 136–40; and Joachim Schlör, *Nachts in der großen Stadt. Paris, Berlin, London 1840–1930* (Munich: Artemis & Winkler, 1991), 70–71.

90. See "Berlin im Licht. Die Reichshauptstadt präsentiert ihr neues Gesicht." *Berliner Morgen-Zeitung* 286 (October 14, 1928).

91. Fischer, "Eine Fahrt durch Berlin im Licht."

92. See *Berliner Morgen-Zeitung* 286 (October 14, 1928).

93. See K. Klöne, "Großstadt im Licht: Hamburg," *Das Licht* 2.10 (October 15, 1931): 230–31; and N. Frühwacht, "Werbende Weltstädte. Eine Lichtplauderei," *Die Reklame* 22 (November 1931): 685–87.

94. Erich Mendelsohn, *Amerika. Bilderbuch eines Architekten* (Berlin: R. Mosse, 1926), 25, 44.

95. Kurt Biebrach, "Aussenreklame," *Die Reklame* 23 (December 1931): 713.

96. See Florian Zimmermann's analysis of Hans Scharoun's design, "*Kennwort: Innen und Außen.* Ankauf," in *Der Schrei nach dem Turmhaus,* ed. Zimmermann et al., 124.

97. Taut, "Die Reklame als Schmuck des Straßenbildes."

98. Jüllig, "Wo nachts keine Lichter brennen," in *Die Kunst zu werben,* ed. Bäumler, 73.

99. For a discussion of the Columbus House, see Regina Stephan, ed., *Erich Mendelsohn. Architekt 1887–1953. Gebaute Welten. Arbeiten für Europa, Palästina und Amerika* (Ostfildern-Ruit: Hatje, 1998), 155–64.

100. As Walter Curt Behrendt noticed in 1927, "so far only electric advertising has been making full use of the new freedom" granted by light-architecture. Behrendt, *Der Sieg des Neuen Baustils* (Stuttgart: Fr. Wedekind, 1927), 47ff.; cited by Oechselin, "Lichtarchitektur," 126.

101. Cited by Kircher, *Das Licht in der Werbung,* 70.

102. One subsequent descendant of Weimar light architecture, namely Mies van der Rohe's Seagram Building in Manhattan, was designed with the total nighttime illumination of all its windows in mind. See Schivelbusch, *Licht Schein und Wahn,* 75.

103. "Die Lichtreklame des Kino-Theaters. Immer wieder: Licht lockt Leute!" *Reichsfilmblatt* 35 (1929): 12.

104. See Schivelbusch, *Licht Schein und Wahn,* 78.

105. Joachim Teichmüller, "Lichtarchitektur," *Licht und Lampe* 13/14 (1927); repr. in *Daidalos* 27 (1988): 68. See also Werner Oechselin, "Lichtarchitektur," in *Expressionismus und Neue Sachlichkeit. Moderne Architektur in Deutschland. 1900 bis 1945,* ed. Vittorio Lampugnani and Romana Schneider (Stuttgart: Hatje, 1994), 117–31; and Oechselin, "Light: A Means of Creation

between Reason and Emotion," *Daidalos* 27 (1988): 23–38. By 1931, however, Teichmüller was voicing his disappointment at the failure of architects to adopt light architecture to its fullest potential: Teichmüller, "Gestaltung durch Schattenwirkung in der Lichtarchitektur," *Das Licht* 1.6 (1931): 170.

106. It was only through indirect lighting that vaulted ceilings in restaurants, cinema auditoriums, hotel lobbies, department stores, and night clubs of the 1920s and 1930s achieved that definitive, postexpressionistic, chiaroscuro look. Fluorescent lighting was not introduced until 1939 at New York's World's Fair. See Schivelbusch, *Licht Schein und Wahn*, 36, 37.

107. Norbert Bolz, *Theorie der Neuen Medien* (Munich: Raben Verlag, 1990), 90.

108. Riezler, "Licht und Architektur," in *Licht und Beleuchtung*, ed. Lotz, 43.

109. Erwin Redslob, introduction to *Berliner Architektur der Nachkriegszeit*, ed. E. M. Hajos and L. Zahn (Berlin: Albertus-Verlag, 1928), x.

110. Redslob, "Das Licht als Maß der Dinge," *Das Licht* 1.1 (October 1930): 3; emphasis in original.

111. "The Skyscraper of Light," unrealized design by "Leo Nachtlicht" for the Berlin Reklameschau (1929), *Reklame und Publikum*, special issue of the *Berliner Tageblatt* 374 (August 10, 1929).

112. Kircher, *Das Licht in der Werbung*, 68.

113. Osborn et al., *Berlins Aufstieg zur Weltstadt*, 216.

114. W. Randt, "Stadtbild und Lichtarchitektur," *Das Licht* 2.6 (1932): 129.

115. Opinion of archivist Sylvia Claus at the Akademie der Künste, Berlin. Personal communication.

116. Riezler, "Umgestaltung der Fassaden," *Die Form* 2.2 (1927): 40.

117. Ernst May, "Städtebau und Lichtreklame," in *Licht und Beleuchtung*, ed. Lotz, 45, 47.

118. Schivelbusch, *Licht Schein und Wahn*, 73.

119. Schivelbusch, *Licht Schein und Wahn*, 73, citing Tom Wolfe's "Car Phantasy Architecture / Electrographic Architecture," *Architectural Design* (July 1969): 380.

120. See Jean Nouvel, "The Meeting Line," in *Berlin Tomorrow: International Architectural Visions*, ed. Vittorio Magnago Lampugnani (London: Academy Editions, 1991), 71. I would like to thank Werner Goehner for pointing out this reference to me.

121. Gustav Brandes, "Die Geschäftsreklame im Stadtbilde" (1922). Staatsarchiv Hamburg: 324–4 Baupflegekommission 127.

122. Von Hartungen, *Psychologie der Reklame*, 1.

123. Benjamin, "Denkbilder," in *Gesammelte Schriften*, 4.1:340.

124. Hans Heinrich Ehrler, "Reise nach Berlin," *Vossische Zeitung* (June 10, 1928); repr. in *Glänzender Asphalt*, ed. Jäger and Schütz, 25.

125. Fritz Giese, *Girlkultur. Vergleiche zwischen amerikanischem und europäischem Rhythmus und Lebensgefühl* (Munich: Delphin Verlag, 1925), 23.

126. Fritz Pauli, *Rhythmus und Resonanz als ökonomisches Prinzip in der Reklame* (Berlin: Verlag des Verbandes Deutscher Reklamefachleute, 1926), 18.

127. Schivelbusch cites as an originating example of this kinetic fascination Muybridge's photographic studies of a bird in flight. Schivelbusch, *Licht Schein und Wahn,* 70. See also "Die Wanderschrift-Lichtreklame," *Seidels Reklame* 10.8 (1926): 358.

128. Reinhardt, *Von der Reklame zum Marketing,* 324.

129. Adolf Behne, *Der moderne Zweckbau,* 39.

130. See "Der Neubau Petersdorff, Breslau," *Architektur und Schaufenster* 25 (1928).

131. See Palmer, *Der Stuttgarter Schocken-Bau von Erich Mendelsohn,* 41–53, 71.

132. Erich Mendelsohn, "Harmonische und kontrapunktische Führung in der Architektur," *Die Baukunst* 1 (1925): 179; cited by Palmer, *Der Stuttgarter Schocken-Bau von Erich Mendelsohn,* 30.

133. Mendelsohn, *Erich Mendelsohn,* 28.

134. Michel Foucault, "Space, Knowledge, and Power," in *The Foucault Reader* (New York: Pantheon, 1984), 244.

135. Paul Virilio, "'Das irreale Monument,'" trans. Hans-Horst Henschen, in *Paris-Berlin 1900–1933,* ed. Centre Georges Pompidou (Munich: Prestel, 1979), 366; emphasis in original.

136. Cited in *From the Great Refractor to the Einstein Tower,* ed. Joachim Krausse, Dietmar Ropohl, and Walter Scheiffele (Giessen: Anabas, 1996), 17.

137. Kracauer, *Straßen in Berlin,* 33. See also Lethen, *Verhaltenslehren der Kälte,* 44–50.

138. For a Simmel-based parallel analysis of the shocks of urban modernity in the turn-of-the-century U.S., see Ben Singer, "Modernity, Hyperstimulus, and the Rise of Popular Sensationalism," in *Cinema and the Invention of Modern Life,* ed. Charney and Schwartz, 72–99.

139. See, for example, *Das Weltreich der Technik. Entwicklung und Gegenwart,* 4 vols., ed. Artur Fürst (Berlin: Ullstein, 1929), esp. 1:345–58 on television.

140. See, for example, Ernst Jünger, *Der gefährliche Augenblick,* ed. Ferdinand Buchholz (Berlin: Jünker & Dünnhaupt, 1931). The best study of Jünger's theory of modernity is Marcus Bullock's *The Violent Eye: Ernst Jünger's Visions and Revisions on the European Right* (Detroit: Wayne State University Press, 1991); see also Lethen's *Verhaltenslehren der Kälte,* particularly 206–15.

141. See Alfred Peyser, "Großstadtlärm," in *Das neue Berlin,* ed. Wagner and Behne, 227–29; and Ludwig Bregmann, "Die Nerven des Grossstädters," *Berliner Tageblatt* 58.120 (March 12, 1929).

142. Harold Nicholson, "The Charm of Berlin" (1929), in *Berlin im "Querschnitt",* ed. Baacke, 174.

143. Le Corbusier, *When the Cathedrals Were White,* 161.

144. Robert Musil, *The Man Without Qualities* (1930–1943), trans. Eithne Wilkins and Ernst Kaiser (London: Picador, 1979), 1:30; cited by Asendorf, *Batteries of Life,* 62.

145. Musil, "Der Riese AGOAG," in *Nachlaß zu Lebzeiten* (Zürich: Humanitas Verlag, 1936). See Lethen's reading of the tank as New Objective symbol of masculinity, *Verhaltenslehren der Kälte,* 202–205.

146. Mike Savage, "Walter Benjamin's Urban Thought: A Critical Analysis," *Environment and Planning. D, Society and Space* 13 (1995): 213.

147. "The Cosmopolis of the Future" was a pictorial series of Manhattan as it might look by the year 1930, drawn by Harry M. Petit in 1908 and published by Moses King. See Koolhaas, *Delirious New York,* 70–71.

148. In Grosz's similar painting *Metropolis* (1917), the façades of buildings cascade furiously at diagonal angles into the paths (and even the bodies) of the unsalubrious city denizens. See the essay by Hanne Bergius on "Berlin, the Dada-Metropolis" in *The 1920's: Age of the Metropolis,* ed. Jean Clair (Montreal: The Montreal Museum of Fine Arts, 1991), 253–69; and Barbara McCloskey, *George Grosz and the Communist Party: Art and Radicalism in Crisis, 1918 to 1936* (Princeton: Princeton University Press, 1997), 44.

149. See Robert Hughes, *The Shock of the New,* rev. ed. (New York: Alfred A. Knopf, 1991).

150. Sigmund Freud, "Beyond the Pleasure Principle," in *The Standard Edition of the Complete Psychological Works* (London: Hogarth Press, 1953—1974), 18:27–29. Cited by Schivelbusch, *The Railway Journey,* 164, 166; emphasis in original.

151. See Freud, "Beyond the Pleasure Principle," 18:13; Benjamin, "On Some Motifs in Baudelaire," in *Illuminations,* 161–63; and Singer, "Modernity, Hyperstimulus, and Popular Sensationalism," 94. See also Hans Prager's related article on the "battle" between eye and ear in the modern city, in "Philosophie des Lärmes," *Der Tag* (October 6, 1928).

152. As Miriam Hansen cautions of the moving camera in the history of cinema: "The mobilization of the gaze promises nothing less than the mobilization of the self, the transformation of seemingly fixed positions of social identity. This mobilization, however, is promise and delusion in one." Hansen, *Babel and Babylon: Spectatorship in American Silent Film* (Cambridge: Harvard University Press, 1991), 112.

153. Benjamin, "On Some Motifs in Baudelaire," in *Illuminations,* 155–200; Buck-Morss, "The City as Dreamworld and Catastrophe," *October* 73 (1995): 8.

154. Buck-Morss, "Aesthetics and Anaesthetics," 22.

155. Bolz, "Design des Immateriellen," 156, 157.

156. Kafka, "Die Stadt im Sommer. Potsdamer Platz, abends," in *Glänzender Asphalt,* ed. Jäger and Schütz, 128.

157. Stadtarchiv Stuttgart C IX 8 Bd. 3 Nr. 6 (Bauregistratur), Reklamegewerbe: 1914–1929.

158. Ernst May, "Städtebau und Lichtreklame," 44.

159. Kracauer, *Straßen in Berlin,* 15. Kracauer's essay corresponds to the post-1929 economic reality: see Carl Foerster, "Wirtschaftskrise—Reklamekrise," *Die Reklame* 22 (November 1931): 700–701.

160. Friedlaender, *Der Weg zum Käufer,* 13, 28.

161. This term is used by Joh. M. Verweyen in his book *Der neue Mensch und seine Ziele. Menschheitsfragen der Gegenwart und Zukunft* (Stuttgart: Walter Hädecke Verlag, 1930), 10.

162. The best study of New Objectivity's "cold *personae*" in Weimar society and literature is Lethen's *Verhaltenslehren der Kälte.*

163. On Biberkopf's experience, see Sabine Hake, "Urban Paranoia in Alfred Döblin's *Berlin Alexanderplatz,*" *The German Quarterly* 67.3 (1994): 347–68; James Donald, *Imagining the Modern City* (Minneapolis: University of Minnesota Press, 1999), 135–37; Erhard Schütz, *Romane der Weimarer Republik* (Munich: Wilhelm Fink, 1986), 217–32; and Hermann Kähler, *Berlin—Asphalt und Licht. Die grosse Stadt in der Literatur der Weimarer Republik* (Berlin: deb/verlag das europäische buch, 1986), 227–48.

164. Döblin, *Berlin Alexanderplatz,* 9.

165. See Eric L. Santner, *My Own Private Germany: Daniel Paul Schreber's Secret History of Modernity* (Princeton: Princeton University Press, 1996); and Christoph Asendorf, *Ströme und Strahlen. Das langsame Verschwinden der Materie um 1900* (Berlin: Anabas, 1989), 139–41.

166. Ernst Toller, *Hoppla, wir leben!* 89.

167. Georg Heym, "Die Dämonen der Städte," *Menschheitsdämmerung. Symphonie jüngster Dichtung,* ed. Kurt Pinthus (Berlin: Rowohlt, 1920), 15. Celebratory-cum-nightmarish visions of Berlin by night also feature strongly in poems in *Um uns die Stadt,* ed. Seitz and Zucker. See Walter H. Sokel's highly influential *The Writer in Extremis* (Stanford: Stanford University Press, 1959); see also Kähler's discussion of the theme of expressionist *Angst* in Weimar city poems, in *Berlin—Asphalt und Licht,* 110–26; and Douglas Kellner, "Expression and Rebellion," in *Passion and Rebellion: The Expressionist Heritage,* ed. Stephen Eric Bronner and Douglas Kellner (South Hadley, Mass.: J. F. Bergin, 1983), 20–28.

168. Ernst Jünger, *Annäherungen. Drogen und Rausch* (Berlin, 1980), 102. Cited by Eckhardt Köln, *Straßenrausch. Flanerie und kleine Form. Versuch zur Literaturgeschichte des Flaneurs bis 1933* (Berlin: Das Arsenal, 1989), 150.

169. Jünger, *Aufzeichnungen bei Tag und Nacht,* 9:77, 78, 79, 90.

170. See also Bruno Seeger, "Die Macht der Finsternis," *Das Licht* 1.9 (June 1931): 225–28.

171. Teichmüller, "Lichtarchitektur," repr. in *Daidalos* 27 (1988): 68.

172. Redslob, "Das Licht als Maß der Dinge," 4; emphasis in original.

173. I thank Werner Goehner for this observation. See also Wolfgang Schivelbusch, *Disenchanted Night: The Industrialization of Light in the Nineteenth Century,* trans. Angela Davies (Berkeley: University of California Press, 1988), 81–134.

174. See H. Lingenfelser, "Verkehrssicherheit und Beleuchtung," *Das Licht* 2.11 (1932): 209–11.

175. For a contemporary analysis of the ways in which the visual language of ads elicits emotions, see Paul Messaris's filmically informed *Visual Persuasion: The Role of Images in Advertising* (London: Sage Publications, 1997).

176. Kracauer, *The Mass Ornament,* 332.

177. Hermann Kesser, "Potsdamer Platz," *Die neue Rundschau* (1929); repr. in *Glänzender Asphalt,* ed. Jäger and Schütz, 131.

178. Kracauer's powerful point is reiterated in the definition of the (post)modern advertising function by the Marxist social theorist Sut Jhally. Jhally deconstructs the decorative basis of the phantasmagoria as a hermeneutics of the void: "The world of goods in industrial society offers no meaning, its meaning having been 'emptied' out of them. The function of advertising is to refill the emptied commodity with meaning. . . . The power of advertising *depends* upon the initial emptying out. Only then can advertising refill this empty void with its own meaning. Its power comes from the fact that it works its magic on a blank slate." Jhally, "Advertising as Religion: The Dialectic of Technology and Magic," in *Cultural Politics in Contemporary America,* ed. Ian H. Angus and Sut Jhally (New York: Routledge, 1989), 221; cited by Celia Lury, *Consumer Culture* (New Brunswick, N.J.: Rutgers University Press, 1996), 62.

179. Friedrich Huth, "Lichtarchitektur," *Schaufenster-Kunst und Technik* (December 1930), 29. Cited by Osterwold, *Schaufenster,* 82.

180. Kracauer, "Lichtreklame," *Frankfurter Zeitung* 71.38 (January 15, 1927).

181. Georg Simmel, "The Berlin Trade Exhibition," trans. Sam Whimster, *Theory, Culture & Society* 8 (1991): 122. Orig. "Berliner Gewerbeausstellung," *Die Zeit* (Vienna) 7.91 (July 25, 1896). I thank Anton Kaes for bringing this essay to my attention.

182. Adorno, "Functionalism Today," in *Rethinking Architecture,* ed. Leach (New York: Routledge, 1997), 9.

183. Sigmund Freud, "Medusa's Head," in *Sexuality and the Psychology of Love* (New York: Macmillan, 1963), 212–13.

184. See Andreas Huyssen, "Mass Culture as Woman: Modernism's Other," 44–62.

185. See Leiss, Kline, and Jhally, *Social Communications in Advertising,* 268. Cited by Friedmann W. Nerdinger, "Strategien der Werbung," in *Die Kunst zu werben,* ed. Bäumler, 300–305.

186. "Plakat- und Lichtsteuer in Nürnberg," *Licht und Lampe* 4 (February 1930): 231.

187. Paul Schmitt, *Die Grenzen der erlaubten Reklame* (Würzburg-Aumühle: Druckerei wissenschaftlicher Werke Konrad Triltsch, 1939), 8, 10.

188. *Die Reklame* 4.2 (February 1933): 119.

189. Buck-Morss, *Dialectics of Seeing,* 309.

190. Schivelbusch, *Licht Schein und Wahn,* 41.

191. Heinrich Hauser, "Das Menschenmeer von Tempelhof," *Neue Rundschau* 1 (1933); repr. in *Glänzender Asphalt,* ed. Jäger and Schütz, 329.

192. The desire to create such an effect stems from nineteenth-century electric usage, as Asendorf notes in *Batteries of Life* (101): Villiers de L'Isle-Adam's story "Advertisement on the Firmament" parodically suggests that the sky could be improved upon by having electric, literally universal advertising beamed up onto it from the ground below.

193. The fact that the memory of Speer's "cathedral of light" has not dimmed at all was highlighted by the media debate, in December 1999, over a proposed light show ("Art in Heaven," by artist Gert Hof) to mark the millennium at the Victory Column (Siegessäule) in Berlin's Tiergarten. Such were the fears of inadvertently staging an homage to Speer that the light show designs were radically altered in color and shape and, effectively, diminished. See "Lichtspektakel wird völlig verändert," *Der Tagesspiegel* (December 18, 1999).

194. Lefebvre, *The Production of Space,* 125.

195. For a study on how Bauhaus architects were tempted into designing for Nazism, see Winfried Nerdinger, ed., *Bauhaus-Moderne im Nationalsozialismus: Zwischen Anbiederung und Verfolgung* (Berlin: Bauhaus-Archiv, 1993).

196. Horkheimer and Adorno, *Dialektik der Aufklärung,* 172, 176.

197. Reinhardt, in *Von der Reklame zum Marketing,* 3–10, gives an account of left-wing postwar German critiques of advertising, but omits any consideration of postmodernist contributions to the debate.

198. One of the more significant recent studies on the ideology of advertising in postwar and post-Wall Germany is *"Ins Gehirn der Masse kriechen!" Werbung und Mentalitätsgeschichte,* by Rainer Gries, Volker Ilgen, and Dirk Schindelbeck (Darmstadt: Wissenschaftliche Buchgesellschaft, 1995).

199. See Reinhardt, *Von der Reklame zum Marketing,* 315.

200. A much-used aspect of the 1907 law passed due to *Heimatschutz* groups in Berlin (*Gesetz gegen die Verunstaltung von Ortschaften und landschaftlich herausragenden Gegenden*) was the clause on whether the advertisement "seriously affects the visual character of the place or street." See Jüllig, "Wo nachts keine Lichter brennen," in *Die Kunst zu werben,* ed. Bäumler, 69.

201. See, for example, "Die Verunstaltung der Straßen durch Reklamen," *Zeitschrift für Polizei- und Verwaltungs-Beamte* 17.6 (February 20, 1909), Staatsarchiv Hamburg 324–4 Baupflegekommission 127; Reinhardt, *Von der Reklame zum Marketing,* 378–86; and Leach on American reform groups, *Land of Desire,* 48–49. See also the Prussian *Volkswohlfahrt* ministry's "Grundsätze für Gestaltung und Anbringung von Werbezeichen im Stadtbilde (Außenreklame)" (October 13, 1925), Staatsarchiv Hamburg 324–4 Baupflegekommission 125.

202. On the cat-and-mouse games between local authorities and advertisers regarding electric advertising, see, for example, Karl Dittmar, "Die Behinderung der Aussen-Reklame," *Die Reklame* 22.1 (1929): 612; and Hermann Kircher, *Das Licht in der Werbung,* 72–78.

203. See Gerhard Engelmann, *Der baurechtliche Verunstaltungsbegriff bei den Anlagen der Aussenwerbung* (Erlangen-Nürnberg: Friedrich-Alexander-Universität Erlangen-Nürnberg, 1986), 16–21.

204. See "Neuregelung im Verdingungswesen und Behinderungen in der Lichtreklame," *Licht und Lampe* 3 (February 1930): 136; "Noch immer keine Lichtreklame in Hamburg möglich," *Hamburger Anzeiger* 160 (July 11, 1924); and Bärbel Hedinger, "Las Vegas an der Alster oder Der Hamburger Reklamestreit," in *Die Kunst zu werben,* ed. Bäumler, 94–102.

205. Stadtarchiv Stuttgart 1500/3 Fasz. 2–8, 1927–1930; letter of June 29, 1928; 6, 1–2. Cited by Palmer, *Der Stuttgarter Schocken-Bau von Erich Mendelsohn*, 75–76.

206. Rolffsen, "Heimatschutz und Heimatpflege in Hamburg," *Deutsche Übersee-Zeitung* 34 (n.d.): 2. Staatsarchiv Hamburg 324–4 Baupflegekommission 116. On the history of the *Heimatschutz* movement, see Uwe Spiekermann, "Elitenkampf um die Werbung. Staat, Heimatschutz und Reklameindustrie im frühen 20. Jahrhundert," in *Bilderwelt des Alltags. Werbung in der Konsumgesellschaft des 19. und 20. Jahrhunderts*, ed. Peter Borscheid and Clemens Wischermann (Stuttgart: Franz Steiner Verlag, 1995), 126–49.

207. See "Reklame und Heimatschutz," *Neue Zürcher Zeitung* 670 (May 6, 1924). Staatsarchiv Hamburg 324–4 Baupflegekommission 127.

208. Hermann Neye, "Lichtreklame und Staat," *Seidels Reklame* 10.8 (1926): 375.

209. Leach, however, gives us two examples of eyes resistant to the Times Square aesthetic: the sociologist Thorstein Veblen, for one, was aghast at the "spectacular display" of what he saw around him in Manhattan: "The wriggly gestures with which certain spear-headed manikins stab the nightly firmament over Times Square may be eloquent and graceful but they are not the goods listed," he complained of the Wrigley Spearmint sign (Veblen, *Absentee Ownership and Business Enterprise in Recent Times* [New York: Viking, 1923], 321–22; Leach, *Land of Desire*, 345). Also, the English author G. K. Chesterton confirms Leach's own thesis when he locates the fault in the system of electric advertising as one of disenfranchisement of the gaze: "The hypnotist of high finance or big business merely writes his commands in heaven with a finger of fire. We are only the victims of his pyrotechnic violence. . . . " Chesterton, "A Meditation in Broadway," *What I Saw in America* (1923), in *The Collected Works of G. K. Chesterton*, ed. Robert Royal (San Francisco: Ignatius Press, 1986), 21:70; Leach, *Land of Desire*, 348.

210. Maria Leitner, *Hotel Amerika* (Berlin: Neuer Deutscher Verlag, 1930), 202, 294.

211. Benjamin, "On Some Motifs in Baudelaire," in *Illuminations*, 194.

212. Benjamin, *Illuminations*, 238.

213. Friedberg, *Window Shopping*, 47.

214. Benjamin, *Gesammelte Schriften*, 4.1:132; Benjamin, "One-Way Street," in *Selected Writings: Volume 1, 1913–1926*, ed. Marcus Bullock and Michael W. Jennings (Cambridge: Harvard University Press, 1996), 476.

215. Benjamin, "On Some Motifs in Baudelaire," *Illuminations*, 194.

216. Benjamin, *Illuminations*, 194.

217. Hans H. Reinsch, "Psychologie der Lichtreklame," in *Das Neue Berlin. Großstadtprobleme*, ed. Wagner and Behne, 154.

218. Fernand Léger, "The Spectacle: Light, Color, Moving Image, Object-Spectacle" (1924), in *Functions of Painting*, ed. Edward F. Fry, trans. Alexandra Anderson (New York: Viking Press, 1973), 36, 35, 46; emphasis in original.

219. Moholy-Nagy offered a textual version of his filmscript in "Dynamik der Grossstadt. Skizze zu einem Filmmanuskript," *Film-Kurier* (September 9, 1925); repr. in *...Film...Stadt...Kino...Berlin...*, ed. Uta Berg-Ganschow and Wolfgang Jacobsen (Berlin: Argon, 1987), 49–50.

220. Benjamin, *Gesammelte Schriften,* 4.1:132; *Selected Writings,* 476.

221. Benjamin, *Gesammelte Schriften,* 4.1:85; *Selected Writings,* 444.

222. Johannes Molzahn, "Nicht mehr lesen! Sehen!" *Das Kunstblatt* 12.3 (1928): 78–82; repr. in *The Weimar Republic Sourcebook,* ed. Kaes, Jay, and Dimendberg, 648.

223. Bolz, *Theorie der neuen Medien,* 69, 106.

224. Benjamin, *Gesammelte Schriften,* 4.1:104; *Selected Writings,* 456.

225. Benjamin, *Gesammelte Schriften,* 4.1:103; *Selected Writings,* 456.

226. See also Benjamin, "The Storyteller," in *Illuminations,* 88.

227. Benjamin, *Gesammelte Schriften,* 4.1:103, 132; *Selected Writings,* 456, 476.

228. See Benjamin, "Thirteen Theses against Snobs," in *Gesammelte Schriften* 4.1:107; *Selected Writings,* 459. Originally published in the *Berliner Tageblatt* (July 10, 1925).

229. Werner Hegemann, *Das steinerne Berlin. Geschichte der grössten Mietkasernenstadt der Welt* (Berlin: G. Kiepenheuer, 1930), 253. Cited by Hans-Georg Pfeifer, in *Architektur für den Handel / Architecture for the Retail Trade,* 48.

230. For a utopian discussion about "intensifying" the metropolis via skyscrapers, see Alfred Gellhorn, "Formung der Großstadt," *Die Form* 2.2. (1927): 56.

231. See Jochen Meyer, "The 'Power that Subjugates Space': Scalar and Formal Problems of the Tall Building," *Daidalos* 61 (1996): 50–61.

232. Koolhaas, *Delirious New York,* 215.

233. Le Corbusier, *Urbanisme/The City of To-Morrow and Its Planning;* see also Le Corbusier, *La Ville Radieuse* (Paris: Vincent Fréal, 1964), 134. Koolhaas includes a facsimile of the *New York Times Magazine*'s coverage of Le Corbusier's criticisms on a visit to Manhattan in 1935 (*Delirious New York,* 221).

234. See Dietrich Neumann, "Das 'Hochhausfieber' der zwanziger Jahre in Deutschland," in *Centrum: Jahrbuch Architektur und Stadt,* ed. Peter Nietzke and Carl Steckenweh (Braunschweig: Vieweg, 1992), 50.

235. Mendelsohn, meanwhile, remained only too happy to construct limpid architectural surfaces on which to parade the new advertising force to the consuming masses.

236. See Buck-Morss's discussion of montage as the constructive principle of *The Arcades Project* and of modern philosophy in general. Buck-Morss, *The Dialectics of Seeing,* 73–77.

237. Benjamin, *Gesammelte Schriften,* 5.1:232.

238. Benjamin, *Gesammelte Schriften,* 5.1:497.

239. Susan Stewart, *On Longing: Narratives of the Miniature, the Gigantic, the Souvenir, the Collection* (Baltimore: The Johns Hopkins University Press, 1984), 101.

240. Baudrillard, *Simulacra and Simulation*, 87, 91–92.

241. Baudrillard, *The Perfect Crime*, trans. Chris Turner (New York: Verso, 1996), 17.

242. Baudrillard, "The Ecstasy of Communication," 130.

243. Ada Louise Huxtable, "Living with the Fake, and Liking It," *The New York Times* (March 30, 1997), 2.1.

244. Baudrillard, "The Ecstasy of Communication," 130, 129.

CHAPTER 3. INTO THE MOUTH OF THE MOLOCH

1. See Anton Kaes, "Film in der Weimarer Republik. Motor der Moderne," in *Geschichte des deutschen Films*, ed. Wolfgang Jacobsen, Anton Kaes, and Hans Helmut Prinzler (Stuttgart: Metzler, 1993), 60. See also Wolfgang Jacobsen and Werner Sudendorf, *Metropolis: A Cinematic Laboratory for Modern Architecture* (Stuttgart: Edition Axel Menges; Oxford: Lavis Marketing, 2000).

2. Cited by Kaes, "Film in der Weimarer Republik," 46.

3. This is Kaes's subtitle to "Film in der Weimarer Republik," 39. See also Kracauer's criticism of Weimar film's generative role in building mass social values in "The Little Shop Girls Go to the Movies," in *The Mass Ornament*, 291–304.

4. Günther Herkt, "Das Ufa-Grossatelier in Neubabelsberg," *Deutsche Bauzeitung* 22 (1929): 201.

5. Paul Rotha, *The Film Till Now* (London: Jonathan Cape, 1930); cited by Lotte H. Eisner, *The Haunted Screen: Expressionism in the German Cinema and the Influence of Max Reinhardt*, trans. Roger Greaves (London: Thames & Hudson, 1969), 160.

6. See Anthony Vidler, "The Explosion of Space: Architecture and the Filmic Imaginary," in *Film Architecture: Set Designs from "Metropolis" to "Bladerunner,"* ed. Dietrich Neumann (New York: Prestel, 1996), 18.

7. Hermann G. Scheffauer, "The Vivifying of Space," *Freeman* (November 24–December 1, 1920), repr. in *Introduction to the Art of the Movies*, ed. Lewis Jacobs (New York: Noonday Press, 1960), 77, 79.

8. See Vidler's analysis of the designs of eighteenth-century architect Etienne-Louis Boullée, in *The Architectural Uncanny*, 168, 171–72.

9. See Karl Sierek, "Regulations and Retrospection: The Rhetoric of Building and Films," *Daidalos* 64 (1997): 114.

10. Neubabelsberg covered 350,000 square meters according to Kracauer in 1926 (*The Mass Ornament*, 281), and 450,000 square meters by 1931, according to Ilya Ehrenburg (*Die Traumfabrik. Chronik des Films* [Berlin: Malik-Verlag, 1931], 91). In a March 6 article for the *Berliner Tageblatt* in 1928, Alfred Polgar refers to it as a wonderful "children's playground" ("Im romantischen Gelände," repr. in *Babelsberg 1912–1992. Ein Filmstudio*, ed. Wolfgang Jacobsen [Berlin: Argon Verlag, 1992], 144). See also Werner Sudendorf's

history of Weimar Babelsberg in "Kunstwelten und Lichtkünste," also in *Babelsberg,* ed. Jacobsen, 45–72; and Hans-Michael Bock's account of the materials needed to build this new "film-city": "Die Filmstadt. Ateliergelände Neubabelsberg," in *Das Ufa-Buch,* ed. Hans-Michael Bock and Michael Töteberg (Frankfurt a.M.: Zweitausendeins, 1992), 86–89.

11. See Sudendorf's summary, in "Kunstwelten und Lichtkünste" (in *Babelsberg,* ed. Jacobsen, 45), of the advantages Neubabelsberg enjoyed over the other Berlin film studios.

12. See Herkt, "Das Ufa-Grossatelier in Neubabelsberg," 201–208; "Die Ufa will bauen!" *Licht-Bild-Bühne* 19.100 (1926): 1–2; Sir Robert Donald, "Englands Lob," *Licht-Bild-Bühne* 19.129 (1926); "Das größte Filmatelier Europas," *Reichsfilmblatt* 51 (1926): 48; "The Film Cities of Germany," *Film Express* 2 (1920).

13. Fred Gehler and Ullrich Kasten, *Fritz Lang. Die Stimme von Metropolis* (Berlin: Henschel Verlag GmbH, 1990), 10.

14. As Karl Prümm remarks in his essay "Empfindsame Reisen in die Filmstadt," reporters soon noted that the film-city produced a "second materiality of the [filmic] medium" (in *Babelsberg,* ed. Jacobsen, 118).

15. *Ufa-Programm* (1925–1926), 6–7; cited by Prümm, "Empfindsame Reisen in die Filmstadt," 117.

16. Bruno Taut, "A Program for Architecture," in Kaes, Jay, and Dimendberg, eds., *The Weimar Republic Sourcebook,* 432.

17. Erich Burger, "Bilder-Bilder," in *Film Photos wie noch nie. 1200 interessante Photos aus den besten Filmen aller Länder,* ed. Edmund Bucher and Albrecht Kindt (Gießen: Kindt & Bucher, 1929), 11.

18. Ehrenburg, *Die Traumfabrik,* 126, 310, 94.

19. For a history of the relationship between the American and German film industries of the 1920s, see Thomas J. Saunders, *Hollywood in Berlin: American Cinema and Weimar Germany* (Berkeley: University of California Press, 1994), particularly 51–83.

20. Hans Buchner, *Im Banne des Films. Die Weltherrschaft des Kinos* (Munich: Deutscher Volksverlag, 1927), 11.

21. Ernst Jünger, *Copse 125: A Chronicle from the Trench Warfare of 1918,* trans. Basil Creighton (New York: Howard Fertig, 1993).

22. Kracauer's semiautobiographical novel *Ginster* (1928) sardonically recalls his years as an architect. See Gerwin Zohlen's essay "Schmugglerpfad. Siegfried Kracauer, Architekt und Schriftsteller," in *Siegfried Kracauer. Neue Interpretationen,* ed. Kessler and Levin, 325–44.

23. Wolfgang Pehnt, *Expressionist Architecture* (London: Thames & Hudson, 1973), 65.

24. Kracauer, *The Mass Ornament,* 281.

25. Kracauer, *The Mass Ornament,* 283.

26. See Nietzsche's 1873 essay, "Über Wahrheit und Lüge im aussermoralischen Sinne": "Truths are illusions about which one has forgotten that they are illusions; worn-out metaphors that have become materially weak; coins

that have lost their image and that now function only as metal and not as coins." Nietzsche, *Sämtliche Werke*, 1:880–81.

27. See the epigraph to Robert Musil's novella of 1905, *Die Verwirrungen des Zöglings Törless.*

28. Kracauer, *The Mass Ornament*, 282.

29. Kracauer, *Das Ornament der Masse*, 274.

30. Kracauer, *The Mass Ornament*, 281, 282. For Kracauer's negative reception of *The Nibelungs* (his first film review), see "Der Mythos im Großfilm," *Frankfurter Zeitung* (May 7, 1924); reprinted in Kracauer's *Schriften 2*, ed. Karsten Witte (Frankfurt a.M.: Suhrkamp, 1979), 397–98.

31. Kracauer, *The Mass Ornament*, 281; *Das Ornament der Masse*, 271.

32. Kracauer, *The Mass Ornament*, 288.

33. Rem Koolhaas, *Delirious Manhattan. A Retroactive Manifesto for Manhattan* (New York: Oxford University Press, 1978), 35.

34. Kracauer, *The Mass Ornament*, 284.

35. See Prümm's comments on Kracauer's narratorial tactics in "Calico-World": "The theoretical discourse is erected like a barrier between the spectator and the spectated event. Coldness and indifference govern this iron text that immediately turns everything seen into elementary reductionism or into philosophical detour." In *Babelsberg*, ed. Jacobsen, 123.

36. Kracauer, *The Mass Ornament*, 284.

37. Kracauer, *The Mass Ornament*, 287.

38. Kracauer, *The Mass Ornament*, 296. See Heide Schlüpmann's "Kinosucht" essay on the feminizing politics involved in the mass experience of Weimar cinema architecture, in *Frauen und Film* 30 (1982): 45–52; and likewise Schlüpmann's "Der Gang ins Kino—ein Ausgang aus selbstverschuldeter Unmündigkeit. Zum Begriff des Publikums in Kracauers Essayistik der Zwanziger Jahre," in *Siegfried Kracauer. Neue Interpretationen*, ed. Kessler and Levin, 267–83.

39. Adolf Loos, "Potemkin City," in *Spoken into the Void*, 95–96.

40. Kracauer describes the Schüfftan technique in the following Platonic manner: "An impressive skyscraper does not tower nearly as dizzyingly as it does in its screen appearance: only the bottom half is actually constructed, while the upper section is generated from a small model using a mirror technique. In this way, such structures refute the colossi: while their feet are made of clay, their upper parts are an insubstantial illusion of an illusion [*Schein des Scheines*], which is tacked on." Kracauer, *The Mass Ornament*, 284; *Das Ornament der Masse*, 274. See also Johannes Rolle, "Der heutige Stand des Schüfftanischen Kombinationsverfahrens," *Reichsfilmblatt* 24 (1926): 23; Eisner, *The Haunted Screen*, 233; and on Schüfftan's own suspicions of sabotage by screen architects, see Werner Sudendorf, "Kunstwelten und Lichtkünste," in *Babelsberg*, ed. Jacobsen, 62.

41. Kracauer, *The Mass Ornament*, 284; *Das Ornament der Masse*, 274; emphasis in original.

42. "Flowing" is Murnau's term, cited by Michael Esser, "Poeten der Filmarchitektur. Robert Herlth und Walter Röhrig," in *Das Ufa-Buch*, ed. Bock and Töteberg, 120.

43. For an account of Ufa's production costs and takeovers, see Bruce A. Murray, "An Introduction to the Commercial Film Industry in Germany from 1895 to 1933," in *Film and Politics in the Weimar Republic*, ed. Thomas G. Plummer, Bruce A. Murray, et al. (Minneapolis: Minnesota University Press, 1982), 29; and also Julian Petley, *Capital and Culture: German Cinema 1933–45* (London: British Film Institute, 1979), 29–46.

44. Cited by Curt Wesse, *Großmacht Film. Das Geschöpf von Kunst und Technik* (Berlin: Deutsche Buch-Gemeinschaft, 1928), 14–17. However, at least according to Buchner's antifilmic, nationalistic tract, Germany still lagged behind the U.S. and the U.K. in the actual percentage of the population going to the cinema in 1927: 10.5 percent of Germans, versus 33.3 percent of Britons and 45 percent of Americans. See Buchner, *Im Banne des Films*, 9, 21.

45. Kracauer, *The Mass Ornament*, 78.

46. Max Horkheimer and Theodor W. Adorno, *Dialectic of Enlightenment*, trans. John Cumming (New York: Continuum, 1944), 120.

47. Alfred Polgar, "Im romantischen Gelände," in *Babelsberg*, ed. Jacobsen, 143–44.

48. Kracauer, *The Mass Ornament*, 79, 78.

49. Kracauer, *The Mass Ornament*, 52.

50. See Jean Baudry, "The Apparatus: Metapsychological Approaches to the Impression of Reality in Cinema" (1975), in *Film Theory and Criticism*, ed. Gerald Mast et al., 4th ed. (New York: Oxford University Press, 1992), 690–707.

51. Kracauer, "Die Notlage des Architektenstandes," *Frankfurter Zeitung* 67 (February 6, 1923).

52. The German term Kracauer uses for plaster here is *Rabitz*—to denote the narrowly woven wire mesh (or expanded metal) that is stretched out over a wall and onto which the plaster is spread (named after its inventor, Karl Rabitz, in 1880).

53. Kracauer, "Über Türmhäuser," *Frankfurter Zeitung* 160 (March 2, 1921). Quoted by Zohlen, "Schmugglerpfad," 332.

54. Kracauer, *From Caligari to Hitler: A Psychological History of the German Film* (Princeton: Princeton University Press, 1947).

55. Rudolf Arnheim, *Kritiken und Aufsätze zum Film*, ed. Helmut H. Diederichs (Munich: Carl Hanser, 1977), 150.

56. Kracauer, "*Frühlicht* in Magdeburg," *Frankfurter Zeitung* 66.30 (January 12, 1922).

57. Kracauer, *The Mass Ornament*, 326. In this sense Kracauer is, by implication, a proponent of the same impulse that fueled the socialist modern architecture of, for example, Hannes Meyer and Ludwig Hilberseimer. See Hays, *Modernism and the Posthumanist Subject*.

58. See Irmgard Keun's *Das kunstseidene Mädchen* (1932), and Kracauer's use of the term *Glanz* as a signifier for Berlin in his essay, "Aus dem Fenster gesehen," *Straßen in Berlin*, 41.

59. Kracauer, *The Mass Ornament*, 327–28.

60. A postwar Kracauer condemned Lang's silent architectonic films as the protofascistic "triumph of the ornamental over the human" (*From Caligari to Hitler*, 95). See Marc Silberman, "Industry, Text, and Ideology in Expressionist Film," in *Passion and Rebellion. The Expressionist Heritage*, ed. Stephen Eric Bronner and Douglas Kellner (New York: J. F. Bergin, 1983), 382.

61. Kracauer, *The Mass Ornament*, 327; emphasis in original.

62. Ken Adam, lecture at the Akademie der Künste, Berlin (June 27, 1994).

63. See, for example, Tim Cornwell, "A Film to Remember," *The Independent on Sunday* (January 11, 1998): 2.1–2.

64. Vidler, "The Explosion of Space," 24.

65. Béla Balázs, *Der sichtbare Mensch, oder die Kultur des Films*, in *Schriften zum Film I* (Munich: Carl Hanser Verlag, 1982), 61.

66. Balázs, *Der sichtbare Mensch*, 90–92. See Frank Kessler's discussion of the debate concerning architectural and painterly *Stimmung* in "Les architectes-peintres du cinéma allemand muet," *Iris* 12 (1990): 51–54; David Bathrick, "Der ungleichzeitige Modernist. Béla Balázs in Berlin," in *Filmkultur zur Zeit der Weimarer Republik*, ed. Jung and Schatzberg, 26–37; and Joseph Zsuffa, *Béla Balázs: The Man and the Artist* (Berkeley: University of California Press, 1987), 114–21.

67. Balázs, *Der sichtbare Mensch*, 91.

68. Balázs, *Der sichtbare Mensch*, 91.

69. Balázs's subsequent book on sound film, *Der Geist des Films* (1930), was criticized by Kracauer for unquestioningly accepting Soviet film theory's valorization of the collective and the masses, and ignoring films in which *das Massenhafte* did not feature. See Kracauer, "Ein neues Filmbuch," *Frankfurter Zeitung* 75.819 (November 2, 1930).

70. Balázs, *Der sichtbare Mensch*, 86, 89.

71. Balázs, *Der sichtbare Mensch*, 90.

72. Citing Kracauer's 1927 review of *Visible Man*, Miriam Hansen states that Balázs's "denial of verbal (i.e. written) language, according to Kracauer a 'serious blunder' (*schlimme Entgleisung*), leads him to a romantic conflation of physiognomy and class struggle, a confusion of mere visibility with genuine concreteness." Hansen, "Decentric Perspectives: Kracauer's Early Writings on Film and Mass Culture," *New German Critique* 54 (1991): 68. See also Sabine Hake's discussion of Balázs's limitations in *The Cinema's Third Machine: Writing on Film in Germany 1907–1933* (Lincoln: University of Nebraska Press, 1993).

73. See Sergei M. Eisenstein, *Schriften* (Munich: Carl Hanser Verlag, 1973). Balázs was to compensate for this in *Der Geist des Films*, with its overt emphasis on montage. In point of fact, nothing tainted Balázs's reputation more for contemporary film studies than his script and help with scenography for Leni Riefenstahl's mountain film, *The Blue Light* (*Das blaue Licht*, 1932).

74. Leo Witlin notes this architectural divide in Weimar cinema in an article entitled "Filmarchitekt oder Filmmaler?" in *Filmtechnik* 3 (1926): 46; cited by Kessler, "Les architectes-peintres," 52–53. The introduction of sound at the end of the 1920s signalled a swift formalization away from architectural monumentalism and a return to indoor shooting in newly equipped studios.

75. *"The so-called picture has given way to the pictorial,"* remarked the film architect Robert Herlth in "Die Aufgaben des Malers beim Film," *Gebrauchsgraphik* 6 (1924—1925); cited by Kessler, "Les architectes-peintres," 53; emphasis in original.

76. Walter Muschg, "Filmzauber," *Neue Zürcher Zeitung* 997 (July 30, 1922); reprinted in *Babelsberg,* ed. Jacobsen, 140.

77. Muschg, "Filmzauber," in *Babelsberg,* ed. Jacobsen, 140; emphasis in original.

78. Muschg, "Filmzauber," in *Babelsberg,* ed. Jacobsen, 140.

79. Muschg, "Filmzauber," in *Babelsberg,* ed. Jacobsen, 142.

80. Virilio, "The Overexposed City," 30.

81. Herlth resigned during production due to a row with May, but his designs nonetheless influenced Kettelhut's subsequent street constructions. See Peter Lähn, "Asphalt (1929)," in *Film Architecture,* ed. Neumann, 108.

82. Erich Kettelhut, "Dekoration," *Reichsfilmblatt* 10 (1929): 12.

83. "Joe May auf dem *Asphalt.* Ein neuer Erich Pommer–Film," *Kinematograph* 23.60 (1929): 1.

84. In his memoirs, Kettelhut states that *Asphalt*'s street could have been three times as long if he had accepted all the firms that wanted their products displayed in the filmset's street. Kettelhut Nachlaß, 841, Stiftung Deutsche Kinemathek.

85. See Bouillon, "The Shop Window," in *The 1920s: Age of the Metropolis,* ed. Clair, 162–63.

86. See Kettelhut Nachlaß, 842, Stiftung Deutsche Kinemathek.

87. See Hans Feld, "Ein Wunderwerk der Filmarchitektur. Die Asphaltstraße im Film-Atelier," *Film-Kurier* 263 (November 1929).

88. "Frontausstattung zu *Asphalt,*" *Reichsfilmblatt* (March 16, 1929): 9.

89. Rolf Nürnberg, *12-Uhr Abendblatt* (March 12, 1929).

90. See Richard W. McCormick, "'New Women' in Crisis: Commodification and Downward Mobility in G. W. Pabst's *Büchse der Pandora* and Irmgard Keun's *Das kunstseidene Mädchen*" (paper presented at the 1996 German Studies Association Conference, Seattle); and McCormick, "From Caligari to Dietrich: Sexual, Social, and Cinematic Discourses in Weimar Film," *Signs* 18.3 (1993): 640–68.

91. Kaes, "Sites of Desire: The Weimar Street Film," in *Film Architecture,* ed. Neumann, 30.

92. Kracauer's review of *Asphalt* appeared in the *Frankfurter Zeitung* 73.235 (March 28, 1929); repr. in Kracauer, *Schriften* 2, 413–14. Other negative reviews include "*Asphalt* im Ufa-Palast," *Berliner Tageblatt* 58.130 (March 17, 1929).

93. Bloch, *Erbschaft dieser Zeit*, 35.

94. Kracauer, "Filmbild und Prophetenrede," *Frankfurter Zeitung* 330 (May 5, 1925). Hansen discusses the role played by Grune's film in Kracauer's metaphysics of film in her "Decentric Perspectives: Kracauer's Early Writings on Film and Mass Culture," *New German Critique* 54 (1991): 47–49.

95. Kracauer, "Ein Film," *Frankfurter Zeitung* 68.93 (February 4, 1924).

96. Kracauer, "Ein Film."

97. Kracauer, "Filmbild und Prophetenrede."

98. See Walter Serner's 1913 essay "Kino und Schaulust," which first coins this term, meaning the voyeuristic urge inherent in watching a film; reprinted in *Kino-Debatte. Texte zum Verhältnis von Literatur und Film 1909–1929*, ed. Anton Kaes (Tübingen: Max Niemeyer Verlag, 1978), 53–58.

99. Karl Prümm notes affinities between Kracauer's description of Neubabelsberg and his notion of the "spatial desert" of modernity in *Der Detektiv-Roman*, written from 1922 to 1925 but not published until 1971 (Prümm, "Empfindsame Reisen in die Filmstadt," 125); but Prümm does not consider the architectural presence of the film-city Neubabelsberg itself in relation to the modern metropolis that provides Kracauer with so much material during his Weimar years.

100. Hans Kafka, "Lunapark. Ein Stück Amerika, versuchsweise . . . " *Berliner Tageblatt* (August 7, 1928); repr. in *Glänzender Asphalt*, ed. Jäger and Schütz, 196.

101. Kracauer, *Straßen in Berlin*, 35.

102. Kracauer, "Über Turmhäuser," *Frankfurter Zeitung* 65.160 (1921): 1.

103. Kracauer, *Straßen in Berlin*, 35.

104. See Hansen's comment: "Kracauer's *Denkbild* implies the vision of a modernity whose spell as progress is broken, whose disintegrated elements have become available for an emancipatory practice." Hansen, "Decentric Perspectives," 76.

105. See Bob Sheue, "New York–New York takes center stage in Nevada's desert," *The Denver Post* (January 19, 1997): 1T, 10T.

106. Koolhaas, *Delirious New York*, 23.

107. See Jeanpaul Goergen, *Walther Ruttmann. Eine Dokumentation* (Berlin: Freunde der Deutschen Kinemathek, 1989), 26, 115.

108. Sabine Hake, "Urban Spectacle in Walther Ruttmann's *Berlin, Symphony of the Big City*," in *Dancing on the Volcano*, ed. Kniesche and Brockmann, 127, 128.

109. Kracauer, "Film 1928," *The Mass Ornament*, 318. Original version published as "Der heutige Film und sein Publikum," *Die Form* 4.5 (1929): 101–104.

110. Kracauer, *The Mass Ornament*, 318. As Miriam Hansen states: "For Kracauer, fascination with the cinema's surface effects and its ideological function are inseparably related: reality assails the boundaries between the two." Hansen, "Decentric Perspectives," 64.

111. See the review "Berlin—die Symphonie der Großstadt," in *Licht-Bild-Bühne* 227 (September 24, 1927): 22.

112. See also Kracauer, "Berliner Lichtspielhäuser," *Das illustrierte Blatt* 14.8 (February 21, 1926): 162.

113. See Dieter Bartetzko, *Illusionen in Stein: Stimmungsarchitektur im deutschen Faschismus. Ihre Vorgeschichte in Theater- und Film-Bauten* (Hamburg: Rowohlt, 1985), 157.

114. Kracauer, *Das Ornament der Masse,* 311 (my translation). Bartetzko cites this emotive phrase of Kracauer's as part of his insightful but essentially overargued thesis of the complicity of Weimar cinema's protofascistic "cultic-suggestive effectiveness" and "atmospheric architecture that stimulated feelings," as if these theatrical factors alone *caused* Nazism—rather than being further used by the same. See Bartetzko, *Illusionen in Stein,* 157.

115. See Sabine Hake, who articulates how late Weimar cinema's "sensory overstimulation" gave rise to an "almost fetishistic attention to theater architecture and design." Hake, *The Cinema's Third Machine,* 266.

116. Kracauer, *The Mass Ornament,* 323; *Das Ornament der Masse,* 311; emphasis in original.

117. The Marmorhaus was built by Hugo Pál (1912–1913), the Universum-Filmpalast by Erich Mendelsohn (1928), the Titania-Palast by Ernst Schöffler, Carlo Schoenbach, and Carl Jacobi (1928), the Mercedes-Palast by Fritz Wilms (1927), and the Capitol and Babylon by Hans Poelzig (1926 and 1929 respectively), while the Gloria-Palast was remodelled in 1926 by Max Bremer and Ernst Lessing. See Peter Boeger, *Architektur der Lichtspieltheater in Berlin. Bauten und Projekte 1919–1930* (Berlin: Arenhövel, 1993); Rolf-Peter Baacke, *Lichtspielhausarchitektur in Deutschland. Von der Schaubude bis zum Kinopalast* (Berlin: Fröhlich & Kaufmann, 1982); Silvaine Hänsel and Angelika Schmitt, eds., *Kinoarchitektur in Berlin 1895–1995* (Berlin: Dietrich Reimer Verlag, 1995); and Michael Töteberg, "Warenhaus des Films. Filmpaläste in Berlin," in *Das Ufa-Buch,* ed. Bock and Töteberg, 106–7.

118. Griebens, *Berlin Reiseführer: Kleine Ausgabe* (1928), 25:49. Deutsches Technikmuseum, Berlin.

119. Kracauer, *The Mass Ornament* 324, 328; *Das Ornament der Masse* 312, 317; emphasis in original.

120. I thank Christian Rogowski for this observation.

121. On this "second skin," see Uta Berg-Ganschow and Wolfgang Jacobsen's comment that the Weimar movie palace "is as living as the film picture. The building is not architecture any more, it is a platform for text and picture . . . " Ganschow and Jacobsen, eds., *. . . Film . . . Stadt . . . Kino . . . Berlin* (Berlin: Argon, 1987), 39–40.

122. Curt Moreck, *Die Sittengeschichte des Kinos* (Dresden: Paul Aretz, 1926), 69; cited by Werner Michael Schwarz, *Kino und Kinos in Wien. Eine Entwicklungsgeschichte bis 1934* (Vienna: Turia & Kant, 1992), 70.

123. Kracauer, *Straßen in Berlin,* 70.

124. Kracauer, *The Mass Ornament*, 332.

125. Starting in 1926, the journal *Der Film* ran a weekly series detailing and judging (albeit in a self-congratulatory manner) the efforts made by the major Berlin cinemas to design film advertisements for their façades. Cited by Boeger, *Architektur der Lichtspieltheater in Berlin*, 148, note 93.

126. See Herkt's comment in "Kinofassade und Filmpropaganda," *Deutsche Bauzeitung* 51 (1929): "The moving poster—with such a complete façade decoration (the girls' legs move mechanically) even the least impressive movie palace façade can be transformed into the most fascinating theater front."

127. Alfred Döblin, "Das Theater der kleinen Leute" (1909), in *Kino-Debatte. Texte zum Verhältnis von Literatur und Film, 1909–1929*, ed. Anton Kaes (Munich: Deutscher Taschenbuch Verlag; Tübingen: M. Niemeyer, 1978), 37.

128. This is what happens to the heroine of Rudolf Braune's popular novel, *Das Mädchen an der Orga Privat. Ein kleiner Roman aus Berlin* (Frankfurt a.M.: Societäts-Verlag, 1930), 24.

129. See G. V. Mendel, "Neuartige Kinoreklame," *Der Kinematograph* 21.1048 (March 20, 1927): 15–16.

130. Mendel, "Neuartige Kinoreklame," 15.

131. Herkt, "Kinofassade und Filmpropaganda," 441.

132. See "Die Silberfassade." *Kinematograph* 21:1039 (January 16, 1927): 38.

133. Anton Kaes, "*Metropolis:* City, Cinema, Modernity," in *Expressionist Utopias: Paradise, Metropolis, Architectural Fantasy*, ed. Timothy O. Benson (Los Angeles: Los Angeles County Museum of Art, 1993), 148.

134. Kaes, "*Metropolis:* City, Cinema, Modernity," 148.

135. Willy Haas, "*Metropolis*," *Film-Kurier* 9 (January 11, 1927); repr. in *The Weimar Republic Sourcebook*, ed. Kaes, Jay, and Dimendberg, 623–25.

136. "Fassadenkultur und Materialfilm," *Reichsfilmblatt* 11 (March 19, 1927): 16–17.

137. "Die Silberfassade," 38.

138. The best introduction to the life and work of Feld is Gabriele Gillner's documentary film *1000 Sterne auf der Straße* (Gillner & HFF Babelsberg, 1995).

139. See Max Paul Erbé's praise of Rudi Feld in "Werbende Ufanale," *Die Reklame* 22 (August 1929): 714–20.

140. "Die Frontreklame der Uraufführungstheater. Ein Interview mit Rudi Feld, dem Leiter des künstlerischen Ateliers der Ufa." No date, no source. Sammlung Rudi Feld, Schriftgutarchiv, Stiftung Deutsche Kinemathek.

141. "1000 Sterne auf der Straße," *Film-Kurier* (October 16, 1929). Stiftung Deutsche Kinemathek.

142. Rudi Feld, "Schrauben Sie eine andere Birne ein . . . und Sie werden volle Kassen haben!" *Licht-Bild-Bühne* 186 (August 5, 1930), 2; and "Fallstrick für das Passanten-Auge. Farbe, Form und Bewegung als Lockmittel. Ein Vortrag Rudi Felds." No date, no source. Sammlung Rudi Feld, Schriftgutarchiv, Stiftung Deutsche Kinemathek. See also Rainer Rother's discussion of Feld in the Stiftung Deutsche Kinemathek's booklet *Metropolis* (Berlin: Stiftung Deutsche Kinemathek, n.d.), 12.

143. See Feld, "Kinofronten für Weihnachten. Licht und Bewegung an der Theaterfront." No date, no source. Sammlung Rudi Feld, Schriftgutarchiv, Stiftung Deutsche Kinemathek.

144. See Max Paul Erbé, "Werbende Ufanale," 717.

145. See Feld, "Schrauben Sie eine andere Birne ein."

146. Feld, "Foyer-Ausstattung und Außenreklame," *Kinematograph* 1038 (November 20, 1927).

147. Feld, "Schrauben Sie eine andere Birne ein."

148. Feld, "Schrauben Sie eine andere Birne ein."

149. Feld, "Schrauben Sie eine andere Birne ein."

150. Heinrich Eduard Jacob, *Blut und Zelluloid. Roman* (Bad Homburg: Oberon Verlag, 1986), 23–34.

151. See "The German Cinema Theatres," *Film-Express* 2 (1920): 16; and Leo Hirsch, "Kinos," *Berliner Tageblatt* (November 15, 1927), repr. in *Glänzender Asphalt*, ed. Jäger and Schütz, 210.

152. Jürgen Schebera, *Damals in Neubabelsberg . . . : Studios, Stars und Kinopaläste im Berlin der zwanziger Jahre* (Leipzig: Edition Leipzig, 1990), 62.

153. Hirsch, "Kinos," in *Glänzender Asphalt*, ed. Jäger and Schütz, 211.

154. Kracauer, *Straßen in Berlin*, 69.

155. See Töteberg, "Europas größtes Kino. Filmtheater und Varieté: Der Ufa-Palast in Hamburg," in *Das Ufa-Buch*, ed. Bock and Töteberg, 290–93; Töteberg, *Filmstadt Hamburg. Von Emil Jannings bis Wim Wenders. Kino-Geschichte(n) einer Großstadt* (Hamburg: VSA-Verlag, 1990), 51–61; and Staatsarchiv Hamburg, 135–1 I–IV Staatliche Pressestelle I–IV 5018.

156. See Osborn et al., *Berlins Aufstieg zur Weltstadt*, 219.

157. Paul Zucker and G. Otto Stindt, *Lichtspielhäuser. Tonfilmtheater* (Berlin: Verlag Ernst Wasmuth A.G., 1931), 130.

158. See P. Morton Shand, *The Architecture of Pleasure: Modern Theatres and Cinemas* (London: B. T. Batsford, 1930), 28–29.

159. Erbé, "Werbende Ufanale," 714.

160. Paul Schaefer, "Arbeiten des Architekten B. D. A. Heinrich Möller Berlin-Dahlem," *Neue Baukunst* 6.3 (1930): 1.

161. See "Großkino in Bielefeld," *Der Film* 12.7 (1927): 7.

162. On this process, see Eugen Schlesinger, "Das deutsche Kino," *Licht-Bild-Bühne* 19.25 (1926): 11–12.

163. Vachel Lindsay, *The Art of the Moving Picture* (1915, New York: Macmillan, 1922).

164. Herkt, "Das Ufa-Lichtspielhaus `Universum' in Berlin," *Deutsche Bauzeitung* 18–19 (1929): 182, 179.

165. "Das modernste Kino Europas in Berlin," *Berliner Westen* (August 16, 1928). Cited by Boeger, *Architektur der Lichtspieltheater in Berlin*, 111.

166. Mendelsohn, "Zur Eröffnung des 'Universum'," *Festprogramm zur Eröffnung des neuerbauten Ufa-Theaters Universum* (September 15, 1928). Stiftung Deutsche Kinemathek. See also *Der Mendelsohn-Bau am Lehniner Platz*, 49.

167. Herkt, "Das Ufa-Lichtspielhaus `Universum' in Berlin," 181.

168. "Ein Lichtspielgebäude," *Die Form* 4.4 (1929): 85.

169. See O. Gerhardt, "Die Beleuchtung des Großen Schauspielhauses," *AEG-Mitteilungen* 16.3 (1920): 29–32; and Shand, *The Architecture of Pleasure*, 5.

170. See Schivelbusch, *Licht Schein und Wahn*, 45–47.

171. Hans Poelzig, "Festbauten," *Kunstblatt* 10 (1926): 200.

172. Hans Poelzig, "Das Capitol," in *Berlin im "Querschnitt"*, ed. Baacke, 165; emphasis in original.

173. Schivelbusch, *Licht Schein und Wahn*, 53.

174. Cited by Marco Biraghi, *Hans Poelzig: Architektur 1869–1936*, trans. Dorothee Friemert and Gabriela Wachter (Berlin: Vice Versa, 1993), 77.

175. Schivelbusch, *Licht Schein und Wahn*, 53.

176. Schivelbusch, *Licht Schein und Wahn*, 56.

177. See Paul Zucker and G. Otto Stindt's comparative discussion of American and German movie palaces in *Lichtspielhäuser. Tonfilmtheater* (Berlin: Verlag Ernst Wasmuth AG, 1931).

178. Mark C. Taylor comments (without geographical specificity): "While the architects whose names are inseparable from the history of modernism were decrying ornamentation and stripping away decoration, other architects whose names have long been forgotten were designing and constructing spectacular movie palaces in which fantasy runs wild." Taylor, *Hiding*, 249.

179. Léger, "New York" (1931), in *Functions of Painting*, ed. Fry, 86.

180. On the Gaumont, see *Das Licht* 2.2 (February 1932): 32; and *Das Licht* 2.11 (November 1932): 220.

181. See Helmut Färber, *Bestands-Aufnahme: Utopie Film. Zwanzig Jahre neuer deutscher Film/Mitte 1983* (Frankfurt a.M.: Zweitausendeins, 1983), 16.

182. For an excellent comparative study of European and American movie theaters of the 1920s, see Shand's *The Architecture of Pleasure*. Kiesler's Film Guild Cinema is shown in Kiesler, *Contemporary Art Applied to the Store and Its Display*, 119.

183. See, for example, Maggie Valentine's book on the cinema architect Charles Lee, *The Show Starts on the Sidewalk: An Architectural History of the Movie Theatre* (New Haven: Yale University Press, 1994).

184. Kracauer, *The Mass Ornament* 324; *Das Ornament der Masse* 312; emphasis in original.

185. See Schlüpmann, "Kinosucht," 44–51.

186. See Nietzsche's attack on Wagner's music for wanting "effect, . . . nothing but effect," for creating a "rhetorics of theater, a medium of expression, of a strengthening of gesture, of suggestion, of the psychologically picturesque." Nietzsche, *Der Fall Wagner*, in *Sämtliche Werke* 6:31, 30.

187. Kracauer, *The Mass Ornament*, 325–26.

188. Kracauer, *The Mass Ornament*, 324.

189. See Schlüpmann, "Der Gang ins Kino," 275.

190. Kracauer, *The Mass Ornament*, 328.

191. Kracauer, *The Mass Ornament*, 326; *Das Ornament der Masse*, 314.

192. Kracauer, *The Mass Ornament*, 325; *Das Ornament der Masse*, 313.

193. Kracauer, *The Mass Ornament*, 327. Bartetzko takes Kracauer at face value here in *Illusionen in Stein*, 172–187, with an oversimplified cause-and-effect argument of Weimar movie palaces leading directly to Nazi applications of *Lichtarchitektur*.

194. The Gloria-Lichtspiele movie palace in Bielefeld was designed by Wilhelm Kreis, and appears in *Moderne Cafés, Restaurants und Vergnügungsstätten* (Berlin: Ernst Pollak Verlag, 1929); reprinted in *Interior Design 1929*, ed. Düttmann, 143.

195. Kracauer, *The Mass Ornament* 324.

196. Indeed, Kracauer's fears regarding the dumbing-down of cinema audiences would appear to be justified in an unrealized project by Bruno Taut for a cinema amphitheater for patients brought in from nearby hospitals ("Bildvorführungen für liegende Zuschauer," *Bauwelt* 15.32 [1924]: 743). This strange design enables prostrate spectators to watch movies by looking up at the screen, rather than down at it, positioned on horizontal, worshipful couches that descend in rows from the screen.

197. Kracauer, "Organisiertes Glück. Zur Wiedereröffnung des Lunaparks," *Frankfurter Zeitung* 74.338 (May 8, 1930).

198. Arnold Höllriegel, "Donnerwetter inbegriffen. Berlin wird so amerikanisch," *Berliner Tageblatt* (November 14, 1929); repr. in *Glänzender Asphalt*, ed. Jäger and Schütz, 212.

199. Kracauer, *Die Angestellten*, 44.

200. Felix Stössinger, "Die verwandelte Tauentzien. Umschichtung im Berliner Westen," *Vossische Zeitung* (April 17, 1932); repr. in *Glänzender Asphalt*, ed. Jäger and Schütz, 107.

201. Cited by Schebera, *Damals in Neubabelsberg . . .*, 171.

202. Letter (October 31, 1925) from lawyer Oskar Arendt to the Capitol's owners. Landesarchiv Berlin: Städtische Baupolizei, Bezirk Charlottenburg: Rep. 207, Acc. 2372, Nr. 1738.

203. From an anonymous protest letter written c. 1924 to the Berlin building authorities. Landesarchiv Berlin: Bauakte Ufa-Palast am Zoo: Rep. 202, Acc. 2834, Nr. 5814: Am Zool. Garten.

204. More strict by far than Berlin was Munich, where the antielectric laws worked to ensure that no neon was allowed on the fronts of movie theaters (see "Kinolicht und Magistratsdunkel," *Film-Kurier* 173 [1926]). On the censorship debate, see, e.g., "Polizeizensur für Kinoreklame," *Licht-Bild-Bühne* 20.134/135 (June 7, 1927); "Ein Anti-Reklamegesetz," *Kinematograph* 21.1045 (February 27, 1927): 14.

205. Letter (March 2, 1926). Landesarchiv Berlin: Städtische Baupolizei, Bezirk Charlottenburg: Rep. 207, Acc. 2372, Nr. 1738.

206. Hans Poelzig, letter to Berlin building code authorities (October 31, 1925). Landesarchiv Berlin: Städtische Baupolizei, Bezirk Charlottenburg: Rep. 207, Acc. 2372, Nr. 1738.

207. The Gloria-Palast's old-style architecture is critiqued by Kracauer as ill-befitting a movie theater: see his "Berliner Lichtspielhäuser," *Das illustrierte Blatt* 14.8 (1926): 162.

208. An agonistic exchange with authorities was a constant for the grand movie theaters: when, for example, the Piccadilly movie palace in Charlottenburg found itself surrounded by a building fence during the U-Bahn installation in the Bismarkstraße in 1928, its owners had to beg permission from the city council to transfer its exterior advertising to the fence, with zealous assurances that this temporary arrangement would be tastefully "irreproachable" and avoid "kitsch" at all costs. Letter from Hein & Kreisle G.m.b.H. to Charlottenburg City Hall (November 12, 1928). Landesarchiv Berlin: (Alhambra) Piccadilly, Rep. 207, Acc. 2552, Nr. 4115.

209. Letter from architects Ernst Lessing and Max Bremer to the mayor of Berlin (June 19, 1926). Landesarchiv Berlin: Bauakte, Rep. 207, Acc. 1039, Nr. 335 (Gloria-Palast).

210. Letters from architects Ernst Lessing and Max Bremer to chief city architects (March 15, December 5, December 7, 1926). Landesarchiv Berlin: Bauakte, Rep. 207, Acc. 1039, Nr. 335 (Gloria-Palast).

211. Josef Goebbels, "Rund um die Gedächtniskirche," *Der Angriff* (January 23, 1928); repr. in *The Weimar Republic Sourcebook,* ed. Kaes, Jay, and Dimendberg, 560–62.

212. Henry James, *The American Scene* (1907); cited by Leach, *Land of Desire,* 39.

213. Hermann Kesser, "Das lineare Berlin. Grundriß eines Aufenthalts," *Berliner Tageblatt* (June 10, 1928); cited in *Glänzender Asphalt,* ed. Jäger and Schütz, 59.

214. Kracauer, "Ansichtskarte," in *Straßen in Berlin,* 37.

215. Kracauer, *The Mass Ornament,* 323.

216. Kracauer, "Straße ohne Erinnerung," in *Strassen in Berlin,* 15.

217. Kracauer, "Aus dem Fenster gesehen," in *Straßen in Berlin,* 41.

218. Hansen, "Decentric Perspectives," 70.

219. See Kracauer, *The Mass Ornament,* 311.

220. See also Kracauer, "Ein Luxushotel," *Frankfurter Zeitung* 73.690 (September 14, 1928); "Abend im Hotel," *Frankfurter Zeitung* 73.963 (December 25, 1928); "Luxushotel von unten gesehen," *Frankfurter Zeitung* 75.964 (December 28, 1930).

221. Kracauer, *The Mass Ornament,* 175; *Das Ornament der Masse,* 160.

222. Kracauer, *The Mass Ornament,* 177.

223. Kracauer, *The Mass Ornament,* 183; *Das Ornament der Masse,* 168.

224. See Vicki Baum, *Menschen im Hotel* (Berlin: Ullstein, 1991), 9, 136.

225. Kracauer, *The Mass Ornament,* 184.

226. Kracauer, *The Mass Ornament,* 177. In accordance with Kracauer's stance is Ernst Toller's late expressionist drama, *Hurrah, We're Alive!* (*Hoppla, wir leben!* 1927), which takes place in the Grand Hotel and is a scathing indictment of Weimar modernity.

227. Kracauer, "Im Luxushotel," *Frankfurter Zeitung* (September 14, 1928); cited by Alfons Arms, "Hotel as Motion Picture," *Daidalos* 62 (1996): 34.

228. See Koolhaas's discussion of the grand hotel as prepackaged "cybernetic universe," and of the revolving door as where the genre of the hotel-movie begins, in *Delirious New York*, 124.

229. Eisner, *The Haunted Screen*, 214.

230. Marc Silberman remarks on this process of reification of the human: "The doorman 'becomes' part of the revolving lobby door and later of the swinging lavatory doors." Silberman, *German Cinema: Texts in Context* (Detroit: Wayne State University Press, 1995), 29.

231. Kracauer, *Die Angestellten*, 93.

232. See, for example, the positive review of this ending in *The Literary Digest* 84 (1925): 26.

233. Willy Haas, "Was wird gebaut" (1924), cited in *Film Architecture*, ed. Neumann, 90. Robert Herlth comments that the street's skyscrapers for *The Last Laugh* were up to fifty-six feet high and gave the illusion of having thirty stories (cited in *Film Architecture*, 90, 33).

234. As Hans-Joachim Neumann states in a retrospective of Berlin's former movie palace world, "The loss of our city culture is shown in the loss of cinema culture." See "Sag mir, wo die Kinos sind," *zitty* 2 (1984): 73.

235. See Coop Himmelb(l)au, "The UFA Cinema Center: Splinters of Light and Layers of Skin," in *Architecture and Film*, special issue of *Architectural Design* 64.11/12 (1994): 55.

236. See Andrea Nelson, "Entertainment Steps Up as a Mall Anchor," *New York Times* (April 16, 1995): 22.

237. See, for example, Cornelia Krause, "Der andere Blick. Multiplex-Kinos in Deutschland," *Deutsche Bauzeitung* 6 (1991): 16–21; and Ingeborg Flagge, Joachim Henkel, and Wolf Rüdiger Seufert, *Entwürfe für das Kino von morgen* (Berlin: Birkhäuser, 1990). See also "Krieg der Kinos," *Cinema* (Hamburg) 11 (1993): 76–81; I thank Rainer Hering for this latter reference.

238. Rudolf Klar, "Der Kinotheaterbau," *Deutsche Bauzeitung* 98 (1928): 835. See also the discussion of building *das ideale Kino* in Jean McGuire, "Kino Grössenwahn," *Zeitmagazin* (*Die Zeit*) 46 (November 8, 1991): 34.

CHAPTER 4. THE DISPLAY WINDOW

1. 1 Corinthians 13, King James Bible.

2. See Plato's *Republic* VII, in Plato, *Collected Dialogues*, ed. Edith Hamilton and Huntingdon Cairns (Princeton: Princeton University Press, 1973), 748.

3. Karl Marx, *Capital: A Critique of Political Economy* (New York: The Modern Library, 1936), 83. Anne Friedberg gives the following comment on the term: "*Phantasmagoria* was an appropriate word: not only did it refer to the illusionistic screen entertainments that manufactured phantoms out of projected light, but it contains the root word *agoria* [*sic*] for the marketplace." Friedberg, *Window Shopping*, 82. See also Terry Castle, "Phantasmagoria:

Spectral Technology and the Metaphorics of Modern Reverie," *Critical Inquiry* 15.1 (1988): 26–61; Jonathan Crary, *Techniques of the Observer: On Vision and Modernity in the Nineteenth Century* (Cambridge: MIT Press, 1990), 132–33; and David Harvey, *The Condition of Postmodernity: An Enquiry in the Origins of Cultural Change* (Cambridge, Mass.: Blackwell, 1989), 100–112.

4. Marx, *Capital,* 83. See also the theory of money in Marx's earlier treatise *A Contribution to the Critique of Political Economy,* trans. N. I. Stone, 2d ed. (Chicago: International Library, 1904), 73–263.

5. Raymond Williams, *Keywords* (London: Fontana, 1976), 68.

6. Theodor W. Adorno, *In Search of Wagner,* trans. Rodney Livingstone (London: NLB, 1981), 91. Cited by Buck-Morss, "Aesthetics and Anaesthetics," 25. See also Miriam Hansen, "Mass Culture as Hieroglyphic Writing: Adorno, Derrida, Kracauer," *New German Critique* 56 (1992): 50; and Norbert Bolz's analysis of Adorno in *Eine kurze Geschichte des Scheins* (Munich: Wilhelm Fink, 1991), 107–109.

7. Buck-Morss states of Benjamin's Paris: "The City of Mirrors—in which the crowd itself became a spectacle—reflected the image of people as consumers rather than producers, keeping the class relations of production virtually invisible on the looking glass' other side." Buck-Morss, *Dialectics of Seeing,* 81.

8. This is noted by Christoph Asendorf in *Batteries of Life,* 30, 193. Likewise, M. Sahlins sees consumer goods (e.g., clothes) as latter-day totems, and consumer groups as tribes (*Stone Age Economics,* London: Tavistock, 1974); quoted by Celia Lury, *Consumer Culture* (Newark: Rutgers University Press, 1996), 16.

9. Walter Benjamin, *Gesammelte Schriften,* IV.1:91; *Selected Writings,* 448.

10. Matheo Quniz comments on this flattening out of class differences in department stores' policy of *entrée libre* in a 1928 article for *Querschnitt:* "Wertheim," repr. in *Berlin im "Querschnitt,"* ed. Baacke, 163. See also Buck-Morss, *Dialectics of Seeing,* 86.

11. Honoré de Balzac, "Gaudissart II," in *The Works of Honoré de Balzac,* intro. George Saintsbury (Freeport: Books for Libraries Press, 1971), vol. 17, bk. 1, 10. Cited by Asendorf, *Batteries of Life,* 45.

12. See Colin Campbell, *The Romantic Ethic and the Spirit of Modern Consumerism* (Cambridge: Blackwell, 1989).

13. Mike Featherstone, *Consumer Culture and Postmodernism* (London: Sage, 1991), 65–82.

14. Susan Stewart continues the Benjaminian-creative vein on the "proper labor of the consumer": "It is a labor of total magic, a fantastic labor which operates through the manipulation of abstraction rather than through concrete or material means" (*On Longing,* 164). This activity can lead to the collection, the consumer's overt presentation of excess materiality.

15. See Walter Benjamin, "Das Kunstwerk im Zeitalter seiner technischen Reproduzierbarkeit," *Illuminationen* (Frankfurt a.M.: Suhrkamp, 1977), 145–47.

16. Rudi Feld, "Foyer-Ausstattung und Außenreklame."

17. See Jean-Paul Bouillon: "The space defined by the shop window is an unreal space, like that of a Cubist painting: it is situated both in front of the glass (due to the reflection) and beyond it (but here compressed and subject to definite constraints)." Bouillon, "The Shop Window," in *The 1920s: Age of the Metropolis,* ed. Clair, 163.

18. See Dietmar Kamper's Lacanian comment on the Platonic fallacy: "The life of appearances in the mirror stage of the picture cave is based on a gross self-misunderstanding. Only on the reverse side of images does the world begin. Only in the film frame can perception begin." Kamper, *Bildstörungen. Im Orbit des Imaginären* (Stuttgart: Cantz Verlag, 1994), 90.

19. Kracauer, *The Mass Ornament,* 326; *Das Ornament der Masse,* 315.

20. Hays, *Modernism and the Posthumanist Subject,* 45.

21. Peter Wollen, introduction to *Visual Display: Culture Beyond Appearances,* ed. Lynne Cooke and Peter Wollen (Seattle: Bay Press, 1995), 9.

22. See Peter Jackson and Nigel Thrift's discussion of Lefebvre's *The Production of Space* in their article "Geographies of Consumption," in *Acknowledging Consumption: A Review of New Studies,* ed. Daniel Miller (New York: Routledge, 1995), 218.

23. Georg Simmel, "The Berlin Trade Exhibition," 122.

24. Paul Mazur, *American Prosperity: Its Causes and Consequences* (New York: The Viking Press, 1928), 24. William Leach disagrees, preferring the pro-agrarian, anticonsumptionist stance of Thorstein Veblen when he judges the onset of modern consumer capitalism and its impersonal business corporations to have been a "nonconsensual" occurrence, a nondemocratic takeover of the social imaginary. See Leach, *Land of Desire: Merchants, Power, and the Rise of a New American Culture* (New York: Vintage, 1993), 290, xv. On Veblen, see Daniel Horowitz, *The Morality of Spending: Attitudes toward the Consumer Society in America, 1875–1940* (Baltimore: The Johns Hopkins University Press, 1985), 37–41.

25. Marx, *Contribution to the Critique of Political Economy,* 87. Cited by Jean Baudrillard, "Consumer Society," in *Reflections on Commercial Life: An Anthology of Classic Texts from Plato to the Present,* ed. Patrick Murray (New York: Routledge, 1997), 450.

26. Jay, *Downcast Eyes,* 120.

27. Victor Fournel, *Ce qu'on voit dans les rues de Paris* (1858); cited by Benjamin, *Charles Baudelaire: A Lyric Poet in the Era of High Capitalism,* trans. Harry Zohn and Quintin Hoare (London, 1973), 69. See also Jay, *Downcast Eyes,* 119.

28. See Andreas Huyssen, "Mass Culture as Woman," 44–62.

29. Mike Davis, *Prisoners of the American Dream: Politics and Economy in the History of the U.S. Working Class* (London: Verso, 1986), 156.

30. On the relationship between Debord's and Baudrillard's theories, see Jonathan Crary, "Eclipse of the Spectacle," in *Art After Modernism: Rethinking Representation,* ed. Brian Wallis (Boston: David R. Godine, 1984), 283–94; and Lury, *Consumer Culture,* 68–72.

31. See Baudrillard, "The Ecstasy of Communication," 131.

32. Baudrillard, "Consumer Society," 461.

33. Debord, *The Society of the Spectacle*, 12.

34. Baudrillard, "Consumer Society," 462. Celia Lury questions both the Marxist production-value theory *and* the Baudrillardian sign-value theory for their equal if mirror-image blanket assumptions of powerlessness on the part of the consumer (*Consumer Culture* 40–48, 71–72).

35. Baudrillard, *The System of Objects*, trans. James Benedict (London: Verso, 1996), 10.

36. Baudrillard, *The System of Objects*, 205. Emphasis in original.

37. Baudrillard, "Consumer Society," 450.

38. Lury, *Consumer Culture*, 68–72.

39. Baudrillard, "The Precession of Simulacra," 30.

40. See Jonathan Crary, "Spectacle, Attention, Counter-Memory," *October* 50 (1989): 97–107.

41. See Georg Lukács, *History and Class Consciousness* (Cambridge: MIT Press, 1971).

42. A 1932 survey indicated that while newspaper advertising was a strong motivational factor for 44.5 percent of respondents, the combined outdoor techniques of display windows, electric advertising, and street posters were considered prime powers of persuasion for 79.2 percent of those interviewed. Cited by Wertheim, *Die Reklame des Warenhauses*, 186.

43. Dr. Berthold, *Volkswirtschaft in Zahlen und Bildern. Eine Erinnerung an die Ausstellung im Herbst 1929. Was, wie, wo kauft die Hausfrau?* (Berlin: Reichsverband Deutscher Hausfrauenvereine e.V., 1930), 35. Geheimes Staatsarchiv, Berlin: Rep. 120 E. XVI.2 Nr. 13.

44. Kiesler, *Contemporary Art Applied to the Window and Its Display*, 71.

45. Jan Gympel, "Abschied vom Bummel," *Der Tagesspiegel* (August 11, 1998). See also Wilhelm Heitmeyer, Rainer Dollase, and Otto Backes, eds., *Die Krise der Städte. Analysen zu den Folgen desintegrativer Stadtentwicklung für das ethnisch-kulturelle Zusammenleben* (Frankfurt a.M.: Suhrkamp, 1998).

46. Paul Virilio, *Open Sky*, trans. Julie Rose (London: Verso, 1997), 65.

47. Christo, undoubtedly aware of the kinship between window display and his own art, designed a "Double Store Front" (1966–1968). See Tilman Osterwold, *Schaufenster—Die Kulturgeschichte eines Massenmediums* (Stuttgart: Württembergischer Kunstverein, 1974), 308–11.

48. See Benjamin's chapter on mirrors in *Gesammelte Schriften*, 5.2:666–73.

49. For a history of department stores, see Klaus Strohmeyer, *Warenhäuser: Geschichte, Blüte und Untergang im Warenmeer* (Berlin: Verlag Klaus Wagenbach, 1980); Rosalind H. Williams, *Dream Worlds: Mass Consumption in Late Nineteenth Century France* (Berkeley: University of California Press, 1982); Johann Friedrich Geist, *Arcades: The History of a Building Type* (orig. 1936), trans. Jane O. Newman and John H. Smith (Cambridge: MIT Press,

1983); Friedberg, *Window Shopping*, 76–81; and Jürgen Schwarz, *Architektur und Kommerz. Studien zur deutschen Kauf- und Warenhausarchitektur vor dem Ersten Weltkrieg am Beispiel der Frankfurter Zeil* (Frankfurt a.M.: Kunstgeschichtliches Inst., 1995).

50. Benjamin, *Gesammelte Schriften*, 5.1:54. In this respect see Anne Friedberg's transformation, in *Window Shopping* (35–37), of Jonathan Crary's male-based analysis of nineteenth-century vision in *Techniques of the Observer* (Cambridge: MIT Press, 1990).

51. See Friedberg, *Window Shopping*, 41–44.

52. Hans Ostwald, in *Kultur und Sittengeschichte Berlins* (Berlin: H. Klemm, 1923), 394, noticed: "There are women, addicted to the high of a daily outing through the streets and department stores, whose most important hours are spent before display windows or in the glittering halls of department stores."

53. As right-wing Wilhelmine economist Werner Sombart commented: "The old specialty shop was static, the department store is dynamic; there everything was fixed, here everything flows. Then small, now big. Then dark, now bright. Then soul, now intellect." Werner Sombart, "Das Warenhaus, Ein Gebilde des hochkapitalistischen Zeitalters," *Probleme des Warenhauses. Beiträge zur Geschichte und Erkenntnis der Entwicklung des Warenhauses in Deutschland* (Berlin: Verband Deutscher Waren- und Kaufhäuser, 1928), 80. See also Paul Göhre's essay "Das Warenhaus" (1907), on the aesthetic ennobling of advertising and architecture in the department store: "Everywhere light, glamor, beauty flow up to one." Quoted by Julius Posener in *Berlin auf dem Wege zu einer neuen Architektur* (Munich: Prestel, 1979), 465.

54. See Benjamin, *Gesammelte Schriften*, 5.1:109.

55. Here Benjamin draws heavily on Sigfried Giedion's *Bauen in Frankreich.* Benjamin, *Gesammelte Schriften*, 5.1:93.

56. Wertheim, *Die Reklame des Warenhauses*, 5. Peter Stürzebecher notes the reciprocal relationship between department stores and metropolitan growth. See Stürzebecher, *Das Berliner Warenhaus. Bautypus, Element der Stadtorganisation, Raumsphäre der Warenwelt* (Berlin: Archibook-Verlag, 1979, 19). See also Stürzebecher, "Warenhäuser," in *Berlin und seine Bauten*, ed. E. Heinrich and F. Mielke, vol. 8.A, *Handel* (Berlin: Wilhelm Ernst & Sohn, 1978), 1–27.

57. Matheo Quintz, "Wertheim," 163. See also Erich Blunck's critique of the extension building for eclipsing Messel's masterpiece: "Erweiterungsbau des Warenhauses Wertheim in Berlin," *Deutsche Bauzeitung* 61.25 (1927): 217–24.

58. Adolf Behne, "Vom Anhalter Bahnhof bis zum Bauhaus. Fünfzig Jahre Deutscher Architektur," *Soziale Bauwirtschaft* 12 (1922): 221. Cited by Strohmeyer, *Warenhäuser*, 67.

59. Sigfried Giedion, in *Space, Time and Architecture* (236–41), states that the first light-court in a department store was built in 1876 as an iron-and-glass achievement for the Magasin au bon Marché in Paris, by Gustave Eiffel

and L. A. Boilleau. On the Bon Marché as Piranesian *Carceri* of glassy infinity, see Asendorf, *Batteries of Life,* 98. As Friedberg notes, the model for department stores's light-courts was that of the central reading room of the Bibliothèque Nationale, where Benjamin wrote his *Arcades Project* under a glass roof, with surrounding stories of stacks/commodities on display for the browser of knowledge/fashion. See Friedberg, *Window Shopping,* 79.

60. Werner Hegemann, *Das steinerne Berlin,* 252; quoted by Stürzebecher, *Das Berliner Warenhaus,* 25.

61. For an analysis of the architectural innovations of the Wertheim and Tietz department stores, see Posener, *Berlin auf dem Wege zu einer neuen Architektur,* 453–64; and Christian Schramm, *Deutsche Warenhausbauten. Ursprung, Typologie und Entwicklungstendenzen* (Aachen: Verlag Shaker, 1995), 46–56, 104–106.

62. Alfred Wiener, "Das Warenhaus," *Jahrbuch des Deutschen Werkbundes* (1913); cited by Posener, *Berlin auf dem Wege zu einer neuen Architektur,* 472.

63. See Friedberg, *Window Shopping,* 65–68, on the development of the storefront from medieval stall to eighteenth-century proscenium to Parisian arcades halfway between a palace gallery and a railway station.

64. The first U.S. trade magazine for display windows was founded in 1897: *The Show Window: A Monthly Journal of Practical Window Trimming,* renamed *The Merchants Record and Show Window* in 1903, and merged with the journal *Display World* (of 1922) in 1938; nowadays it is *Visual Merchandising. The Show Window* was first edited by *Wizard of Oz* author L. Frank Baum, founder in 1898 of the National Association of Window Trimmers of America. See Leach's reading of Baum's bestselling *The Wonderful Wizard of Oz* as a tale of the wizard as capitalist promoter and conjurer for the masses, in *Land of Desire,* 248–60. For histories of window display in the United States, see Leonard S. Marcus, *The American Store Window* (New York: Whitney Library of Design, 1978), 12–54; and Leach, *Land of Desire,* 55–70.

65. See Leo Kern, "Von Früh bis Abend. Ein Tag im Schaufenster und für das Schaufenster," *Das Schaufenster* 2.1 (1929): 5. In London, the spectacular window displays of the new Selfridges store, which opened in 1909, promptly forced Harrod's to follow suite. On the impact of Selfridges, see Erika D. Rappaport, "'A New Era of Shopping': The Promotion of Women's Pleasure in London's West End, 1909–1914," in *Cinema and the Invention of Modern Life,* ed. Charney and Schwartz, 130–55.

66. Hans Schliepmann, "Das Moderne Geschäftshaus," *Berliner Architekturwelt* 3 (1901): 425; cited by Reinhardt, *Von der Reklame zum Marketing,* 272.

67. See Dirk Reinhardt, "Beten oder Bummeln? Der Kampf um die Schaufensterfreiheit," in *Bilderwelt des Alltags,* ed. Borscheid and Wischermann, 116–25. In the U.S., this Sunday covering lasted until the 1930s; see Reinhardt, *Von der Reklame zum Marketing,* 278–79; and Leach, *Land of Desire,* 70.

68. See Osterwold, *Schaufenster,* 234–48.

69. Elisabeth von Stephani-Hahn, *Schaufenster-Kunst* (Berlin: Verlag L. Schottlaender & Co., 1919).

70. Reinhardt, *Von der Reklame zum Marketing,* 281. See also Osterwold, *Schaufenster* 60–62.

71. See Arthur Korn, ed., *Glas im Bau und als Gebrauchsgegenstand* (Berlin: Ernst Pollak, 1926); trans. as *Glass in Modern Architecture of the Bauhaus Period* (New York: George Braziller, 1968).

72. A similar recognition was occurring in France, if on a less radical scale of architectural renovation: Henri Verne and René Chavance noted, for example, that the "shop is one big window" (*Pour comprendre l'art décoratif Moderne en France* [Paris: Hachette, 1925]). The French journal *Présentation* proclaimed in 1927: "The shop front must give pride of place to the display window, so that the public gaze is never disturbed by the slightest architectural detail. We should be focusing our efforts on the window, so as to give it all the space it needs." *Présentation 1927: Le décor de la rue, les magasins, les étalages, les stands d'exposition, les éclairages* (Paris: Les Editions de Parade, 1927), 32; cited by Bouillon, "The Shop Window," in *The 1920s: Age of the Metropolis,* ed. Clair, 163, 173. But Bouillon's emphasis on the Parisian 1920s brings about his totally erroneous claim (179) that "in Mendelsohn's works in Stuttgart and Breslau, as in most German architecture of the period, the window was not treated as significant in itself, but integrated into a compact and uniform block; it was the interiors, the sales floors, that attracted most of the attention."

73. Posener, *Berlin auf dem Wege zu einer neuen Architektur,* 473, citing Alfred Wiener, "Das Warenhaus," in *Jahrbuch des Deutschen Werkbundes* (1913).

74. Paul Scheerbart, *Glasarchitektur,* 59.

75. Benjamin, "Erfahrung und Armut" (1933), in *Illuminationen,* 294.

76. See Scheerbart's ecstatic predictions of the imminent rise of glass culture, such as: "'The new glass-milieu will completely transform mankind,'" in *Glasarchitektur;* and Ludwig Hilberseimer's "Glasarchitektur," in *Die Form* 4:19 (1929): 521–22, in which Hilberseimer cites Scheerbart's 1914 treatise as the expressionist creative source for the Weimar shift toward glass architecture.

77. Baudrillard, *The System of Objects,* 41.

78. Bruno Taut, *The Crystal Chain Letters: Architectural Fantasies by Bruno Taut and His Circle,* ed. and trans. Iain Boyd Whyte (Cambridge: MIT Press, 1985), 24.

79. Christoph Asendorf comments: "A crystal is a regular solid body bounded by flat surfaces. Owing to its symmetrical nature, which effects a mathematical resolution in the very moment of petrification, it has been predestined from the start to be a carrier of notions of harmonious and ideal order." Asendorf, *Batteries of Life,* 22.

80. Michel Foucault, "The Eye of Power," in *Power/Knowledge: Selected Interviews and Other Writings, 1972–1977,* ed. Colin Gordon (Brighton: Har-

vester Press, 1980), 152. See also Foucault, *Discipline and Punish: The Birth of the Prison,* trans. Alan Sheridan (New York: Pantheon, 1970).

81. Graeme Davison, "Exhibitions," *Australian Cultural History* 2 (1982/83): 7; cited by Tony Bennett, "The Exhibitionary Complex," in *Thinking About Exhibitions,* ed. Reesa Greenberg, Bruce W. Ferguson, and Sandy Nairne (New York: Routledge, 1996), 87.

82. Scheerbart, *Glasarchitektur,* 56, 102.

83. See Janet Lungstrum (now Ward), "'Ein Käfig ging einen Vogel suchen': Architectural Imaging in Kafka and Wittgenstein," *Journal of the Kafka Society of America* 16.2 (1992): 29–44.

84. Paul Mahlberg, "Die Soziale Mission des Schaufensters," *Schaufenster-Kunst und -Technik* (February 1934). Cited by Osterwold, *Schaufenster,* 70.

85. Schivelbusch, *Licht Schein und Wahn,* 133. See also Gerhard Auer, "The Desiring Gaze and the Ruses of the Veil," *Daidalos* 33 (1989): 36–53.

86. See Kracauer, "Das Neue Bauen. Zur Stuttgarter Werkbund-Ausstellung: 'Die Wohnung,'" *Frankfurter Zeitung* 72.561 (July 31, 1927).

87. Ernst Bloch, *Erbschaft dieser Zeit* (Frankfurt a.M.: Suhrkamp, 1962), 216; emphasis in original.

88. Bloch, *Erbschaft dieser Zeit,* 34.

89. Bloch, *Erbschaft dieser Zeit,* 216.

90. Bloch, *Erbschaft dieser Zeit,* 216.

91. Nietzsche, *Die Geburt der Tragödie aus dem Geiste der Musik,* in *Sämtliche Werke,* 1:65.

92. Kracauer, *The Mass Ornament,* 75; *Das Ornament der Masse,* 50.

93. See "Immer Neues . . . Immer Anderes!" *Zeitschrift für Waren- und Kaufhäuser* 26.27 (July 1, 1928): 12.

94. Kracauer, "Das Neue Bauen."

95. "Ochse, siehste Wertheim nicht?" *Der Angriff* (September 12, 1927). Landesarchiv Berlin.

96. "Der 'Reklamegoj' der Warenhäuser," *Der Angriff* (December 31, 1928). Landesarchiv Berlin.

97. See Leo Colze, *Berliner Warenhäuser,* orig. 1908 (Berlin: Fannei & Walz, 1989), 62–63.

98. Wertheim, *Die Reklame des Warenhauses,* 1.

99. Noted by Stürzebecher, *Das Berliner Warenhaus,* 23.

100. See Heinrich Müller, "Psychologisches von der Schaufensterreklame," *Seidels-Reklame* 9.6 (1925): 260. The French Cubist artist Fernand Léger termed this the "aesthetic of the isolated object." Léger, "The Street: Objects, Spectacles" (1928), in Léger, *Functions of Painting,* ed. Edward F. Fry, trans. Alexandra Anderson (New York: Viking Press, 1973), 79.

101. The fact that Germany's first democracy was such an overachiever in technical innovation has been linked by Peter Fritzsche to Weimar Germany's post-WWI status as a "landscape of danger" and crisis that gave simultaneous birth to a "landscape of design." Fritzsche, "Landscape of Danger, Landscape of

Design: Crisis and Modernism in Weimar Germany," in *Dancing on the Volcano,* ed. Kniesche and Brockmann, 29–46.

102. Cited by Leach, *Land of Desire,* 304. Leach also gives an account of the American window dresser Arthur Fraser of Marshall Field's, whose pictorial display windows in the 1910s and 1920s set the tone for the country (68–70).

103. The 1930s—when there were up to two million display windows in Germany—recycled the basic principles of Weimar window design, adding more neon but introducing little else save an emphasis on themes intended to forge a collective spirit, and Party symbols. In the initial euphoric period of Nazism, display windows were so overstocked with Nazi symbolism (especially at Christmas) that a law had to be passed in December 1933 to prevent the Nazi *Hoheitszeichen* being used except for official purposes. See Reinhardt, *Von der Reklame zum Marketing,* 283, 286; and Osterwold, *Schaufenster,* 126.

104. See Kiesler, *Contemporary Art Applied to the Store and Its Display,* 146. For a discussion of America's relation to European modernist design, see Terry Smith, *Making the Modern: Industry, Art, and Design in America* (Chicago: University of Chicago Press, 1993), 353–84.

105. See *Devantures et installations de magasins. Exposition internationale des arts décoratifs, Paris 1925* (Paris: Edition d'Art Charles Moreau, 1925). For a discussion of this exhibition and the impact of French window display in the 1920s, see Bouillon, "The Shop Window," in *The 1920s: Age of the Metropolis,* ed. Clair, 162–81. It was the Paris exhibition that influenced John Parkinson, Donald Parkinson, and Percy Winnett, architects of the new Bullocks Wilshire in Los Angeles (1929), the first explicitly car-oriented department store in the world, to drop what would have been an overblown ornamentation of the mock-cathedral of commerce and adopt instead the starker lines of art deco; and the interior of the store was designed in New Objective style by a German architect, Jock Peters. See Margaret Leslie Davis, *Bullocks Wilshire,* 38–44.

106. See Leach, *Land of Desire,* 313–14.

107. Kiesler, *Contemporary Art Applied to the Store and Its Display,* 108.

108. In 1928, Amedée Ozenfant enthused about European window display's links to the entire modern architectural movement:

> Nowadays the window dressing of small or great shops is very agreeable to see. A sane geometry derived from Purism and Léger directs the composition: dresses, boots, casseroles, all play their eager parts in the equations to which they provide a solution.
>
> The art of window dressing is an important factor in that town planning to which Le Corbusier brought so much clear vision and power.

Amedée Ozenfant, *Foundations of Modern Art* (1928), trans. John Rodker (London: John Rodker, 1931), 162. Quoted by Bouillon, "The Shop Window," in *The 1920s: Age of the Metropolis,* ed. Clair, 163; also cited by Marcus, *The American Store Window,* 24–25.

109. Le Corbusier noted in 1912 how German display windows understood the "order," "rhythm," and "*art of presentation.*" Ch-E. Jeanneret (Le Corbu-

sier), *Étude sur le mouvement d'art décoratif en Allemagne* (New York: Da Capo, 1968), 45; emphasis in original. See also Bouillon, "The Shop Window," in *The 1920s: Age of the Metropolis*, ed. Clair, 169–70.

110. Gustav Brandes, "Die Geschäftsreklame im Stadtbilde" (1922). Staatsarchiv Hamburg 324–4 Baupflegekommission 127.

111. Kiesler, *Contemporary Art Applied to the Store and Its Display*, 79.

112. Gerhard Schatte, "Fassade und Schaufenster als Werbemittel," *Architektur und Schaufenster* 25 (1928). See Gerta-Elisabeth Thiele's praise of Mendelsohn in "Der Einfluß neuzeitlicher Architektur auf das Schaufenster," *Farbe und Form* 13.10/11 (1928): 186.

113. Ernst Pollak, "Modern Shop Constructions," in *Interior Design 1929*, ed. Düttmann.

114. Paul Mahlberg, untitled, in *Moderne Ladenbauten*, 108; repr. in *Interior Design 1929*, ed. Düttmann, 174, 176.

115. H. K. Frenzel, "Die Reklameschau in Berlin 1929," *Das Schaufenster* 2.3 (1929): 7; see also "Das neue Schaufenster auf der Reklameschau Berlin 1929," *Schaufenster-Kunst und -Technik* 5.1 (1929): 7.

116. Bruno Zevi, *Erich Mendelsohn* (New York: Rizzoli, 1985) 68.

117. See Erich Mendelsohn, "Harmonische und kontrapunktische Führung in der Architektur," *Die Baukunst* 1 (1925): 179; discussed by Renate Palmer, *Der Stuttgarter Schocken-Bau von Erich Mendelsohn*, 30.

118. Posener, *Berlin auf dem Weg zu einer neuen Architektur*, 481.

119. "Das Deukonhaus-Umbau," *Die Form* 3.2 (1928): 42.

120. Rainer Stommer, "Vom Traumpalast zum Warencontainer. Die Warenhausarchitektur der zwanziger Jahre," *Deutsche Bauzeitung* 10 (1990).

121. Mia Klein, *Die Reklame des Warenhauses*, 31. See also Schöndorff, "Der moderne Geschäftsbau und seine Einrichtungen," in Georg Grimm, *Kauf- und Warenhäuser aus aller Welt. Ihre Architekur und Betriebseinrichtungen* (Berlin: Verlag L. Schottlaender & Co., 1928), 13–20.

122. On the store generally, see the booklet published for its grand opening: *Rudolph Karstadt Berlin am Hermannplatz.* # 8771, Landesarchiv Berlin. The store (minus towers) received its post-Wall renovation in the fall of 2000.

123. "Steuerhinterziehungen Berliner Warenhäuser," *Der Angriff* (December 12, 1927). Landesarchiv Berlin.

124. "Bauakrobatik am Hermannplatz," *Berliner Lokal-Anzeiger* (January 13, 1929).

125. Introduction by Werner Hegemann to Philipp Schaeffer, *Neue Warenhausbauten der Rudolph Karstadt AG* (Berlin: Friedrich Ernst Hübsch Verlag, 1929), vi.

126. Hegemann, in *Neue Warenhausbauten der Rudolph Karstadt AG*, v; cited by Stürzebecher, *Das Berliner Warenhaus*, 42; see also Christian Schramm, *Deutsche Warenhausbauten*, 84–87.

127. On the opening of Germany's first cinema in a department store, in Düsseldorf, see *Licht-Bild-Bühne* 20.108 (May 6, 1927): 1. The Eaton's depart-

ment store in Toronto had a movie auditorium seating 1,500 on its eighth floor; see *Das Licht* 2.5 (May 1932): 111–12.

128. Kracauer, "Der Dichter im Warenhaus," *Frankfurter Zeitung* 75.707 (September 9, 1930).

129. Max Osborn et al., eds., *Berlins Aufstieg zur Weltstadt* (Berlin: R. Hobbing, 1929), 205. The official cut-off mark for what actually "defined" a German department store, according to Prussian tax laws, was a minimum in annual turnover of 400,000 Reichmarks. J. Wernicke, "Zum Begriff des Warenhauses," *Zeitschrift für Waren- und Kaufhäuser* 25.35 (August 26, 1927): 1.

130. See Klein, *Die Reklame des Warenhauses,* 7. Salman Schocken's opinion about the rankings of department stores in 1930 is cited by Konrad Fuchs, *Ein Konzern aus Sachsen. Das Kaufhaus Schocken als Spiegelbild deutscher Wirtschaft und Politik 1901–1953* (Stuttgart: Leo Baeck Institute, 1990), 154.

131. Wertheim, *Die Reklame des Warenhauses,* 7. In the late 1920s, for every one hundred RM spent by the average German housewife, most was spent in small shops, and less than four RM in the department stores of the big cities, despite their enormous pulling power as sites of spectacle. Berthold, *Volkswirtschaft in Zahlen und Bildern,* 30. See also Peukert, *Die Weimarer Republik. Krisenjahre der klassischen Moderne,* 176.

132. See Klein, *Die Reklame des Warenhauses,* 37; and Berthold, *Volkswirtschaft in Zahlen und Bildern,* 1, 4.

133. See Stürzebecher, *Das Berliner Warenhaus,* 38. The Ka De We was too expensive for Germans, and full of foreigners, especially Russians; see Andrei Bely, "Wie schön es in Berlin ist," in *Russen in Berlin: Literatur, Malerei, Theater, Film 1918–1933,* ed. Fritz Mierau (Leipzig: Reclam, 1991), 58.

134. E. Alber, "Die Symphonie im Schaufenster," *Architektur und Schaufenster* 25 (1928): 25.

135. "Linienharmonie im Schaufenster," *Zeitschrift für Waren- und Kaufhäuser* 25.35 (1927): 36.

136. See Bruno Seydel, "Die Innenausstattung des Schaufensters," *Zeitschrift für Waren- und Kaufhäuser* 25.34 (1927): 81–82.

137. Robert Schulhof, "Die Psychologie des Schaufensters," *Schaufenster und Dekoration* 2.12 (1929): 7; see also "Die psychologische Brille," *Die Auslage* 26 (1928): 6–10.

138. Marbe, *Psychologie der Werbung,* 65–66, 68–70, citing respectively W. Blumenfeld's "Zur Psychotechnik der Werbewirkung des Schaufensters," *Praktische Psychologie* 2 (1920/1921): 81, and E. Lysinski, in *Zeitschrift für Handelswissenschaft und Handelspraxis* (1919/1920): 6.

139. H. Schmidt-Lamberg, "Das Schaufenster," *Die Reklame* 1 (1925): 670–72.

140. "Die 'neue Sachlichkeit' im Schaufenster," *Architektur und Schaufenster* 25 (1928): 11.

141. Wertheim, *Die Reklame des Warenhauses,* 188, 40.

142. Georg Fischer, "Sachlichkeit im Schaufenster," *Farbe und Form* 11.10/11 (1926): 126.

143. A. Kling, "Rationelle Gestaltung der Schaufensterreklame," *Das Schaufenster* 1 (1926).

144. Sergei Tretiakov (Tretjakow), "Schaufensterreklame" (1931), in *Russen in Berlin*, ed. Mierau, 543.

145. "Das Erbsen-Fenster," *Seidels Reklame* 9.4 (1925): 142–43.

146. Rudolf Schulhof, "Die Zeit fordert Entwicklung," *Schaufenster und Dekoration* 2.11 (1929): 3. See also Osterwold, *Schaufenster*, 8.

147. "Immer Neues . . . immer Anderes!" *Zeitschrift für Waren- und Kaufhäuser* 26.27 (July 1, 1928): 12.

148. See the photographs taken of the "Then and Now" display window competition, in Stephani-Hahn, *Schaufenster Kunst*, 232–33.

149. Lavoby, "Einst und Jetzt im Schaufenster," *Seidels Reklame* 9.3 (1925): 102.

150. Kracauer, "Der Verkaufs-Tempel," *Frankfurter Zeitung* 76.548 (July 25, 1931).

151. Kracauer, "Straße ohne Erinnerung" (1932), in *Straßen in Berlin*, 16.

152. Kracauer, "Reise im Schaufenster," *Frankfurter Zeitung* 74.440 (June 16, 1930).

153. Reinhardt, *Von der Reklame zum Marketing*, 280.

154. See H. Moos, "Das 'rechte Licht,'" *Seidels Reklame* 9.1 (1925): 15.

155. Döblin, *Berlin Alexanderplatz*, 124.

156. Hannes Meyer, "Die neue Welt," *Das Werk* 13.7 (1926): 222; repr. in *The Weimar Republic Sourcebook*, ed. Kaes, Jay, and Dimendberg, 448.

157. Baudrillard, "Consumer Society," in *Reflections on Commercial Life*, ed. Murray, 450.

158. Tretiakov, "Schaufensterreklame," in *Russen in Berlin*, ed. Mierau, 543.

159. Tretiakov, "Schaufensterreklame," in *Russen in Berlin*, ed. Mierau, 544.

160. See Tom Gunning, "The Cinema of Attraction(s): Early Film, Its Spectator and the Avant-Garde," *Wide Angle* 8.3–4 (1986): 63–70; and "The Whole Town's Gawking: Early Cinema and the Visual Experience of Modernity," *The Yale Journal of Criticism* 7.2 (1994): 189–201. As Gunning relates: "We need to investigate these scenarios of attraction not only as reflections of what we *already* know about the culture of consumption, but for what they can reveal about the experience of modernity that has not yet come to the surface." Gunning, "The Whole Town's Gawking," 196–97.

161. Buck-Morss (*Dialectics of Seeing*, 82) likens the viewing of nineteenth-century panoramas located in the arcades to the experience of actually passing by a series of display windows. This walking, mobile film-experience for urban dwellers is further explored by Anne Friedberg in her analysis of modern consumerism in *Window Shopping*.

162. Asendorf, in *Batteries of Life* (94), suggests that this process began earlier, with the impressionists' foregrounding of color and light at the expense

of sharp outlines and causal perspective as a direct result of commodity fetishism's primacy of the visual.

163. Tretiakov, "Schaufensterreklame," in *Russen in Berlin,* ed. Mierau, 541.

164. "Ein Lichtjournal im Schaufenster," *Schaufenster und Dekoration* 2.11 (1929): 16.

165. Kiesler, *Contemporary Art Applied to the Store and Its Display,* 73.

166. Hörnig Reichenberg, "Architektur von Heute, das Schaufenster von Morgen," *Schaufenster und Dekoration* 2.11 (1929): 11.

167. Kiesler explains the "dream of a kinetic window" and its relation to stage, film, and even TV. See *Contemporary Art Applied to the Store and Its Display,* 110–13, 120–22.

168. Friedberg (*Window Shopping,* 66–67) cites the prevalence among such film theorists as Mary Ann Doane and Jane Gaines of the use of "window shopping" as a term for cinema spectatorship. See Doane, *The Desire to Desire: The Woman's Film of the 1940s* (Bloomington: Indiana University Press, 1987), and Gaines, "The Queen Christina Tie-Ups: Convergence of Show Window and Screen," *Quarterly Review of Film and Video* 11.1 (1989): 35–60.

169. Recounted in *Schaufenster-Kunst und -Technik* (April 1927), 25. Cited by Osterwold, *Schaufenster,* 114. See also Kiesler, *Contemporary Art Applied to the Store and Its Display,* 120.

170. Klein, *Die Reklame des Warenhauses,* 23.

171. Friedberg, *Window Shopping,* 68.

172. Sara K. Schneider, citing Duchamp and the surrealists as *fenêtriers,* states in *Vital Mummies* that the show window as theater helped make twentieth-century art into a display form. Schneider's approach, while insightful, neglects the closer kinship of film (over theater) to the window art form (especially in that the transparent wall of window glass behaves rather like the lens of the camera or the literal screen of the film). Schneider's book title also indicates her anthropomorphic bias, which downplays how show window display of the German 1920s focused equally on nonmannequin scenes; she also seems unaware of Weimar German predominance in the field, implying instead that it was a uniquely "'American' [modern] art form." Schneider, *Vital Mummies: Performance Design for the Show-Window Mannequin* (New Haven: Yale University Press, 1995), 14.

173. Herbert N. Casson, "Dramatisieren Sie Ihr Schaufenster!" *Schaufenster-Kunst und -Technik* (January 1930): 14. Cited by Osterwold, *Schaufenster,* 100.

174. Bolz, "Design des Immateriellen," 160.

175. See Rob. Mallet-Stevens, *Le décor moderne au cinéma* (Paris: C. H. Massin & CIE, 1928).

176. Bouillon states: "The space defined by the [modern] shop window is an unreal space, like that of a Cubist painting: it is situated both in front of the glass (due to the reflection) and beyond it (but here compressed and subject to definite constraints)." Bouillon, in "The Shop Window," in *The 1920s: Age of the Metropolis,* ed. Clair, 163.

177. Sara K. Schneider points up futurism's links, in the Marinetti essay "Futurist Cinema," to show window display. See Schneider, *Vital Mummies*, 150.

178. See Léger, "The Machine Aesthetic: The Manufactured Object, the Artisan, and the Artist" (1924), in *Functions of Painting*, ed. Fry, 56–58.

179. Bouillon, "The Shop Window," in *The 1920s: Age of the Metropolis*, ed. Clair, 177.

180. See Featherstone, *Consumer Culture and Postmodernism*, 25.

181. This is the gist of Stephani-Hahn's *Schaufenster-Kunst*.

182. Kiesler, *Contemporary Art Applied to the Store and Its Display*, 73.

183. *Présentation 1927. Le décor de la rue, les magasins, les étalages, les stands d'exposition, les éclairages*, foreword by Henri Clouzot (Paris: Les Editions de "Parade," 1927), 38.

184. Dr. Perl, "Der rechtliche Schutz der Schaufensterdekoration," *Schaufenster-Kunst und -Technik* 4.5 (1929): 14.

185. Stephani-Hahn has photographs of the top seventeen "window display artists" of the day (including two women) in her *Schaufenster-Kunst*, 270–71.

186. Klein, *Die Reklame des Warenhauses*, 16.

187. "Künstler oder Kaufmann?" *Schaufenster-Kunst und -Technik* 4.5 (1929): 15.

188. See Pierre Bourdieu's comparison between Kant's refinement of aesthetic judgement and the taste of the masses for the emotional, immediate, and physical, in his *Distinction: A Social Critique of the Judgement of Taste*, trans. R. Nice (New York: Routledge, 1984), 488–91.

189. Featherstone, *Consumer Culture and Postmodernism*, 77.

190. Dr. Krentz, "Die kulturelle Bedeutung der Schaufenster-Dekoration," *Schaufenster-Kunst und -Technik* (November 1929), 9; emphasis in original. Cited by Osterwold, *Schaufenster*, 260.

191. Kiesler, foreword to *Contemporary Art Applied to the Store and Its Display*.

192. Celia Lury, for example, following Zygmunt Bauman (in *Thinking Sociologically* [Cambridge: Blackwell, 1990]), inclines somewhat toward the laws of dispossession and nonparticipation among consumers. Lury, *Consumer Culture*, 5–7. Featherstone, on the other hand, construes both modern and postmodern consumerism as an active, participatory aesthetic of self-invention for consumers. See Featherstone, *Consumer Culture and Postmodernism*, 65–82.

193. Debord, *The Society of the Spectacle*, 30.

194. Baudrillard, "Consumer Society," 463, 464, 465.

195. Baudrillard, "Consumer Society," 465, 467, 471.

196. Horkheimer and Adorno, *Dialektik der Aufklärung*, 176.

197. Baudelaire, "Short Poems in Prose," in *My Heart Laid Bare and Other Prose Writings*, ed. Peter Quennell, trans. Norman Cameron (New York: The Vanguard Press, 1951), 147.

198. Tretiakov, "Schaufensterreklame," in *Russen in Berlin,* ed. Mierau, 542.

199. Colomina, *Privacy and Publicity,* 8. See also Schivelbusch, *Licht Schein und Wahn,* 125–37.

200. Colomina, *Privacy and Publicity,* 9.

201. Benjamin, *Gesammelte Schriften,* 5.2:1008; emphasis in original. See also Buck-Morss (*Dialectics of Seeing,* 80) on Benjamin's reading of the sleight of hand that the City of Light's show windows performed on the production process.

202. Schneider's critique is apt here: "The simplest explanation of how the window works on its public is as façade, as representation of what the passerby might expect to find inside the store. At a deeper level, and implicit in the overtones of the world 'façade,' hums the suggestion of false self-representation. The window may present a grandiose image of who the customer considers herself to be; it may also stand as an image of how the world is supposed to work." Schneider, *Vital Mummies,* 154. Schneider then moves away from this view, preferring to locate in the process of visual desire enflamed by the display window a certain degree of active role-play for the consumer.

203. Leach blames the display window for the "new culture of class" of the twentieth century, by its "permitting everything to be seen yet rendering it all beyond touch": "Glass was a symbol of the merchant's unilateral power in a capitalist society to refuse goods to anyone in need, to close off access without being condemned as cruel and immoral. . . . At the same time, the pictures behind the glass enticed the viewer. The result was a mingling of refusal and desire that must have greatly intensified desire, adding another level of cruelty. Perhaps more than any other medium, glass democratized desire even as it dedemocratized access to goods." Leach, *Land of Desire,* 62, 63.

204. See Reinhardt, *Von der Reklame zum Marketing,* 275–76.

205. Franz Hessel, *Heimliches Berlin* (Frankfurt a.M.: Suhrkamp, 1982), 98–100.

206. Joseph Roth, "Philosophie des Schaufensters," *Vorwärts* (April 3, 1923); repr. in Roth, *Der Neue Tag: Unbekannte Politische Schriften. 1919 bis 1927. Wien, Berlin, Moskau,* ed. Ingeborg Sültemeyer (Berlin: Kiepenheuer & Witsch, 1970), 128. Emphasis in original. My thanks to Ian Foster for pointing out this reference.

207. An example of this is related in "Der Schaufenstereinbrecher im Auto," *Berliner Morgen-Zeitung* (October 20, 1928).

208. Alliez and Feher, "The Luster of Capital," 350.

209. Debord, *The Society of the Spectacle,* 30.

210. Baudrillard, *The System of Objects,* 41–42.

211. Baudrillard, *The System of Objects,* 160; see also 193–96.

212. Baudrillard, *The System of Objects,* 159; emphasis in original. Helga Dittmar extends this criticism of the contradiction in consumer culture: a false magic is projected that all are equal to participate, when that is evidently not so. See Dittmar, *The Social Psychology of Material Possessions: To Have Is To Be* (Hemel Hempstead, UK: Harvester Wheatsheaf, 1992).

213. Kracauer, "On Employment Agencies: The Construction of a Space," trans. David Frisby, in *Rethinking Architecture*, ed. Leach, 60.

214. Hans Fallada, *Kleiner Mann—Was nun?* (Hamburg: Rowohlt, 1950), 129.

215. See chapter 3 in Asendorf, *Batteries of Life.*

216. Alfred Döblin, "Der Geist des naturalistischen Zeitalters," *Die neue Rundschau* 35.2 (1924); repr. in Döblin, *Schriften zu Ästhetik, Poetik und Literatur,* ed. Erich Kleinschmidt (Olten: Walter-Verlag, 1989), 189. More emphatically than Döblin, Karl Kraus was offended by the "obscene erotic impertinence" of commodity exchange. Karl Kraus, *Die Fackel,* 457–61 (May 10, 1917): 39; cited by Asendorf, *Batteries of Life,* 1.

217. Freud's "Fetishism" essay (1927) draws attention to the ironic fore-fronting of surface in this mode of desire—the bilingual meanings of a patient's *Glanz auf der Nase* (translatable, as Freud writes, as both a "*shine* on the nose" and a "*glance* at the nose") constitute the "necessary special brilliance" of a fetishist's self-expression. Sigmund Freud, "Fetishism," trans. Joan Riviere, in Freud, *Sexuality and the Psychology of Love* (New York: Collier, 1963), 214.

218. Kurt Tucholsky, *Deutschland Deutschland über alles,* with photos by John Heartfield (Hamburg: Rowohlt, 1994), 123.

219. Kracauer, "Heißer Abend," *Frankfurter Zeitung* 439 (June 15, 1932).

220. Benjamin, *The Arcades Project* (*Das Passagen-Werk*), in *Gesammelte Schriften,* 5.1:516.

221. Le Corbusier, *When the Cathedrals Were White* (1937), 165.

222. See Friedberg, *Window Shopping,* 66.

223. See Marina Warner's history of Madame Tussaud's, "Waxworks and Wonderlands," in *Visual Display,* ed. Cooke and Wollen, 179–201.

224. See Barry James Wood, *Show Windows: 75 Years of the Art of Display* (New York: Congdon & Weed, Inc., 1982), 14.

225. Emile Zola, *Au bonheur des dames* (1883), in *Oeuvres Complètes* (Paris: François Bernouard, 1927), 12:11.

226. Bouillon calls this abstraction of the mannequin's body "its true nature: a presence/absence behind the window that encompasses and encourages all fantasies." Bouillon, "The Shop Window," in *The 1920s: Age of the Metropolis,* ed. Clair, 181.

227. See Gerta-Elisabeth Thiele, "Das Schaufenster," *Die Form* 1 (1925/1926): 146–48; and Elisabeth von Stephani-Hahn, *Schaufenster Kunst,* 262.

228. In a *Filmkurier* article in fetishistic praise of a film star's legs, a commentator demanded that a film be made of her legs alone. Cited by Buchner, *Im Banne des Films,* 117–18.

229. "Die Figur im Schaufenster," *Das Schaufenster* 10 (October 1926).

230. Zola, *Au bonheur des dames,* 83.

231. Kracauer, "Der Verkaufs-Tempel," *Frankfurter Zeitung* 76.548 (July 25, 1931).

232. Benjamin, *Gesammelte Schriften,* 4.1:105; Benjamin, *One-Way Street,* 64 (modified translation).

233. Benjamin, *Gesammelte Schriften,* 5.1:427, 438. In *Les Fleurs du Mal* (1857), Charles Baudelaire speaks of a *flâneur's* desire for a woman passer-by, whose eyes are "lit up like shops to lure their trade" with a "borrowed power" from the commodities on display. Baudelaire, *Les Fleurs du Mal,* poem 26, trans. Richard Howard (Boston: David R. Godine, 1983); cited by Friedberg, *Window Shopping,* 34.

234. *Die Auslage* 32 (1928): 9.

235. "Bestrafung wegen lebender Schaufensterreklame," *Zeitschrift für Waren- und Kaufhäuser* 26.29 (July 1928): 12.

236. See L. Frank Baum's *The Art of Decorating Dry Goods Windows* (1900), cited by Friedberg, *Window Shopping,* 66. Schneider, in *Vital Mummies,* 52–54, refers to Freud's reading of "The Sandman" (1817) as a prototype of the uncanny live show window dummy—whether automaton or human.

237. Cited by Osterwold, *Schaufenster,* 286–88.

238. See Mataja, *Die Reklame,* 322–31.

239. Rudolph Seyffert, *Allgemeine Werbelehre* (Stuttgart: C. E. Poeschel Verlag, 1929), 390–91, 596–97. A similar study by Seyffert showed less differentiation between men and women, but still with longer viewing time by the latter; also couples looked longer than individuals, and mixed pairs looked longer than did pairs of women. Cited by Fritz Wertheim, Seyffert's pupil, in *Die Reklame des Warenhauses,* 195.

240. Richard Huelsenbeck, "Bejahung der modernen Frau," in *Die Frau von morgen,* ed. Huebner, 36.

241. Stephani-Hahn, "Kultur oder Unkultur im Schaufenster? Sammlung zu neuem Wollen!" *Farbe und Form* 13.10/11 (1928): 174.

242. Stephani-Hahn, "Kultur oder Unkultur im Schaufenster?" 182, 183.

243. Stephani-Hahn, "Kultur oder Unkultur im Schaufenster?" 182, 183.

244. Stewart, *On Longing,* 168–69.

245. Jane Gaines, "Introduction: Fabricating the Female Body," in *Fabrications: Costume and the Female Body,* ed. Gaines and Charlotte Herzog (New York: Routledge, 1990), 15.

246. See, for example, Susan Buck-Morss, "The Flâneur, The Sandwich-Man, and the Whore: The Politics of Loitering," *New German Critique* 39 (1986): 99–140; and Janet Wolf, "The Invisible Flâneuse: Women and the Literature of Modernity," *Theory, Culture, and Society* 2.3 (1985): 37–46.

247. See Janet Lungstrum (now Ward), "*Metropolis* and the Technosexual Woman of German Modernity," in *Women in the Metropolis,* ed. von Ankum, 128–44.

248. Baudrillard, *The System of Objects,* 177.

249. Katharina Sykora mentions the inside/outside boundary-breaking that goes on in *Die Straße:* the street enters the home (literally, in the protagonist's city-vision at the beginning of the film) and beckons the man into "her"

world of dangerous surfaces. See Sykora, "Die Neue Frau," in *Die Neue Frau*, ed. Sykora et al., 135.

250. John Wanamaker, "Editorials of John Wanamaker" (November 9, 1916), Wanamaker Archive, Pennsylvania Historical Society. Cited by Leach, 39.

251. Baudrillard, *The System of Objects*, 166–67. Emphasis in original.

252. Baudrillard, *The System of Objects*, 171, 167, 171.

253. Baudrillard, *The System of Objects*, 173 (note 31), 173.

254. Baudrillard, *The System of Objects*, 177.

255. Michel de Certeau, *The Practice of Everyday Life*, 91–110.

256. See Anton Kaes's reading of *M:* "The Cold Gaze: Notes on Mobilization and Modernity," *New German Critique* 59 (1993): 105–17.

257. Karl Ernst Osthaus, in *Jahrbuch des Deutschen Werkbundes* (1913), 62. Cited by Posener, *Berlin auf dem Wege zu einer neuen Architektur*, 470.

258. See also Gérard Legrand's discussion of this scene in *M le maudit*, ed. Noel Simsolo (Paris: Editions Plume, 1990), 50–52.

259. Schulhof, "Die Psychologie des Schaufensters," 10.

260. Seyffert, *Allgemeine Werbelehre*, 596–99. Lest we think such psychotechnical studies are far-fetched, the current burgeoning field of retail anthropology is the latest version of Weimar-era experiments on the shopping experience, nowadays focusing on such minutiae as in-store time-lapse photography of browsing shoppers. See the *New Yorker*'s essay on Paco Underhill: Malcolm Gladwell, "The Science of Shopping" (November 4, 1996): 66–75.

261. See Jonathan Crary's discussion of toys and displays in his *Techniques of the Observer*.

262. See Heide Schönemann, *Fritz Lang. Filmbilder, Vorbilder* (Berlin, Edition Hentrich, 1992) 62–63.

263. See Maria Tatar, "The Killer as Victim: Fritz Lang's *M*," in Tatar, *Lustmord: Sexual Murder in Weimar Germany* (Princeton: Princeton University Press, 1995), 160–61.

264. The Salamander was designed by the architectural firm of von Gerkan, Marg and Partner, in 1992; and the Galeria by Quick-Bäckmann-Quick, in 1995. See Duane Phillips, *Berlin. Ein Führer zur zeitgenössischen Architektur* (Cologne: Könemann, 1997), 56–57, 88–89.

Illustration Sources

Fig. 1. © Lucia Moholy (Dr. Vital Hauser), Bauhaus Archiv, Berlin.
Fig. 2. Author's personal archive.
Fig. 3. In "Die Straßen der Stadt Stuttgart" (1930), 5. Bauregistratur C.X A1 Bd. 1 Nr. 5. Courtesy Stadtarchiv Stuttgart.
Fig. 4. *Die Form* 1.1 (1925): 84. Courtesy Museum der Dinge.
Fig. 5. In *Filmfotos wie noch nie. 1200 interessante Photos aus den besten Filmen aller Länder*, ed. Edmund Bucher & Albrecht Kindt (Gießen: Kindt & Bucher, 1929).
Fig. 6. *Berliner Illustrirte Zeitung* 38.49 (December 8, 1929): 2232. © Stadtbibliothek Berlin.
Fig. 7. In "Ecken von gestern und heute," *Berliner Tageblatt* 58.153 (March 31, 1929). Courtesy Zentral- und Landesbibliotek, Berlin.
Fig. 8. © Akademie der Künste (Bauabteilung), Berlin.
Fig. 9. © Museum of Modern Art, New York.
Fig. 10. In *Das Kunstblatt* 5 (1921): 10; original artwork now lost. Courtesy VAGA, New York, and Deutsche Bücherei Leipzig.
Fig. 11. *Seidels Reklame* 10.11 (November 1926): 498. Courtesy Staatsbibliothek Unter den Linden, Berlin.
Fig. 12. © Museum of Modern Art, New York.
Fig. 13. © Akademie der Künste, Berlin.
Fig. 14. Reprinted in *Architektur für den Handel / Architecture for the Retail Trade* (Basel: Birkhäuser, 1996), 58.
Fig. 15. Front cover for *Die Reklame* 22, (December 1929). Courtesy Deutsche Bücherei Leipzig.
Fig. 16. *Berliner Illustrirte Zeitung* 40.14 (1931): 576. © Berliner Bibliothek.
Fig. 17. *Berliner Illustrirte Zeitung* 38.41 (October 13, 1929): 1832. Courtesy Zentral- und Landesbibliotek, Berlin.

Fig. 18. Cover design for *Die Reklame* 23 (December 1931). Courtesy Deutsche Bücherei Leipzig.
Fig. 19. *Die Reklame* (October 1925): 1180/1181. Courtesy Deutsche Bücherei Leipzig.
Fig. 20. *Die Reklame* 22 (September 1929): 708. Courtesy Deutsche Bücherei Leipzig.
Fig. 21. Osram Sammlung #5544. III SSg.2 Firmenschriften. © Deutsches Technikmuseum, Berlin.
Fig. 22. *Seidels Reklame* 10 (August 1926). Courtesy Staatsbibliothek Unter den Linden, Berlin.
Fig. 23. *Die Reklame* 22 (August 1929): 618/619. Courtesy Deutsche Bücherei, Leipzig.
Fig. 24. © Landesbildstelle Berlin.
Fig. 25. Author's personal collection.
Fig. 26. *Berliner Tageblatt* 58.153 (March 31, 1929). Courtesy Zentral- und Landesbibliotek, Berlin.
Fig. 27. © Akademie der Künste, Berlin.
Fig. 28. In Gerhard Schmidt, "Vom Werbenachtbild Berlins," *Die Reklame* 22.1 (1929): 578. Courtesy Deutsche Bücherei, Leipzig.
Fig. 29. *Siemens-Zeitschrift* 7.11 (November 1927): 737–38. Courtesy Deutsches Technikmuseum, Berlin.
Fig. 30. Cover page of *Architektur und Schaufenster* 25 (May 1928). Courtesy Deutsche Bücherei, Leipzig.
Fig. 31. © Stiftung Deutsche Kinemathek.
Fig. 32. © Stadtarchiv Stuttgart: Bauregistratur C IX 8 Bd. 3, Nr. 6, Reklamegewerbe: 1914–1929.
Fig. 33. *Die Reklame* 2 (February 1926): VIII. Courtesy Deutsche Bücherei, Leipzig.
Fig. 34. © Bundesarchiv-Filmarchiv, Berlin.
Fig. 35. Author's personal collection.
Fig. 36. © Stiftung Deutsche Kinemathek, Berlin.
Fig. 37. © Stiftung Deutsche Kinemathek, Berlin.
Fig. 38. *AEG-Mitteilungen* 19.2 (February 1923): 91. Courtesy Deutsches Technikmuseum, Berlin.
Fig. 39. *Die Reklame* 22 (September 1929): 717. Courtesy Deutsche Bücherei, Leipzig.
Fig. 40. *Berlin. Berliner Wochenspiegel für Leben, Wirtschaft und Verkehr der Reichshauptstadt* 4 (January 22–28, 1927): 7. Courtesy Staatsbibliothek unter den Linden, Berlin.
Fig. 41. © Stiftung Deutsche Kinemathek, Berlin.
Fig. 42. *Die Reklame* 22 (September 1929): 716. Courtesy Deutsche Bücherei, Leipzig.
Fig. 43. © Landesbildstelle Berlin.
Fig. 44. © Deutsches Technikmuseum, Berlin.
Fig. 45. © Landesbildstelle Berlin.

Fig. 46. © Landesarchiv Berlin.
Fig. 47. *Die Reklame,* special issue for Reichs-Reklame-Messe (1925): 74. Courtesy Deutsche Bücherei, Leipzig.
Fig. 48. *Das neue Berlin. Großstadtprobleme,* ed. Martin Wagner and Adolf Behne (Berlin: Deutsche Bauzeitung, 1929), 93; repr. with an introduction by Julius Posener (Boston: Birkhäuser Verlag, 1988).
Fig. 49. *Der Reklame* 22 (December, 1929): 864/865. 74. Courtesy Deutsche Bücherei, Leipzig.
Fig. 50. *Die Auslage* 30 (1928). Courtesy Deutsche Bücherei, Leipzig.
Fig. 51. © Berlinische Galerie. Landesmuseum für moderne Kunst, Photographie und Architektur.
Fig. 52. *Der Angriff* (December 10, 1928). Courtesy Landesarchiv Berlin.
Fig. 53. In *Moderne Ladenbauten* (Berlin: Ernst Pollak Verlag, 1928). Repr. in *Interior Design 1929. Vom Opp-Laden in die Kakadu-Bar / From Opp Shop to Cockatoo Bar,* ed. Martina Düttmann, trans. M. M. Barkei (Berlin: Birkhäuser Verlag, 1989), 175.
Fig. 54. © Bauhaus-Archiv, Berlin.
Fig. 55. In *Berliner Architektur der Nachkriegszeit,* ed. E. M. Hajos & L. Zahn (Berlin: Albertus, 1928), 15.
Fig. 56. *Berliner Illustrirte Zeitung* 38.27 (July 7, 1929): 1178. Courtesy Zentral- und Landesbibliotek, Berlin.
Fig. 57. In *Das Kaufhaus des Westens* (Berlin: Kaufhaus des Westens, 1932): 45. Courtesy Landesarchiv Berlin.
Fig. 58. *Zeitschrift für Waren- und Kaufhäuser* 25.35 (November 26, 1927): 43. © Staatsbibliothek unter den Linden, Berlin.
Fig. 59. Courtesy Landesarchiv Berlin (Außenstelle).
Fig. 60. *Die Auslage* 32 (1928): 9. Courtesy Deutsche Bücherei, Leipzig.
Fig. 61. © Museum of Modern Art, New York.
Fig. 62. Rudolf Seyffert, *Allgemeine Werbelehre* (Stuttgart: C. E. Poeschel Verlag, 1929), 599.
Fig. 63. © Bundesarchiv-Filmarchiv, Berlin.

Index

Text: 10/13 Aldus
Display: Aldus
Composition: Impressions Book and Journal Services, Inc.
Printing and binding: Edwards Brothers, Inc.